TO EVERYONE AN ANSWER

A CASE FOR THE CHRISTIAN WORLDVIEW

ESSAYS IN HONOR OF *Norman L. Geisler*

EDITED BY *Francis J. Beckwith,*
William Lane Craig
and J. P. Moreland

InterVarsity Press
Downers Grove, Illinois

InterVarsity Press
P.O. Box 1400, Downers Grove, IL 60515-1426
World Wide Web: www.ivpress.com
E-mail: mail@ivpress.com

InterVarsity Press® is the book-publishing division of InterVarsity Christian Fellowship/USA®, a student movement active on campus at hundreds of universities, colleges and schools of nursing in the United States of America, and a member movement of the International Fellowship of Evangelical Students. For information about local and regional activities, write Public Relations Dept., InterVarsity Christian Fellowship/USA, 6400 Schroeder Rd., P.O. Box 7895, Madison, WI 53707-7895, or visit the IVCF website at <www.intervarsity.org>.

All Scripture quotations, unless otherwise indicated, are taken from the Holy Bible, New International Version®. NIV®. Copyright ©1973, 1978, 1984 by International Bible Society. Used by permission of Zondervan Publishing House. All rights reserved.

Cover design: Cindy Kiple

Cover images: Harnett/Hanzon/Getty Images

ISBN 0-8308-2735-8

Printed in the United States of America ∞

Library of Congress Cataloging-in-Publication Data

To every one an answer: a case for the Christian worldview: essays
in honor of Norman L. Geisler / edited by Francis J. Beckwith,
William Lane Craig, and J.P. Moreland.
   p. cm.
Includes bibliographical references and index.
ISBN 0-8308-2735-8 (hardcover: alk. paper)
  1. Apologetics. I. Geisler, Norman L. II. Beckwith, Francis III.
Craig, William Lane. IV. Moreland, James Porter, 1948-
BT1103.T6 2004
239—dc22

                                  2004008465

P	19	18	17	16	15	14	13	12	11	10	9	8	7	6	5	4	3
Y	20	19	18	17	16	15	14	13	12	11	10	09	08	07	06	05	

CONTENTS

FOREWORD

Josh McDowell

"APOLOGETICS IS SIMPLY TO DEFEND THE FAITH, AND THEREBY DESTROY ARGU-
ments and every proud obstacle against the knowledge of God (2 Cor
10:5). It is opening the door, clearing the rubble, and getting rid of the
hurdles so that people can come to Christ."

This is how Dr. Norman L. Geisler described the main purpose of
apologetics. And after fifty-three years of faithful ministry, there is no
one who could speak with more authority on the subject. The apostle
Paul wrote, "Let your speech always be with grace, seasoned with salt,
that you may know how you ought to answer each one" (Col 4:6 NKJV).
Norm says apologetics, then, is just an attempt to get answers to everybody's questions in order to tear down the obstacles keeping them from
Christ.

Norm Geisler was raised in an antireligious home but came to Christ
at the age of seventeen. The following day, he went door to door, sharing his newfound faith with those who had yet to hear about Christ.
Evangelism was a passion from the beginning of his Christian life. But it
didn't take long before he realized that in order to be more effective in
sharing the gospel, he would need to be better equipped with knowledge of the Scripture and better prepared to answer difficult questions.

"One Friday evening," Norm remembers of his early days as a Christian, "we were witnessing at the city rescue mission in Detroit and a
drunk staggered up to me. 'I'm a graduate of Moody Insti-bible-tute,' the
man slurred. Then he took the Bible out of my hand and said, 'You're

not supposed to be doing this.' He turned to the Gospels and pointed out a verse where Jesus said to *go and tell no man*. 'Get out of here,' the inebriated man said with confidence. 'Jesus doesn't want you to be doing this.'

"This really threw me," Norm remembered. "I didn't have the foggiest idea what the verse meant. But I decided then after being twisted up by Jehovah's Witnesses and Mormons and now this drunk, I had better get some answers or else stop witnessing. I'm convinced that most Christians stop witnessing because they don't want to take the time to get answers to all of these people. Instead, I've dedicated my life to getting answers."

Norman Geisler has been at the forefront of the study and teaching of Christian apologetics for decades. His conviction and passion for truth over the years have made a tremendous impact on the body of Christ. His work has provided countless skeptics with solid evidence for the truth of the gospel. And the resources he has faithfully labored over have equipped many believers with confidence to stand firm in the faith and share the truth with others.

Looking at today's cultural climate, we see that the need for apologetics is greater than ever. When Norm started out in ministry more than fifty years ago, most people in America believed that God existed. They believed there were miracles and that Christianity is the true religion; they just hadn't made a commitment to Christ. "Today," Norm said, "with cultural trends leaning toward naturalism, relativism and pluralism, along with all their subcategories, people no longer believe in God, miracles, truth or any of the prerequisites that help make sense out of the gospel."

"Nietzsche said that God is dead," Norm continued. "So for the last century, we've been living under the shadow of the death of God in the culture. And when God dies, all truth dies. If you don't have an absolute moral lawgiver, you can't have any moral laws. When God dies, all truth dies and all meaning dies. So in this culture, the church is faced with reestablishing that there is absolute truth, absolute meaning, absolute morals, and that the opposite of true is false. We have to do more apologetics today than ever before."

This book you hold in your hand is a powerful tool for young people who want to be better prepared to "make a defense to everyone who asks [them] to give an account for the hope that is in [them]" (1 Pet 3:15 NASB). The essays contained herein come from some of the greatest Christian minds of our time, many of whom have been trained and influenced by Dr. Norman L. Geisler. It is only appropriate, then, that the book is compiled in Dr. Geisler's honor.

Personally, Norm Geisler has had a major impact on my life and ministry. In the many years I have been able to call him my friend, Norm has consistently shown me the value of pursuing truth and apologetics. He has shown me the value of biblically based and Christ-centered ministry. And through it all, I have been inspired and challenged by his commitment to excellence.

I have known few people with such a passion for the truth of God's Word and commitment to sharing the claims of Christ with others as Norm Geisler. "It's a life or death issue," he recently said. "In fact, it's an eternal life or eternal death issue, to put it in blunt language. . . . And if we can't get passionate about that, then we're not going to get passionate about anything!"

Thank you, Norm, for all you have done and continue to do for the cause of Christ. Your faithful service to the Lord will influence generations to come with the knowledge of the one true God. May this book help continue the work to which you have devoted your life, until every tribe and tongue will truly know the Answer.

Norm—to you we are all indebted.

INTRODUCTION

Francis J. Beckwith

THE APOSTLE PETER INSTRUCTED HIS FELLOW CHRISTIANS TO "BE READY AL-
ways to give an answer to every man that asketh you a reason of the
hope that is in you with meekness and fear" (1 Pet 3:15 KJV). This command is just as relevant today as it was during the days of the first-century church. Some of the questions asked of today's church are similar
to ones raised during Peter's time (e.g., How do you know Jesus rose
from the dead?) while others are quite different (e.g., Has Darwinism re-
futed the belief that God may have designed the universe?). The intent
of this volume is to offer to the church a collection of essays that addresses some of the questions raised by those outside the church and to
provide the ordinary Christian a resource so that he or she may be able
to fulfill Peter's command. Responding to such challenges and offering
reasons for one's faith is called *apologetics*. This term derives from the
Greek word *apologia*, which is a legal term referring to one's defense in
court.

This volume is a festschrift to honor the career of Norman L. Geisler,
a philosopher and theologian who has been a teacher, friend and colleague to and/or important influence on all the contributors of this volume. Dr. Geisler's career has been dedicated to offering to the world and
equipping the church with a defense "of the hope that is in you" and
doing so by addressing, in his books, articles, lectures and courses, an
array of questions in such diverse fields as theology, philosophy, biblical
studies, jurisprudence and religion. This volume attempts, in a modest
way, to touch on issues in each of these areas in order to present a de-

fense of the Christian faith as a worldview.

What do we mean when we say that Christianity is a worldview? What we mean is that the Christian faith is a philosophical tapestry of interdependent ideas, principles and metaphysical claims that are derived from the Hebrew-Christian Scriptures as well as the creeds, theologies, communities, ethical norms and institutions that have flourished under the authority of these writings. These beliefs are not mere utterances of private religious devotion but are propositions whose proponents claim accurately instruct us on the nature of the universe, human persons, our relationship with God, human communities and the moral life. The following is a summary of some of these beliefs.

First, there exists an eternally self-existing moral agent named God, who created the universe *ex nihilo*. The universe is completely and absolutely contingent upon God for its beginning as well as its continued existence. He is, among other things, personal, omnipotent, omniscient, omnipresent, perfectly good, necessary and infinitely wise. God is not only the Creator of the visible and physical universe but also the source of the invisible and nonphysical one. He is the creator of human souls and the ontological source of the moral law, logic and mathematics.

Second, God created human beings in his image. A human being is not merely a collection of physical parts but has an underlying unity or soul.[1] A human being's life is sacred from the moment that human being comes into existence; the value of a human being is not something acquired when he or she reaches a certain level of physical complexity, as many secular thinkers maintain. Because human beings are moral agents, they have the capacity to make decisions and judgments within the larger framework of family and community. Thus, for the Christian worldview, marriage, government and church are not merely social constructions that can be shaped in any way consistent with some utopian vision of justice but rather are natural institutions in which and by which human beings ought to learn what is good, true and beautiful. However differently expressed throughout human history and/or better under-

---

[1]For a philosophical defense of this viewpoint from a biblical perspective, see J. P. Moreland and Scott B. Rae, *Body and Soul: Human Nature and the Crisis in Ethics* (Downers Grove, Ill.: InterVarsity Press, 2000). See also chapter thirteen in this volume.

stood as the result of moral reflection, they are part of the furniture of the universe, and their continued existence is essential to maintaining the moral ecology of human society. Thus the end of the community should be to produce good citizens and therefore provide a privileged position for these natural institutions.

Third, God reveals himself in special revelation (2 Tim 3:14-17), the Bible, as well as general revelation. Concerning the former, if the Bible is truly God's Word, then it must be without error, for God is perfect (Mk 10:18; Heb 6:18), and it follows logically that his Word must be as well. The Bible provides us with an account of humanity's genesis and fall; a history of God's chosen people; the institution of the law of Moses and its inadequacy to redeem; prophecy; prayer; wisdom and poetry; the good news and story of the first coming of the Messiah; and the establishing of his church on earth.

The latter is the cornerstone of Chrisitan faith. According to the Bible, human beings have violated the moral law of God and need to be made right with him. That is, human beings are in need of salvation but are powerless to achieve this on their own. This is why God became a human being in Jesus of Nazareth: so that he may pay the sacrifice necessary to atone for our sins—his death on the cross. Christians believe that Jesus rose bodily from the grave three days after his death and forty days later ascended into heaven. Shortly after that Jesus' apostles and disciples established his church, a body of believers that continues to grow to this day. This church is diverse in its membership, including men and women and people from every race, nationality and region of the globe. Christianity attracts such a wide range of people because it offers to the world good news that touches the human heart in a way that is not contingent on cultural idiosyncracies or racial or nationalistic affiliations: God loves us so much that he became a human being and suffered and died so that he may forgive us our sins and by his grace offer us the free gift of eternal salvation.

According to Scripture, God has not left himself without a witness among the unbelievers (Acts 14:17). This is called general revelation, since it is something that all people have the capacity to access through observation, reason and reflection apart from the Bible. J. Budziszewski outlines the five forms in which general revelation is presented in Scripture:

> (1) The testimony of creation, which speaks to us of a glorious, powerful and merciful Creator (Psalm 19:1-6; Acts 14:17; Romans 1:20); (2) the fact that we are made in the image of God, which not only gives us rational and moral capacities but tells us of an unknown Holy One who is different from our idols (Genesis 1:26-27; Acts 17:22-23); (3) the facts of our physical and emotional design, in which a variety of God's purposes are plainly manifest (Romans 1:26-27); (4) the law of conscience, written on the heart, which, like the law of Moses, tells us what sin is but does not give us power to escape it (Romans 2:14-15); (5) the order of causality, which teaches us by linking every sin with consequences (Proverbs 1:31).[2]

Because the editors of this volume believe that general revelation is a legitimate means by which human beings may acquire knowledge of theological truths, we have asked the contributors of this volume to provide arguments that may be understood and appreciated by those who do not share our Christian faith. Consequently, we do not share the conviction of some Christians that theological knowledge is impossible apart from special revelation.

It is fashionable today to speak of the theological posture of Western civilization, and American intellectual culture in particular, as post-Christian. Our most important, influential and culture-shaping institutions and professions—law, medicine, education, science, media and the arts—no longer accept the presuppositions of the biblical worldview as part of their philosophical frameworks. Thus, for example, it is not unusual—in fact, it is quite common—to hear academic luminaries from different disciplines in assorted venues defend points of view that presuppose that theological claims, and Christian ones in particular, are not claims of knowledge but rather religious opinions no different in nature than matters of taste. The ease by which these points of view are presented, and the absence of a call to justify them by the same standards of philosophical rigor that are required of their opposition, is testimony to how po-

---

[2]J. Budziszewski, *Written on the Heart: The Case for Natural Law* (Downers Grove, Ill.: InterVarsity Press, 1997), pp. 180-81.

tently certain views antithetical to the Christian worldview have shaped the ideas, opinions and policies of those who occupy the seats of cultural influence in our society.

Although there are numerous technical works that respond to these challenges, there are few if any that are offered to the ordinary Christian and the wider public as an accessible volume that can be understood by the informed churchgoer and used at Christian colleges, universities, parachurch ministries and Sunday schools throughout North America. *To Everyone an Answer* is an attempt to address this neglect. Its contributors include many well-known Christian apologists, some of whom have made important strides in their professional work in defending differing aspects of the Christian worldview. Virtually all the contributors have worked within the church, especially in parachurch organizations and local congregations. Because of this experience, they are particularly gifted in teaching laypeople and students on how to defend the Christian worldview in the public square. In fact, some of the contributors work exclusively in this area. Others have a foot in each realm. Nearly all of the contributors have a regular academic appointment at a college, university or seminary at which they teach on a regular basis an apologetics course or one in which there is an apologetics component.

This book is divided into five parts, each of which has a brief introduction written by one of the editors. Each essay includes a brief section of suggested works for further reading. Part one concerns the relationship between faith and reason, and the importance of apologetics to Christian witness. Arguments for God's existence are the focus of part two, in which contemporary versions of five classical arguments are presented. The central claims of the Christian faith are dealt with in part three. Here the contributors cover the possibility of miracles and the claims of Christ. Part four concerns philosophical and cultural challenges to the Christian worldview. A broad range of issues, including the problem of evil and postmodernism, is covered in this section. In part five the contributors respond to religious challenges to the Christian worldview, including Islam and the problem of Christian exclusivism. J. P. Moreland summarizes the book's case in a concluding essay, which is followed by a biographical timeline of the career of Dr. Geisler as well as a bibliography of his published works.

If not for the influence, encouragement, mentorship and personal virtue of Dr. Geisler, many of the contributors of this volume would have
taken a much different and less fulfilling path in their professional lives.
For this reason, we offer to our friend, colleague and teacher this volume
in his honor. Well done, good and faithful servant.

PART 1

FAITH, REASON AND THE NECESSITY OF APOLOGETICS

William Lane Craig

APOLOGETICS IS THAT BRANCH OF CHRISTIAN THEOLOGY THAT SEEKS TO PRO-
vide rational warrant for Christianity's truth claims. It contains offensive
and defensive elements, on the one hand presenting positive arguments
for Christian truth claims and on the other refuting objections brought
against Christianity's truth claims.

Is apologetics necessary? That depends. Necessary for whom? And for
what? The question is not as simple as it first appears.

Usually people who ask this question have something like the following in mind: "Is apologetics necessary for rational belief in Christianity
on the part of a normal adult?" Theological rationalists, or evidentialists,
as they are often called today, maintain that in the absence of positive
evidence for Christian truth claims faith is irrational for a normally functioning adult. Such a position, however, is difficult to square with Scripture, which seems to teach that faith in Christ can be immediately
grounded by the inner witness of the Holy Spirit (Rom 8:14-16; 1 Jn 2:27;
5:6-10), so that argument and evidence become unnecessary.

It might be thought that in the case of a person who believes Christian
truth claims immediately through the witness of the Holy Spirit, one
must have at least the defensive apologetic resources to defeat the various objections with which one is confronted, as happens so frequently

in Western culture. But even that more modest claim is hasty, for if the witness of the Holy Spirit in a person's life is sufficiently powerful (as it should be), then it will overwhelm the objections brought against that person's Christian beliefs, thus obviating the need even for defensive apologetics. Since beliefs grounded in the objective, veridical witness of the Spirit are part of the deliverances of reason, believers are rational in their faith even if they are bereft of apologetic arguments, as is the case with most Christians today and throughout the history of the church.

Is then apologetics an utterly trivial pursuit, of no value or relevance to Christian faith, as fideists claim? Such a conclusion would again be hasty. For apologetic arguments may be sufficient for rational faith, even if they are not necessary. There may be persuasive, cogent arguments for Christian faith, even if such arguments are not indispensable for rational belief. The Holy Spirit can use such arguments and evidence as a means of drawing people to himself. Sometimes apologetic arguments will give the honest seeker permission, so to speak, to believe what the Holy Spirit immediately delivers to him, so that they serve as a sort of catalyst to faith, even if they do not become the basis of faith. Moreover, apologetic arguments can confirm the witness of the Holy Spirit, providing a valuable backup in times of spiritual dryness when the believer is not as sensitively attuned to the Spirit or is struggling with doubt.

But suppose we reframe the question. For even if apologetics is not necessary for rational faith, it could still be necessary with respect to other ends. For example, apologetics may well be necessary for the gospel to be effectively heard in Western society today. In general Western culture is deeply post-Christian. It is the product of the Enlightenment, which introduced into European culture the leaven of secularism that has by now permeated the whole of Western society. The hallmark of the Enlightenment was free thought, that is, the pursuit of knowledge by means of unfettered human reason alone. While it is by no means inevitable that such a pursuit must lead to non-Christian conclusions and while most of the original Enlightenment thinkers were themselves theists, it has been the overwhelming impact of the Enlightenment mentality that Western intellectuals do not consider theological knowledge to be possible. Theology is not a source of genuine knowledge and therefore is not a science. Reason and religion are thus at odds with each other. The deliverances of the physical sciences are alone taken as authoritative guides to our understanding of the world, and the confident assumption is that the picture of the world that emerges from the genuine sciences is a thoroughly naturalistic picture. The person who follows the pursuit of reason unflinchingly toward its end will be atheistic or at best agnostic.

There have been countercurrents to Enlightenment rationalism in Western thought—one thinks of Romanticism, for example—but these have been no more sympathetic to Christianity than the Enlightenment project. Indeed, they have sometimes served to offer a mystical, pantheistic nature religion as an alternative to traditional theism, in order that one's religious yearnings, which Enlightenment rationalism tended to treat dismissively, might not go unfulfilled.

On the current scene, self-proclaimed postmodernism is such a movement. The Enlightenment is associated with the modern age, dominated by science and technology, and hence is sometimes called modernity. Postmodernism rejects the all-sufficiency of human reason championed by free thought. This might seem at first blush a welcome development for Christian believers, weary of centuries of attacks by Enlightenment rationalists. But in this case the cure is worse than the disease. For postmodernists deny that there are universal standards of logic, rationality and truth. This claim is incompatible with the Christian idea of God, who, as the Creator and Sustainer of all things, is an objectively existing reality and who, as an omniscient being, has a privileged perspective on the world, grasping the world as it is in the unity of his intellect. There is thus a unity and objectivity to truth that is incompatible with postmodernism. Postmodernism is therefore no more friendly to Christian truth claims than is Enlightenment rationalism. Christianity is reduced to but one voice in a cacophony of competing claims, none of which is objectively true.

In any case, Enlightenment rationalism is so deeply imbedded in Western intellectual life that these antirationalistic currents like Romanticism and postmodernism are doomed, it seems, to be mere passing fashions. After all, no one adopts a postmodernist view of literary texts when reading the labels on a medicine bottle or a box of rat poison!

Clearly we ignore the objective meaning of such texts only at peril to our lives. In the end, people turn out to be subjectivists only about ethics and religion, not about matters provable by science. But this is not postmodernism; this is nothing else than classic Enlightenment naturalism—it is the old modernism in a fashionable new guise.

Why are these considerations of culture important? Simply because the gospel is never heard in isolation. It is always heard against the background of the cultural milieu in which one lives. A person reared in a cultural milieu in which Christianity is still seen as an intellectually viable option will display an openness to the gospel that a person who is secularized will not. For the secular person you may as well tell him to believe in fairies or leprechauns as in Jesus Christ! What awaits us in North America is already evident in Europe. Although the overwhelming majority of Europeans retain a nominal affiliation with Christianity, only about 10 percent are practicing believers. The most significant trend in European religious affiliation is the growth of those classed as nonreligious from effectively 0 percent of the population in 1900 to more than 22 percent today. Evangelical Christians, for example, appear almost as weird to persons on the streets of Bonn, Stockholm or Paris as do the devotees of Krishna.

It is for that reason that Christians who depreciate the value of apologetics because "no one comes to Christ through arguments" are so shortsighted. For the value of apologetics extends far beyond one's immediate evangelistic contact. It is the broader task of Christian apologetics to help create and sustain a cultural milieu in which the gospel can be heard as an intellectually viable option for thinking men and women. It is not implausible that robust apologetics is a necessary ingredient in fostering a milieu in which evangelization can be most effectively pursued in contemporary Western society and those societies increasingly influenced by it.

In this opening section of our book, we shall take a closer look at the various roles apologetics has to play—in rational faith, in knowledge of Christianity's truth, in discipleship—as well as provide some useful advice on its practical application.

1

KNOWING CHRISTIANITY IS TRUE

The Relationship Between Faith and Reason

Thomas A. Howe and Richard G. Howe

IN THE POPULAR CLASSIC CHRISTMAS MOVIE *MIRACLE ON THIRTY-FOURTH Street,* little Suzie Walker, played by Natalie Wood, is perplexed about how some of those around her are reacting to the enigmatic Santa Claus figure who has recently come into their lives. Her mother, Doris, played by Maureen O'Hara, tries to explain to her the need to have faith in Kris Kringle. Frustrated, little Suzie exclaims, "But that doesn't make any sense, Mommy," to which her mother responds, "Faith is believing in something when common sense tells you not to."

Unfortunately, too many people think this is exactly what faith is: accepting something against the evidence. But is it really better to believe something despite what our common sense tells us? In our culture today and throughout church history there have been several ways of understanding the nature of faith and its relationship to reason. What we want to do in this essay is to look at those various approaches to the issue of faith and reason and defend a view that we believe is biblical and does justice to who we are as God's creatures.

Before we can jump into the subject of the relationship between faith and reason, it is necessary that we define a few terms. Notice the essay title: "Knowing Christianity Is True: The Relationship Between Faith and Reason." This title suggests a number of notions that need to be examined: truth, knowing, faith and reason. What do we mean by the use of such terms?

What Is Truth?

As Christians, what are we claiming when we say our faith is true? This may seem like an unnecessary question if we ask it about most things. If someone said, "It is raining," and someone else said, "That's true," most of us would know exactly what is being said about the rain. But for some reason, when it comes to subjects like religion, the meaning of terms like "truth" becomes confused.

If unbelievers do not understand what we are saying when we say Christianity is true, this confusion can hamper our ability to effectively communicate the claims of Christ. What they need to understand is that when we as Christians maintain that Christianity is true, we are not merely claiming that it fulfills a certain function in our lives. Our contention is that religion is more than something to give us peace of mind, a purpose for life, and happiness. It should certainly do this, but there is something more. We believe that true religion must be grounded in reality, that it must make true claims about reality—who we are as human beings, who God is, and how we relate to God. The religion that cannot truthfully answer these questions is false, not because it fails to give one peace of mind, but because it makes false claims about the way things are.

What Is Knowing?

There are two familiar lines from two famous Christian songs that may help illustrate two different ways that our culture understands how to know something: "Jesus loves me, this I know, for the Bible tells me so," and "You ask me how I know he lives, he lives within my heart." Sometimes these two types of knowing are referred to as objective (or public, external, factual) and subjective (or private, internal, personal), respectively. As far as they go, there is nothing wrong with thinking of things being known in these ways. After all, surely there are some things that are publicly known, such as the distance the earth is from the sun, or who is the current president of the United States. Just as surely there are some things that are known privately, such as whether I have a headache or whether I am comfortable.

These examples are perhaps not controversial. What is controversial is when some people insist that certain broad issues are necessarily relegated to one realm of knowing or the other. For example, a popular notion is that science deals with the objective, public, external and factual and that religion deals with the subjective, private, internal and personal. Now, while it may be the case that there could be certain aspects of religion that are subjective, private, internal and personal, our contention is that there are important aspects of Christianity that are objective, public, external and factual. Christianity is a worldview that makes claims about reality. These claims are either true or false. If they are true, then there is evidence that can be given to support them. We discovered in the section on "What Is Truth?" that for Christianity to be true means that the claims of Christianity correspond to reality. Likewise, to know that Christianity is true must mean more than knowing it in some subjective, private, internal and personal way. It means that we can know that it is true in an objective, public, external and factual way.

WHAT IS REASON?

To understand what we mean when we talk about reason, let us consider reason in two ways, in terms of the acts of reason and the objects of reason.

Acts of reason. The expression "acts of reason" indicates all those subjective and personal acts of our mind by which we discover, understand or seek to demonstrate truth. The classical designations of these acts of reason are simple apprehension, judgment and reasoning. Although we are considering these as separate acts, we may never experience them as distinct acts of the mind. They normally occur almost simultaneously and automatically. We must not confuse the analysis of reason with the experience of reason.

Simple apprehension is the act of reason whereby the mind lays hold of a thing. This laying hold makes the thing present in and to our mind.

However, in simple apprehension, the mind is not engaged in affirming or denying. We simply lay hold of what a thing is. Apprehension may be extremely vague and general. We may lay hold only of the fact that something is a substance. Thorough knowledge of what something is will involve study and experience, and we may never fully comprehend any given thing we apprehend. As the first act of reason, simple apprehension is a simple laying hold of or grasping what something is.

Judgment, the second act of reason, is the act whereby we affirm or deny that the thing apprehended is or was or will be. This may be a simple affirmation or negation, or it may be according to some mode of necessity or possibility. Also, the act of judgment may involve negation, in which we deny that a thing is or was, and so forth. The act of judgment differs from a simple apprehension in that the act of judgment involves knowing the thing we have apprehended in terms of affirming or denying its existence.

The third act of reason, reasoning, is that act whereby the mind proceeds from known truth to new truth. The new truth will be distinct from the previously known truth, but the latter is implied in the former. However, reasoning involves not only logical movement from premises to conclusion. Reasoning may also involve a movement from question to answer. For example, one might inquire of a trusted colleague concerning the state of affairs in a foreign country. On the basis of trust in the person's honesty, we can gain new knowledge by moving from inquiry to response. Also, reasoning may be a movement from rhetoric to persuasion. On the basis of authoritative testimony and the persuasive presentation of evidence we might move from the knowledge of the existence of particles and waves to accepting the new knowledge of the nature of light. Any progress of the mind from knowledge possessed to knowledge gained is an act of reasoning, and the act of reasoning may involve more than the strictly logical relations of premises to conclusions.

Objects of reason. The objects of reason are whatever the mind can know by reason. The objects of reason correspond to the three acts of reason. Any object of reason can be grasped, understood either to be or not to be, and demonstrated, without any assumptions based on faith in divine revelation, to be true or false. Peter Kreeft and Ronald K. Tacelli have made a helpful chart delineating these acts of reason and their relation to faith.[1] This chart is represented in table 1.1.

Table 1.1

	Laying Hold/ Simple Apprehension	Understanding/ Judgment	Proving/ Reasoning
By reason alone and not part of revelation	What a star is	That the universe of stars exists	The Pythagorean theorem
By reason and by faith in divine revelation	That the universe is well ordered	That Jesus existed in historical space-time	That the universe was created
Not by reason, only by faith in divine revelation	God's plan of salvation	How much God loves us	God is a Trinity

Concerning the objects of reason corresponding to the first act of reason, simple apprehension, by human reason alone and without any relation to divine revelation, we can apprehend what a star is. This is not something that is revealed in Scripture but is apprehended by the mind. By human reasoning accompanied by faith in divine revelation, we can apprehend that the universe is well ordered and why it is so ordered. That the universe is well ordered is something we can discover and judge to be true by rational investigation. However, this is also something that is revealed in Scripture, and we can accept it by faith. By divine revelation we can apprehend what God's plan is for our salvation. This is not something that we can apprehend by observing the world, but only by hearing the Word of God (Rom 10:17).

Concerning the objects of reason corresponding to the second act of reason, judgment, by human reason alone and without any relation to divine revelation, we can judge that the universe of stars exists. By human reason accompanied by faith in divine revelation, we can judge that

---

[1]Peter Kreeft and Ronald K. Tacelli, *Handbook of Christian Apologetics: Hundreds of Answers to Crucial Questions* (Downers Grove, Ill.: InterVarsity Press, 1994), p. 33.

Jesus actually existed in space-time history. Now the fact that Jesus existed as a human is something that we can discover by historical investigation. But it is also something that is revealed in Scripture. By divine revelation, we can know how much God loves us. We cannot judge that God loves us by simply observing the universe. We must come to know this through divine revelation.

Concerning the objects of reason corresponding to the third act of the mind, reasoning, we can, by human reason alone and without any relation to divine revelation, discover and demonstrate the truth of the Pythagorean theorem. This is not something revealed in Scripture. By human reason accompanied by faith in divine revelation, we can demonstrate that the universe was created. This is something we can demonstrate by philosophical arguments, but it is also something that is revealed in Scripture. So, we can accept it as a conclusion of reasoning, or we can accept it by faith as a truth revealed in Scripture. By divine revelation, we can accept the truth that God is a Trinity. However, we cannot prove this by philosophical reasoning. We can demonstrate that it is not an irrational belief, but we cannot comprehend it or prove it, nor could we have apprehended it apart from divine revelation. We have come to know it through divine revelation, and we must accept it by faith.

What Is Faith?

Definition of faith. Faith is a personal trust in someone or something. Saving faith is a personal trust in God, who is true to his Word. In the book of Romans, Abraham is presented as an example of saving faith (Rom 4:1-5). Abraham believed God when, in Genesis 15, God promised that Abraham would have an heir from his own loins and that God would give to him all the land that he surveyed. Genesis 15:6 (NASB) says, "Then he believed in the LORD; and He reckoned it to him as righteousness." The basic idea of the assertion in Genesis 15:6, "he believed in," is the idea of certainty and firmness, holding something to be certain. Abraham accepted God's word as a promise that would certainly be fulfilled. Abraham trusted God to give him a son and the land. Faith is not an amorphous wish or hopeful desire for something that one is not certain will be realized. Faith is a firm certainty grounded in the faithfulness of God and a certain expectation of the fulfillment of all of the promises which God has made to those who would trust him.

As was observed above, sometimes people will argue that faith is contrary to reason—the notion of believing in something in spite of reason. But this is not accurate. Faith is not contrary to reason or irrational. In fact, trusting in God is eminently reasonable. God has demonstrated his faithfulness and trustworthiness again and again. Even in those times when it seems that the promises of God will not be fulfilled, it would in fact be unreasonable not to believe in God. Faith is trusting God to do what he says he will do. Faith is a personal trust.

Act of faith. We must distinguish between the act of faith and the object of faith. Faith is more than simply believing something to be true. Kreeft and Tacelli present four helpful aspects of faith that we will summarize.[2] First of all there is the emotional aspect of faith. This involves the feeling of assurance, trust or confidence in a person. The emotional aspect of faith is characterized in the Bible as hope, but this is not simply wishful thinking. Rather, hope in this sense is the confident expectation of ultimately receiving that which has been promised.

The intellectual aspect of faith is belief. The intellectual aspect of faith is the stable and unchanging commitment that is grounded in truth. This is perhaps what people are talking about when they say they believe in spite of reason. Often, the circumstances of life may influence us to question the truth of God's Word. The intellectual aspect of faith, however, is not grounded in the appearances of the moment but in the truths about God and reality. Although I may not feel strong in faith, my mind can remain committed to trusting in God because of what I know to be true about him. This is not mere opinion but is a firm commitment of trust in God based on who he is.

The volitional aspect of faith is the act of the will by which I make a commitment to live, think and act on the basis of God's Word. The volitional aspect of faith is often characterized as faithfulness. It is realized in one's life and actions. Not only do I have a feeling of assurance, not only do I have a firm commitment to the truth about God, but also I act

---

[2]Kreeft and Tacelli, *Handbook*, pp. 30-31.

on that belief. My choices, values, pursuits and goals are based on that to which I am committed.

The act of faith is more than simply accepting something to be the case. The act of faith in the biblical sense involves the whole person, emotions, intellect, will and heart, in a total commitment of trust in another. This is what distinguished Joshua and Caleb from the rest of Israel. "Joshua the son of Nun and Caleb the son of Jephunneh, of those who had spied out the land, tore their clothes; and they spoke to all the congregation of the sons of Israel, saying, 'The land which we passed through to spy out is an exceedingly good land. If the LORD is pleased with us, then He will bring us into this land, and give it to us—a land which flows with milk and honey. Only do not rebel against the LORD; and do not fear the people of the land, for they will be our prey. Their protection has been removed from them, and the Lord is with us; do not fear them'" (Num 14:6-9 NASB). Without fear, Joshua and Caleb trusted God and were willing, based on their trust in God, to enter the land and take it from the inhabitants, because they trusted God when he said, "I will be with you" (Deut 31:23 NASB).

Object of faith. The object of faith is the person or the thing in which one trusts. This includes not only the person of God but the words of God as well. The words of God include all that we hold to be taught by the Word of God, including the doctrines that the Bible teaches. In other words, the object of our faith is not only God but everything he has revealed in the Bible. But what is revealed in the Bible are truths that can be expressed in propositions. The Bible teaches that there are certain things that we should believe. For example, the Bible teaches that the God of Israel is the only true and living God: "Remember the former things long past, For I am God, and there is no other; I am God, and there is no one like Me" (Is 46:9 NASB). But the statement "I am God" is a proposition that is presented to the person as something to be accepted as true and believed.

However, the propositions themselves are not the ultimate objects of faith. Rather, they are the proximate objects of faith. The ultimate object of faith is God, whose nature insures the truthfulness of the propositions he asserts. Simply to accept that a proposition is true is not the same as trusting in the one who makes the assertion. One must not only believe the truth of the propositions, but one must actually trust in him who is the Author and Guarantor of the truth of these propositions. In Numbers 14, Israel knew (believed) God was able to bring them into the land, but they did not trust him to do it for them.

THREE VIEWS ON THE RELATIONSHIP BETWEEN FAITH AND REASON

Faith absent reason. One view on the relationship between faith and reason that we believe is an inadequate view has already been examined. It is the view that matters of faith are private and matters of reason are public. It is probably the most common view that people have about such matters. We have argued that when it comes to the Christian faith, while there are indeed aspects that are private, the claims that Christianity makes are claims about reality and as such are objective claims. Christianity claims that there is a God who is the Creator and Sustainer of the entire universe and to whom every person will have to give an account one day. Christianity claims that Jesus Christ lived a life of miracles, was crucified and rose from the dead. These claims are such that they can be investigated philosophically, scientifically and historically. These claims are such that philosophical, scientific and historical evidence can be marshaled to support them. These claims are such that they can be reasoned about. We see that this is the case not only because of the nature of the claims themselves but also because that is what the Bible says about them and that is how the apostles treated them.

Faith against reason. Another view of the relationship between faith and reason that we believe is inadequate has shown itself at various times throughout church history, namely, the claim that reason is useless in spiritual matters. Fideism (from Latin, *fides,* meaning "faith") asserts that a person cannot reason about matters of faith. You must simply believe. There is perhaps no better example of this kind of perspective than that proposed by Søren Kierkegaard (1813-1855). Kierkegaard is popularly held to be the father of modern existentialism. For several reasons, he asserted that the human mind was unable to discover any divine truth. The reason that is most relevant here is that Kierkegaard claimed that though human reason could be used to identify and reject the absurd or irrational, it could not make any positive advance toward attaining divine truth. For Kierkegaard, God was so utterly transcendent, "wholly other," that truths about God equally transcend the capacities of human reason. Consequently there is no way for the human mind to know any truth about God by the exercise of human reason.

However, the Bible declares that we must believe in the right things, not in the wrong things. If fideism is true, then how can we know what to believe in and what not to believe in? In fact, why should we accept fideism? If fideism offers no reasons why we should accept it, then there is no reason to accept fideism over some other system. But if fideism offers any reasons why we should accept fideism, then it is using reason to say that we should not use reason, which is self-defeating. It uses reason to make statements about divine truth and spiritual matters. Though there are many things about God that are beyond our capacity to reason about, there are many things about God that are within the grasp of our reason, like the reasons the Bible gives for trusting God for our salvation. In fact, Jesus commanded us to love God with our whole mind: "'Teacher, which is the great commandment in the Law?' And [Jesus] said to him, 'You shall love the Lord your God with all your heart, and with all your soul, and with all your mind'" (Mt 22:36-37 NASB).

Faith and reason. We believe that there is a better way to understand the relationship between faith and reason. Various aspects of our view have been touched on throughout this essay. It would be helpful at this point to pull these various aspects together and fill them out into a fuller picture. Our contention is that the best way to understand the relationship between faith and reason is to see that each has its proper role to play and that faith and reason complement each other in their respective roles. Let us put the pieces together regarding each of them.

THE RELATIONSHIP BETWEEN FAITH AND REASON: PUTTING THE PIECES TOGETHER

The role of reason. You may ask yourself why there is a need at all for reasoning with someone about the Christian faith. After all, if it is the case that one can come to faith in Christ only by the work of the Holy Spirit, then what place does reason play? We think that there are a number of good reasons why a Christian can and should give evidence for his faith in Christ. First, the Bible is clear about the mandate to give reasons. First Peter 3:15 (NASB) says, "But sanctify Christ as Lord in your hearts, always being ready to give a defense to everyone who asks you an account for the hope that is in you, yet with gentleness and reverence." The word translated "defense" is *apologia,* from which we get the word *apologetics.* Another verse that commands us to defend the faith is Jude 3 (NASB), which says, "Beloved, while I was making every effort to write to you about our common salvation, I found the necessity to write to you appealing that you contend earnestly for the faith which was once for all handed down to the saints."

Second, not only does the Bible say that we should give reasons, but as the other chapters in this book will show, there is every reason to give reasons because the reasons are there. The evidence is strong for defending the faith. Since Christianity is rooted in history and is corroborated by science and philosophy, Christians have at their disposal ample evidence for its truthfulness.

A third reason why we should give evidence is that we find that the apostles contended for the faith by giving reasons. Throughout the book of Acts we see numerous examples of the apostles reasoning about the truths of Christianity. A look at a number of passages in Acts shows instances of disputing, proving, explaining, demonstrating, reasoning and persuading.[3]

While it is the Holy Spirit who enables someone to believe, he may sometimes use the presentation of evidence for the Christian faith as the means whereby someone can come to see the truth of the gospel. There is no conflict between the work of the Holy Spirit and the use of evidence and reason. The evidence and reason as such were never intended to supplant the work of God's Spirit but rather are intended to be the means by which the Holy Spirit brings someone to faith in Christ.

---

[3]Note Acts 9:22; 15:2; 17:2-4; 17:17; 18:4, 19, 27-28; 19:8-10; 28:23-24.

What Evidence Can Do

As anticipated in the last discussion, we can see that evidence can answer honest intellectual questions. Throughout the history of the church as the gospel has spread around the world, many who have been confronted with the claims of Christ have had honest questions, if not objections, about what we are presenting. The marshaling of evidence and the use of reason enable Christians to give honest answers to these questions and responses to these objections.

Second, evidence can expose dishonest intellectual questions as spiritual problems. In John 10:24-28 (NASB) we discover that the recalcitrance of some of the Jews was not due to any lack of evidence or information but rather was due to their darkened hearts.

> The Jews then gathered around Him, and were saying to Him, "How long will You keep us in suspense? If You are the Christ, tell us plainly." Jesus answered them, "I told you, and you do not believe; the works that I do in My Father's name, these testify of Me. But you do not believe because you are not of My sheep. My sheep hear My voice, and I know them, and they follow Me; and I give eternal life to them, and they will never perish; and no one will snatch them out of My hand."

A third thing that evidence can do is build up the faith of the believer. Take a look at what Acts 18:24-28 (NASB) says about Apollos and how he "greatly helped" those who believed:

> Now a Jew named Apollos, an Alexandrian by birth, an eloquent man, came to Ephesus; and he was mighty in the Scriptures. This man had been instructed in the way of the Lord; and being fervent in spirit, he was speaking and teaching accurately the things concerning Jesus, being acquainted only with the baptism of John; and he began to speak out boldly in the synagogue. But when Aquila and Priscilla heard him, they took him aside and explained to him the way of God more accurately. And when he wanted to go across to Achaia, the brethren encouraged him and wrote to the disciples to welcome him; and when he had arrived, he greatly helped those who had believed through grace, for he powerfully refuted the Jews in public, demonstrating by the Scriptures that Jesus was the Christ.

THE ROLE OF FAITH

Reason prior to faith. Reason precedes faith in that it is able to demonstrate the preambles of faith, such as God's existence, the reliability of the Bible and that the Word of God is trustworthy. But reason does not produce faith. As Norman Geisler puts it, "Discursive thought, or reasoning from premises to conclusions, is not the cause of the assent of faith. Nonetheless, such reasoning 'can accompany the assent of faith.' The reason they are parallel but one does not cause the other is that 'faith involves will (freedom) and reason doesn't coerce the will.' That is, a person is free to dissent even though there may be convincing reasons to believe."[4] Remember, faith is a personal trust in someone or something. Faith in God is a personal trust in him. Even though there are convincing reasons to trust God, some will not, but it is precisely because they *will* not. In summary, table 1.2 illustrates the relation between faith and reason and the role of each.

Table 1.2

Reason	Faith
Believing those things demonstrated by appropriate disciplines, e.g., philosophy, science, mathematics	Believing those things revealed by God through Christ and Scripture that could not be discovered by reason alone
God's existence and certain attributes	The Trinity
The nature of light waves	Human fallenness
Pythagorean theorem	The Gospel
General revelation	**Special revelation**
Romans 1:19-20	2 Peter 1:21
Psalm 19:1-4	Colossians 2:9; John 14:9

CONCLUSION

Ultimately there is an essential agreement between faith and reason. The

---

[4]Norman L. Geisler, *Thomas Aquinas: An Evangelical Appraisal* (Grand Rapids, Mich.: Baker, 1991), p. 58.

very fact that we, as Christians, study the Bible and discuss it and that we seek to understand how the Bible applies to our lives shows that we attempt to understand (reason) what we believe (faith). Reason does not cause faith, but our faith is not unreasonable.

FOR FURTHER READING

Beckwith, Francis J., and Stephen Parrish. *See the Gods Fall: Four Rivals to Christianity*. Joplin, Mo.: College Press, 1997.

Craig, William Lane. *Reasonable Faith: Christian Truth and Apologetics*. 2nd ed. Wheaton, Ill.: Crossway, 1994.

Geisler, Norman L. *Christian Apologetics*. Grand Rapids, Mich.: Baker, 1976.

———. *Thomas Aquinas: An Evangelical Appraisal*. Grand Rapids, Mich.: Baker, 1991.

Kreeft, Peter, and Ronald K. Tacelli. *Handbook of Christian Apologetics: Hundreds of Answers to Crucial Questions*. Downers Grove, Ill.: InterVarsity Press, 1994.

Moreland, J. P., and William Lane Craig. *Philosophical Foundations for a Christian Worldview*. Downers Grove, Ill.: InterVarsity Press, 2003.

2

DEFENDING THE DEFENSE
OF THE FAITH

Craig J. Hazen

THE APOSTLE PETER PROBABLY TOLD THE STORY ON MANY OCCASIONS AS HE preached his way to Rome in the decades that followed the earthly ministry of Jesus. Mark, a close companion of Peter during his journeys, recorded Peter's account of this event in the New Testament Gospel that bears Mark's name. The event to which I refer is the miraculous healing of a man who could not walk, probably paralyzed for many years if not from birth, recorded in Mark 2. There are many healing miracles recorded in the Scriptures, but this one has a special twist in that this miracle illustrates, in a dramatic fashion and early in the ministry of Jesus, a key method our Lord utilized in communicating and confirming the central points of his message.

JESUS AND THE ETHOS OF DEMONSTRATION

As Mark relates the story, Jesus had already garnered a large following that made it difficult for him to move around in populated areas. In Capernaum, Jesus began to teach in a local home, and a huge crowd quickly gathered so there was no room left even outside the door. Reports of Jesus' healing activities certainly added to the interest, and it is likely that many in attendance were anxious for a touch from this extraordinary rabbi. Four men in particular sought healing from Jesus, not for themselves but for their companion, who was unable to walk. They could not get though the crowd to Jesus inside so they climbed up on top of the structure, burrowed through the roof and lowered the "paralytic" down on his mat to Jesus in the room below.

Now comes the twist. When Jesus saw the paralytic and the faith of the men who had brought him, Jesus said, "Son, your sins are forgiven." Even the parallel passages recorded in Matthew and Luke do not tell us the reaction of the man on the mat, or those who brought him, to this unexpected statement by Jesus. All three Synoptic Gospels, however, record the reaction of some "teachers of the law" who were likely following Jesus around in order to scrutinize his teaching and activities. Indeed, the text implies that the looks on their faces may have told the whole story, because they clearly thought Jesus had crossed a very serious line with his utterance to the paralytic. In their view, Jesus had blasphemed. After all, who could forgive sins but God alone?

Jesus' response to the "teachers of the law" is the climax of this passage. Peter, who was likely an eyewitness and the source of Mark's account, probably knew enough about the religious law of his day to sense that a conflict was looming. Ironically, and certainly the reason that this incident stayed so prominently in Peter's mind, Jesus did not dispute the thinking of the teachers of the law on the point that God alone could forgive sins—simply because the point was a valid one. Instead, Jesus replied, "that you may know that the Son of Man has authority on earth to forgive sins, get up, take your mat and go home" (Mk 2:10). The man got up in full view of the throng that had gathered and walked out leaving everyone amazed.

I suppose any religious teacher could have wandered into Capernaum and made spiritual statements such as "your sins are forgiven" and convinced at least a few people to believe that a real activity in the unseen, spiritual world had taken place. But Jesus' goal on this occasion and on many that followed (e.g., Mt 11:2-5; Lk 7:18-23; Jn 3:2; 5:31-36; 10:38; 15:24-25) was to help those in attendance have good reason to "know" that he had authority from God and, by implication in the case of the paralytic, that he was the divine Son of God. Jesus provided reasons to believe through many different means, the most dramatic of which were miracles done in public as authentication of his message, identity and authority. Of course Jesus' prediction of his death and resurrection (Mt

12:39-40; Lk 11:29-30; Jn 2:18-22; etc.), which he overtly labeled "*the sign*" to a wicked generation, took this to the highest level. New Testament scholar R. V. G. Tasker called the sign of the resurrection spoken of by Jesus "the supreme sign, which would be the Father's unmistakable vindication of his Son."[1]

It is very important to understand that in justifying the task of Christian apologetics throughout the history of the church, it was Jesus himself who set the stage. He did this not by writing apologetic tracts and treatises but by creating what I shall call here an "ethos of demonstration" among his followers. Jesus demonstrated the truth of his message and his identity over and over again using nearly every method at his disposal, including miracle, prophecy, godly style of life, authoritative teaching *and* reasoned argumentation.[2] And although Jesus clearly authorized the apologetic ethos for his followers by living it out himself, it is also important to note that he did not create this approach *ex nihilo* during his three years of ministry. Indeed, Jesus was really just reaffirming an ages-old ethos of demonstration that had been well established in the Old Testament tradition. From the miracles of Moses in Pharaoh's court (Ex 7) to Elijah's contest with the prophets of Baal (1 Kings 18) to God himself calling for his opponents to "present your case . . . set forth your arguments" (Is 41:21), a divine pattern was already fixed by the time Jesus came on the scene.

THE APOSTLES AND THE EARLY CHURCH

Perhaps there is no stronger argument that Jesus himself was an extraordinary source for the apologetic impulse in Christianity than the fact that his closest followers, those who so deeply desired to emulate their Master, were such ardent proponents of Jesus' ethos of demonstration. In-

---

[1]R. V. G. Tasker, *The Gospel According to Matthew: An Introduction and Commentary* (Grand Rapids, Mich.: Eerdmans, 1961), p. 131.

[2]As for Jesus and "reasoned argumentation," several recent books have given special attention to the reasoning skills and intellectual prowess of Jesus. See Dallas Willard, *The Divine Conspiracy: Rediscovering Our Hidden Life in God* (New York: HarperSanFrancisco, 1998); J. P. Moreland, *Love Your God with All Your Mind: The Role of Reason in the Life of the Soul* (Colorado Springs, Colo.: NavPress, 1997); and James W. Sire, *Habits of the Mind: Intellectual Life as a Christian Calling* (Downers Grove, Ill.: InterVarsity Press, 2000).

deed, Paul, John and Peter seemed almost obsessed with offering evidence, testimony and argument at every turn in order to establish the truth of the gospel message. The case for the apostolic support for the full range of apologetic activity is very well known and has been affirmed by scores of preeminent Christian scholars in the last fifty years.[3] Anyone wishing to downplay the significance of the defense of the faith to the apostles and the early church is truly swimming upstream against an overwhelming current. Since it has been so well covered, I shall choose only a few of the most compelling examples to highlight.

Peter, who along with James and John was a member of the inner circle of Christ's apostles, was greatly influenced by the apologetic thrust of Jesus' ministry and offers a direct command for all believers likewise to follow this model. In what remains today as a touchstone verse for those with a calling to defend the faith, Peter wrote, "But in your hearts set apart Christ as Lord. Always be prepared to give an answer to everyone who asks you to give the reason for the hope that you have. But do this with gentleness and respect" (1 Pet 3:15). Jude, who was likely the brother of Jesus, also gives a very straightforward command to his brothers and sisters in the Way to defend the faith against false teachers. "I felt I had to write and urge you to contend for the faith that was once for all

---

[3]Kenneth D. Boa and Robert M. Bowman, Jr., *Faith Has Its Reasons: An Integrative Approach to Defending Christianity* (Colorado Springs, Colo.: NavPress, 2001); F. F. Bruce, *The Defense of the Gospel in the New Testament* (Grand Rapids, Mich.: Eerdmans, 1959); Avery Dulles, *A History of Apologetics* (New York: Corpus Instrumentorum, 1971); William Dyrness, *Christian Apologetics in a World Community* (Downers Grove, Ill.: InterVarsity Press, 1983); Norman L. Geisler, *Baker Encyclopedia of Christian Apologetics* (Grand Rapids, Mich.: Baker, 1999), pp. 37-41; Norman L. Geisler and Ronald M. Brooks, *When Skeptics Ask* (Wheaton, Ill.: Victor, 1990); Frederic R. Howe, *Challenge and Response: A Handbook of Christian Apologetics* (Grand Rapids, Mich.: Zondervan, 1982); Gordon R. Lewis, *Testing Christianity's Truth Claims: Approaches to Christian Apologetics* (Lanham, Md.: University Press of America, 1990); Ronald B. Mayers, *Balanced Apologetics: Using Evidences and Presuppositions in Defense of the Faith* (Grand Rapids, Mich.: Kregel, 1984); John Warwick Montgomery, *Faith Founded on Fact: Essays in Evidential Apologetics* (Nashville: Thomas Nelson, 1978); Clark J. Pinnock, *Set Forth Your Case: Studies in Christian Apologetics* (Chicago: Moody Press, 1971); Bernard Ramm, *Varieties of Christian Apologetics* (Grand Rapids, Mich.: Baker, 1962); J. K. S. Reid, *Christian Apologetics* (Grand Rapids, Mich.: Eerdmans, 1969); and R. C. Sproul, John Gerstner and Arthur Lindsley, *Classical Apologetics: A Rational Defense of the Christian Faith and a Critique of Presuppositional Apologetics* (Grand Rapids, Mich.: Zondervan, 1984). Even those apologetics texts that do not begin with a biblical case for defending the faith, and there are hundreds in this time frame, invariably assume it at the outset.

entrusted to the saints" (Jude 3). The apostle Paul makes it clear that anyone who is to be considered for eldership in the church should be pro-
ficient in arguing against those who hold false doctrine. Paul wrote that
an elder "must hold firmly to the trustworthy message as it has been
taught, so that he can encourage others by sound doctrine and refute
those who oppose it" (Tit 1:9).[4]

Even if Christ's closest followers had not given direct commands to
engage in apologetic activities, they modeled these activities so frequently and unmistakably in Scripture that their actions amount to a
clear exhortation for all Christians to go and do likewise. The Gospel
writers themselves were carefully attuned to this. Luke, for instance, had
explicit apologetic purposes in the construction of his Gospel—a special
focus that he lays out in the prologue to his book. Here he highlights
the importance of eyewitness testimony, careful investigation and accurate reporting all with an eye toward helping his reader, Theophilus, to
know "the certainty" of the things he had been taught (Lk 1:1-4). Luke's
book of Acts begins by mentioning the "many convincing proofs" Jesus
had given his followers to confirm the truth of the resurrection (Acts 1:3).
Jesus was therefore portrayed as the first among many in Acts who
would offer reasons for belief at every opportunity. Later in Acts, Luke
focuses in on the apostle Paul and describes a key *modus operandi* of
Paul for his missionary activity in his travels throughout the Mediterranean world as reasoning, proving and persuading on behalf of the truth
of the gospel. Luke describes Paul's regular method in Acts 17:2-4, as
well as the result. "As his custom was, Paul went into the synagogue,
and on three Sabbath days he reasoned with them from the Scriptures,
explaining and proving that the Christ had to suffer and rise from the
dead. 'This Jesus I am proclaiming to you is the Christ,' he said. Some of
the Jews were persuaded and joined Paul and Silas, as did large numbers
of God-fearing Greeks and not a few prominent women."In addition to
confirming that it was his "custom," Luke gives direct accounts of Paul

---

[4]I am not going to make a distinction here between polemics—the traditional term used for
disputation over differing views on doctrine among believers or those who claim to be believers—and apologetics. Both terms support the idea of offering reasons for beliefs and fit well
into the ethos of demonstration.

reasoning and persuading in Thessalonica (Acts 17:2), Athens (Acts 17:17), Corinth (Acts 18:4) and Ephesus (Acts 19:8). Indeed, in Ephesus Paul not only "had discussions" daily in the lecture hall of Tyrannus but was also a vehicle for God's "extraordinary miracles" among the people (Acts 19:11). For the apostles, as for Jesus, there was no ultimate line of demarcation between miracles and reasoning in that both were powerful tools in the hands of the Holy Spirit to persuade and lead humanity to salvation in Christ. Jesus' ethos of demonstration was thriving among the New Testament figures and set in place a tradition of defending the faith that would be carried on by the church fathers in the centuries immediately following the founding of Christianity.[5]

OBJECTIONS TO APOLOGETIC ENGAGEMENT AND RESPONSES

Because of the steady encroachment of secular culture onto the church's turf and the tremendous increase in the felt need by evangelicals for responses to the intellectual issues that challenge the gospel and the Christian view of the world, objections by Christians to apologetic activity seem to be raised far less frequently. There are still objections, but it is my experience that even these seem to be formulated somewhat differently from those in the recent past.[6] I shall offer responses to four objections to apologetic engagement that I have heard most often in recent years. I will present the objections I have heard in the same language with which I normally encounter them at public events.

I've never seen anybody come to faith in Christ through apologetics. Of course one would immediately wonder why the apostle Paul was so enamored of reasoning, proving and persuading if these methods were desperately ineffective, or why Peter and Jude would command the practice of giving reasons for faith. Indeed, in the passage from Acts 17:2-4 quoted above, Paul's explaining, proving and persuading is directly associated with "large numbers" of converts and undoubtedly

---

[5]For more on the defense of the faith in the church fathers, see Dulles, *History of Apologetics,* and Reid, *Christian Apologetics.*

[6]Responses to similar objections to apologetic activity can be found in Lewis, *Testing Christianity's Truth Claims,* pp. 21-34, and Geisler, *Encyclopedia of Christian Apologetics,* pp. 38-41.

played a role. People always come to Christ through the work of the Holy Spirit, but there are many tools the Holy Spirit uses to do his work. One of those tools is apologetic reasoning. There are many who give serious personal testimonies to the value of apologetics in assisting their movement toward salvation—Augustine of Hippo and C. S. Lewis, to name two easily recognizable and influential figures. Occasionally apologetics is the primary tool that brings people to the foot of the cross. This would be true of my own conversion and of many I've shared the gospel with over the years. Other times apologetics plays a secondary or tertiary role, helping to make the gospel message more plausible in a world that has serious doubts about its veracity. However, given the explicit commands and clear examples in Scripture to offer reasons for faith, I would guess that those who offer this objection have either rarely tried robust but gentle apologetic engagement or perhaps are not "prepared" in the way that the apostle Peter exhorted us to be (1 Pet 3:15).

But without faith it is impossible to please God. This objection derives from a common misinterpretation of Hebrews 11:6: "And without faith it is impossible to please God, because anyone who comes to him must believe that he exists and that he rewards those who earnestly seek him." The misunderstanding of this verse is based on a weak notion of the word *faith*. The only way this verse can be a problem for the task of apologetics is if one equates saving faith with "blind faith"—something that is illegitimate but done far too often by Christians today. Christian faith is not "blind faith," that is, it is not opposed to reason, evidence, logic or knowledge. In fact, the apostle Paul allows no room for blind faith in a very provocative passage in 1 Corinthians. Paul wrote that if Christ did not rise from the dead, our faith is useless and futile (1 Cor 15:12-19). Here he locks together the resurrection of Christ, a knowable historical event—the truth of which can be determined through evidence and reason—with saving faith. He had a marvelous opportunity in this passage to decouple reason and faith. He could have encouraged us to have faith no matter what the evidence showed. But he did exactly the opposite. Paul confirmed that if we have no valid resurrection, then we have no valid faith. Christian faith is not blind in the least; rather it is dependent upon a historical event that can be thoroughly investigated with eyes wide open. A good synonym for genuine faith in the Christian tradition is simply "trust," and we can certainly trust that which we can know to be true—indeed, it is the wise thing to do. Our trust or faith is stronger when we have excellent reason to believe in whom we are trusting.

Just preach the Word because it will not return void. The Bible verse from which this objection is derived (Is 55:11) does not contain the word *just*. But it is the word *just* that really creates the problem because it implies that nothing else is ever needed in order to have the Word of God begin its regenerative work in the unbeliever. But Jesus and his apostles demonstrated to us that other elements could act as a catalyst for the gospel. As I showed earlier, miracle, prophecy, godly style of life *and* reasoned argumentation were all employed to authenticate their message with great effect. And once again the commands of Peter and Jude to defend the faith do not make sense if the only tool permissible is direct gospel proclamation.

Let me look at this from another angle for a moment because this objection actually made a lot more sense in previous generations. In years past it was not unusual that a believer could quote the Bible or "preach the Word" and have a good chance of engendering respect and perhaps deep reflection on the part of the unbeliever. This was possible because the Bible still carried significant cultural authority. An unbeliever would be likely to consider its words because there was a widespread recognition that the Bible was at the foundation of western civilization and brought wise counsel on many issues—even if the whole text was not considered true or without error by the skeptical recipient. Those days, however, are gone. There is a better than ever chance today that a person will actually consider you immoral for quoting the Bible because the Bible is often viewed, inappropriately of course, as misogynist, racist, violent, religiously exclusive and the basis for much of the conflict in our world. Clearly, the Scriptures are still "living and active" and "sharper than any double-edged sword" (Heb 6:12) and able to make us "wise for salvation through faith in Christ Jesus" (2 Tim 3:15). However, the armor that the opposition is wearing may need to be lowered for the sword to penetrate. A robust defense of Scripture as the Word of God—a pillar of modern apologetic work—can be used by the Holy Spirit to do this and is needed now more than ever.

What really matters is that you love Jesus and are willing to be used. It is difficult to argue with this sentiment, because there is so much truth in it. After all, if we do not put loving Jesus first and are not willing to be used, we are way out of touch with Christianity and are in serious need of discipleship. However, on close inspection this objection, like the one just before it, is problematic in that it is in principle excluding as unimportant a whole area of God-ordained activity. Putting this objection in a slightly different way, loving Jesus is where our focus should be and not on ivory-tower dialogue. Of course, once again we run into the problem of the commands and examples of Jesus and his followers. If they valued reasoned argumentation on behalf of the gospel, then so should we. Moreover, since loving Jesus entails obedience to him and to the commands of his inspired apostles, then engaging in apologetic activity would certainly be a mark of obedience and therefore consistent with loving Jesus.

When I hear this objection to apologetic activity I can't help but think there is something lying beneath it—something not stated clearly or completely forthrightly. I shall conclude with a brief word about this underlying issue. As one can quickly tell, the popular objections that I have addressed here are not particularly precise or persuasive. Very often when Christians dispute the validity of defending the faith, they may not be reacting to the legitimacy of the apologetic task but rather to their negative experiences with some who take up the apologetic task. This has been at times a serious problem with the effectiveness of our overall Christian witness. Apologists are sometimes out to win arguments and not souls, impatient with illogic from their counterparts, and arrogant in their demeanor. I am convinced that this can strip even the brightest apologists of their effectiveness for the Lord. Indeed, the "ethos of demonstration" that I identified in the daily ministry of Christ and his apostles included living out the second greatest commandment, to "love your neighbor as yourself" (Mt 22:39). The most effective apologist is not one who has the greatest academic prowess alone, but the one who has excellent intellectual preparation *and* reflects Christ's love in every way.

When Peter penned his great apologetics command (1 Pet 3:15), he was compelled to attach a qualifier that captures this notion: "But do this with gentleness and respect." Paul likewise confirmed this when he explained to Timothy that "the Lord's servant must not quarrel; instead, he must be kind to everyone, able to teach, not resentful. Those who oppose him he must gently instruct, in the hope that God will grant them repentance leading to a knowledge of the truth" (2 Tim 2:24-25).[7]

Christians who are able to bring it all together—a bright mind, comprehensive intellectual preparation for the proclamation and defense of the faith, the deepest devotion to and emulation of our Lord, and an unflinching commitment to the Great Commission—are instruments of great power in the hands of the Holy Spirit for furthering the kingdom. It should be our goal to raise up apologists such as these. I am convinced that even in small numbers they will foment a spiritual revolution in a world that is so thirsty for knowledge of the truth.

FOR FURTHER READING

Boa, Kenneth D., and Robert M. Bowman Jr. *Faith Has Its Reasons: An Integrative Approach to Defending Christianity.* Colorado Springs, Colo.: NavPress, 2001.

Bruce, F. F. *The Defense of the Gospel in the New Testament.* Grand Rapids, Mich.: Eerdmans, 1959.

Lewis, Gordon R. *Testing Christianity's Truth Claims: Approaches to Christian Apologetics.* Lanham, Md.: University Press of America, 1990.

Mayers, Ronald B. *Balanced Apologetics: Using Evidences and Presuppositions in Defense of the Faith.* Grand Rapids, Mich.: Kregel, 1984.

Sproul, R. C., John Gerstner and Arthur Lindsley. *Classical Apologetics: A Rational Defense of the Christian Faith and a Critique of Presuppositional Apologetics.* Grand Rapids, Mich.: Zondervan, 1984.

Stackhouse, John G., Jr. *Humble Apologetics: Defending the Faith Today.* New York: Oxford University Press, 2002.

---

[7]Many key apologetics texts make mention of this balanced approach to Christian character, gentle communication and the apologetic task. Of special interest, though, are David K. Clark, *Dialogical Apologetics: A Person-Centered Approach to Christian Defense* (Grand Rapids, Mich.: Baker, 1993), and John G. Stackhouse Jr., *Humble Apologetics: Defending the Faith Today* (New York: Oxford University Press, 2002).

3

TACTICS

Applying Apologetics to Everyday Life

Gregory P. Koukl

APOLOGETICS HAS A QUESTIONABLE REPUTATION AMONG NONAFICIONADOS. By definition apologists "defend" the faith. They defeat false ideas. They destroy speculations raised up against the knowledge of God.

Those sound like fightin' words to many people: Circle the wagons. Hoist the drawbridge. Fix bayonets. Load weapons. Ready, aim, fire. It's not surprising, then, that believers and unbelievers alike associate apologetics with conflict. Defenders don't dialogue. They fight.

In addition to the image problem, apologists face another barrier. The truth is that effective apologetics in the twenty-first century requires more than having the right answers. It's too easy for postmoderns to ignore our facts, deny our claims or simply yawn and walk away from the line we've drawn in the sand.

But sometimes they don't walk away. They think they know a few things, so they stand and fight. We wade into battle only to face a barrage we can't handle. We've ignored one of the first rules of engagement: never make a frontal assault on a superior force. Caught off balance, we tuck our tails between our legs and retreat, maybe for good.

I'd like to suggest a "more excellent way." Jesus said that when you find yourself a sheep amid wolves, be innocent but be shrewd (Mt 10:16). This calls for a tactical approach. Even though there is real warfare going on (note Paul's comments in Eph 6:10-20), our engagements should look more like diplomacy than combat.

Think of it this way. There are two critical elements of any encounter: strategy and tactics. Strategy involves the big picture, one's positioning prior to actual engagement. In our case, Christianity is well positioned (we have strategic superiority, in a sense) because we have superior ideas: the best answers to life's most important questions.

Tactics involve the actual details of engagement, literally "the art of arranging"—maneuvering in the face of an enemy, deploying assets, putting them into action to gain an advantage. Often a clever commander has the advantage over a superior opponent through deft tactical maneuvering.

This is where we must give our attention. We must learn to artfully manage the details of dialogue. This does not mean using tricks or slick ruses but finding clever ways to exploit another's bad thinking for the purpose of guiding him to truth.

TAKE A TIP FROM COLUMBO

There are many ways to accomplish this,[1] but my favorite is what I call the "Columbo tactic." It's the simplest device imaginable to stop a challenger in his tracks, turn the tables and get him thinking. It's an almost effortless way to put you in the driver's seat.

This tactic is typified by Lieutenant Columbo, the bumbling and seemingly inept TV detective whose remarkable success was based on an innocent query: "Do you mind if I ask you a question?"

The key to Columbo is to go on the offensive by advancing the conversation—and eventually dismantling another person's viewpoint—with carefully selected questions which move the discussion along in an interactive way. The tactic is best played out Columbo style—halting, head-scratching and apparently harmless.

Simply put, instead of making assertions, ask questions. If you hit a roadblock when witnessing, ask a good question. With practice this can become second nature, especially if you plan questions in advance.

---

[1]Stand to Reason has an entire course on "Tactics in Defending the Faith," available at <www.str.org>.

Hugh Hewitt, a secular radio talk show host who is also a superb Christian ambassador, is a master of this technique. He advises asking at least a half-dozen questions in every conversation.

> Once developed, the habit of asking questions will inevitably give you advantages in every setting. You will obviously leave most situations with more information (and friends) than when you arrived, and being an asker allows you control of situations that statement-makers rarely achieve. Once you learn how to guide a conversation, you have also learned how to control it.[2]

There are literally hundreds of fun ways to do this, and it offers tremendous advantages. For one, questions are interactive by nature, inviting others to participate in dialogue. They are also neutral; no "preaching" is involved. The Columbo tactic allows you to make good headway without actually stating your case. More importantly, a carefully placed question shifts the burden of proof to the other person where it often belongs.

Jesus used this method frequently. When facing a hostile crowd he often asked challenging or leading questions meant to silence his detractors: "Show Me a denarius. Whose likeness and inscription does it have?" (Lk 20:22-26 NASB); "Was the baptism of John from heaven or from men?" (Lk 20:4 NASB).[3]

Columbo is most powerful when you have a plan of attack. Generally when I ask a question I have one of three goals: to gain information, to reverse the burden of proof or to exploit a weakness I see in another's view.[4]

"WHAT DO YOU MEAN BY THAT?"

Sometimes you need more information to know how to proceed, so your initial probe will be open-ended. The most effective question you can ask in most circumstances is a clarification question, some variation of "What do you mean by that?" It's delivered in a mild, genuinely in-

---

[2]Hugh Hewitt, *In, but Not Of* (Nashville: Thomas Nelson, 2003), p. 173.

[3]See also Mt 17:25; 18:12; 21:28-32; Jn 18:22-23.

[4]Kevin Bywater of Summit Ministries was very helpful in my formulation of this three-step approach. His website is www.kevinbywater.com

quisitive fashion. It's a natural opening with absolutely no pressure. For example, when they say . . .

"There is no God," you ask, "What do you mean by 'God'?"

"Reincarnation was taken out of the Bible," you ask, "What do you mean it 'was taken out'?"

"All religions are basically the same," you ask, "Really? In what way?"

"You shouldn't force your views on me," you ask, "Specifically, how am I forcing my views on you?"

"The Bible has been changed over the years," you ask, "How exactly do you think it's been altered?"

"It's only your interpretation," you ask, "What exactly do you mean by only my 'interpretation'?"

Questions like these accomplish a few important things. First, they immediately engage the other person in an interactive way. Second, they're flattering because questions show that you are genuinely interested in another's view. Third, they force her to think more carefully—maybe for the first time—about exactly what she does mean. Finally, questioning uncovers valuable information, revealing precisely what she thinks so you don't misunderstand or misrepresent her.

Be sure to pay attention to the response. If it's unclear, follow up with more questions. Say, "Let me see if I understand you on this," then feed back the view to make sure you got it right.

Once while on vacation in Wisconsin, the woman helping my wife and me at the one-hour photo had a large pentagram—a five-pointed star generally associated with the occult—dangling from her neck.

"Does that have religious significance," I asked, "or is it just jewelry?"

"It has religious significance," she answered. "The five points stand for earth, wind, fire, water and spirit. I'm a pagan."

My wife, unaware that "pagan" referred to Wicca (witchcraft) and earth worship, laughed in amazement at what seemed like a remarkably candid confession. "I've never heard anyone actually admit right out they were pagan," she explained. She knew the term only as a pejorative, used by girlfriends yelling at their kids: "Get in here, you bunch of pagans."

"It's an earth religion," the woman explained, "like the Native Americans."

"So you're Wiccan?" I continued. She nodded. This led to a productive conversation made possible by noticing a piece of jewelry and asking a very simple question, a variation of "What do you mean by that?"

How Did You Come to That Conclusion?

The first Columbo question helps you know more precisely what another person thinks. Next, you want to know why he thinks that way. That takes a second question: "How did you come to that conclusion?"

An alternate might be, "Why do you say that?" or "What are your reasons for saying that?" These questions charitably assume that the non-Christian has actually thought through the issue carefully instead of just making an assertion or expressing feelings.

This question accomplishes something else vitally important. It forces your opponent to give an account for his own beliefs. The responsibility to defend or give evidence for a view is called "burden of proof." The basic rule governing this responsibility is: the one who makes the claim bears the burden.

Christians should not be the only ones who have to defend what they believe. In the immortal words of Ricky Ricardo, the other side has "a lot of splainin' to do" themselves. Reject the impulse to counter every assertion someone manufactures. Don't try to refute every tale spun out of thin air. It's not your job to answer his claim. It's his job to defend it.

For example, I was once on the top-rated secular talk radio show in Los Angeles making a case for intelligent design over evolution. When a caller used the big bang theory to argue against a Creator, I said the big bang worked in my favor. It seemed to me, I told him, that a big bang needs a Big Banger.

The caller disagreed. The big bang doesn't need God, he claimed. Then leading off with the phrase "One could say," he spun a lengthy science-fiction tale for the audience on how everything came from nothing.

"You're right," I responded. " 'One could say' anything he wants. But giving good reasons why we should believe the story you just told is another thing altogether."

It wasn't my job to disprove his fairy tale. He bore the burden of proof for his own claim. It was his job to demonstrate why anyone should take his something-from-nothing musings seriously.

THE PROFESSOR'S PLOY

The Columbo tactic is a good one to use in the classroom. Some professors are fond of taking potshots at Christianity with remarks like "The Bible is just a bunch of fables." Well-meaning believers sometimes take up the challenge and attempt a head-to-head duel with the professor. This rarely works.

There is another rule of engagement that governs exchanges like these: the person with the microphone wins. The professor always has the strategic advantage. It's foolish to get into a power struggle when you're outgunned. There's a better way. Use your tactics.

Simply ask your Columbo questions: "Professor, what do you mean by that? How did you come to that conclusion?" Make him shoulder the burden of proof. After all, he's the teacher, and he's the one making the claim. With this approach you are able to stay engaged while deftly sidestepping the power struggle.

At this point the professor may sense your maneuver and respond, "Oh, you must be one of those fundamentalists who thinks the Bible is inspired by God. Okay, I'm a fair man. Why don't you take a few minutes and prove that to the rest of the class?"

What has he done? In one quick move he's cleverly switched the burden of proof back on you, the student.

If you find yourself facing the challenge "Why don't you try to prove me wrong?" don't take the bait. Falling into this trap is fatal. Instead, shift the burden back where it belongs, on the professor. After all, he made the claim.

Respond this way. "Professor, I haven't said anything about my own view, so you don't know what it is. More to the point, it's irrelevant. It doesn't matter what I believe. Your view is the issue, not mine. I'm just a student. I'm here to learn. You've made a strong claim. I simply want clarification and reasons."

If he gives you an answer, thank him for explaining himself and either ask another question or let it go for the time being.

Don't miss this point: Christians don't have to be experts in everything. If we keep the burden on the other side when they're making the claim, we don't have to have all the answers. In fact, we can be effective even when we know very little if we ask the right questions.

When someone says to you, "The Bible's been changed so many times," or "No one can know the truth about religion," or "All religions are basically the same," don't retreat in silence. Instead, simply raise your eyebrows and say, "Oh? What do you mean by that?" and "How did you come to that conclusion?" Everyone in the discussion has a point of view. There's no reason to let the other side have a free ride.

Don't allow yourself to be thrust into a defensive posture when others are making the claim. Remember, they are the ones who bear the burden of proof. Why let them ignore her responsibility?

For far too long non-Christians have contrived fanciful challenges, then sat back and watched us squirm, and we've let it happen. Others must defend their own unbelief. If they make the claim, it's not our job to refute it; it's their job to answer for it. The simple question "How did you come to that conclusion?" puts the responsibility right where it belongs. The pressure is on them, not you.

HAVE YOU EVER CONSIDERED . . . ?

The information you gather with the first two questions puts you in a better position to move to the final stage of Columbo. Now that you know both what the other person believes and why he believes it, you can move on to questions that challenge his ideas.

This step is more demanding because it requires some insight into what has gone wrong; you have to be able to see the flaw. The key is to pay close attention to the reasons. Look, observe, reflect. Ask yourself if the conclusion follows from the evidence. What are the weaknesses of the view? Is there a misstep, a non sequitur, a fallacy or a failing of some sort? If so, how can it be exposed with a question instead of a statement?

It's not always easy to flush out the error, so don't be surprised if you find yourself stalled out. This takes a little practice, but with time you'll improve.

You may find that in some conversations you don't have the resources to go further. Or you'll sense the person you're talking to is losing interest. If so, don't feel compelled to force the conversation; let the encounter die a natural death. Consider it a fruitful, interactive learning experience nonetheless. You don't have to hit home runs. Sometimes just getting up to bat will do, and the first two questions accomplish that.

In the process of conversation you may be alerted to some weakness, flaw or contradiction that can be exposed and exploited. There's no special formula for acting on your discovery. When you see something wrong, point it out with a question rather than a statement.

For example, when they say . . .

"The fetus may be a human being, but it's not a person," you ask, "What's the difference?"

"You shouldn't push your morality on me," you ask, "Why not?" (It's going to be very hard for them to answer this without them pushing their morality on you.)

"How can God exist when there's so much evil in the world?" you ask, "But if there is no God, how can we call anything evil in the first place?"

Your approach can be softened a bit by using your question to suggest an alternative. Ask, "Have you ever considered," then offer a different view that gently challenges his beliefs or confronts the weakness of his argument. For example, have you ever considered . . .

the difficulty of removing something like teaching on reincarnation from every existing handwritten copy of the New Testament in circulation in the Roman world by the fourth century?

that the existence of evil is actually evidence *for* the existence of God, not *against* it?[5]

that if the Bible were "merely written by men" it would be very hard to account for fulfilled prophecy?

that if partial-birth abortion is morally acceptable, it's going to be hard to condemn infanticide, since the only difference between the two is the

---

[5]C. S. Lewis opens with this argument in *Mere Christianity* (New York: Macmillan, 1952), his fine introduction to the faith. See also the talk by Gregory Koukl, "Evil, Suffering and the Goodness of God," available through Stand to Reason at <www.str.org>.

baby's location—partially out of the womb or completely out?

that if Jesus was wrong about being the only way of salvation, it becomes difficult to call him a good man, a prophet or a wise religious teacher?

Initially you will not be quick on your feet with responses like the ones above. Your best ideas will come afterward, when the pressure is off. Make note of them. Practice them out loud. Try to anticipate the rejoinder and what your counter will be. I have made this a regular habit, and it's paid off. Next time around, the new responses are right at my fingertips.

TWENTY-FIRST-CENTURY AMBASSADORS

Defending the faith in the new millennium requires more than knowledge. It's not enough for followers of Christ to have accurately informed minds. They also need an artful method. They need to combine their knowledge with wisdom and diplomacy. They need the tools of an ambassador, not the weapons of a warrior, tactical skill, not brute force.

Asking simple, leading questions is an almost effortless way to accomplish balance. You can advance the dialogue and make capital of the conversation for spiritual ends without seeming abrupt, rude or pushy. Questions are engaging and interactive, probing yet amicable. Most important, they keep you in the driver's seat while someone else does all the work.

Most critics are not well-equipped to defend their own faith. They have rarely thought through what they believe and have relied more on generalizations and slogans than on careful reflection. To expose their error, take your cue from Columbo. Scratch your head, rub your chin, pause for a moment, then say, "Do you mind if I ask you a question?"

FOR FURTHER READING

Beckwith, Francis J., and Gregory P. Koukl. *Relativism: Feet Firmly Planted in Mid-Air.* Grand Rapids, Mich.: Baker, 1998.
Koukl, Gregory P. *Tactics in Defending the Faith.* Compact disc. Available for purchase at <www.str.org>.

Hewitt, Hugh. *In, But Not Of*. Nashville: Thomas Nelson, 2003.

Kreeft, Peter. *Between Heaven and Hell*. Downers Grove, Ill.: InterVarsity Press, 1982.

———. *Socrates Meets Jesus*. Downers Grove, Ill.: InterVarsity Press, 1987.

———. *The Unaborted Socrates*. Downers Grove, Ill.: InterVarsity Press, 1983.

PART 2

GOD'S EXISTENCE

Francis J. Beckwith

IN THE LATE 1960S, PRESIDENT JAMES MCCORD OF PRINCETON THEOLOGICAL Seminary declared that Protestant theology's death-of-God movement was ushering in a "whole new era in theology."[1] Nevertheless, *Time*'s ominous front cover, which asked the question "Is God Dead?" was not really as prophetic as President McCord had thought. For only five years later *Time* heralded on its front cover the sudden revival of evangelical faith among Roman Catholic and Protestant young people with a psychedelic portrait of Jesus of Nazareth, labeled "The Jesus Revolution."[2] Some of these "Jesus People," as they matured in their faith, began to take seriously the philosophical and theological traditions of the Christian church and became part of the burgeoning movement in professional philosophy that has produced two important academic organization, the Evangelical Philosophical Society (EPS) and the Society of Christian Philosophers (SCP). Both groups produce first-rate academic journals, *Philosophia Christi* and *Faith & Philosophy,* which have received high praise from the wider philosophical community.

Many of these Christian philosophers offer new and improved versions of the traditional arguments for God's existence. In this portion of the book, we include five such arguments: the *kalam* cosmological argument (R. Douglas Geivett), an argument from design (William A.

---

[1]"Toward a Hidden God: Is God Dead?" *Time,* April 8, 1966, pp. 82ff.
[2]"Rebel Cry: Jesus Is Coming!" *Time,* July 21, 1971, pp. 56ff.

Dembski), a Thomistic cosmological argument (W. David Beck), a moral argument (Paul Copan) and an ontological argument (William Lane Craig).

Arguments 1 and 3 (chapters four and six) are cosmological arguments. They are called cosmological because defenders of these arguments make a case for God being the cause of the universe (or cosmos) from the fact of its contingent existence. That is, because the universe cannot account for its own existence, there must exist a being who exists in such a way that he does not depend on anything for his existence.

Design (or teleological) arguments are offered to support belief in God's existence by appealing to the apparent design of the universe as a whole or aspects of it. For example, some philosophers argue that because the universe seems fine-tuned for the arising of human life, and because such fine-tuning requires an agent powerful enough to design a universe, the universe was likely designed by a superior agent with attributes we typically associate with a being called God. In chapter five, Dembski offers a much more modest version of the design argument, one that does not claim to prove God's existence but rather shows that certain aspects of the natural universe that exhibit design cannot be accounted for by naturalism. According to Dembski, "Design arguments can tell us that certain patterns exhibited in nature reliably point us to a designing intelligence. . . . A design argument can clear away materialistic stumblingblocks to belief in God (for example, it can refute the claim that science has shown that all the patterns in nature can be explained without recourse to intelligence). Clearing away such stumbling blocks has immense apologetic value, especially in the current cultural and intellectual climate."

Chapter seven is a moral argument for God's existence, a version of which was made popular by C. S. Lewis in the first five chapters of *Mere Christianity*. Defenders of this type of argument maintain that the reality of moral law in the world cannot be accounted for in a naturalist universe. In this book, Paul Copan offers a version of the moral argument that is in the tradition of Lewis but engages contemporary atheistic critics such as Michael Martin.

Probably the most difficult argument to understand for God's existence is the ontological argument. First offered to the Christian church by the medievel philosopher Anselm of Canterbury and recently reformulated by Norman Malcolm and Alvin Plantinga, this argument maintains that once one understands what is meant by the term *God,* then one is driven to the conclusion that God must exist. Although it is a highly controversial argument rejected by some Christian philosophers, William Lane Craig defends a version of it in chapter eight.

4

THE *KALAM* COSMOLOGICAL ARGUMENT

R. Douglas Geivett

I FIRST LEARNED OF THE *KALAM* COSMOLOGICAL ARGUMENT FROM NORM Geisler some twenty years ago. What struck me then was that Norm, an unrepentant Thomist, was genuinely enthusiastic about an argument that had been repudiated by St. Thomas. From the beginning, I was drawn to Norm's thoughtful approach to Christian belief and to the *kalam* argument that I learned at his knee. For two decades, this argument has figured prominently in my own conception of a viable program of natural theology. This chapter is written as a tribute to Norm for the generosity of spirit he has always shown me. Thank you, Norm, for turning the key that unlocked my passion to become a philosopher.

WHAT IS THE *KALAM* COSMOLOGICAL ARGUMENT?

I've structured this chapter as a series of reflections on questions pertaining to the *kalam* cosmological argument. The first and most obvious question must be, what *is* the *kalam* cosmological argument?

First, it is an argument for the existence of God. In the final section of this chapter, I'll clarify the sense in which God is contained in the conclusion.

Second, the *kalam* argument is a cosmological argument for God's existence. There are various versions of the cosmological argument. Their family resemblance is determined by what they all have in common. Cosmological arguments for the existence of God conclude that God exists as the cause of the universe. Each version of cosmological argument focuses on some feature of the cosmos that implies that the cosmos was caused to exist. Some versions hold that the universe is contingent rather than necessary, so that some necessary being must exist and be the ultimate cause of the universe. The *kalam* argument infers the existence of God from a different fact about the universe—namely, that the universe began to exist a finite time ago.

Third, this argument was first christened the *kalam* argument by William Lane Craig, because of its historical pedigree stretching all the way back to medieval Islamic philosophy and the *kalam* tradition of natural theology.[1]

Fourth, the basic structure of the *kalam* argument may be captured in the following straightforward manner:

1. Whatever begins to exist has a cause.
2. The universe began to exist.
3. Therefore, the universe has a cause.[2]

While this is not, as it stands, an explicit argument for the existence of God, it is an argument that the beginning of the universe implies the existence of a First Cause.[3] All that remains for this to qualify as an argument for the existence of God is to show that the First Cause must, if it is to be such a cause, have properties that usually are uniquely ascribed to God. At the very least, the argument suggests that the First Cause is the personal Creator of the universe, a being who decided to create and did so for reasons.

---

[1]For a masterful survey of the history of this argument, see William Lane Craig, *The Kalam Cosmological Argument* (London: Macmillan, 1979), pp. 1-60.

[2]This is William Craig's customary way of formulating the argument. See his article "Philosophical and Scientific Pointers to *Creatio ex Nihilo*," in *Contemporary Perspectives on Religious Epistemology*, ed. R. Douglas Geivett and Brendan Sweetman (New York: Oxford University Press, 1992), p. 186, and his remarks in *Does God Exist? The Craig-Flew Debate*, ed. Stan W. Wallace (Aldershot, England: Ashgate Publishing, 2003), p. 20. See also "The Finitude of the Past and the Existence of God," in a book jointly written by William Lane Craig and Quentin Smith, *Theism, Atheism and Big Bang Cosmology* (Oxford: Clarendon Press, 1993), p. 4, where the first premise is recast in only slightly different form: "Everything that begins to exist has a cause of its existence."

[3]Capital letters are used here to emphasize the ultimacy of the cause in question.

Fifth, while all versions of the *kalam* argument share the same basic structure, they vary in several respects. They differ, first, with respect to the support offered for each of the major steps in the argument. For example, there are at least two philosophical arguments and two scientific arguments that the universe began to exist.[4] Those who are convinced by all four arguments often integrate them into a single multipart argument for the premise that the universe began to exist. Different arguments have also been offered in support of the claim that "whatever begins to exist has a cause." This premise has been variously grounded in a metaphysical intuition, an induction from empirical observation, and a practical principle of rationality. Again, some proponents of the *kalam* argument seem to favor a plurality of defenses of this premise.

Versions of the *kalam* argument also differ in the way they seek to exhibit the theistic content of the final conclusion of the argument. Related to this, they may also be said to differ in the way they are integrated into a cumulative case for theism. Some proponents of the argument treat the argument as a stand-alone argument for the existence of God, having pretty much the same conclusion as any other standard argument for the existence of God, so that a plurality of arguments is thought to strengthen the case for belief in the shared conclusion "God exists." Other *kalam* proponents regard the scope of its final conclusion as somewhat more restricted and having a content that overlaps without being identical to that of other standard arguments for the existence of God, so that a combination of arguments, perhaps bearing certain logical relations to one another, is needed to generate the full content of the concept of God characteristic of classical theism.[5]

Sixth, the distinctive feature of the *kalam* argument, setting it apart from other cosmological arguments for the existence of God, is the central role it attributes to the claim that the universe began to exist. This gives the argument at least four advantages. First, the claim that the uni-

---

[4]For concise introductory statements of these four arguments, see Craig, "Philosophical and Scientific Pointers to *Creatio ex Nihilo*," and William Lane Craig, *Reasonable Faith: Christian Truth and Apologetics* (Wheaton, Ill.: Crossway, 1994), pp. 91-122.

[5]This is the approach I tend to favor. See R. Douglas Geivett, *Evil and the Evidence for God* (Philadelphia: Temple University Press, 1993), chaps. 6 and 7.

verse began to exist comports nicely with what the Bible says in Genesis 1:1, "In the beginning, God created the heavens and the earth." Second, the claim that the universe began to exist is initially more intuitively accessible than, say, the claim that the universe is contingent. Third, that the universe had a beginning is one indication that the universe is contingent. And fourth, the claim that the universe began to exist enjoys both philosophical support and corroboration from science.

DID THE UNIVERSE BEGIN TO EXIST?

The central feature of the *kalam* cosmological argument is the claim that the universe began to exist a finite time ago. It is this claim that receives the most development and defense in expositions of the argument. On this occasion I shall consider only one philosophical argument for this claim and set aside the special scientific evidence that supports the claim.[6]

The argument I have in mind has been stated by William Craig as follows:

1. The temporal series of events is a collection formed by successive addition.
2. The collection formed by successive addition cannot be an actual infinite.
3. Therefore the temporal series of events cannot be an actual infinite.[7]

It follows that the temporal series of events is finite and therefore has a beginning.

---

[6]The philosophical argument that I do not consider here reasons (according to one variant) that actually infinite sets are impossible and that the universe must therefore have a beginning, for otherwise the events that constitute the history of the universe would form an actually infinite set. Since I have not been able to convince myself that actually infinite sets are impossible, I find that I cannot endorse this version of the *kalam*. The first problem is that the reasonable supposition that the set of all natural numbers actually exists constitutes a good reason to think that actually infinite sets of a certain type are possible. The second problem is that the more telling paradoxes that are generated by the supposition that there are actual infinites of this or that sort all happen to pertain to objects or states that differ from abstract objects in important ways. My misgivings are spelled out a bit more fully in my commentary on the existence of God debate between William Lane Craig and Antony Flew, "Reflections on the Explanatory Power of Theism," in *Does God Exist? The Craig-Flew Debate*, ed. Stan W. Wallace (Aldershot, England: Ashgate Publishing), p. 51.
[7]Craig, *Kalam Cosmological Argument*, p. 103.

Perhaps a simple illustration will help. Suppose that before you, the reader, reached this page in your reading of the present book you had first to read the page before it, and that before you read that page you had to read the one before it, and so on, going all the way back to the first page. Since the book has a first page, your coming to this page requires that you first read only a finite number of pages. More pages could be added to the front of this book to lengthen the time it would take for you to get to this page.

Let us suppose that you are a better than average reader and that it takes only two minutes for you to read each page; and let us suppose that you read continuously until you get to this page. Then, if there are only ten pages to complete before this page, it will take you twenty minutes to get to this page in your reading. How long will it take if you must first read twenty pages, or fifty pages, or a hundred pages, or ten thousand pages?

I'll let you do the math. The important thing to notice is that in every case there is always only a finite amount of time it will take. When will you get to this page if you must first read 200,000 pages? In about 66,667 hours! That's a long but finite amount of time. But suppose we now add an infinity of pages to the front of this book. When will you get to this page if you must first read all of those pages? Answer: never. So if you find yourself reading this page after completing all the pages before it, you know you've read only a finite number of pages.

The same sort of thing holds for the series of events making up the total history of the universe. Take some event in the actual history of the universe, like the birth of my daughter Erin. That event can occur only if a finite number of events must occur first. If an infinite number of events must occur before her birth, then she would never be born. So, either I have hallucinated her birth, or only a finite number of events occurred prior to her birth. If only a finite number of events occurred before her birth, then the universe has not always existed but had a beginning. Since I am not hallucinating, the universe must have had a beginning.

Of course, the possibility of hallucinating is introduced for humorous effect. The point is that no particular event whatsoever would ever occur if it had first to be preceded by the occurrence of an infinite number of events, one after the other in temporal sequence.

The most common objection to this argument is due to a confusion. Here's the objection as stated by philosopher Paul Draper:

> As it stands, the argument is unconvincing. For while it is true that one cannot start with a finite collection and then by adding one new member at a time turn it into an infinite collection (no matter how much time one has available), nothing of the sort is required in order for the past to be infinite. For if the temporal regress of events is infinite, then the universe has never had a finite number of past events. Rather, it has always been the case that the collection of past events is infinite. Thus, if the temporal regress of events is infinite, then the temporal series of events is not an infinite collection formed by successively adding to a finite collection. Rather, it is a collection formed by successively adding to an infinite collection. And surely it is not impossible to form an infinite collection by successively adding to an already infinite collection.[8]

Draper seems to think that if we ask, "How long will it take for a particular event to occur if it is preceded by a chain of infinitely many events?" the answer will simply be, "An infinite amount of time." But the question is ill-formed in the case of a supposed infinite chain of events. The more revealing (and less question-begging) question is, "When will event E occur if it is preceded by an infinite chain of events?" One might think that the answer would simply be, "After an eternity." But when is that? How can anything come after an eternity? An eternity is an always incomplete series. But on our supposition, event E occurs only when the series is completed.

WHO MADE GOD?

"Who made God?" I once asked my older daughter, Kaitlyn. She must have been about two years of age at the time. The way she said, "Dad!" in two syllables—"Da-ad!!"—told me she considered the question impertinent. We all know that if God exists, he's always existed.

---

[8]Paul Draper, "A Critique of the *Kalam* Cosmological Argument," in *Philosophy of Religion: An Anthology,* ed. Louis P. Pojman, 3rd ed. (Belmont, Calif.: Wadsworth, 1997), p. 43.

Or do we? After I've sketched the *kalam* cosmological argument for an audience of skeptics, I'm almost always asked, "So what caused God?" It might be easy to dismiss the question as sophomoric, except that some impressive minds have pressed it pretty persistently.

Of course, there's an initially promising reply. "God does not need a cause. God is not an event. I have argued that events have causes and that the beginning of the universe must be caused because it is an event." This isn't always enough to silence the obstreperous. And here's why.

When the universe begins to exist, time itself begins. God *sans* creation is timeless, but begins to exist in time when he creates the universe and time itself. God's beginning to exist in time entails that God begins to exist.

So far, this doesn't sound as clever as it should. Who can't see the difference between *beginning to exist* and *beginning to exist in time?* Surely, God could begin to exist in time without beginning to exist.

But the objection is more subtle than it first appears. The *kalam* argument uses the locution "begins to exist" a certain way. The argument appeals to our ordinary intuitions about what it means for something to begin to exist. So, it seems committed to the usual way we think about something beginning to exist. The objection we are considering goes one step further in referencing our intuitions. It supposes either that our intuitions leave out something crucial for the *kalam* argument, or that we have the intuition that anything that begins to exist in time begins to exist as such. If we suppose that God begins to exist in time but does not begin to exist as such, then our ordinary intuitions about "begins to exist" are unreliable and must be corrected. But then the original authority for the statement "everything that begins to exist has a cause" is compromised. It will no longer be enough to observe that this conviction is justified on the basis of ordinary intuition.

Notice, the problem is not that, on any construal of "begins to exist," God must begin to exist as such precisely when God begins to exist in time. It is intelligible to distinguish between beginning to exist and beginning to exist in time. But for that distinction to carry freight for the *kalam* argument, "begins to exist" must be glossed a certain way. Craig, the best-known sponsor of the *kalam* argument, has suggested the following more precise analysis of "*x* begins to exist (as such)":

x exists at *t*; there is no time immediately *prior* to *t* at which *x* exists; and the actual world contains no state of affairs involving *x*'s timeless existence.[9]

The complaint is that this goes far beyond our intuitions. While it may not be "counterintuitive," it "is not obviously supported by any widely shared metaphysical intuition."[10] And if this precise analysis of "*x* begins to exist (as such)" cannot be grounded in ordinary intuition, then the original grounds for asserting "Whatever begins to exist has a cause" proves to be inadequate. We simply don't have the intuition about what it means for something to begin to exist, as required by the *kalam* argument if it is to avoid the question, "What caused God?"[11]

It may now seem that the question "What caused God?" is insincere, since the objector may very well allow that because God himself is not an event he does not have a cause. But the question only seems insincere because it is code for an objection to the way the *kalam* proponent supports his claim that "whatever begins to exist has a cause."

What are we to make of this concern? That depends on whether we're dealing with the moderate version of the complaint or a more virulent form of the objection, which holds that Craig's gloss on "begins to exist" is actually counterintuitive.

The moderate version of the complaint does not asseverate that Craig's gloss is opposed to our intuitions. It maintains only that the gloss is not explicitly countenanced by our intuitions. As Wes Morriston has suggested, the gloss is an amendment to our intuitions about what it means for something to begin to exist. Now if this is right, then we don't have clear intuitions about whether "begins to exist in time" entails "begins to exist as such." But this in no way compromises the intuition that "whatever begins to exist (as such) has a cause of its existence." The

[9]William Lane Craig, "The Existence of God and the Beginning of the Universe," *Truth Journal* 3 (1991), posted online at <http://www.iclnet.org/clm/truth/3truth11.html>, and cited by Wes Morriston, "Must the Beginning of the Universe Have a Personal Cause? A Critical Examination of the Kalam Cosmological Argument," *Faith and Philosophy* 17 (April 2000): 155.
[10]Morriston, "Must the Beginning of the Universe Have a Personal Cause?" p. 155.
[11]This seems to be Morriston's complaint in ibid., pp. 154-55.

kalam proponent who supports the latter statement by appealing to metaphysical intuition does not need the same sort of support for the altogether different claim that something may begin to exist in time without beginning as such.

On the contrary, our intuitions about such things seem to supply a premise for deducing that there is a timeless being that comes to exist in time without being caused to exist as such. We have the intuition, let us say, that everything that begins to exist as such has a cause. For the time being, we'll allow, we don't know what to think about whether something could come to exist *in time* without being caused as such. Our intuition tells us that if the universe began to exist as such (and time itself began to exist), then the universe has a cause. But this cause must be something. Whatever it is, it must be timeless, at least relative to the origin of the universe. But if the cause creates the universe and time, and this means that the cause begins to exist in time, then it must be possible for something to begin to exist in time without beginning to exist as such. The "metaphysical intuition," as it has been called, that "whatever begins to exist has a cause," grounds an inference to the sort of gloss that Craig has proposed.[12]

What about the stronger claim that the Craig gloss on "begins to exist" is counterintuitive? Well, if it is counterintuitive, then that would be a problem for supporting the premise "Whatever begins to exist has a cause" by suggesting that it is a metaphysical intuition. But is the gloss counterintuitive? Not by a long shot.

First, whether something that begins to exist in time must begin to exist as such is not at all part of the intuition that whatever begins to exist has a cause. Second, there is no widely shared intuition that "if *x* begins to exist in time, then *x* must begin to exist as such." Indeed, as we have noted, it seems perfectly natural to speak of something beginning to exist in time without supposing that it began to exist as such. The strong version of the objection errs in loading our intuitions about "begins to exist" with questionable baggage.

---

[12]The theist should acknowledge that God's beginning to exist in time (or God's "putting himself in time") is an event, and that this event, like any other, must have a cause.

I conclude that the reasoning behind the question, "What caused God?" turns out to be specious, even if it is subtle and sincere.

MUST THE BEGINNING OF THE UNIVERSE HAVE A CAUSE?

"Whatever begins to exist has a cause" is a key premise in the *kalam* cosmological argument. We've just seen that the question "What caused God?" may be motivated by skepticism about the support sometimes offered for this premise. Some *kalam* proponents hold that justification of this premise is grounded in a "metaphysical intuition."[13] That is, we know it to be true by a kind of direct rational awareness.

"Intuition" here does not refer to a special sixth sense or a gut feeling. It refers, rather, to an ordinary faculty of cognition, common to all normally functioning human persons. It is by means of this faculty that we are supposed to apprehend the so-called truths of reason, including analytic truths, such as "The same physical object cannot be both red all over and green all over at the same time," and possibly some synthetic statements, such as "Everything that begins to exist has a cause."

It's easy enough to find sophisticated thinkers who deny that we have an epistemically secure metaphysical intuition that "whatever begins to exist has a cause." Most who deny this deny that we have any synthetic *a priori* knowledge. They are called empiricists.

It would be worthwhile to consider the question, how does an empiricist know there are no synthetic *a priori* truths? The statement "there are no synthetic *a priori* truths" is not itself analytically true, and it's not at all clear how such a statement could be empirically confirmed. The best evidence that there are synthetic *a priori* truths is that we know them. And that we know them is good evidence that we have the requisite faculty for knowing them.

The empiricist may be willing to allow that for every instance—that we have so far examined—of something beginning to exist, it has a cause. But the *kalam* argument needs the more general claim that for *every* instance—without qualification—of something beginning to exist,

---

[13]See, for example, William Lane Craig, "A Reply to Objections," in *Does God Exist? The Craig-Flew Debate*, p. 157.

it has a cause. Empirical observation can't get that for us. First, empirical observation does not warrant the belief that if something begins to exist, then it *must* have a cause. The necessity of a cause for something that begins to exist is not available for empirical observation. Second, the sample of observed instances of something beginning to exist *and* having a cause is too small to warrant the empirical generalization (induction) that in all likelihood everything that begins to exist has a cause.

The empiricist, however, is faced with some awkward questions. As Hume showed, it's not clear how an empiricist could justify inferring the existence of a cause for any event whatsoever, unless "cause" is reduced to "constant conjunction," in which case, reference to causes will have no explanatory power. In other words, it's hard to take the empiricist seriously.

It's also relevant that when we witness an event, our confidence that it has a cause does not depend on our ability to see or infer its cause. Quite often our confidence that an event has a cause precedes our awareness of the cause itself. (Something similar happens in reverse as well. We observe a set of conditions and expect an event of a certain sort.) Now this might be due to custom or habit. But I doubt it. Even if it is, the expectation is routinely rewarded with precisely what we expected—a particular cause.

And why should some events have causes and not others? What, indeed, is it for something to be the cause of some event? What do we know about events that implies that some of them may not have a cause? Absolutely nothing. As Dallas Willard has remarked, "even if it were neither self-contradictory nor counter-intuitive to suppose that something originated without a cause, the probability of it relative to our data would be exactly zero."[14]

But wait, aren't we told by physicists that there is a species of event that occurs without a cause? It's true—some physicists believe that "quantum indeterminacy" is evidence that subatomic events have no cause.

---

[14]Dallas Willard, "The Three-Stage Argument for the Existence of God," in *Contemporary Perspectives on Religious Epistemology,* ed. R. Douglas Geivett and Brendan Sweetman (New York: Oxford University Press, 1992), p. 216.

The *kalam* proponent is free to quibble with this by noting that physicists and philosophers of physics disagree about quantum indeterminacy.[15] But let us suppose that quantum events are indeterminate so that they are not *causally necessitated* by antecedent states of affairs. It does not follow that they are not *causally conditioned*. In fact, they are. If they were not at all causally conditioned, they wouldn't be repeatable under controlled circumstances in the physicist's laboratory.

Furthermore, the typical example of a quantum event is said to be indeterminate relative to a set of possible events, given certain specifiable conditions (though not necessarily exhaustively specifiable conditions). But such an event is not indeterminate with respect to the disjunction of all the members of the set of events made possible by conditions C. Consider a simple case where there is exactly one alternative to a particular quantum event, E1, that actually occurs under conditions C. The rule would seem to be roughly as follows: if conditions C is obtained, then either event E1 or event E2 will occur. That one or the other quantum event will occur is determined by conditions C, even if conditions C don't determine which event will occur.

Some physicists will generalize from "garden variety" quantum events that occur *within* the universe to the origin of the universe itself, supposing that the big bang singularity is a quantum event that has no cause. Such a universe is said to be "inflationary."

Alan Guth has developed a highly celebrated model of how the big bang went "bang." Listen as he summarizes the potential significance of his stunning achievement:

> While attempts to describe the materialization of the universe from nothing remain highly speculative, they represent an exciting enlargement of the boundaries of science. If someday this program can be completed, it would mean that the existence and history of the universe could be explained by the underlying laws of nature. That is, the laws of physics would imply the existence of the universe. We would have accomplished

---

[15]For an accessible discussion of this debate, see Nick Herbert, *Quantum Reality: Beyond the New Physics* (New York: Anchor, Doubleday, 1985).

the spectacular goal of understanding why there is something rather than nothing—because, if this approach is right, perpetual 'nothing' is impossible. If the creation of the universe can be described as a quantum process, we would be left with one deep mystery of existence: What is it that determined the laws of physics?[16]

Never mind that Guth ends with a question that may itself invite a theistic reply. Notice the central idea of his hypothetical model: "the creation of the universe can be described as a quantum process." If he means that we can extrapolate from particle physics to the physics of the early universe and from there to the instant of the big bang itself, then we should wonder how what he calls "nothing" could match the conditions for garden variety indeterminacy. We are far from having any empirical basis for believing that events occur in a totally conditionless void.

In the more familiar quantum context of the everyday world (I use the word *familiar* advisedly), what is indeterminate is which event will occur given the specified conditions. I doubt that we know enough to know that such "indeterminacy" is ontic and not merely epistemic.[17] But even if it is, this does nothing to show that there are events that are strictly causally indeterminate.

It is helpful to keep in mind that the *kalam* can be formulated as an inference to the best explanation. "What is the cause of the beginning of the universe?" is a perfectly natural and intelligible explanation-seeking question. As long as something identifiable can be reasonably proposed as the cause of the beginning of the universe, it will be more reasonable to infer the existence of that than to suppose that there is no cause at all. This is a principle of rationality. Reasonable belief is guided by what it makes the most sense to believe. A best explanation in terms of a cause provides better guidance about what to believe than no explanation at all. While it's true that the best explanation for some puzzling state of affairs is not always the correct explanation, the best explanation

---

[16]Alan Guth, *The Inflationary Universe: The Quest for a New Theory of Cosmic Origins* (Reading, Mass.: Perseus Books, 1997), p. 276.
[17]Craig makes the same point in "A Reply to Objections," p. 161.

is at least the one most likely to be true, all things considered—until more is known and some other explanation commends itself as better.[18]

MUST THE CAUSE BE GOD?

I've just suggested that something identifiable can be reasonably proposed as the cause of the beginning of the universe. By this I mean that there is something that falls under a certain description, such that it fulfills the requirements of an adequate causal explanation for the origin of the universe. I am referring, of course, to God.

It's important to be clear about the scope of the term *God* as it appears in the conclusion of the *kalam* cosmological argument. The argument infers that there must be some personal and timeless being, powerful and intelligent enough to cause the universe to begin to exist. This fully transcendent Agent presumably acted for reasons when creating the universe. Even if that is all that can be said about the most likely cause of the beginning of the universe, it already appears to be a good candidate for the appellation *God*.

First, there must be more to this Agent than what meets the eye trained only on the evidence of the origin of the universe. We know from the description warranted by the *kalam* argument that there's much more that we don't know on the basis of this evidence only. We should not conclude that there is nothing more to the Creator than what is specifically implied by the evidence featured in the *kalam* argument.

Second, the above description of the Agent credited with creating the universe is compatible with the fuller description of God as expressed in classical theism. Indeed, it overlaps the tradition of classical theism in important respects. Classical theism embraces a rich and complex description of God. It should not be surprising if a plurality of evidences will be required to exhibit the strength of classical theism in all its richness and complexity.

Third, there are specific parallels between this being and the God of the Bible. Most notably, both are presented as the Creator of the uni-

---

[18]For more on the nature of inference to the best explanation and its relation to the *kalam* cosmological argument, see Geivett, "Reflections on the Explanatory Power of Theism," pp. 50-52.

verse. If there is one Creator of the universe, as both the *kalam* and the Bible suggest,[19] then the *kalam* and the Bible can be harmonized only on the assumption that the *kalam* and the Bible refer to the same Agent.

Fourth, the Agent exposed in the *kalam* is "fully transcendent" in that it stands apart from the created world as a timeless being, apparently self-subsistent, and the universe and its inhabitants depend entirely on the good will of this Agent for their own existence. This Agent is self-subsistent in that it is timeless and uncaused. It is not "self-caused."

Fifth, as a personal being, acting from the intention to create a physical universe, this Agent is a mindful being. It can be presumed that this mindful Agent acted for a purpose in creating the universe. There is, in principle, a way to test this presumption and even to discover what that purpose may be. The Creator of the universe may have left signposts of his creative purposes in the world he created. And he may arrange for direct communication of his purposes. (See point seven below.)

Sixth, the production of a physical universe out of nothing implies unimaginable intelligence and power. It's difficult to say whether a being that is not quite omnipotent and/or not quite omniscient could do such a thing. But if such a being did create the universe and eventually claimed to be omnipotent and omniscient, I'd be reluctant to disagree with him.

Seventh, since our actual physical universe would not exist if this Agent had not created it, the whole of the physical universe is a source of evidence to be further excavated and developed, with the very good prospect of finding out more about the Creator and learning something about the Creator's intentions. In other words, the *kalam* sets the stage for a fuller inquiry into the nature of God and God's relationship to the world, a world especially remarkable for being inhabited by other agents. The evidence of design, of moral responsibility, of beauty, of consciousness, of the human hankering for the Transcendent, of religious experience, of patterns in history, and so forth, all acquire a compelling cumulative force pointing to a fuller composite description of the

---

[19]The Bible is explicit about this. The *kalam* relies on an application of Ockham's razor to draw out this point. See Craig, "A Reply to Objections," p. 162.

Creator of the universe.[20]

Paul Draper, an agnostic philosopher who has reflected deeply and written extensively on the *kalam* argument, asks, "Must we . . . conclude that the *kalam* argument succeeds?" "This would be a profound result," he says. "Granted, this argument doesn't quite get all the way to God's existence. But accepting its conclusion does require rejecting naturalism."[21]

While I appreciate Draper's candor regarding the trouble that would confront naturalism by a successful *kalam* argument, and I agree that only a proper part of the biblical description of God is contained in the conclusion of the *kalam,* I must say that his acknowledgment of the potential force of the *kalam* is much too guarded and understated. Yes, the *kalam,* if successful, entails that naturalism is false. But it also frames the project of further exploration into the nature of the Creator in a way that is highly suggestive of even deeper parallels with the God of Abraham, Isaac and Jacob—not to mention Jesus.

For Further Reading

Craig, William Lane. *The Kalam Cosmological Argument*. London: Macmillan, 1979.

Craig, William Lane, and Quentin Smith. *Theism, Atheism and Big Bang Cosmology*. Oxford: Clarendon Press, 1993.

Geivett, R. Douglas. *Evil and the Evidence for God*. Philadelphia: Temple University Press, 1993.

Wallace, Stan W., ed. *Does God Exist? The Craig-Flew Debate*. Aldershot, England: Ashgate Publishing, 2003.

---

[20]In various places I have described how this rich panoply of evidence might be combined into a systematic case for Christian theism, including especially "The Evidential Value of Miracles," in *In Defense of Miracles,* ed. R. Douglas Geivett and Gary R. Habermas (Downers Grove, Ill.: InterVarsity Press, 1997), and in "The Evidential Value of Religious Experience," in *The Rationality of Theism,* ed. Paul K. Moser and Paul Copan (London: Routledge, 2003).

[21]Draper, "A Critique of the Kalam Cosmological Argument," pp. 45-46.

5

AN INFORMATION-THEORETIC DESIGN ARGUMENT

William A. Dembski

THE DESIGN ARGUMENT BEGINS WITH FEATURES OF THE NATURAL WORLD THAT exhibit evidence of purpose and from there attempts to establish the existence and attributes of an intelligent cause responsible for those features. Just what features signal an intelligent cause, what the nature of that intelligent cause is (for example, personal agent or teleological process) and how convincingly those features establish the existence of an intelligent cause remain subjects for debate and account for the variety of design arguments over the centuries. In this chapter I formulate the design argument in terms of information theory. To set the stage, I want first to provide a brief historical overview of design arguments.

HISTORICAL SYNOPSIS

Perhaps the best known design argument is William Paley's. According to Paley, if we find a watch in a field, the watch's adaptation of parts to telling time ensures that it is the product of an intelligence. So too, according to Paley, the marvelous adaptations of means to ends in organisms (like the human eye) ensure that organisms are the product of an intelligence. Paley published this design argument in 1802 in a book titled *Natural Theology*. The subtitle of that book is revealing: *Evidences of the Existence and Attributes of the Deity, Collected from the Appear-*

ances of Nature. Paley's project was to examine features of the natural world ("appearances of nature") and from there draw conclusions about the existence and attributes of a designing intelligence responsible for those features (whom Paley identified with the God of Christianity).

Paley was too optimistic about how much theological mileage could be obtained from the design argument. As Immanuel Kant noted in his *Critique of Pure Reason,* the most the design argument can establish is "an architect of the world who is constrained by the adaptability of the material in which he works, not a *creator* of the world to whose idea everything is subject." Far from rejecting the design argument, Kant objected to overextending it. For Kant, the design argument legitimately establishes an "architect" (that is, an intelligent cause whose contrivances are constrained by the materials that make up the world), but it can never establish a creator who originates the very materials which the architect then fashions.

We need here to draw a clear distinction between creation and design. Creation is always about the source of being of the world. Design is about arrangements of preexisting materials that point to an intelligence. Creation and design are therefore quite different. One can have creation without design and design without creation. For instance, one can have a doctrine of creation in which God creates the world in such a way that nothing about the world points to design. Richard Dawkins has a book titled *The Blind Watchmaker: Why the Evidence of Evolution Reveals a Universe Without Design.* Suppose Dawkins is right about the universe revealing no evidence of design. It would not logically follow that it was not created. It is logically possible that God created a world that provides no evidence of his handiwork. By contrast, it is logically possible that the world is full of signs of intelligence but was not created. This was the ancient Stoic view, in which the world was eternal and uncreated, and yet a rational principle pervaded the world and produced marks of intelligence in it.

There's a joke that clarifies the difference between design and creation. Scientists come to God and claim they can do everything God can do. "Like what?" asks God. "Like creating human beings," say the scientists. "Show me," says God. The scientists say, "Well, we start with some dust and then—." God interrupts, "Wait a second. Get your own dust." Just as a carpenter must take preexisting wood to form a piece of furniture, so these scientists have to take preexisting dust to form a human being. But where did the dust—the raw materials—come from to make a human being? From stars? And where did stars come from? From the big bang? And where did the big bang come from? From a quantum vacuum fluctuation? And where did that quantum fluctuation come from? At some point such questions must end. Creation asks for an ultimate resting place of explanation—the source of being of the world. Design, by contrast, inquires not into the ultimate source of matter and energy but into the cause of their present arrangements, particularly those entities, large and small, that exhibit signs of intelligence.

Even Thomas Aquinas admitted the need for modesty in design reasoning. In his *Summa Contra Gentiles,* Aquinas wrote: "By his natural reason man is able to arrive at some knowledge of God. For seeing that natural things run their course according to a fixed order, and since there cannot be order without a cause of order, men, for the most part, perceive that there is one who orders the things that we see. But who or of what kind this cause of order may be, or whether there be but one, cannot be gathered from this general consideration." Aquinas here was not doing first philosophy or metaphysics. He was simply noting that our natural reason readily infers some sort of "orderer" or "designer" behind nature. Aquinas calls this designer God, but he was clearly speaking of this designer very loosely—the nature and even plurality of that designer could for Aquinas not be settled simply by studying nature.

Design arguments can tell us that certain patterns exhibited in nature reliably point us to a designing intelligence. But there's no inferential chain that leads from such finite design-conducing patterns in nature to the infinite, personal, transcendent Creator God of Christianity. Nevertheless, a design argument can clear away materialistic stumbling blocks to belief in God (for example, it can refute the claim that science has shown that all the patterns in nature can be explained without recourse to intelligence). Clearing away such stumbling blocks has immense apologetic value, especially in the current cultural and intellectual climate. A particularly effective way to cash out the design argument is with the concept of information. Such an information-theoretic design argument is the subject of the remainder of this chapter.

INFORMATION AND MATTER

To develop this argument, let's start by elucidating the distinction between information and matter. Imagine you are an interior decorator. Bill Gates hires you to decorate his mansion. You decide to put a big marble bust of the composer Ludwig van Beethoven in the music room. You therefore contract with Laszlo, a promising if eccentric young sculptor, to make the bust and deliver it to the mansion. The next day he drops by the mansion and tells you he's finished. Naturally you're skeptical, but he rolls an imposing crate into the music room and with some fanfare removes the "sculpture." You find yourself staring at a big marble cube. Shocked, you ask the sculptor where the bust of Beethoven is. "The bust is there all right," he says, handing you his bill. "You just have to scoot aside the excess marble." When you protest, he grows red-faced and yells, "I defy you to find a single, solitary molecule of Beethoven's bust that isn't in that block of marble! Now pay what you owe me!"

The quarrel escalates, each of you growing increasingly red-faced until who should walk into the room but Bill Gates himself. He calms the two of you and gets first your side of the story and then the sculptor's. "Tell you what," Gates says after he's heard the sculptor out. "I'm so impressed with your sculpture, Laszlo, that instead of paying you what we agreed I'll trade you an advance copy of the next generation of Microsoft Windows." Here Gates produces an unmarked compact disc. "This is it, and you're free to sell the operating system on the black market to whomever you wish as often as you wish." "Are you crazy?" you shout, forgetting yourself. "That's worth billions!" "Deal!" Laszlo shouts, snatches the disc from Gates's hand and rushes to a nearby computer. After some pointing and clicking, the sculptor turns on Mr. Gates. "The disc is blank! Give me the operating system!" "Oh, but friend," Gates says, resting an avuncular hand on the young sculptor's shoulder. "I defy you to find a single, solitary molecule of the operating system that isn't on that disc. You just have to scoot aside the excess polycarbonate and there it is."

This story illustrates the difference between information and matter. Matter is raw stuff that can take any number of shapes. Information is what gives shape to matter, fixing one shape to the exclusion of others. Both the words *matter* and *information* derive from Latin. Matter (from the Latin noun *materia*) initially referred to the raw timber used in building houses. Later it came to mean any raw stuff or material with the potential to assume different shapes, forms or arrangements. Information (from the Latin verb *informare*) literally means to give form or shape to something. Unlike passive or inert matter, which needs to be acted upon, information is active. Information acts on matter to give it its form, shape, arrangement or structure. (Note that I'm using these terms loosely and interchangeably. Aristotle would distinguish form, in the sense of substantial form or essence, from mere shape or arrangement. It's enough for my purposes here, however, that shape or arrangement be correlated with form in Aristotle's sense. Thus for marble to express the form [*sensu* Aristotle] of Beethoven's likeness, it must be shaped or arranged in very particular ways.)

As an interior decorator, you were paying the sculptor to "inform" a slab of marble—to take an unformed slab of marble and give it the form or shape of Ludwig van Beethoven. For the sculptor to tell you that the cube of marble contains the promised bust of Beethoven (you just have to remove some excess marble) is therefore totally unacceptable. That's what you were paying the sculptor to do. Yes, the marble cube has the potential to become a bust of Beethoven. But it also has the potential to take on countless other shapes. It was the sculptor's job to give the marble the shape you requested.

The relation between matter, with its potential to assume any possible shapes, and information, with its restriction of possibilities to a narrow range of shapes, is fundamental to our understanding of the world. Certainly this relation holds for all human artifacts. This is true not only for human artifacts composed of physical stuff (like marble busts of Beethoven) but also for human artifacts composed of more abstract stuff (like poetry and mathematics). Indeed, the raw material for many human inventions consists not of physical stuff but of abstract stuff like alphabetic characters, musical notes and numbers. For instance, the raw material for a Shakespearean sonnet consists of the twenty-six letters of the alphabet. Just as a bust of Beethoven is only potential in a slab of mar-ble, so a Shakespearean sonnet is only potential in those twenty-six let-ters. It takes a sculptor to actualize the bust of Beethoven, and it takes a Shakespeare to arrange those twenty-six letters appropriately so that one of his sonnets emerges.

The relation between matter and information that we are describing here is old and was understood by the ancient Greeks, especially the Stoics. What's more, nothing said so far about the relation between mat-ter and information is especially controversial. The world consists of a lot of raw material waiting to be suitably arranged. There's matter, pas-sive or inert stuff waiting to be arranged, and there's information, an ac-tive principle or agency that does the arranging. This is a perfectly straightforward and useful way of carving up experience and making sense of the world. Much of our knowledge of the world depends on understanding the relation between matter and information.

Nonetheless, the relation between matter and information does be-come controversial once we add another dimension to it. That happens when we place matter and information in combination with design and nature:

Information
|
|
Nature — — — — — Design
|
|
Matter

So far the examples of information that we've considered have focused on the activity of a designing intelligence (a sculptor or writer) informing or giving shape to certain raw materials (a slab of marble or letters of the alphabet). But designing intelligences are not the only causal powers ca-pable of structuring matter and thereby conferring information. Nature, too, is capable of structuring matter and conferring information.

Consider the difference between raw pieces of wood and an acorn. Raw pieces of wood do not have the power to assemble themselves into a ship. For raw pieces of wood to form a ship requires a designer to draw up a blueprint and then take the pieces of wood and, in line with the blueprint, fashion them into a ship. But where is the designer that causes an acorn to develop into a full-grown oak tree? There isn't any. The acorn has within itself the power to transform itself into an oak tree.

Nature and design therefore represent two different ways of producing information. Nature produces information, as it were, internally. The acorn assumes the shape it does through powers internal to it—the acorn is a seed programmed to produce an oak tree. But a ship assumes the shape it does through powers external to it—a designing intelligence imposes a suitable structure on pieces of wood to form a ship.

Not only did the ancient Greeks know about the distinction between information and matter, but they also knew about the distinction between design and nature. For Aristotle, for instance, design consisted in capacities external to an object for bringing about its form with outside help. Nature, however, consisted in capacities internal to an object for transforming itself without outside help. Thus in book twelve of the *Metaphysics* Aristotle wrote, "[Design] is a principle of movement in something other than the thing moved; nature is a principle in the thing itself." In book two of the *Physics* Aristotle referred to design as completing "what nature cannot bring to a finish." (Note that Thomas Aquinas took this idea and sacramentalized it into grace completing nature).

The Greek word here translated "design" is *technē,* from which we get our word *technology.* In translations of Aristotle's work, the English word most commonly used to translate *technē* is "art" (in the sense of "artifact"). Design, art and *technē* are synonyms. The essential idea behind these terms is that information is conferred on an object from outside the object and that the material constituting the object, apart from that outside information, does not have the power to assume the form it does. For instance, raw pieces of wood do not by themselves have the power to form a ship.

This contrasts with nature, which does have the power within itself to express information. Thus in book two of the *Physics* Aristotle wrote, "If

the ship-building art were in the wood, it would produce the same results by nature." In other words, if raw pieces of wood had the capacity
to form ships, we would say that ships come about by nature. The Greek
word here translated "nature" is *physis,* from which we get our word
physics. The Indo-European root meaning behind *physis* is growth and
development. Nature produces information not by imposing it from outside but by growing or developing informationally rich structures from
within. Consider again the acorn. Unlike wood that needs to be fash-
ioned by a designer to form a ship, acorns produce oak trees naturally—
the acorn simply needs a suitable environment in which to grow.

The central question that an information-theoretic design argument
needs to resolve can therefore be stated as follows: Is nature complete
in the sense of possessing all the resources needed to bring about the
information-rich structures we see in nature or does nature also require
some contribution of design to bring about those structures? Aristotle
claimed that the art of ship building is not in the wood that constitutes
the ship. We've seen that the art of sonnet composing is not in the letters
of the alphabet. Likewise, the art of statue making is not in the stone out
of which statues are made. Each of these cases requires a designer. So
too, an information-theoretic design argument contends that the art of
building certain information-rich structures in nature (like biological organisms) is not in the physical stuff that constitutes these structures but
requires a designer.

COMPLEX SPECIFIED INFORMATION

I want next to describe the particular type of information required for an
information-theoretic design argument, namely, *complex specified information.* To understand this concept we need briefly to review contemporary information theory as employed by mathematicians (don't worry,
I'll keep the discussion user-friendly). Ordinarily when we think of information, we think of meaningful statements that we communicate to
each other. The vehicle of communication here is language, and the information is the meaning communicated by some utterance or linguistic
expression. This picture of information diverges sharply from the picture
of information associated with the mathematical theory of information.

The ordinary picture of information focuses on meaning and treats the linguistic vehicle by which that meaning is transmitted as secondary. The mathematical picture of information, by contrast, focuses exclusively on the vehicle and ignores the meaning entirely.

Consider a spy who needs to determine the intentions of an enemy—whether that enemy intends to go to war or preserve the peace. The spy agrees with headquarters about what signal will indicate war and what signal will indicate peace. Let's imagine that the spy will send headquarters a radio transmission and that each transmission takes the form of a bit string (i.e., a sequence of 0s and 1s). The spy and headquarters might therefore agree that 0 means war and 1 means peace. But because noise along the communication channel might flip a 0 to a 1 and vice versa, it might be good to have some redundancy in the transmission. Thus the spy and headquarters might agree that 000 represents war and 111 peace and that anything else will be regarded as a garbled transmission. Or perhaps they will agree to let 0 represent a dot and 1 a dash and let the spy communicate via Morse code in plain English whether the enemy plans to go to war or maintain peace.

This example illustrates how information, in the sense of meaning, can remain constant whereas the vehicle for representing and transmitting this information can vary. In ordinary life we are concerned with meaning. If we are at headquarters, we want to know whether we're going to war or staying at peace. Yet from the vantage of mathematical information theory, the only thing that's important here is the mathematical properties of the linguistic expressions we use to represent the meaning. If we represent war with 000 as opposed to 0, we require three times as many bits to represent war, and so from the vantage of mathematical information theory we are utilizing three times as much information. The information content of 000 is three bits whereas that of 0 is just one bit.

Claude Shannon invented the mathematical theory of information shortly after World War II. The inspiration for his theory derived from his work on cryptography during the war. In cryptography, meaningful messages get encrypted to prevent an enemy from reading one's mail. The important thing in cryptography is to have a secure encryption-decryption scheme, to be able to code messages efficiently as character strings from some alphabet, and then to be able to move those character strings efficiently across communication channels.

The actual meaning of a character string therefore takes second seat in the mathematical theory of information. Think of the mathematical theory of information as an internet service provider. The internet service provider is not concerned with the meaning of your email messages or what product you're trying to sell on your website. What they're concerned about is that the character strings you use to convey meaning in your emails or on your website is faithfully stored and transmitted. That's what the mathematical theory of information is all about. Specifically, it is about quantifying the information in such character strings, characterizing the statistical properties of such strings when they are sent across a noisy communication channel (noise typically is represented as a stochastic process that disrupts the strings in statistically well-defined ways), preserving the strings despite the presence of noise (i.e., the theory of error-correcting codes), compressing the strings to improve efficiency, and transforming the strings into other strings to maintain their security (i.e., cryptography).

Although Shannon's theory started out as a syntactic theory concerned with character strings based on a fixed alphabet, it quickly became a statistical theory. Characters from an alphabet will often have different probabilities of occurrence (for instance, the letters from our ordinary alphabet occur with widely varying frequencies—in English the letter *e* occurs roughly 13 percent of the time, the letter *q* less than 1 percent of the time; what's more, *u* follows *q* with probability one). These probabilities in turn determine how much information any given string can convey. In general, the quantity of information contained in a character string corresponds to the improbability of that character string. Thus, the more improbable the string, the more information it contains.

To see why this should be the case, consider the claim "it's raining outside." This claim will be more informative (now in a loose semantic sense) depending on how improbable it is. If it refers to weather in the Sahara desert during the summer when the chance of rain is very low, then this claim will be both highly improbable and highly informative—

it's telling you something you wouldn't otherwise have guessed. But if this claim refers to weather in Seattle during the spring when the chance of rain is very high, then it will be both probable and uninformative— it's telling you something you could easily have guessed. The mathematical theory of information models this feature of our ordinary understanding of information, making high probability claims have low information content and low probability (high improbability) claims have high information content.

Given this characterization of high and low information in terms of probability, there's no reason to confine the mathematical theory of information to character strings. Indeed, any reference class of possibilities over which there is a probability distribution is fair game for the mathematical theory of information. For information to be generated therefore means identifying one possibility and ruling out the rest. The more possibilities get ruled out and, correspondingly, the more improbable the possibility that actually obtains, the greater the information generated. To rule out no possibilities is to assert a tautology and provide no information. "It's raining or it's not raining" is true but totally uninformative. But "it's raining" is informative because it rules out "it's not raining." Moreover, "it's raining" is informative to the degree that this claim is improbable (this claim is therefore going to be more informative in the Sahara desert than in Seattle).

To generate information is therefore to rule out possibilities. Moreover, the amount of information generated here corresponds to the probability of that possibility (or range of possibilities) that wasn't ruled out. But who or what rules out possibilities? In practice, there are two sources of information: intelligent agency and physical processes. An intelligent agent may explicitly identify a pattern within the reference class of possibilities and thereby generate information. Alternatively, a physical process can produce an event, represented as a possibility within the reference class of possibilities, and thereby generate information. Let us refer to the former type of information as *agent-induced* or *conceptual information* and to the latter as *event-induced* or *physical information*.

Now, what happens when conceptual information and physical information coincide? Consider, for instance, the Search for Extraterrestrial In-

telligence (SETI), which looks for signs of intelligence in radio signals
from outer space. What happens if, as a conceptual act, SETI researchers
identify a sequence of prime numbers, and then, lo and behold, as in
the movie *Contact,* that very sequence is transmitted, as a physical event,
to the radio telescopes that these same SETI researchers are monitoring?
As in the movie, they would conclude that an extraterrestrial intelligence
had established contact. Now it's precisely such a coincidence between
conceptual and physical information that constitutes complex specified
information.

Yet within Shannon's theory of information, such a coincidence plays
no role. Shannon's theory is simply concerned with generating information from a reference class of possibilities. It is immaterial to Shannon's
theory whether the information generated is agent-induced or event-induced. Complex specified information, by contrast, requires a dual ruling out of possibilities, one by an intelligent agent who identifies a pattern and one by physical processes that induce an event. Provided these
coincide, the probability is small, and the pattern can be identified independently of the event, we say the event exhibits complex specified information.

Complex specified information is therefore a souped-up form of information. To be sure, complex specified information is consistent with
the basic idea behind information, which is the reduction or ruling out
of possibilities from a reference class of possibilities. But whereas the
traditional understanding of information is unary, conceiving of information as a single reduction of possibilities, complex specified information
is a binary form of information. Complex specified information depends
on a dual reduction of possibilities, a conceptual reduction (i.e., conceptual information) combined with a physical reduction (i.e., physical information). Moreover, these dual reductions must be coordinated so that
the physical information matches the pattern set by the conceptual information. When they match, we have complex specified information.

FROM COMPLEX SPECIFIED INFORMATION TO DESIGN
Complex specified information reliably detects design. To see this, we
need to consider the nature of intelligent agency and, specifically, what

it is about intelligent agents that makes them detectable. The principal characteristic of intelligent agency is choice. The very etymology of the word *intelligent* makes this clear. "Intelligent" derives from two Latin words, the preposition *inter*, meaning "between," and the verb *lego*, meaning "to choose or select." Thus, according to its etymology, intelligence consists in *choosing between*. For an intelligent agent to act is therefore to choose from a range of competing possibilities.

This is true not just of humans but of animals as well as of extraterrestrial intelligences. A rat navigating a maze must choose whether to go right or left at various points in the maze. When SETI researchers attempt to discover intelligence in the extraterrestrial radio transmissions they are monitoring, they assume an extraterrestrial intelligence could have chosen any number of possible radio transmissions and then attempt to match the transmissions they observe with certain patterns as opposed to others. Whenever a human being utters meaningful speech, a choice is made from a range of possible sound-combinations that might have been uttered. Intelligent agency always entails discrimination, choosing certain things, ruling out others.

Given this characterization of intelligent agency, the crucial question is how to recognize it. Intelligent agents act by making a choice. How, then, do we recognize that an intelligent agent has made a choice? A bottle of ink spills accidentally onto a sheet of paper; someone takes a fountain pen and writes a message on a sheet of paper. In both instances ink is applied to paper. In both instances one among an almost infinite set of possibilities is realized. In both instances a contingency is actualized and others are ruled out. Yet in one instance we ascribe agency, in the other chance.

What is the relevant difference? Not only do we need to observe that a contingency was actualized, but we ourselves need also to be able to specify that contingency. The contingency must conform to an independently given pattern, and we must be able independently to construct that pattern. A random ink blot is unspecified; a message written with ink on paper is specified. To be sure, the exact message recorded may not be specified. But orthographic, syntactic and semantic constraints will nonetheless specify it.

Actualizing one among several competing possibilities, ruling out the rest and specifying the one that was actualized encapsulates how we recognize intelligent agency, or equivalently, how we detect design. Experimental psychologists who study animal learning and behavior have known this all along. To learn a task, an animal must acquire the ability to actualize behaviors suitable for the task as well as the ability to rule out behaviors unsuitable for the task. Moreover, for a psychologist to recognize that an animal has learned a task, it is necessary not only to observe the animal making the appropriate discrimination but also to specify the discrimination.

Thus, to recognize whether a rat has successfully learned how to traverse a maze, a psychologist must first specify which sequence of right and left turns conducts the rat out of the maze. No doubt, a rat randomly wandering a maze also discriminates a sequence of right and left turns. But by randomly wandering the maze, the rat gives no indication that it can discriminate the appropriate sequence of right and left turns for exiting the maze. Consequently, the psychologist studying the rat will have no reason to think the rat has learned how to traverse the maze.

Only if the rat executes the sequence of right and left turns specified by the psychologist will the psychologist recognize that the rat has learned how to traverse the maze. Now it is precisely the learned behaviors we regard as intelligence in animals. Hence it is no surprise that the same scheme for recognizing animal learning recurs for recognizing intelligent agency generally, to wit: actualizing one among several competing possibilities, ruling out the others and specifying the one actualized.

Note that complexity is implicit here as well. To see this, consider again a rat traversing a maze, but now take a very simple maze in which two right turns conduct the rat out of the maze. How will a psychologist studying the rat determine whether it has learned to exit the maze? Just putting the rat in the maze will not be enough. Because the maze is so simple, the rat could by chance just happen to take two right turns and thereby exit the maze. The psychologist will therefore be uncertain whether the rat actually learned to exit this maze or whether the rat just got lucky.

But contrast this with a complicated maze in which a rat must take just the right sequence of left and right turns to exit the maze. Suppose the rat must take one hundred appropriate right and left turns and that any mistake will prevent the rat from exiting the maze. A psychologist who sees the rat take no erroneous turns and in short order exit the maze will be convinced that the rat has indeed learned how to exit the maze and that this was not dumb luck.

This general scheme for recognizing intelligent agency mirrors complex specified information. In general, to recognize intelligent agency we must observe an actualization of one among several competing possibilities, note which possibilities were ruled out and then be able to specify the possibility that was actualized. What's more, the competing possibilities that were ruled out must be live possibilities and sufficiently numerous so that specifying the possibility that was actualized cannot be attributed to chance. This is just another way of saying that the possibility that was actualized is complex. All the elements in this general scheme for recognizing intelligent agency (i.e., actualizing, ruling out and specifying) therefore find their counterpart in complex specified information. It follows that complex specified information formalizes what it is that all along has enabled us to recognize intelligent agency. Complex specified information pinpoints how we detect design.

DISPLACEMENT

Not everyone agrees. Darwinian naturalists, for instance, accept that biological systems exhibit complex specified information but deny that it results from intelligence. Rather, they contend that it results from a non-teleological process or mechanism (typically the Darwinian mechanism of natural selection and random variation). In effect, the Darwinian naturalist claims that nature is capable of generating complex specified information apart from intelligence. To see that nature has no such capacity, we need to understand the concept of *displacement* as it applies to information generally and complex specified information in particular.

The basic idea behind displacement is this: Suppose you need to search a space of possibilities. The space is so large and the possibilities individually so improbable that an exhaustive search is not feasible and a random search is highly unlikely to conclude the search successfully. In consequence, you need some constraints on the search—some information to help guide the search to a solution (think of an Easter egg hunt where no one provides hints or guidance versus one where someone directs you by saying "warm," "warmer" and "hot"). All such information that assists your search, however, resides in a search space of its own—an informational space. So the search of the original space gets *displaced* to a search of an informational space in which the crucial information for successfully searching the original space resides. Now it is a mathematical fact that such a higher-order informational space ("higher" with respect to the original search space) is always at least as big and at least as hard to search as the original space (for the details see chapter four of my book *No Free Lunch*). I call this *the displacement problem.*

Think of it this way. Imagine an island with buried treasure. You can scour the island trying to find the buried treasure. Alternatively, you can try to find a map that tells you where the treasure is buried. Once such a map is in hand, finding the treasure is no problem. But how to find such a map? For every place on the island there is a map with an "x" marking where the treasure could be located. There are also maps with directions such as "turn here, walk ten paces, then start to dig." The vast majority of such maps will be misleading and provide no help in locating the treasure. Indeed, a map that accurately informs us where the treasure is will be mixed among a huge assortment of misleading maps. The huge assortment of maps is the informational space associated with the original search space. Finding the right map within that huge assortment is no easier than simply searching the island directly (and in fact, mathematics tells us it will be more difficult).

It follows that constraining the search of an original space by employing information does not provide a nonteleological, design-free explanation for the success of that search. Instead, the solution found in the original space merely reflects the solution already in hand in a higher-order informational space. And if the one solution exhibits complex specified information, then so does the other (this follows from the simple fact that any information that identifies complex specified information is itself complex specified information—for the details see chapter three of *No Free Lunch*). In particular, when nonteleological processes output complex specified information, it is because they take preexisting complex specified information and merely re-express it. They are not generating it for free or from scratch. To claim otherwise is like filling one hole by digging another. If the problem was to be rid of holes period (i.e., design), then the problem hasn't been resolved but merely relocated.

Displacement implies that if you have some naturalistic process whose output exhibits complex specified information, then that process was front-loaded with complex specified information. The task of the information theorist in that case is to "follow the information trail" and show where the complex specified information that was outputted was first inputted. Displacement is essentially a bookkeeping device for keeping science honest about the sources of information. It forces us to show where complex specified information supposedly gotten for free has in fact been front-loaded, smuggled in or hidden from view.

The existence of complex specified information in nature argues for real design in the world. But that raises the question, who designed the designer? If the designer exhibits complex specified information, this would imply a design regress in which attributions to design based on complex specified information always give way to some other explanation. But in fact there is no reason to suppose that the designer responsible for complex specified information in nature is part of nature and therefore in turn exhibits complex specified information. Complex specified information refers to patterns embodied in physical structures. But if the designer is not a physical structure, the designer, though capable of bringing about complex specified information, would not in turn exhibit complex specified information. The very definition of complex specified information therefore precludes the design regress in which— to stay consistent with our methods of design detection—we must answer whether the designer is designed. The designer responsible for the complex specified information in nature is, as best we can tell, not an event, object or structure. Consequently, the designer, though capable of producing phenomena that exhibit complex specified information, does not in turn exhibit complex specified information.

Who is the designer? As a Christian I hold that the Christian God is the ultimate source of design behind the universe (though that leaves open that God works through secondary causes, including derived intelligences such as angels or teleological processes). But there's no way for design inferences based on features of the natural world to reach that conclusion. Design inferred from complex specified information in nature is compatible with Christian belief but does not entail it. This is as it should be. Nature is silent about the revelation of Christ in Scripture. At the same time, nothing prevents nature from independently testifying to the God revealed in the Scripture. The complex specified information exhibited in natural phenomena is perhaps best thought of as God's fingerprints. Fingerprints never tell us the character of the one whose fingers are in question. But they can tell us that we are dealing with the fingers of an intelligence, and this in turn can lead us to inquire into the character of that intelligence. An information-theoretic design argument therefore doesn't so much lead us to God as remove us from paths that lead away from God.

FOR FURTHER READING

Behe, Michael. *Darwin's Black Box: The Biochemical Challenge to Evolution.* New York: The Free Press, 1996.

Dembski, William A. *The Design Inference: Eliminating Chance Through Small Probabilities.* Cambridge Studies in Probability, Induction and Decision Theory. New York: Cambridge University Press, 1998.

———. *No Free Lunch: Why Specified Complexity Cannot Be Purchased Without Intelligence.* Lanham, Md.: Rowman & Littlefield, 2002.

Dembski, William A., and Michael Ruse, eds. *Debating Design: From Darwin to DNA.* New York: Cambridge University Press, 2004.

Ratzsch, Del. *Nature, Science and Design: The Status of Design in Natural Science.* Philosophy and Biology Series. Albany: State University of New York Press, 2001.

Rea, Michael C. *World Without Design: The Ontological Consequence of Naturalism.* New York: Oxford University Press, 2002.

6

A THOMISTIC COSMOLOGICAL ARGUMENT

W. David Beck

THE TERM "COSMOLOGICAL ARGUMENT" (HEREAFTER CA) REFERS TO A WHOLE class of arguments or patterns of thinking that have in common the conclusion that God is real because the things we see around us never exist unless something makes them exist. So, roughly, the CA concludes to God as a first cause or initiating source of things because there cannot be an infinite sequence of causes of the existence of the things around us, those things that we observe as existing only because they are caused to do so.

We can distinguish types of the CA in several ways. First, most have been based on observations of the real world. Some, however, have been argued strictly on the basis of what is logically possible and necessary (see below).

A second critical distinction is between arguments that imply that God is chronologically first in time versus those that conclude to a God as the first cause in a concurrent sequence of dependent causes, all at the same time. A third distinction is between those arguments that refer to the whole universe as a single dependent object and those that refer only to individual causal chains as the basis for needing a first cause.

Fourth, some arguments attempt to conclude to a full-blown concept of God. This demands a rather complex argument. By contrast, many rather simple arguments arrive at the minimal conclusion of a first cause. They will then add supplemental arguments that provide a fuller conclusion as to the nature of this cause.

This chapter is concerned with the classic form of the CA, first fully stated by Aristotle and best known as developed by Thomas Aquinas. We will begin with a historical overview.

A Little History

Looking at the development of Greek philosophy, we see a step-by-step unfolding of an argument delineating the source of the universe. What drives it is the recognition of change, motion, the combining and recombining of chemical elements, that is, the dependency of things on an organizing, designing and driving cause. In Heraclitus it is a *logos* or lawfulness; in Anaxagoras it has become Mind.

The first time, however, that this becomes a real argument for an actual agent is in Plato. In his *Phaedrus* and in *Laws,* we have the key elements of the CA: (1) the things we observe are arranged in sequences of causes and effects; (2) such sequences cannot go on endlessly; and (3) the beginning point, or initiating cause, will be different from the other causes in not being caused by something else. For Plato it is Soul.

Aristotle, Plato's student, carefully refines this argument into its standard format in his *Metaphysics.* He has a clearer concept of "infinite" and provides a subargument as to precisely why there cannot be an infinite sequence of causes of dependent things. He also provides some implications about the nature of this first cause that follow just because it cannot itself be caused but is precisely uncaused.

Little knowledge of Aristotle is preserved for Roman and early Christian Europe. It is, however, maintained in Arab culture and is central in the development of Islamic philosophy. The version of the CA put forward by al-Ghazali, Ibn Rushd and others understands the sequence of causes as a chronological argument for a first cause of the universe backwards in time. This CA has come to be known as the *kalam* argument and is the subject of another chapter.

By the twelfth century, Aristotle's *Metaphysics* had been brought to Europe by way of the Muslim conquest of Spain. Enter Thomas Aquinas.

What is most significant is his development of the argument within the context of Christian theology. In the *Summa Theologica* and in the *Summa Contra Gentiles* he gives five brief statements of the CA that have come to be known as the Five Ways, though they are not the same in each book.

Following Thomas, the CA develops in a number of different directions. One is initiated by Duns Scotus. What he does is preface each premise of the CA with "it is possible." The conclusion then is that it is possible that an uncaused first cause exists. This is a quite different argument in that it proceeds solely on the basis of what is logically possible. Scotus argues that if an uncaused being is possible, then it is actual, since nothing could limit its being. There are contemporary versions of this form found in the work of James Ross and others.[1]

By far the most important direction taken by the CA comes in the eighteenth century at the hands of G. W. F. Leibniz and Samuel Clarke. The notable addition to the CA is what Leibniz calls the principle of sufficient reason: nothing happens or exists without a reason. This transforms the CA into a significantly different argument. First, it is now an argument about the reason for the entire universe rather than its cause. Second, it concludes to a God whose existence is necessary, that is, who exists in such a way that it makes no sense to ask the reason for the necessary being's existence.

It is precisely this second point that forms the basis for an attack by Immanuel Kant in his *Critique of Pure Reason* (1781). He holds that the very concept of a necessarily existing being is incoherent. The debate over Kant's criticism continues, but its effect on the entire discussion of the CA in the nineteenth century was devastating, even though Kant's criticism only affects Leibniz's version of the CA.

A renewed discussion begins in the 1960s as a result of the work of Bruce Reichenbach, William Rowe and others.[2] Since then, the volume

---

[1]See James Ross, *Philosophical Theology* (Indianapolis: Bobbs-Merrill, 1969).

[2]See Bruce Reichenbach, *The Cosmological Argument: A Reassessment* (Springfield, Ill.: Charles Thomas Press, 1972), and William Rowe, *The Cosmological Argument* (New York: Fordham University Press, 1998). The latter is an excellent source on the entire history of the Leibnizian argument. First published in 1975, this new edition keeps the discussion current.

of published literature on this form of the CA and the principle of sufficient reason has exploded.

Another direction is taken by a tradition of late nineteenth and early twentieth century philosophers known as Personalists. They actually combined the CA with the teleological argument. Peter Bertocci, for example, argued that in fact there must be a self-sufficient source of our universe and that what directs our search is its design. We must conclude that there is a self-sufficient designing intelligence/creator of the universe. What was important to Bertocci and is to current philosophers like Richard Gale, who uses a similar approach, is that this argument demands only a finitely intelligent God, which provides them an answer to the vexing problem of evil.[3]

These three lines of development should not cloud the fact that the standard CA itself continues to be developed following Thomas. This process comes to an almost virtual standstill with the apparently successful critique leveled by Kant.

A renewed interest begins with the pronouncement of Vatican I, which directed Catholic philosophers and theologians to resume the study of Thomas Aquinas. This brought about a renewed discussion and appreciation of the CA in the early twentieth century. Catholic philosophers like Etienne Gilson and Jacques Maritain were crucial here. Within broader philosophical circles, and particularly among evangelicals, this renewal of interest in Thomas's CA had to wait until the 1960s and the work of Norman Geisler and others.[4]

THE ARGUMENT

Our purpose in this chapter is to examine the traditional argument of Aristotle and Thomas. This argument is based on simple observations of the world around us. It looks at causal connections as a concurrent series and not one going back in time. It focuses on individual, actual se-

---

[3]See Richard Gale, "A New Argument for the Existence of God: One That Works, Sort Of," in *The Rationality of Theism*, ed. Godehard Bruentrup and Ron Tacelli (Dordrecht: Kluwer, 1999).

[4]A good example of Norman Geisler's treatment is his *Philosophy of Religion* (Grand Rapids: Zondervan, 1974).

quences and does not need to talk of the universe as a whole. Finally, its conclusion is simple, with a minimal conception of God, and leaves a fuller concept of God to subsequent conclusions.

The briefest and most general statement of Thomas's argument is found in chapter fifteen of the *Summa Contra Gentiles*. It is also close to its predecessor in Aristotle.

> We see things in the world that can exist and can also not exist. Now everything that can exist has a cause. But one cannot go on *ad infinitum* in causes. . . . Therefore one must posit something the existing of which is necessary. (*Summa Contra Gentiles* 15.124, excerpts)

There are three basic points in this argument.

Premise 1: What we observe in this universe is contingent. This argument begins with a simple observation concerning the things we see and know about in the real world around us. It is not intended to be about everything in the universe, let alone every possible entity, only those things we have actually observed. The key element in this first premise is the notion of contingency. In this context this means that something owes its existence to something else; it does not exist in and of itself.

So these causal relations are transferring not initiating. That is, A is caused by B, but only as B is caused by C. Everything we know of possesses this sort of contingency: it exists and functions only as it is caused by other factors in its causal chain. We know of nothing that by itself spontaneously initiates causal activity. But note that nothing here turns on our knowing about everything. Even if something does turn out to spontaneously initiate, it would have no effect on the CA.

Premise 2: A sequence of causally related contingent things cannot be infinite. The point of the second premise is to show that regardless of how complex and interconnected, and regardless of how extensive they may be, the sequence of causally related contingent things is not infinite. Thomas at one point uses the picture of a hand moving a stick moving a ball. Perhaps the most frequently used analogy in recent discussions is the train.

Imagine seeing a train moving past you for the first time. Baffled, you wonder how the boxcar is moving. You come to realize that it is being pulled by another boxcar in front of it, and so on, and so on down the tracks.

This allows us to visualize the various naturalistic scenarios, so commonly heard in our society, that describe how it is that things exist in the real world. "The cosmos is a great circle of being," we are told. But stringing boxcars all the way around in a circle until the last one hooks up to the first will still not explain the motion even of the first boxcar. And likewise, if contingent things cause each other to exist in a circle, there is no initiating of the causality. The naturalist offers another more promising scenario: "The cosmos is an intricately evolved ecosystem in which everything is related causally to everything else." So boxcars clutter the world in an unimaginably complex system of railroads such that in some way every boxcar is coupled to and pulling the first one. We still have no accounting for the motion of that first boxcar and likewise for the existence of actual things.

It is always tempting, of course, to say that it is just enough to know that the one in front of it is pulling each boxcar. In one sense it is clearly true that boxcar A is pulled by boxcar B. But B can pull A only because at the same time C is pulling B. The pulling action of B is transferred from C. And so it is also true that A is being pulled by C. The same is true, of course, about D, and about E, and so on.

One last option suggests itself. Suppose that there are infinite boxcars, or as the naturalist says: "The intricacy of the universe is lost in infinite complexity." But infinite boxcars, no matter how complexly arranged, still leave unexplained why our first boxcar is moving and hence why any are. Letting the sequence go to infinity fails to explain anything. It just puts off infinitely the question of what initiates the causality.

Premise 3: The sequence of causally dependent contingent things must be finite. The rest of the CA simply draws the obvious conclusion from premise 2. If the sequence cannot be infinite, then it must be finite. There is, of course, one other alternative, just as there is one way in which the line of boxcars can be infinite, namely, if they are not moving at all. There might of course be infinite boxcars in the train, but there could not be a moving train that consisted only of an infinity of boxcars. Just so, there might exist infinite things but not an infinite network of concurrently causally dependent, contingent things.

Conclusion: There must be a first cause in the sequence of contingent causes. If the causal sequence is finite, then there is a first cause regardless of how many causes there might be in the series. This concept of "first cause" involves two component concepts. To say that it is the *first* cause is to say that it neither requires nor has a cause itself. First is first! Thus it is fundamentally different from every other cause in the system: it is not contingent. It depends on, is limited by, or exists because of absolutely nothing else. It does not pass on causality it receives in a transferring relation; rather it strictly initiates causality. It is itself uncaused.

To say of the conclusion that it is the first *cause* is to define its relation to everything else in the sequence: namely, that it is their cause. It is the cause of all things in that it initiates all of the causal activity in the sequence, without negating that each cause is, in fact, a cause in its own right of the following one in the sequence, and is an effect of the proceeding one.

The only explanation for the moving line of boxcars is that somewhere there is a locomotive powerful enough to pull the whole train while itself not needing to be pulled. And so the concept of a first cause is richer than it might at first appear. It is the initiating cause of existence of everything in the series of causes and exists without any cause or dependency whatsoever. It is strictly an uncaused cause.

WHAT FOLLOWS ABOUT GOD'S NATURE?

The fairly simple argument of Aristotle and Thomas gives us no more than a first cause. It does, however, set up a series of subsequent arguments that fill in a good deal of content and provide a preface of something we are more justified in calling God.

For the most part, these subarguments go back to Parmenides. He was something of an oddity in Greek philosophy by thinking that the universe is just one simple uncaused thing and not a network of casually connected things. It is precisely this notion that pushed him to ask what characteristics the universe must possess if it is in-and-of-itself or necessary. But notice that this is exactly where the CA leaves us too. What follows from the fact that something is a first cause, that is, entirely without cause while causing all relevant effects?

Uniqueness. Why think that there is only one first cause? It seems to me that in fact many of the versions of the CA have been directed at precisely this goal. The obvious way to do it is to find a way to make the CA an argument about the entire universe, and the best way to do that is to incorporate some principle that includes all possible reality, for example, the principle of sufficient reason. But this is not the tactic taken by Aristotle and Thomas.

The subargument they use can be simplified like this. Imagine there are two first and uncaused causes. Call them FC1 and FC2. What is it that distinguishes them and hence determines that they are two, not one? What controls our thinking here is the logical principle that two things that do not differ in any respect at all are just the same thing.

Put briefly, the only way FC2 could differ from FC1 would be for it to have some characteristic that FC1 does not. But if FC1 lacks something that is available (since FC2 has it) then it is limited or caused not to have it. But that is impossible since FC1 is not caused in any way. And so we have to conclude that any two—or more for that matter—uncaused first causes would have to be identical in the strict sense, and therefore there could only be one of them.

Simplicity. That God is "simple" is a difficult but crucial concept. It means at least the following: (a) God has no parts and is therefore not material (made of measurable units); (b) God does not change, that is, he cannot add or subtract parts of what he is; (c) God is all one thing. There is not one part of him that is distinguishable from others. He simply is what he is.

All of the meanings given to simplicity imply that God has parts, that is, that God has internal differences. The Bible sometimes seems to refer such things to God, just as we correctly do to human persons, such as changing his mind, or being somewhere (such as a burning bush) but not somewhere else. With some people he seems to act judgmentally. With others he is loving and forgiving. How are we to understand this?

The argument here is a version of the argument for God's uniqueness. Any differences between parts would involve a lack of something in one of them. Such a lack would have to be a limit due to some cause, but that is impossible for an uncaused first cause.

These two arguments might seem abstract or irrelevant at first glance, but they play quite important roles in a larger conception of God. That there is only one God is crucial enough, and so is the point that God is what he is without change. Put together, these arguments form boundaries for the Christian doctrine of the Trinity. That is, there is only one God, not three, and he does not have internal divisions or parts. The biblical data has to be compiled in a way that fits these logical boundaries.

Perfection. An uncaused first cause, existing in and of itself, must therefore be perfect. This is simply the reverse of the argument used in the first two points above. If God has no limitations in what he is, then he is simply unlimited.

The difficulty here is that we do not have any really positive meaning to this notion. When I say that I am 5'11" tall or that I am sitting at my desk, I am actually describing my limitations. My size is confined in certain ways, as is my presence in the room, as well as in the world. God, it turns out, must be described avoiding any limitations. Expressing that, however, can be accomplished only by consistently denying definitions of God. For example, God is *not* spatial. We say this by using the term *omnipresent*. But that should not be taken to mean that God is located in every space. Rather, he is just not located in any sense. And this is to be applied to every description of God. Thus a seemingly empty term, applied to God, turns out to generate a great deal of important theology. We have come to call it "perfect being theology."

Personhood. We are still left with a rather abstract, nonrelational or, in general, nonpersonal being at best. Does anything follow from the CA that would indicate that God has personal characteristics?

Both Aristotle and Thomas do have subarguments that God possesses knowledge and will. Aristotle's God, however, is nonrelational, knowing only himself. Thomas, however, shows that God's knowing of himself as first cause of all things does in fact involve a perfect knowing that is truly relational.

I want, however, to mention here a simpler argument for personhood that flows from the CA. Among recent philosophers, it can be found in Norman Geisler's discussions. Put briefly, since the universe contains persons who are rational, social, moral and free, how could the first cause of all things be any less than a person? In particular, if the first cause is both uncaused and explains itself, then it must be free, not determined.

There is much more to be said here as to what can be developed out of the CA. This, however, is enough to show that Thomas's simple argument does provide the basis for a fuller concept of God.

Some Basic Objections to the Argument

During our discussion of the argument we have dealt with a number of problems, objections or alternate views. Here I want only to bring up two very general objections to the CA.

First, certainly the most frequent criticism of the CA is that there is no reason to think that it concludes to God. Even if it were a sound argument, the objection typically goes, it only gives us a first cause. This could well be some space/time factor, say, the big bang or elementary particles of some sort, but not an infinite creator God who loves us and desires relationship and worship.

Any response to this objection will first have to pose the question of what it takes to identify someone. Specifically, what characteristics do you have to know in order to identify someone? Clearly one answer is that you need only one, if it is a uniquely identifying characteristic. If only one object in the universe has a specific property, and even if that is the only property I know, then I am able to correctly identify that object.

Given that principle, we should say that strictly speaking the minimal CA discussed above, by itself, does not uniquely identify God in its conclusion. However, that there must be finite links in every causal network and thus a first, uncaused cause is already enough to defeat most forms of atheistic naturalism which hold that the universe is a closed causal network.

More important, of course, the CA has immediate implications that do provide unique identifiers. So a good strategy is to leave the argument as simple as possible rather than burden it with all sorts of complex premises that only demand additional, often difficult and only moderately probable premises.

There are those who still object, including some Christian theists, that even with all the subarguments we are left with an abstract, impersonal something that does not demand religious worship. The best response is to agree: the CA proves only what it proves. Certainly we will want more and different kinds of input, including revelation and experience. This further objection often supposes that unless we know everything about God, we know nothing. But this is not only obviously false—I certainly know many things without knowing everything about any of them—it is also self-contradictory since the objector clearly does not know everything about the objection. I conclude that the argument yields a little but crucial and uniquely identifying knowledge of God.

A second frequent objection makes the point that infinite series are possible. Since the CA depends on a denial of an infinite series of causes, the argument fails. It is, of course, true that infinite series are possible. The sequence of cardinal numbers, as we all learned in elementary school, is infinite. We could assign a cardinal number to each member of any causal sequence, and we would then have an infinite sequence of causes.

This objection occurs in many forms, but they all overlook the specifics of the sequence of causes in the CA. There are four characteristics of this series and each is crucial to eliminating the possibility of infinity. (1) It is a sequence, a connected series of causes to effects. (2) Each cause is itself contingent. It, in turn, needs a cause. (3) The dependency in the Aristotelian/Thomistic CA is concurrent not chronological. It refers to concurrent dependency relations of cause and effect. (4) The specific relation to which the generic CA refers is the causing of existence itself. The key point in the CA is that there cannot be an infinite series of causes with all four of the above characteristics, not that there cannot be infinite series of other types.

Note that, given this point, it is irrelevant to the argument whether the universe itself might be infinite. Thomas thought that it is at least possible that the universe exists in infinite time, as Aristotle had held. That God created the beginning of time we know only by revelation. Many objections attempt to show that in some respects the universe is infinite, so the CA must be wrong. Attached to this is typically that Thomas's physics is just wrong. But this is all irrelevant to the CA. It shows only that there cannot be an infinite sequence of concurrent dependent causes of existence.

CONCLUSION: WHY IS THIS ARGUMENT IMPORTANT?

It is clear that Thomas intended this argument to play a critical role in our understanding, not just of God and religion but, as it did for Aristotle, of everything. We cannot make sense of our reality at all apart from God. The God of the CA best explains life as we experience it.

At the same time this argument is not a starting point. It is based on other arguments and observations, and so God is also a conclusion from the evidence. My point here is that one way in which the CA is important is that it demonstrates that God is not a belief or a creation of faith but part of our true description of things. So the CA is tremendously valuable for apologetics.

This argument along with its subarguments is also vital in setting logical guidelines for theology. We mentioned earlier how it helps us in regard to the doctrine of the Trinity, but there are many other applications. The CA demands that God is unchanging. Applied to God as knowing, choosing, willing or acting in any way at all, we will have to see "unchangingly" as a filter that always modifies our understanding of how God is to be conceptualized. If we extend this to all of the aspects of God's nature that are identified in the various subarguments of the CA and then apply them in turn to each of God's actions, we have built a framework for theology: a perfect being theology.

Finally, the CA is important for us in doing science. It specifies the relationship between God's acting and the processes of science, including the behaviors of human beings. It says that God is the true source— the first cause—of all processes, every event and even every free action. We must note that this concept does not eliminate, replace or reduce the necessity of doing science. It is not a god-of-the-gaps view. It respects the proper place of science; in fact, it grounds science by explaining why it is even possible.

This brings us back to the original question of how the universe operates and the subsequent moves in philosophy that culminate in Aristotle's and Thomas's arguments. The CA can be seen as establishing or underwriting a worldview: a big-picture understanding of how everything works—namely, theism, as opposed to naturalism.

I have argued that cosmological thinking is important to our large understanding of everything. There is much work yet to be done on the CA, and it may well be that faults will be found with our current ways of wording this argument. The objections that have been brought against it over virtually the entire history of both western and eastern philosophy either fail or only point out the obvious limitations of the CA. It remains an essential part of a Christian apologetic.

FOR FURTHER READING

Burrill, David, ed. *The Cosmological Arguments*. Garden City, N.Y.: Anchor, 1967.

Davis, Stephen. *God, Reason and Theistic Proofs*. Grand Rapids, Mich.: Eerdmans, 1997.

Davies, Brian. *The Thought of Thomas Aquinas*. Oxford: Clarendon Press, 1992.

Edwards, Paul. "The Cosmological Argument." Published in 1959, it can be found in many anthologies, including Burrill's mentioned above.

Geisler, Norman L. *Thomas Aquinas: An Evangelical Appraisal*. Grand Rapids, Mich.: Baker, 1991.

Geisler, Norman L., and Winfried Corduan. *Philosophy of Religion*. 2nd ed. Grand Rapids, Mich.: Baker, 1988.

7

A MORAL ARGUMENT

Paul Copan

WHAT MORAL DIFFERENCE WOULD IT MAKE IF GOD DID NOT EXIST? SOME WILL say, "Not much. After all, atheists can be just as moral as believers. We can be good without God." The United Nations Universal Declaration of Human Rights (1948) simply assumes this point of view without any reference to God: "All human beings are born free and equal in dignity and rights. They are endowed with reason and conscience and should act towards one another in a spirit of brotherhood." By contrast, the U.S. Declaration of Independence (1776) asserts: "We hold these truths to be self-evident, that all men are created equal, that they are endowed by their Creator with certain unalienable rights."

An obvious point of departure between these two declarations is that the Declaration of Independence grounds human rights and dignity in our having been created by God whereas the UN declaration simply posits human equality and dignity without offering any basis or foundation for intrinsic human value.

Norman Geisler, to whose major work in contemporary Christian apologetics many others and I owe a great debt, observes that God serves as this crucial foundation. He is the "infinite and necessarily good" Source of all finite goods.[1] Indeed, the good ("that which is desired for its own sake") is inescapable. Persons want to be treated as persons, not as objects, and they act as though intrinsic goods exist (even in express-

---

[1] Norman L. Geisler, *Christian Apologetics* (Grand Rapids, Mich.: Baker, 1976), p. 249.

ing the right to dissent from such a view).[2]

Indeed, the difference God makes is momentous. Indeed, if God doesn't exist, then we simply do not have an adequate foundation for objective ethics—including intrinsic human dignity and rights, personal responsibility and moral obligation. Furthermore, if the divine grounding for morality is lacking, then (as Nietzsche argued) it is not a far step to undercut moral motivation as well.

In this chapter I want to argue, first, that basic moral values exist, and there is no good reason to deny them. Second, humans have dignity because they are made in the image of God, the source of goodness. Naturalism cannot adequately account for moral obligation or human rights since valueless processes cannot conceivably produce valuable personal beings. If God doesn't exist, then objective moral values and rights don't exist. Third, the theistic basis for objective moral values and human dignity is further supported by the fact that many atheists recognize the intrinsic connection between God and objective moral values/human rights. Fourth, morality is not the byproduct of evolutionary forces that enable us to survive and reproduce. The naturalistic mechanisms behind evolutionary ethics would undermine not only virtue but rational thought itself. Finally, nontheists (following Plato's Euthyphro argument) may argue that if God exists, then God's commands or character must be subject to nonarbitrary principles of goodness that are independent of God; so moral values can exist independently of God. As we'll see, this is a weak argument.

A strong case can be made for the difference God makes for both moral foundations and motivation. The general argument we'll be using can be summarized as follows:

> If objective moral values exist, then God exists.
> Objective moral values do exist.
> Therefore, God exists.

OBJECTIVE MORAL VALUES AS PROPERLY BASIC

Pro-Nazi philosopher Martin Heidegger said of Hitler, "He alone is the

---

[2]Ibid., pp. 248-49.

German reality of today, and of the future, and of its law." But when the Germans were defeated in World War II, the French confiscated his property because of his Nazi sympathies. In response, he wrote an indignant letter to the commander of the French forces: "What justice there is in treating me in this unheard of way is inconceivable to me."[3] To Heidegger's mind, there was not a "German morality" and a different "French morality." Despite being mesmerized by Hitler, he was assuming some universal standard of justice that even the French could understand!

Here's a good rule of thumb about morality: *Don't believe people who say murder or rape may not really be wrong.* Such people haven't looked deeply enough into the basis for moral belief; they just aren't functioning properly. Just as color-blind persons need help distinguishing red from green, morally malfunctioning persons (who can't "see" basic moral truths) need help psychologically and spiritually; they don't need arguments! Like sense perception, we have certain moral intuitions or instincts that are basic to properly functioning humans. If we don't have them, something's wrong with us. And in the absence of strong reasons to overturn these intuitions, they should be taken seriously. The *credulity principle* is appropriate both with regard to our sense perceptions as well as our moral intuitions/perception—they are innocent until proven guilty. I am wise to accept their testimony unless I have a strong, overriding reasons to doubt them.

I was speaking at a university in New York, and during the question-and-answer time a female student stood up and charged me with being ethnocentric. (At least she believed that ethnocentrism is wrong for all people everywhere!) When I asked why, she replied, "You believe that your morality should be imposed on other people." I asked her, "If you're walking down a dark alley and you're about to be raped and there is a bystander who could help you, would you want that bystander to impose his morality on your attacker?" I added that it's easy to claim morality is relative when it doesn't immediately affect me, but when

---

[3]Martin Heidegger, *"Mit welchem Rechtsgrund ich mit einem solchen unerhörten Vorgehen betroffen werde, ist mir unerfindlich."* Quoted in Hugo Ott, *Martin Heidegger: Unterwegs zu seiner Biographie* (Frankfurt: Campus Verlag, 1988), p. 296.

someone violates my rights, deeply humiliates me or steals my property, then I respond to this personal affront as morally wrong.

As C. S. Lewis has documented in *The Abolition of Man*,[4] the same sorts of moral standards—don't murder, don't take another's property, don't defraud—continually surface across civilizations and cultures and throughout history. We don't need to look far to find commonalities. Such moral principles are discovered, not invented. Without them, the idea of moral reform makes no sense. Furthermore, properly functioning persons generally know when they're being treated like an object (e.g., child abuse, rape, the torture of innocent people for fun) rather than with dignity and respect. If one can't see this, something's malfunctioning (e.g., self-deception, hard-heartedness). As part of God's general self-revelation, all people—unless they ignore or suppress their consciences—can and should have basic moral insight, knowing truths generally available to any morally sensitive person (Rom 2:14-15). We just know the rightness of virtues (kindness, trustworthiness, unselfishness), and the burden of proof falls on those who deny this.

Atheist philosopher Kai Nielsen comments on the vileness of child abuse and wife beating: "It is more reasonable to believe such elemental things to be evil than to believe any skeptical theory that tells us we cannot know or reasonably believe any of these things to be evil. . . . I firmly believe that this is bedrock and right and that anyone who does not believe it cannot have probed deeply enough into the grounds of his moral beliefs."[5]

Objective moral values do exist, and we can recognize them. The existence of gray areas doesn't mean that we can't readily recognize general moral principles. In making moral judgments, we must begin with the clear and move to the unclear, not vice versa. Just because moral uncertainty or ambiguity exists, this doesn't eclipse the morally obvious. As Dr. Samuel Johnson put it, "The fact that there is such a thing as twilight does not mean that we cannot distinguish between day and night."

---

[4]C. S. Lewis, *The Abolition of Man* (San Francisco: Harper, 2001), appendix.
[5]Kai Nielsen, *Ethics Without God,* rev. ed. (Buffalo, N.Y.: Prometheus, 1990), pp. 10-11.

THE CONNECTION BETWEEN GOD AND OBJECTIVE MORAL VALUES/HUMAN DIGNITY

In writing an essay presenting an argument for God's existence from morality, why am I citing Nielsen—an atheist—for support? The short answer is: atheists have been made in the image of God and can therefore recognize the same sorts of moral values Christians can. Atheists don't need the Bible to recognize basic objective moral values. They have been created or constituted to be able to recognize them, even if they disbelieve. All humans are hard-wired the same way: they are made to function properly when living morally. This moral awareness is part of God's general self-revelation. We see something of God in the moral order of the universe.

Atheist Michael Martin asks, "Why would the nonexistence of God adversely affect the goodness of mercy, compassion, and justice? . . . One could affirm the objective immorality of rape and deny the existence of God with perfect consistency."[6] Martin claims that even if God didn't exist, we could still know that objective morality exists. The Christian will cite the same reasons as the atheist about the wrongness of rape: "It violates the victim's rights and offends her dignity. It also contributes to the destruction of society." The atheist appears to be vindicated. He can say to the theist: "See? Your reasons didn't even appeal to God's existence. The very reasons you give are the ones I give."

This is too hasty. We must distinguish between *knowing* and *being*—and get clear on which is more fundamental. At one level (knowing), Martin's argument appears to make sense. Because human beings have been made in God's image as intrinsically valuable (endowed with rights, dignity, conscience, moral responsibility and the basic capacity to recognize right and wrong), we should not be surprised that an atheist holds similar beliefs about human rights, dignity and obligation. But Martin's defense of objective morality only works at one level—knowledge.[7] The more fundamental level of being—that is, the actual ground

---

[6]Michael Martin, "Atheism, Christian Theism and Rape (1977)," <www.infidels.org/library/modern/michael_martin/rape.html> p. 4.

[7]For further support of this thesis, see Paul Copan, "The Moral Argument," in *The Rationality of Theism,* ed. Paul Copan and Paul K. Moser (London: Routledge, 2003), pp. 149-74.

or basis (which makes moral knowledge possible)—is inadequate.[8]

Ironically, we live in a time when many claim everything is relative, yet they believe they have rights. But if morality is just the product of naturalistic evolution or cultural development or personal choice, then rights do not truly exist. But if they do exist and if human persons truly have value in and of themselves—regardless of what their culture or the high priests of science (or better, scient*ism*) say—then what is the basis for this value? Did this intrinsic value come from impersonal, nonconscious, unguided, valueless processes over time (naturalism)? The contextual fit isn't a good one.[9] A more natural context for moral values and human dignity is the theistic one—in which we've been made by a personal, self-aware, purposeful, good God to resemble him in certain important ways.

In table 7.1, note how theism offers a superior explanatory context than naturalism to account for objective moral values, human dignity and other important phenomena we readily recognize or observe.

Theism is the more natural context for these features. Given materialistic, impersonal, nonconscious, valueless, deterministic processes, the atheist is hard pressed to account for personal, self-conscious, valuable, morally responsible persons. Theism offers a better fit, and this fit is one important basis for affirming one context (in this case, theism) and rejecting another (naturalism).

The reason theism makes more sense here is that personhood and morality are necessarily connected. That is, moral values are rooted in personhood. Without God (a personal Being), no persons—and thus no moral values—would exist at all. The moral argument points to a personal, good Being to whom we're responsible. Only if God exists can moral properties be realized or instantiated.

---

[8] See Paul Copan, "Is Michael Martin a Moral Realist? *Sic et Non,*" *Philosophia Christi* n.s. 1/2 (1999): 45-72; "Atheistic Goodness Revisited: A Personal Reply to Michael Martin," *Philosophia Christi* n.s. 2/1 (2000): 91-104. Martin offers an online response that brings up charges and issues already addressed in the aforementioned essays. See "Copan's Critique of Atheistic Objective Morality" <www.infidels.org/library/modern/michael_martin/copan.html>. For a partial response, see Paul Copan, "The Moral Argument," in *The Rationality of Theism*.

[9] I'm not here dealing with Eastern monism (sometimes called pantheism = everything is God/divine), which claims that no ultimate distinction between good and evil exists—an outlook that serves to support relativism.

Table 7.1 Naturalism versus theism: which context best explains the phenomena we observe?

Phenomena We Observe	Theistic Context	Naturalistic Context
(Self-)consciousness exists.	God is supremely self-aware/self-conscious.	The universe was produced by mindless, non-conscious processes.
Personal beings exist.	God is a personal Being.	The universe was produced by impersonal processes.
We believe we make free personal decisions/choices.	God is spirit and a free Being, who can freely choose to act (e.g., to create or not).	We have emerged by material, deterministic processes and forces beyond our control.
We trust our senses and rational faculties as generally reliable in producing true beliefs.	A God of truth and rationality exists.	Because of our impulse to survive and reproduce, our beliefs would only help us survive, but a number of these could be completely false.
Human beings have intrinsic value/dignity and rights.	God is the supremely valuable Being.	Human beings were produced by valueless processes.
Objective moral values exist.	God's character is the source of goodness/moral values.	The universe was produced by nonmoral processes.
First life emerged.	God is a living, active Being.	Life somehow emerged from nonliving matter.
Beauty exists (e.g., not only in landscapes and sunsets but in "elegant" or "beautiful" scientific theories).	God is beautiful (Ps 27:4) and capable of creating beautiful things according to his pleasure.	Beauty in the natural world is superabundant and in many cases superfluous (often not linked to survival).
The universe is finely tuned for human life (known as "the Goldilocks effect"—the universe is "just right" for life).	God is a wise, intelligent Designer.	All the cosmic constants just happened to be right; given enough time and/or many possible worlds, a finely tuned world eventually emerged

So when atheists like Martin[10] appeal to objective ethical systems that make no reference to God (e.g., Immanuel Kant or Aristotle),[11] the theist can affirm much of what they have to say but show that their ethical systems are still incomplete, lacking sufficient grounding.

NONTHEISTS' RECOGNITION OF THE GOD-AND-MORALITY CONNECTION

What further reinforces the connection between God and objective morality is the fact that many atheists and skeptics have observed that a Godless world would entail an absence of objective moral values. But if objective moral values exist, then this would be an argument for God's existence.

Let's look at what some naturalists have said in this regard.

Bertrand Russell stood on the "firm foundation of unyielding despair."[12] He claimed, "The whole subject of ethics arises from the pressure of the community on the individual."[13]

J. L. Mackie found moral properties "queer" in a naturalistic universe: "If . . . there are . . . objective values, they make the existence of a god more probable than it would have been without them. Thus we have . . . a defensible argument from morality to the existence of a god."[14]

Agnostic philosopher Paul Draper agrees with Mackie: "A moral world is . . . very probable on theism."[15]

Ethicist James Rachels insists, "Man is a moral (altruistic) being, not because he intuits the rightness of loving his neighbor, or because he responds to some noble ideal, but because his behavior is comprised of

---

[10]For example, Martin points to Immanuel Kant in *The Big Domino in the Sky* (Amherst, N.Y.: Prometheus, 1996), pp. 43, 68. See also Michael Martin, *Atheism, Morality and Meaning* (Amherst, N.Y.: Prometheus, 2002). See my forthcoming review of the latter in *Philosophia Christi*.

[11]On Aristotle, see Stephen Layman, *The Shape of the Good* (Notre Dame, Ind.: University of Notre Dame Press, 1991), pp. 138-44.

[12]Bertrand Russell, "A Free Man's Worship," in *Why I Am Not a Christian* (New York: Simon and Schuster, 1957), p. 107.

[13]Bertrand Russell, *Human Society in Ethics and Politics* (London: Allen & Unwin, 1954), p. 124.

[14]J. L. Mackie, *The Miracle of Theism* (Oxford: Clarendon Press, 1982), pp. 115-16.

[15]Cited in Greg Ganssle, "Necessary Moral Truths and the Need for Explanation," *Philosophia Christi* series 2, 2/1 (2000): 111.

tendencies which natural selection has favoured."[16]

Zoologist Richard Dawkins declares, "The universe we observe has precisely the properties we should expect if there is, at bottom, no design, no purpose, no evil and no good, nothing but blind pitiless indifference."[17]

The list goes on and on.

If the divine foundation for moral obligation and human dignity is removed, then the moral motivation may actually be undermined. For example, despite being brought up to believe in God and that human beings are intrinsically valuable, Jeffrey Dahmer was exposed to naturalistic evolution. The result was devastating. This sexual predator and cannibal "placed the blame for [his] murders on his atheistic beliefs and the theory of evolution." Given naturalism, he found no basis for affirming intrinsic human dignity. His father, Lionel Dahmer, expressed Jeffrey's rationale: "If it all happens naturalistically, what's the need for a God? Can't I set my own rules? Who owns me? I own myself."[18]

That said, many theistic philosophers and theologians, past and present, have made the necessary connection between God's existence and objective moral values—that somehow God and objective moral values/human dignity are intrinsically connected.

Furthermore, Nielsen recognizes the inadequacy of grounding objective morality from a naturalistic point of view:

> We have not been able to show that reason requires the moral point of view or that all really rational persons, unhoodwinked by myth or ideology, not be individual egoists or classic amoralists. Reason doesn't decide here.
>
> The picture I have painted for you is not a pleasant one. Reflection on it depresses me. . . . The point is this: pure practical reason, even with a good knowledge of the facts, will not take you to morality.[19]

---

[16]James Rachels, *Created from Animals: The Moral Implications of Darwinism* (Oxford: Oxford University Press, 1990), p. 77.

[17]Richard Dawkins, *River Out of Eden: A Darwinian View of Life* (New York: Basic Books/ Harper Collins, 1995), pp. 132-33.

[18]These quotations are documented in *Jeffrey Dahmer: The Monster Within,* A&E Biography (1996). I am grateful to Ronald Tacelli for pointing this out to me.

[19]Kai Nielsen, "Why Should I Be Moral? Revisited," *American Philosophical Quarterly* 21 (January 1984): 90.

There is an important connection between God and objective moral values. Negatively stated, naturalism/God's nonexistence entails that there are no objective moral values, and it is no surprise that many nontheists take this entailment for granted.

GOD AND EVOLUTIONARY ETHICS

Naturalists generally claim that moral values are just the result of human evolutionary development. For some (naturalistic moral realists), moral values are objective because moral properties "supervene" upon nonmoral (or physical) ones—that is, moral properties emerge once the human brain and nervous system reach a certain level of complexity. (We've already dealt with this serious unlikelihood of value's emerging from valuelessness.) Other naturalists claim that moral values are simply subjective. Philosopher of science Michael Ruse asserts that we have developed an "awareness of morality—a sense of right and wrong and a feeling of obligation to be thus governed—because such an awareness is of biological worth."[20] Such a subjectivistic view reduces to ethical relativism.

The naturalist of Ruse's stripe might say to the theist, "You take moral belief as properly basic, but what if we're just hard-wired to believe what contributes to our fitness and survival? Belief in moral values helps us to survive and nothing more." I want to deal with this potential objection to the existence of objective moral values.

The question to ask here is this: Can we trust our minds if we are nothing more than the products of naturalistic evolution trying to fight, feed, flee and reproduce? Charles Darwin was deeply troubled by this: "With me the horrid doubt always arises whether the convictions of man's mind, which has been developed from the mind of the lower animals, are of any value or at all trustworthy. Would any one trust in the convictions of a monkey's mind, if there are any convictions in such a mind?"[21]

---

[20]Michael Ruse, *The Darwinian Paradigm* (London: Routledge, 1989), p. 262.
[21]Letter to William Graham Down, July 3, 1881, in *The Life and Letters of Charles Darwin Including an Autobiographical Chapter,* ed. Francis Darwin (London: John Murray, 1887), 1:315-16.

The evolutionary process is interested in fitness and survival, not in true belief.[22] The problem with naturalistic evolution is that not only is objective morality undermined, but so is rational thought. Our beliefs—moral or epistemic—may help us survive, but there is no reason to think they are true.[23]

So we may believe that human beings are intrinsically valuable, and this belief may help *homo sapiens* to survive, but it may be wholly false. We may believe with full conviction that we have moral obligations, and this belief may help us survive, but it may be completely wrong. We may have the belief that our wills are free and that our choices do make a difference, but, again, we may be in serious error. If we are blindly hard-wired by nature to accept certain beliefs because of their survival-enhancing value, then we would not have access to the truth-status of these beliefs. They may help us to survive, but how could we know whether they are true or false?

Every waking hour, we depend upon our rational faculties to make basic inferences and to guide us toward truth. We take our sense perceptions as basically reliable. Many of us assume moral intuitions to be generally trustworthy. But if we're hard-wired to reproduce and survive, then the reliability of our reason, sense perceptions and moral intuitions must be called into question. The scandal of such skepticism is this: I am relying on the very cognitive faculties whose unreliability is the conclusion of my skeptical argument.[24] I am assuming a trustworthy reasoning process to arrive at the conclusion that I can't trust my reasoning.

Moreover, we believe lots of things that don't help us survive but are still true (e.g., the current temperature at the North Pole). The fact that we seek to know the truth about many things apart from their survival value indicates that we are living according to a theistic worldview rather

---

[22]Alvin Plantinga, *Warrant and Proper Function* (New York: Oxford University Press, 1993), p. 219.

[23]George I. Mavrodes, "Religion and the Queerness of Morality," in *Rationality, Religious Belief and Moral Commitment,* ed. Robert Audi and William Wainwright (Ithaca, N.Y.: Cornell University Press, 1986), p. 219.

[24]Alvin Plantinga, *Warranted Christian Belief* (New York: Oxford University Press, 2000), p. 219.

than a naturalistic one. We have been made in the image of a truthful, rational Being. So it would make sense that we would be functioning properly when our cognitive faculties are directed at the truth. In our very nature, we are interested in more than just survival.

So the evolutionary ethics argument to explain away objective moral values is inadequate. Our basic moral intuitions—along with our faculties of reason and sense perception—are generally reliable (unless we're malfunctioning); there is no good reason to deny them. And if we claim that such basic beliefs should be questioned in the name of our impulse to survive and reproduce, then this skeptical conclusion is itself the result of those same impulses.

Naturalism does not inspire confidence in our belief-forming mechanisms. Indeed, naturalism has the potential to undermine our conviction that rationality and objective moral values exist. If our beliefs—moral or epistemic—are survival-enhancing byproducts of Darwinistic evolution, why think that we actually have dignity, rights and obligations—or that we are thinking rationally? A theistic worldview, by contrast, does assure us that we can know moral and rational truths—even if they may not contribute one whit to our survival.

THE EUTHYPHRO PROBLEM

In Plato's *Euthyphro* dialogue, Socrates asks, "Is what is holy holy because the gods approve it, or do they approve it because it is holy?"[25] Skeptics like to raise this dilemma: Either (a) God's commands are arbitrary (something is good because God commands it—and he could have commanded "You *shall* murder/commit adultery") or (b) there must be some autonomous moral standard (which God consults in order to command).[26] Are we left with divine "caprice," as Russell suggested,[27] or with a moral standard completely independent of God?

---

[25] *Euthyphro* 10a, Plato, "Euthyphro," trans. Lane Cooper, in Plato, *The Collected Dialogues of Plato*, ed. Edith Hamilton and Huntington Cairns (Princeton, N.J.: Princeton University Press, 1961), p. 178.

[26] These terms are taken from Mark D. Linville, "On Goodness: Human and Divine," *American Philosophical Quarterly* 27 (April 1990): 143-52.

[27] Bertrand Russell, *Human Society in Ethics and Politics* (New York: Simon & Schuster, 1962), p. 38.

Although God's commands may serve as a partial guide to living rightly (e.g., God's civil laws given at Mount Sinai to theocratic Israel), God's character is the more ultimate and underlying reality. Indeed, the final resolution to the Euthyphro dilemma is that God's good character/ nature sufficiently grounds objective morality. So we don't need to look elsewhere for such a standard. We have been made in the divine image, without which we would neither (a) be moral beings nor (b) have the capacity to recognize objective moral values.[28] The ultimate solution to the Euthyphro dilemma shifts the grounding of morality from the commands of God to something more basic—that is, the nature or character of God. Thus, we human beings (who have been made to resemble God in certain ways) have the capacity to recognize them, and thus his commands—far from being arbitrary—are in accordance with that nature.[29]

The atheist may push the Euthyphro dilemma further by questioning whether the very character of God is good because it is God's character or it is God's character because it is good. Several responses are in order to this revised Euthyphro dilemma.

First, if a good God does not exist, why think that morally responsible, intrinsically valuable, rights-bearing beings would exist at all? Without God, moral properties would never be instantiated or realized. Personhood is the locus of objective moral values, and without God, no persons would exist. Contextually, theism—not naturalism—favors such moral obligations and human dignity.

Second, if the naturalist is correct, then she herself cannot escape a similar dilemma; her argument offers her no actual advantage. Atheist Robin Le Poidevin declares that "we can, apparently, only make sense of these doctrines [that God is good and wills us to do what is good] if

---

[28]Robert Adams remarks: "It matters what God's attributes are. . . . It makes a difference if you think of commands as coming from someone who completely understands both us and our situation. It matters not only that God is loving but also that he is just" ("Divine Commands and Obligation," *Faith and Philosophy* 4 [July 1988]: 272).

[29]See Thomas V. Morris's essays, "Duty and Divine Goodness" and "The Necessity of God's Goodness" in *Anselmian Explorations* (Notre Dame, Ind.: University of Notre Dame Press, 1987), pp. 26-41 and pp. 42-69; William P. Alston, "Some Suggestions for Divine Command Theorists," in *Christian Theism and the Problems of Philosophy,* ed. Michael D. Beaty (Notre Dame, Ind.: University of Notre Dame Press, 1990).

we think of goodness as being defined independently of God."[30] But the theist could reply that we can make sense of these doctrines if humans have been made in the image of the Source of goodness. Further, we can ask the naturalistic moral realist: "Are these moral values good simply because they are good, or is there some independent standard of good to which *they* conform?" She faces the *same* alleged dilemma of arbitrariness or some (additional) autonomous standard. So it is difficult to see why the theist's stopping point—God—is arbitrary and the naturalist's is not. The sword cuts both ways. Le Poidevin's comment that we must think of goodness as defined independently of God is merely posited, and there's no good reason to accept it. And if we remember that two entities are sufficient to establish a relation—namely, God's character and objective moral values—the third, some standard independent of God to assess the connection between them, becomes superfluous.

Third, the naturalist's query is pointless since we must eventually arrive at some self-sufficient and self-explanatory stopping point beyond which the discussion can go no further. Imagine that God does not exist and that we have a Platonic form of the Good from which all values derive. At this point it would appear silly to ask, "Why is *the Good* good?" Rather, we have an ultimate ground for morality, and everything is good in approximation to this. Again, why is the "independent moral standard" any less arbitrary a stopping point than God's nature?[31]

Fourth, God, who is essentially perfect, does not have obligations to some external moral standard; God simply acts, and what he naturally does is good.[32] The revised Euthyphro dilemma wrongly assumes God has moral obligations. If such an external standard existed, God would be obligated to it. But God's actions and will operate according to the divine nature. So God's goodness should not be viewed as his fulfilling moral obligations but as expressing the way he is: "No preliminary stage of checking the relevant principles is required."[33]

Fifth, the idea that God could be evil or command evil is utterly con-

---

[30]Robin Le Poidevin, *Arguing for Atheism* (London: Routledge, 1996), p. 85.
[31]William Alston asks this question in "Some Suggestions," pp. 303-26.
[32]See Morris, "Duty and Divine Goodness," pp. 35, 38.
[33]Alston, "Some Suggestions for Divine Command Theorists," p. 320.

trary to the very definition of God; otherwise, such a being would not be God and would not be worthy of worship. Worshiping God because of his great power or knowledge alone is inadequate. A being worthy of worship must also be essentially good. As Robert Adams states, "Belief in the existence of an evil or amoral God would be morally intolerable."[34] So when atheists like Martin suggest God may be an evil being,[35] this is a straw man.

Sixth, the acceptance of objective values assumes a kind of ultimate goal or cosmic design plan for human beings, which would make no sense given naturalism but makes much sense given theism (which presumes a design plan for humans). Objective moral values presuppose (a) a fixed human nature (all human beings have a moral nature and possess dignity/rights) and (b) that a certain kind of life is better than another and thus ought to be pursued by every human being. It is exceedingly difficult to make sense of a brute cosmic purpose for all human beings apart from a transcendental purposive Creator. The brute fact of the value of human beings and the corresponding overarching purpose (and thus the demand) for their living excellently—another brute fact— are for naturalism nothing more than, as noted philosopher John Rist suggests, an "ethical hangover from a more homogeneous Christian past."[36]

In light of these points, there seems to be no good reason to see the Euthyphro dilemma as a serious threat to a theistically rooted ethic.

CONCLUSION

Unlike the United Nations Universal Declaration of Human Rights, which takes human rights and moral obligations for granted, the Declaration of Independence presents the essential grounding for human rights and dignity as being rooted in "our Creator"—a personal Being who has made us in his image. Without God, there would be no moral values, no

---

[34]Robert Adams, "Moral Arguments for Theistic Belief," in *Rationality and Religious Belief,* ed. C. F. Delaney (Notre Dame, Ind.: University of Notre Dame Press, 1979), p. 135.

[35]Martin suggests this alternative in "Patrick Glynn's God: The Evidence," <www.infidels.org/library/modern/michael_martin/glynn.html> p. 3.

[36]John M. Rist, *Real Ethics* (Cambridge: Cambridge University Press, 2002), p. 2.

moral obligations, no human rights, no human dignity. Rist observes that there is "widely admitted to be a crisis in contemporary Western debate about ethical foundations."[37] Without a return to the God of the Jewish-Christian tradition as the "infinite and necessarily good" Source of all finite goods, the crisis will only become more pronounced.

FOR FURTHER READING

Beckwith, Francis J., and Gregory P. Koukl. *Relativism: Feet Firmly Planted in Mid-Air.* Grand Rapids, Mich.: Baker, 1998.

Copan, Paul. "Atheistic Goodness Revisited: A Personal Reply to Michael Martin." *Philosophia Christi* n.s. 2/1 (2000): 91-104.

———. "Is Michael Martin a Moral Realist? *Sic et Non.*" *Philosophia Christi* n.s. 1 (1999).

———. "The Moral Argument," in *The Rationality of Theism.* Edited by Paul Copan and Paul K. Moser. London: Routledge, 2003.

Mavrodes, George I. "Religion and the Queerness of Morality," in *Rationality, Religious Belief and Moral Commitment.* Edited by Robert Audi and William Wainwright. Ithaca, N.Y.: Cornell University Press, 1986.

Moreland, J. P., and Kai Nielsen. "Does Ethics Need God?" in *Do the Right Thing: Readings in Applied Ethics and Social Philosophy.* Edited by Francis J. Beckwith. 2nd ed. Belmont, Calif.: Wadsworth, 2002.

[37]Ibid., p. 1.

8

THE ONTOLOGICAL ARGUMENT

William Lane Craig

IN 1078 A BENEDICTINE MONK NAMED ANSELM, LATER TO BECOME THE ARCH-
bishop of Canterbury, broached a novel and bold argument for the existence of God which has now fascinated philosophers for over a millennium. A year earlier, in 1077, Anselm had finished a treatise entitled
the *Monologium,* a soliloquy in which he argued for the existence of
God by means of moral and cosmological arguments. But Anselm remained dissatisfied with the complexity of his demonstration and
yearned to find a single argument which would on its own prove that
God exists in all his greatness. It was then that he hit upon the conception of God as "the greatest conceivable being" *(aliquid quo nihil maius
cogitari possit),* which provided the key to his new argument. In his discourse entitled *Proslogium* Anselm argued that once a person truly understands the notion of a greatest conceivable being, then he will see
that such being must exist, since if it did not, it would not be the greatest
conceivable being. A greatest conceivable being must be an existent being. God's existence, then, is truly inconceivable for him who rightly understands the word *God* (*Proslogium* 2-3). For that reason the Scripture
calls him who "hath said in his heart there is no God" a "fool" (Ps 14:1
KJV), for anyone who properly understands the word *God* will see that
God cannot fail to exist.

Anselm's argument, which has come to be known as the ontological
argument (from the Greek word *ontos,* "being"), went on to assume a

variety of forms, being defended by such notable thinkers as Duns Scotus, Descartes, Spinoza, Leibniz and others. What is the common thread in all these arguments that makes them versions of the ontological argument? Although Graham Oppy in his very thorough study *Ontological Arguments and Belief in God* identifies six basic types of ontological argument, his identification of an argument as ontological is based on a criterion far too vague for useful classification (namely, an argument is a form of the ontological argument if it proceeds from considerations that are entirely internal to the theistic worldview).[1] Rather the common thread in ontological arguments is that they try to deduce the existence of God from the very concept of God, together with certain other necessary truths. Proponents of the argument claim that once we understand what God is—the greatest conceivable being or the most perfect being or the most real being—then we shall see that such a being must in fact exist.

The argument tends to sharply polarize philosophers. Many would agree with Arthur Schopenhauer's dismissal of the argument as "a charming joke," but a number of recent, prominent philosophers such as Norman Malcolm, Charles Hartshorne and Alvin Plantinga not only take the argument seriously but even consider it to be sound. Since the formulation and defense of the argument provided by Plantinga are by far the most sophisticated in the long history of the ontological argument, profiting from the missteps and oversights of his predecessors, Plantinga's version of the argument has the best chance of being cogent and will therefore serve as the springboard for our discussion.

In his version of the argument, Plantinga appropriates the insight of Gottfried Wilhelm Leibniz that the ontological argument assumes that the concept of God is possible.[2] That is to say, the argument assumes that the concept "God" or "greatest conceivable being" is a coherent concept or, employing the semantics of possible worlds, that there is a possible world in which God exists.

---

[1] Graham Oppy, *Ontological Arguments and Belief in God* (Cambridge: Cambridge University Press, 1995), p. 1.

[2] G. W. F. Leibniz, *New Essays Concerning the Human Understanding,* trans. A. G. Langley, 3rd ed. (LaSalle, Ill.: Open Court, 1949), pp. iv, 10.

For those who are unfamiliar with the semantics of possible worlds, we should explain that by "a possible world" one does not mean a planet or even a universe but rather a maximal description of reality or a way reality might be. Perhaps the best way to think of a possible world is as a huge conjunction $p \& q \& r \& s \ldots$ ("&" means "and"), whose individual conjuncts are the propositions $p, q, r, s \ldots$. A possible world is a conjunction which comprises every proposition or its contradictory, so that it yields a maximal description of reality—nothing is left out of such a description. By negating different conjuncts in a maximal description ("−" means "it is not the case that"), we arrive at different possible worlds:

W1: $p \& q \& r \& s \ldots$
W2: $p \& -q \& r \& -s \ldots$
W3: $-p \& -q \& r \& s \ldots$
W4: $p \& q \& -r \& s \ldots$

Only one of these descriptions will be composed of conjuncts all of which are true and so will be the way reality actually is, that is to say, the actual world.

Since we are talking about possible worlds, the various conjuncts which a possible world comprises must be capable of being true both individually and together. For example, the proposition *The prime minister is a prime number* is not even possibly true, for numbers are abstract objects which could not conceivably be identical with a concrete object like the prime minister. Therefore, no possible world will have that proposition as one of its conjuncts. Such a proposition is necessarily false, that is to say, it is false in every possible world. By contrast, the proposition *George McGovern is the president of the United States* is false in the actual world but could be true and so is a component of some possible worlds. To say that George McGovern is the president of the United States in some possible world is to say that there is a maximal description of reality having the relevant proposition as one of its conjuncts. Similarly, to say that God exists in some possible world is to say that the proposition *God exists* is comprised by some maximal description of reality. Leibniz's insight into the ontological argument was that the argument assumes that the proposition "God exists" (or "A greatest conceivable being exists" or "A perfect being exists") is possibly true, that is to say, God exists in some possible world. For if the concept of God is incoherent or impossible, then the word *God* cannot possibly refer to anything, anymore than the words *square circle* could refer to something. The expression *greatest conceivable being* would in that case just be an incoherent combination of words.

Now in his version of the argument, Plantinga conceives of God as a being which is "maximally excellent" in every possible world. Plantinga takes maximal excellence to entail such excellent-making properties as omniscience, omnipotence and moral perfection. A being which has maximal excellence in every possible world would have what Plantinga calls "maximal greatness." Now the property of maximal greatness, Plantinga avers, is possibly exemplified, that is to say, there is a possible world in which a maximally great being exists. But then this being must exist in a maximally excellent way in every possible world, including the actual world. Therefore God exists.

Although Plantinga thinks that the ontological argument is sound and non-question-begging, still he did not initially regard it as "a successful piece of natural theology" because the key premise, "Possibly, maximal greatness is exemplified," can be rationally denied.[3] Plantinga later confessed that he had set the bar for "success" in natural theology unreasonably high. He muses,

> I employed a traditional but wholly improper standard: I took it that these arguments are successful only if they start from propositions that compel assent from every honest and intelligent person and proceed majestically to their conclusion by way of forms of argument that can be rejected only on pain of insincerity or irrationality. Naturally enough, I joined the contemporary chorus in holding that none of the traditional arguments was successful. (I failed to note that no philosophical arguments of any consequence meet that standard; hence the fact that theistic arguments do not is of less significance than I thought.)[4]

---

[3]Alvin Plantinga, *The Nature of Necessity,* Clarendon Library of Logic and Philosophy (Oxford: Clarendon Press, 1974), p. 219.
[4]Alvin Plantinga, *Warranted Christian Belief* (Oxford: Oxford University Press, 2001), p. 69.

In fact, Plantinga believes that "the ontological argument provides as good grounds for the existence of God as does any serious philosophical argument for any important philosophical conclusion."[5] George Mavrodes rightly remarks, "But if natural theology can be *that* good, as good as the best arguments anywhere in serious philosophy, . . . why should we not put forward these powerful arguments as *proofs* of God?"[6]

We can formulate Plantinga's version of the ontological argument as follows:

1. It is possible that a maximally great being exists.
2. If it is possible that a maximally great being exists, then a maximally great being exists in some possible world.
3. If a maximally great being exists in some possible world, then it exists in every possible world.
4. If a maximally great being exists in every possible world, then it exists in the actual world.
5. If a maximally great being exists in the actual world, then a maximally great being exists.

The principal issue to be settled with respect to Plantinga's ontological argument is what warrant exists for thinking the key premise "It is possible that a maximally great being exists" to be true. In dealing with this issue, it is crucial that we keep clear on the difference between metaphysical and merely epistemic possibility. One is tempted to say, "It's possible that God exists, and it's possible that he doesn't exist!" But this assertion is true only with respect to epistemic possibility: for all we know, God may exist or he may not exist. But if God is conceived as a maximally great being, then his existence is either necessary or impossible, regardless of our epistemic uncertainty. To illustrate: some extraordinarily difficult mathematical equation may be beyond our ability to

---

[5]Alvin Plantinga, "Reason and Belief in God," typescript dated in October 1981, pp. 18-19. This paragraph was inadvertently omitted in the published version of the essay, with the result that Mavrodes's reference to it has no referent. Fortunately, a nearly identical paragraph appears in Alvin Plantinga, "Self-Profile," in *Alvin Plantinga,* ed. James E. Tomberlin and Peter Van Inwagen, Profiles 5 (Dordrecht: D. Reidel, 1985), p. 71.

[6]George Mavrodes, "Jerusalem and Athens Revisited," in *Faith and Rationality,* ed. Alvin Plantinga and Nicholas Wolterstorff (Notre Dame, Ind.: University of Notre Dame Press, 1983), pp. 205-6.

grasp, and so we say that it is possible that the equation is true and it is possible that it is false. But we thereby merely confess our epistemic uncertainty concerning the equation's truth value. As a piece of mathematics, the equation itself is either necessarily true or necessarily false. In the same way, the epistemic entertainability of the ontological argument's key premise (or its denial) does not guarantee its metaphysical possibility.

That being said, however, it remains the case that the concept of a maximally great being is intuitively a coherent notion and, hence, it might be argued, possibly instantiated. In order for the ontological argument to fail, the concept of a maximally great being must be incoherent, like the concept of a married bachelor. The concept of a married bachelor is not a strictly self-contradictory concept (as is the concept of a married unmarried man), and yet it is obvious, once one understands the meaning of the words *married* and *bachelor,* that nothing corresponding to that concept can exist. By contrast, the concept of a maximally great being does not seem even remotely incoherent. This provides some prima facie warrant for thinking that it is possible that a maximally great being exists.

But will this appeal to intuition not lead to a sort of ontological overkill? One of the most important strategies employed by detractors of the ontological argument ever since Anslem's fellow monk Gaunilo wrote a response "On Behalf of the Fool" (who, it will be remembered, says that there is no God) has been the construction of parodies of the argument designed to defeat the prima facie warrant which the argument's main premise is said to enjoy. By showing that analogous notions like that of "a most perfect island" or "a necessarily existent lion" also seem prima facie to be coherent concepts, critics have tried to show that one is forced by the logic of the argument to postulate the existence of all sorts of ridiculous beings.

But the argument's defender may plausibly argue that the idea of God differs from supposedly parallel notions traditionally put forward by the argument's detractors. For one thing, the properties that go to make up maximal excellence as Plantinga defines it have intrinsic maximum values, whereas the excellent-making properties of things like islands do not. For example, omniscience is the property of knowing only and all truths. It is impossible to know any more truths than that. By contrast, in the case of islands, there could always be more palm trees or native dancing girls! Thus there cannot be a most perfect or greatest conceivable island. Moreover, it is far from clear that there even are objective excellent-making properties of things like islands, for the excellence of islands seems to be relative to one's interests—does one prefer a desert island or an island boasting the finest resort hotels?

The idea of something like a necessarily existent lion also seems incoherent. For as a necessary being, such a beast would have to exist in every possible world we can conceive. But any animal which could exist in a possible world in which the universe is composed wholly of a singularity of infinite space-time curvature, density and temperature just is not a lion. By contrast, a maximally excellent being, if it is immaterial, could transcend such physical limitations and so be conceived as necessarily existent.

Perhaps the greatest challenge to the appeal to intuition to warrant the premise that maximal greatness is possibly exemplified is that it seems intuitively coherent in the same way to conceive of a quasi-maximally great being—for example, one which is in every other respect maximally excellent save that it does not know truths about future contingents (for example, the truth about what you will be doing ten years from now). Why is the key premise of the ontological argument more plausibly true than a parallel premise "It is possible that a quasi-maximally great being exists"? If we are warranted in thinking that a maximally great being exists, are we not equally warranted in thinking that a quasi-maximally great being exists?

Perhaps not; for maximal greatness is logically incompatible with quasi-maximal greatness. Since a maximally great being is by definition omnipotent, no concrete object can exist independently of its creative power. As an omnipotent being, a maximally great being must have the power to freely refrain from creating anything at all, so that there must be possible worlds in which nothing other than the maximally great being exists. But that entails that if maximal greatness is possibly exemplified, then quasi-maximal greatness is not. A quasi-excellent being may exist in many worlds (worlds in which the maximally great being has chosen to create it), but such a being would lack necessary existence and thus not be quasi-maximally great. Hence, if maximal greatness is possibly exemplified, quasi-maximal greatness is impossible. Thus our intuition that a maximally great being is possible is not undermined by the claim that a quasi-maximally great being is also intuitively possible, for we see that the latter intuition depends on the assumption that a maximally great being cannot possibly exist, which begs the question.

Still, modal skeptics will insist that we have no way of knowing *a priori* whether maximal greatness or quasi-maximal greatness is possibly exemplified. It cannot be both, but we have no idea if either is possible. Our intuitions about modality are unreliable guides. In the face of such skepticism, can anything more be said in defense of the ontological argument's key premise? Plantinga provides a clue when he says that if we "carefully ponder" the key premise and the alleged objections to it, if we "consider its connections with other propositions we accept or reject" and we still find it compelling, then we are within our rational rights in accepting it.[7] Such a procedure is a far cry from the sort of *a priori* speculations decried by the modal skeptic. Even if we cannot determine *a priori* whether maximal greatness is possibly exemplified, we may come to believe on the basis of a posteriori considerations that it is possible that a maximally great being exists.

For example, other theistic arguments like Leibniz's cosmological argument, certain versions of the moral argument and the so-called conceptualist argument may lead us to think that it is plausible that a maximally great being exists. A simple statement of a Leibnizian cosmological argument might run as follows:[8]

1. Every existing thing has an explanation of its existence, either in the necessity of its own nature or in an external cause.
2. If the universe has an explanation of its existence, that explanation is God.
3. The universe is an existing thing.
4. Therefore the explanation of the existence of the universe is God.

---

[7]Plantinga, *The Nature of Necessity*, p. 221.
[8]Cf. Stephen Davis, "The Cosmological Argument and the Epistemic Status of Belief in God," *Philosophia Christi* n.s. 1 (1999): 5-15.

Many philosophers have objected to Leibniz's own formulation of the argument because his Principle of Sufficient Reason that "no fact can be real or existent, no statement true, unless there be a sufficient reason why it is so and not otherwise"[9] seems too strong to be plausible. Some theists such as Richard Swinburne have responded to this objection by agreeing that one must ultimately come to some explanatory stopping point which is simply a brute contingent, which they identify as God. But the above formulation of the Leibnizian argument avoids the objection without retreating to the dubious position that God is a contingent being. For premise 1 merely requires any existing thing to have an explanation of its existence, either in the necessity of its own nature or in some external cause. This premise is compatible with there being brute facts or states of affairs about the world. What it precludes is that there could exist things—substances exemplifying properties—which just exist inexplicably. This principle seems quite plausible, at least more so than its contradictory, which is all that is required for a successful argument. On this analysis, there are two kinds of beings: necessary beings, which exist of their own nature and so have no external cause of their existence, and contingent beings, whose existence is accounted for by causal factors outside themselves. Numbers might be prime candidates for the first sort of being, while familiar physical objects fall under the second kind of being.

Premise 2 is, in effect, the contrapositive of the typical atheist response to Leibniz that on the atheistic worldview the universe simply exists as a brute contingent thing. Atheists typically assert that, there being no God, it is false that everything has an explanation of its existence, for the universe, in this case, just exists inexplicably. In so saying, the atheist implicitly recognizes that if the universe has an explanation, then God exists as its explanatory ground. This premise also seems quite plausible in its own right, for since the universe, by definition, includes all of physical reality, its explanation must be found in some external, transcendent cause which exists beyond space and time. The only things we know of that could possess such a mode of existence are either abstract objects

---

[9]G. W. F. Leibniz, "The Monadology," in *Leibniz Selections,* p. 539.

or a mind. But abstract objects do not stand in causal relations. So the cause of the universe must be found in a transcendent mind. This is what we normally mean by *God*.

Finally, premise 3 states the obvious, that there is a universe.[10] Since the universe is obviously an existing thing (especially evident in its very early stages when its density was so extreme) possessing many unique properties such as a certain density, pressure, temperature, space-time curvature, and so on, it follows that God exists and does so by a necessity of his own nature, that is to say, God is a metaphysically necessary being.

A plausible version of the moral argument may be formulated as follows:

1. If God does not exist, objective moral values and duties do not exist.

2. Objective moral values and duties do exist.

3. Therefore God exists.

Consider premise 1. If God does not exist, then what is the foundation for moral values? More particularly, what is the basis for the value of human beings? If God does not exist, then it is difficult to see any reason to think that human beings are special or that their morality is objectively valid. Moreover, why think that we have any moral obligations to do anything? Who or what imposes moral duties upon us? As a result of socio-biological pressures, there has evolved among *homo sapiens* a sort of herd morality which functions well in the perpetuation of our species in the struggle for survival. But if there is no God, then any ground for regarding the herd morality evolved by *homo sapiens* as objectively true seems to have been removed. Human beings are just accidental byproducts of nature which have evolved relatively recently on an infinitesimal speck of dust lost somewhere in a hostile and mindless universe and which are doomed to perish individually and collectively in a relatively short time. Some action, say, rape, may not be socially advantageous and so in the course of human evolution has become taboo; but on the athe-

---

[10]I do not mean to pronounce here on ontological debates as to what constitutes an object but merely to claim that the universe is just as much a thing as are other familiar entities which we recognize to have causes, such as chairs, mountains, planets and stars.

istic view it is difficult to see why there is really anything wrong about raping someone. Crudely put, on the atheistic view human beings are just animals, relatively advanced primates; and animals are not moral agents.

Few philosophers have the stomach for the moral nihilism which atheism seems to imply. Many therefore try to salvage the existence of objective moral principles or properties in the context of a naturalistic worldview. But the advocates of such theories are typically at a loss to justify their starting point. If their approach to metaethical theory is to be serious metaphysics rather than just a shopping list approach, whereby one simply helps oneself to the moral properties or principles needed to do the job, then some sort of explanation is required for why moral properties supervene on certain natural states or why such principles are true. It is insufficient for the naturalist to point out that we do, in fact, apprehend the goodness of some feature of human existence, for that only goes to establish the objectivity of moral values and duties, which the proponent of the moral argument is eager to affirm.

Much more deserves to be said about this,[11] but if we do think that objective moral values exist, as premise 2 states, then we shall be led logically to the conclusion that God exists. And surely we do apprehend a realm of objective moral values. There is no more reason to deny the objective reality of moral values than the objective reality of the physical world. If moral values are gradually discovered rather than invented, then our gradual and fallible apprehension of the moral realm no more undermines the objective reality of that realm than our gradual, fallible perception of the physical world undermines the objectivity of that realm. The best way to make sense of our moral obligations is in terms of agreement or disagreement of certain acts with the will or commands of an essentially holy and loving God.

Now the interesting thing about moral principles is that at least some of them seem to be necessary truths. As one naturalist philosopher confesses, "The man who says that it is morally acceptable to rape little children is just as mistaken as the man who says, 2+2=5."[12] Hence, if God's

---

[11]See the chapter in this volume by Paul Copan on the moral argument for God's existence.

nature and will ground such necessary moral principles, it follows that God exists not just in the actual world but in every possible world, that is to say, his existence is necessary.

Moreover, we may find ourselves persuaded by a conceptualist argument for God's existence that the best metaphysical grounding for the existence of abstract objects is an infinite mind whose concepts they are. Such an argument might be formulated as follows:

1. Abstract objects, such as numbers and propositions, are either independently existing realities or else concepts in some mind.
2. Abstract objects are not independently existing realities.
3. If abstract objects are concepts in some mind, then an omniscient, metaphysically necessary being exists.
4. Therefore an omniscient, metaphysically necessary being exists.

A defense of premise 1 will involve a refutation of nominalism, the view that abstract objects do not exist at all. Premise 2 rejects Platonism with respect to abstract objects, most plausibly on the grounds of their causal isolation and hence irrelevance to what exists or transpires in the world. Premise 3 excludes the grounding of abstract objects in some human mind, for there are too many such objects to be grounded in anything less than an infinite intelligence, and since many of these objects exist necessarily, they cannot in any case be grounded in the mind of a merely contingent being. Thus one is brought to the existence of an omniscient, necessary mind as the foundation of the existence of abstract objects.

Thus the cosmological argument leads to a metaphysically necessary being which is the ground of existence for any concrete reality, the moral argument to a locus of moral value which must be as metaphysically necessary as the moral values it grounds, and the conceptualist argument to an omniscient, metaphysically necessary intelligence as the foundation of abstract objects.

Considerations of simplicity might also come into play here. For example, it is simpler to posit one metaphysically necessary, infinite, omniscient, morally perfect being than to think that three separate neces-

---

[12]Michael Ruse, *Darwinism Defended* (London: Addison-Wesley, 1982), p. 275.

sary beings exist exemplifying these respective excellent-making properties. Similarly, with respect to quasi-maximally great beings, Swinburne's contention seems plausible that it is simpler (or perhaps less ad
hoc) to posit either zero or infinity as the measure of a degreed property
than to posit some inexplicably finite measure. Thus it would be more
plausible to think that maximal greatness is possibly instantiated than
quasi-maximal greatness. On the basis of considerations like these, we
might well consider ourselves to be warranted in believing that it is possible that a maximally great being exists.

The question which arises at this point is whether the ontological argument has not then become question begging. An argument is question
begging if one's only reason for accepting a premise in the argument is
that one already accepts the conclusion, so that one in effect reasons in
a circle. In the present case it might seem that the reason one thinks that
it is possible that a maximally great being exists is that one has good reasons to think that a maximally great being does exist.

But this misgiving may arise as a result of thinking of the project of
natural theology in too linear a fashion. The theistic arguments need not
be taken to be like links in a chain, in which one link follows another
so that the chain is only as strong as its weakest link. Rather they are like
links in a coat of chain mail, in which all the links reinforce one another
so that the strength of the whole exceeds that of any single link. The ontological argument might play its part in a cumulative case for theism, in
which a multitude of factors simultaneously conspire to lead one to the
global conclusion that God exists. In that sense Anselm was wrong in
thinking that he had discovered a single argument which, standing independently of all the rest, served to demonstrate God's existence in all his
greatness. Nevertheless, his argument does encapsulate the thrust of all
the arguments together to show that God, the Supreme Being, exists.

FOR FURTHER READING

Davis, Stephen. "The Ontological Argument." In *The Rationality of Theism*. Edited by Paul Copan and Paul K. Moser. London: Routledge, 2003.
Geisler, Norman L. "The Missing Premise in the Ontological Argument." *Religious Studies* 9, no. 3 (September 1973).

Hick, John H., and Arthur C. McGill. *The Many-faced Argument*. New York: Macmillan, 1967.

Oppy, Graham. *Ontological Arguments and Belief in God*. Cambridge: Cambridge University Press, 1995.

Plantinga, Alvin. *The Nature of Necessity*. Oxford: Clarendon Press, 1974.

Plantinga, Alvin, ed. *The Ontological Argument*. Garden City, N.Y.: Doubleday, 1965.

PART 3

CHRIST AND MIRACLES

William Lane Craig

IN 1985 A PROMINENT NEW TESTAMENT SCHOLAR NAMED ROBERT FUNK founded a think tank in Southern California which he called the Jesus Seminar. The ostensible purpose of the seminar was to uncover the historical person Jesus of Nazareth using the best methods of scientific, biblical criticism. In Funk's view the historical Jesus has been so overlaid by Christian legend, myth and metaphysics that he scarcely resembles the Christ figure presented in the Gospels and worshiped by the church today. The goal of the seminar was to strip away these layers and to recover the Jesus who really lived and taught.

The historical Jesus uncovered by the seminar turns out to have been a sort of itinerant social critic, the Jewish equivalent of a Greek Cynic philosopher. He never claimed to be the Son of God or to forgive sins or to inaugurate a new covenant between God and man. His crucifixion was an accident of history; his corpse was probably thrown into a shallow dirt grave where it rotted away or was eaten by wild dogs.

Now if these conclusions are correct, we who are Christians today are the victims of a massive delusion. To continue to worship Jesus today in light of these conclusions would be either idolatry or mythology—idolatry if we worship the merely human figure who actually lived, mythology if we worship the figment of the church's imagination. None of us, I hazard to think, wants to be either an idolater or a mythologizer. Therefore it is of utmost importance to assess whether the claims of the radical critics are true.

Crucial to any examination of the historical Jesus will be the question of presuppositions. Skeptical critics, like those in the Jesus Seminar, have certain presuppositions which determine how they look at the evidence. Fortunately, scholars in the Jesus Seminar have been commendably forthright in stating some of their presuppositions. The introduction to the seminar publication *The Five Gospels* states:

> The contemporary religious controversy turns on whether the worldview reflected in the Bible can be carried forward into this scientific age and retained as an article of faith. . . . the Christ of creed and dogma . . . can no longer command the assent of those who have seen the heavens through Galileo's telescope.[1]

This is an expression of scientific naturalism, which holds that every event in the world has a natural cause. There are no events with supernatural causes. In other words, miracles cannot happen.

Now this presupposition constitutes an absolute watershed for the study of the historical Jesus. If we presuppose naturalism, then events like the incarnation, the virgin birth, Jesus' miracles and his resurrection go out the window before we even sit down at the table to look at the evidence. As supernatural events, they *cannot* be historical. Even a relatively moderate critic like John Meier, who claims to eschew naturalism, has not entirely succeeded in escaping its thrall, for he declines even to discuss the historicity of Jesus' alleged resurrection "because the restrictive definition of the historical Jesus I will be using does not allow us to proceed into matters that can be affirmed only by faith."[2]

---

[1]R. W. Funk, R. W. Hoover and the Jesus Seminar, introduction to *The Five Gospels* (New York: Macmillan, 1993), p. 2.

[2]John P. Meier, *A Marginal Jew*, vol. 1, *The Roots of the Problem and the Person* (New York: Doubleday, 1991), p. 13. On his definition of "the historical Jesus" see note 5 below. What clause in that definition precludes the resurrection as a feature of the historical Jesus? Meier denies that the resurrection "is in principle open to the observation of any and every observer" (John P. Meier, *A Marginal Jew*, vol. 2, *Mentor, Message and Miracle* [New York: Doubleday, 1994], p. 525). That would exclude its belonging to the historical Jesus as well as, perversely, its qualifying as a miracle under Meier's definition of the latter. But why think that the resurrection is not observable in this way? Meier endorses O'Collins's view that "although the 'resurrection is a real, bodily event involving the person of Jesus of Nazareth,' the resurrection of Jesus 'is not an event *in* space and time and hence should not be called historical,' since 'we should require an historical occurrence to be something significant that is known to have hap-

But why, we might ask, must we in a scientific age presuppose a purely naturalistic Jesus? After all, a good many scientists are Christian believers, and contemporary physics shows itself quite open to the possibility of realities which lie outside the domain of physics. What justification is there for a purely naturalistic approach to Jesus of Nazareth?

Here things become very interesting from a philosophical point of view. According to the Jesus Seminar, the historical Jesus by definition must be a nonsupernatural figure. By way of justification they appeal to D. F. Strauss, the nineteenth-century German biblical critic, whose *The Life of Jesus, Critically Examined,* was based squarely in a philosophy of naturalism. According to Strauss, God does not act directly in the world; he acts only indirectly through natural causes. With regard to the resurrection, Strauss states that God's raising Jesus from the dead "is irreconcilable with enlightened ideas of the relation of God to the world."[3]

Now consider carefully what the Jesus Seminar says about Strauss: "Strauss distinguished what he called the 'mythical' (defined by him as anything legendary or supernatural) in the Gospels from the historical. . . . The choice Strauss posed in his assessment of the Gospels was between the supernatural Jesus—the Christ of faith—and the historical Jesus."[4]

Anything that is supernatural is by definition not historical. No argument is given for that conclusion; it is simply a matter of definition. As a result we have a radical divorce between the Christ of faith, or the su-

---

pened in our space-time continuum'" (Meier, *Marginal Jew,* 1:201; cf. G. G. O'Collins, "Is the Resurrection an 'Historical' Event?" *Heythrop Journal* 8 [1967]: 381-87). But O'Collins thinks that the resurrection, which he defines as Jesus' passing "out of the empirical sphere of this world to a new mode of existence," did not occur in the space-time continuum only in a very Pickwickian sense: the same sense in which it can be said that someone's exiting a building does not occur in the building. But if the resurrection was a real, bodily event that happened to Jesus, then that event must be temporally located sometime around A.D. 30, and moreover, spatially located as well, in Palestine near Jerusalem (rather than, say, in Wilmette, north of Chicago). More fundamentally, how can Meier know the nature of Jesus' resurrection so as to say that it did not happen in our space-time continuum apart from a historical investigation? He must be presupposing some prior theological knowledge of the event. But this a priori theorizing contradicts Meier's historical methodology, which positions itself as theologically neutral.

[3]David Friedrich Strauss, *The Life of Jesus, Critically Examined,* ed. with an introduction by Peter C. Hodgson, trans. George Eliot, Lives of Jesus Series (London: SCM Press, 1973), p. 736.
[4]Funk et al., "Introduction," p. 3.

pernatural Jesus, and the real, historical Jesus. The Jesus Seminar gives a ringing endorsement of Strauss's bifurcation: they say that the distinction between the historical Jesus and the Christ of faith is "the first pillar of scholarly wisdom."[5]

But now the whole quest of the historical Jesus becomes a charade. If we begin by presupposing naturalism, then of course what we wind up with is a purely natural Jesus. This reconstructed, naturalistic Jesus is not based on evidence but on mere definition. What is remarkable is that the Jesus Seminar makes no attempt at all to defend this naturalism; it is just presupposed.

Those who have read Strauss know that he appealed to the arguments of the Scottish skeptic David Hume to justify his rejection of miracles. But those who are familiar with contemporary philosophy also know that Hume's arguments are today widely rejected as fallacious.[6]

If we are at least open to supernaturalism, then miraculous events cannot be ruled out in advance. We have to be open to looking honestly at the evidence that they occurred.[7] In fact, if we do not presuppose natu-

---

[5]Ibid., pp. 2-3. Meier struggles to avoid collapsing Jesus to a purely naturalistic figure by drawing a further distinction between "the real Jesus" (roughly, the man who actually lived) and "the historical Jesus" (a construct of historians employing the scientific tools of modern historical research). Meier seems to agree with the Jesus Seminar that "in the historical-critical context, the 'real' has been defined—and has to be defined—in terms of what exists within this world of time and space, what can be experienced in principle by any observer, and what can be reasonably deduced and inferred from such experience" (Meier, *Marginal Jew,* 1:197). Meier apparently takes this definition to exclude the affirmation that the historical Jesus performed miracles and rose from the dead. It seems, then, that the historical Jesus is an abstraction constructed on the presupposition of methodological naturalism, but this abstraction may be quite different from the person who actually lived.

[6]For a recent devastating critique by a prominent philosopher of science who is an agnostic, see John Earman, *Hume's Abject Failure* (Oxford: Oxford University Press, 2000). See further George Campbell, *Dissertation on Miracles* (1762; repr. ed.: London: T. Tegg & Son, 1834); William Paley, *A View of the Evidences of Christianity,* 2 vols., 5th ed. (London: R. Faulder, 1796; repr. ed.: Westmead, England: Gregg, 1970); Richard Swinburne, *The Concept of Miracle* (New York: Macmillan, 1970); John Earman, "Bayes, Hume and Miracles," *Faith and Philosophy* 10 (1993): 293-310; George Mavrodes, "Miracles and the Laws of Nature," *Faith and Philosophy* 2 (1985): 333-46; William Alston, "God's Action in the World," in *Divine Nature and Human Language* (Ithaca, N.Y.: Cornell University Press, 1989), pp. 197-222.

[7]Despite his refusal to examine historically the resurrection of Jesus, Meier does not decline to investigate the historicity of the events comprised by the Gospel miracles, even affirming after detailed study that some of those events do belong to the historical Jesus; he merely prescinds from the verdict that such events were genuine miracles, that is, that they are inexplicable by means of human abilities or natural causes but were the result of special acts of God (Meier,

ralism, then the Gospels come out looking pretty good as historical sources for the life of Jesus. R. T. France, a British New Testament scholar, has written,

> At the level of their literary and historical character we have good reason to treat the Gospels seriously as a source of information on the life and teaching of Jesus. . . . Indeed many ancient historians would count themselves fortunate to have four such responsible accounts [as the Gospels], written within a generation or two of the events, and preserved in such a wealth of early manuscript evidence. Beyond that point, the decision to accept the record they offer is likely to be influenced more by openness to a supernaturalist worldview than by strictly historical considerations.[8]

In other words, skepticism about the Gospels is not based so much on historical considerations as on the presupposition of naturalism.

In this section of the book we shall examine the feasibility of investigating the historical Jesus without the prejudicial assumption of naturalism, as well as the self-understanding of the historical Jesus and finally the credibility of his resurrection as an event of history.

A Marginal Jew, 2:512). But then the historical researcher wants to know why a similar investigation of Jesus' alleged resurrection is off-limits to the historian. Historians of the American Civil War trace the fascinating misadventures of Lincoln's corpse following his assassination. Are contemporary Jesus scholars employing the scientific tools of modern historical research unable to probe the question of how Jesus' corpse was disposed of following his crucifixion? Are they incapable of assessing the historical credibility of the traditions that women visited the tomb of Jesus and found it empty? Can they not inquire whether the early disciples did or did not experience a series of apparitions of Jesus and whether the Jesus movement was not founded on the belief of these first disciples that Jesus had risen from the dead? All of these questions and more seem perfectly open to the contemporary historian, even given methodological naturalism, and there seems no good reason for abruptly terminating one's study of the historical Jesus with his crucifixion. O'Collins, whom Meier cites to prove that the resurrection was not an event *in* space-time, insists that all these events "can be the object of investigation by the historian" (O'Collins, "Resurrection," p. 386). Even if one agrees with Meier that the historian, *qua* historian, cannot utter the verdict, "God raised Jesus from the dead" or even "Jesus rose from the dead," there still remains a great deal that the historian can say concerning the events of the resurrection narratives.

[8]R. T. France, "The Gospels as Historical Sources for Jesus, the Founder of Christianity," *Truth* 1 (1985): 86.

9

THE CHRISTOLOGY
OF JESUS REVISITED

Ben Witherington III

WHEN *THE CHRISTOLOGY OF JESUS* WAS WRITTEN NOW ALMOST FIFTEEN YEARS ago,[1] the reaction of scholars was predictably mixed. There was some awkward silence, there was some enthusiastic acceptance, and there was some rather vehement rejection.[2] I remember well the wry smile of one member of the SNTS (Studiorum Novi Testamenti Societas) Historical Jesus section when I suggested the christology of Jesus as a topic for discussion. It was assumed that Rudolf Bultmann had long ago pronounced the benediction on this topic when he said that we could know next to nothing with any certainty about the historical Jesus other than that he was crucified under Pontius Pilate. As things have turned out, quite a lot of New Testament scholars, including a wide variety of contributors to the Third Quest for the Historical Jesus, have chosen to disagree with Bultmann not only in general about the historical Jesus but on the specific question of Jesus' self-understanding. To choose but one example, John P. Meier has argued, as I did, that there is much to be learned about Jesus' self-understanding by examining him in his relationships with various other significant figures such as John the Baptist, the Pharisees and the first disciples.[3]

---

[1]Ben Witherington III, *The Christology of Jesus* (Minneapolis: Fortress, 1990).
[2]This chapter appeared in a somewhat different form in a festschrift for Jack Kingsbury.
[3]See John P. Meier, *A Marginal Jew: Rethinking the Historical Jesus*, vol. 2, *Mentor, Message and Miracle* (New York: Doubleday, 1994).

One of the questions I have pondered a good deal of late is whether we really have framed the questions about Jesus' relationships properly. Have we not simply assumed that ancient persons related to one another much as we do today? Have we not presumed that ancient persons and personality were not essentially different from ourselves and our personas, and thus that we can evaluate Jesus as if he were a candidate for modern or postmodern western psychological evaluation?[4] The problem of anachronism has all too often been insufficiently conjured with, even though we know that nurture as well as nature, culture as well as genetics affect the sort of person one turns out to be. It is in this area of the social and cultural conditioning of human personality that I think the exploration of Jesus' self-understanding has been lacking. I propose then in this study to do two things: to try to more closely focus the discussion of Jesus in his social context and relationships and to try and make some introductory suggestions about how this sort of social data and approach might illuminate the discussion of the so-called christological titles found in the Synoptic Gospels.

TO KNOW AS ONE IS KNOWN

One of the areas in which distinct progress has been made in Gospel studies since *The Christology of Jesus* was written is in genre studies. The crucial work of R. A. Burridge has provided a strong case that at least three of the four Gospels fall into the category of ancient Greco-Roman biographies.[5] One of the most striking features of these sorts of ancient biographical works, whether one thinks of Plutarch's *Lives* or Josephus's *Life of Apion* or Tacitus's *Agricola* or Mark's Gospel, is that instead of presenting womb-to-tomb analyses of the development of a particular human personality, the authors regularly assume that a per-

---

[4]This seems, surprisingly enough, to be the assumption behind the recent effort by John W. Miller, *Jesus at Thirty: A Psychological and Historical Portrait* (Minneapolis: Fortress, 1997). There are some helpful insights in the work, in spite of trying to explain Jesus on the basis of a midlife crisis.

[5]See R. A. Burridge, *What Are the Gospels? A Comparison with Greco-Roman Biography* (Cambridge: Cambridge University Press, 1992). The case for Luke as biography is not convincing, not least because of the preface and opening chapter to that Gospel which are crucial in defining its literary kind. See the introduction to Ben Witherington III, *The Acts of the Apostles: A Socio-Rhetorical Commentary* (Grand Rapids, Mich.: Eerdmans, 1997).

son's character does not develop over time. To the contrary, time is thought to simply reveal the character a person has always had. Human personality was viewed as static, and therefore a change in one's personality, a conversion or chameleon-like behavior would be viewed with extreme skepticism by most. Knowing what we now know on this front, it becomes very difficult to psychoanalyze Jesus on the basis of texts that by and large don't believe in developmental theories of personality and do not present us with anything like adequate data about things such as Jesus' "early childhood influences."[6] What we can say about the historical Jesus must stand or fall on the data of what is revealed in the Gospels about the adult Jesus during the last three or so years of his life. It is not the stuff of modern biographical portraits, for it provides us few opportunities to speculate about how he grew or changed over time.

The study of ancient Mediterranean persons and personalities reveals that it was assumed that normal persons were not what we'd call unique individuals but rather mirrors of the virtues and vices, the strengths and flaws of some particular ancient group. What we might call stereotypes, ancients would see as character types or traits that explain both individuals and the groups of which they are a part. The remarks we find at Titus 1:12, "Cretans are always liars, vicious brutes, lazy gluttons" (a quotation from a famous Cretan no less), and at John 1:46 are frankly typical of this sort of ancient literature. Human identity was established by the group and was confirmed to the individual by members of the group. Life was not by and large about establishing one's unique place in the world, discovering one's distinctive character or making personal claims for oneself.

In antiquity it was widely assumed that gender, generation and geog-

---

[6]On this latter front we would be able to deduce next to nothing from Mark or John, and even in Matthew's and Luke's birth narratives there is very little to work with. Lk 2:41-52, especially Luke 2:52, is a very slender foundation on which to build and it sends a mixed signal. On the one hand Jesus sees it as his duty to be doing what he was doing in the temple even after his parents have left. On the other hand he obeys his parents and comes home with them. On the one hand it is said he grew in wisdom and stature, after noting his obedience to parents. On the other hand he responds to the "your father and I" remarks with a distinguishing reference to "my Father." In short, this is not a typical picture of a dutiful son enmeshed in the social and patriarchal webs of his culture.

raphy for the most part determined one's identity,[7] and with good reason. Corporate or group identity rather than individual identity was primary. A person who sought to stand out from his ethnic, familial, geographical or gender group was seen as a deviant, not as a person simply being himself. In this sort of environment, even a remarkable and somewhat distinctive person like Jesus would seek to identify himself by indicating the relationships that were formative for him and would seek to have his identity confirmed to him by his most intimate dialogue partners since it was normal that someone other than oneself had a crucial say in who one was and could be (cf., e.g., Mk 1:11; 8:27-30).

As it turns out there is nothing very surprising about a first-century person choosing only to speak indirectly or eliptically about himself, if at all. This is what one would expect in a culture where corporate identity was not merely prominent but dominant. If Mark's messianic secret and silencing motif does to some degree go back to the historical Jesus' situation, it would not suggest that Jesus had doubts about his identity or was seeking to veil it or was being coy. It would merely indicate that Jesus was an ancient person who played out his life in a setting where whose child one was was far more important than who one was (in one's inner self or uniqueness).

Something must be said at this juncture about Jesus as a change agent in a patriarchal world and then about Jesus' relationships with his family. It has become a commonplace of discussion of Jesus' environment that he lived in a male-dominated and androcentric world. Slim evidence to the contrary, coming from Jewish colonies outside of Israel, does not change the basic picture that has been usually painted of Galilee and Judea.[8] I know of no evidence of women as synagogue leaders or elders or teachers of Torah with disciples in the Holy Land prior to or during the time of Jesus. Still extant traditional Near Eastern or Far Eastern cultures in our world are far closer analogies to what we find in Jesus' en-

---

[7]See now the discussion of this matter in B. J. Malina and J. H. Neyrey, *Portraits of Paul: An Archaeology of Ancient Personality* (Louisville, Ky.: Wesminster, 1996). I owe the summary triad of gender, generation and geography to them.

[8]See Ben Witherington III, *Women and the Genesis of Christianity* (Cambridge: Cambridge University Press, 1990).

vironment than anything in the West today. In this sort of environment it is no surprise that Jesus had twelve male disciples as his inner circle. What is very surprising is that he also apparently had various women disciples, something that would have scandalized many in his setting.

Clearly enough, Jesus was not a person who simply followed the flow of his culture, but equally clearly he was able to relate to others in this male-dominated environment, and in various cases do so successfully. This must tell us something about how Jesus viewed himself and his place in his Jewish world. His social approach to relationships was such that he could relate well to both men and women and could attract both men and women to his circle of disciples. This is in part why I have suggested in my earlier work on women in Jesus' ministry that he must be seen as some sort of reformer within Judaism,[9] creating a community with differing values within that society, not a revolutionary building base camps in Galilean villages in preparation for a revolt against the dominant Roman or client king power structures.[10] He is eschatological and theocratic in orientation in a somewhat similar fashion to the way the Qumran community was and unlike the way the Zealots were.[11]

One must admit that in Jesus' culture his gender is probably a reason why he was able to attract a following of both men and women in his social setting, why he was able to be a public person and build his social network as he did, why he was able to conjure up conjectures by various people about whether he was some sort of a messianic figure or not. Note, however, that his own teaching and way of relating suggests that

---

[9]This same sort of give and take with the dominant Jewish culture can also be seen in Jesus' approach to the Law. Sometimes he affirms it, sometimes he intensifies it, sometimes he offers new teaching, sometimes he suggests by deeds or words that portions of the Law have been fulfilled or have had their day and no longer apply now that the dominion of God is breaking in. It is precisely because Jesus does believe that God is bringing about divine rule by eschatological intervention that he feels no compulsion to lead a revolt.

[10]Compare Ben Witherington III, *Women in the Ministry of Jesus* (Cambridge: Cambridge University Press, 1984) to what is said by E. P. Sanders, *The Historical Figure of Jesus* (London: Penguin, 1993).

[11]Note that if it is the case that Jesus envisioned himself and his Twelve playing a role in the future in the judging of the twelve tribes of Israel, and in the judgment that would come on sin in Israel, this would not distinguish him from the Qumranites, who like Jesus were not taking such action in the present but were prepared to be a part of it as the sons of light later when the final intervention came.

he believed that the inbreaking dominion of God was in the process of changing some of the social stereotypes and constrictions that especially plagued women and other subordinant members of society in this culture. This Jesus still does not fit neatly into modern pigeonholes of chauvinist or feminist.

If his gender may have been something of an asset as he strove to be some sort of leader figure in Israel, Jesus' geographical location and family connections would seem to have been liabilities on the whole. Jesus lived in a culture where people had no last names to distinguish them from others. Rather a patronymic or a geographical tag was used to distinguish one person from another who had the same personal name. From start to finish in the Gospels Jesus is regularly identified as Jesus of Nazareth (e.g., Jn 1:45-46; Mk 16:6). This cannot be accidental. The initial impression for some will have been that this determined his identity, and more specifically it ruled out any likelihood of Jesus being some kind of messianic figure (Jn 1:46). Yet what is striking is that in spite of this geographical tag, Jesus managed to raise eyebrows and messianic questions anyway. This suggests, albeit in an indirect fashion, that Jesus' words, deeds and relationships must have been extraordinarily suggestive to overcome this sort of geographical identity marker. Surely no one was looking for God's eschatological Anointed One to come from a backwater town in Galilee like Nazareth, and yet Jesus' followers enshrined this part of his identity repeatedly in the Gospels. One must ask how Jesus overcame this geographical determinism to still stir up hopes and fears, curses and blessings during his ministry. That Jesus was not simply dismissed by all and sundry suggests he did overcome this initial obstacle, at least in the minds of some.

Perhaps most importantly there is the whole question of Jesus' family. What do we make of the fact that Jesus is rarely identified by a patronymic, indeed is sometimes identified by a matronymic, in a culture where the question, who is your father and/or mother? was always critical to figuring out the identity of someone? True enough, we have texts like John 1:45 or the variant reading in Mark 6:3, but in both cases it would appear that we are meant to think that those speaking are not necessarily in the best position to know the full truth about Jesus' relationship with Mary's husband, Joseph. Indeed, both texts are laden with irony, for in Mark 6 the hometown crowd goes on to reject Jesus on the basis of what they think they know about his true identity, and in John 1 we have just begun a Gospel-long trek through various attempts to properly name Jesus, a trek that does not come to a fully satisfactory conclusion until finally a confession of Thomas in John 20 matches up with that of the prologue in John 1.[12]

Furthermore, the most likely reading in Mark 6:3 is "the carpenter, the son of Mary," and there is some reason to suspect that this is meant as a disparaging identity statement.[13] In this sort of setting, when a man's parentage was either open to disparaging remarks or open to question, or the issue was left open, it is very hard to see how Jesus could have suggested to anyone that he might be a messianic figure unless there was something dramatically impressive about his words, deeds and relationships that suggested that the identity markers of geography and generation would prove inadequate in his case. The overcoming of traditional identity markers and boundaries is a telltale sign that Jesus did not present himself as just one of the crowd.

If we probe a bit further in regard to Jesus' relationship with his family, note that it is plainly admitted in both the Synoptic and Johannine traditions that there was a certain distance between Jesus and his family during his ministry (Mk 3:21, 31-35; Jn 7:5); indeed they could not really be said to be followers of Jesus at this time. This is frankly a shocking admission in an environment where family, including extended family, was perhaps the chief building block of Jewish society and where, after the death of a father, the eldest son, in this case presumably Jesus, would be expected to take over as head of the kinship group. This was a critical matter in the times in which Jesus lived, precisely because, as Richard Horsley has suggested, there was enormous pressure on such lower- or artisan-class family units in Galilee and elsewhere in Israel because of the way the economy worked in Jesus' day and the pressures brought to bear on the economy by tax farmers, client rulers and others trying to

---

[12]See Ben Witherington III, *John's Wisdom: A Commentary on the Fourth Gospel* (Louisville, Ky.: Westminster, 1995).

[13]See Witherington, *Women in the Ministry of Jesus,* pp. 85-92.

raise funds to satisfy the various demands for taxes.

To make matters worse, the Gospels suggest that Jesus actually be-friended some of the tax and toll collectors in the region, even discipling some. This would surely have been seen as a betrayal by many Jews, perhaps even by members of Jesus' own family.[14] What one must ask is, How did Jesus during his itinerant ministry overcome the negative stigma of being considered a bad Jew, one who was a social deviant, one who associated with the wrong sorts of people, one who did not properly honor his parents and family by living among them and serving them? How, in spite of the fact that the text freely admits that Jesus ap-parently refused to be taken home by his family when he was causing too much controversy (Mk 3:31-35), did Jesus implant positive impres-sions in the minds and hearts of early Jews that suggested to some of them that he was a messianic figure?[15] Again, the more we know about the social matrix out of which Jesus came, the more it looks likely that Jesus must indeed have made some sort of messianic claims, indirectly or directly, to overcome so much and so many ordinary ancient beliefs about what established identity.

It needs to be understood that it was expected to some degree that prophets and kingly figures and sages would deviate somewhat from the norm. For example, John the Baptist would still be seen by many in Israel as a true prophet despite his abnormal lifestyle. I would argue that only a strongly implanted suggestion during Jesus' lifetime that Jesus was more than an ordinary person, that he was at least some sort of prophet or sage or messianic figure, could have likely overcome all these obstacles, including especially the crucifixion, and could have led those who knew Jesus before his death to proclaim him after the

---

[14]See Richard Horsley, *Galilee: History, Politics, People* (Valley Forge, Pa.: Trinity Press Interna-tional, 1995), and Richard Horsley, *Archaeology, History and Society in Galilee* (Valley Forge, Pa.: Trinity Press International, 1996).

[15]There is nothing in the Gospels to suggest that we should think that Jesus' parents were not good and loving parents. A text like Lk 2:41-52 should not be read with modern eyes. This is not about child neglect by Mary and Joseph. It is about the fact that Jesus was part of an ex-tended family, not just a nuclear family, and in that situation it was perfectly understandable why the parents would assume Jesus was with other relatives and town folk pilgrimaging home from Jerusalem. The story also, as a side note, suggests strongly how Torah true Ga-lilean Jews actually were, that they came and went from feasts in Jerusalem in great numbers.

Easter events as the Jewish messiah.[16]

We must ask then, what sort of person in this androcentric culture built on extended families leaves home and family; itinerates with women and men; calls his own followers his family; fraternizes with women, slaves, minors, tax collectors; and overcomes geographical and familial drawbacks to announce the arrival of the dominion of God? With this set of credentials and list of activities it is not surprising so many saw Jesus as someone out of the ordinary either in a good way or a bad way;[17] what is surprising is that the positive viewpoint prevailed even after Jesus' execution.

The so-called big bang theory of Easter, which suggests that the appearances of Jesus are what created much of the later christological speculation, does not account for the social matters we have just discussed, it does not adequately deal with Jesus in his own social setting, and it is especially inadequate to deal with the fact that the first post-Easter witnesses for Jesus had previously been pre-Easter followers of Jesus whose hopes had been shattered, as the Gospels freely admit, on Good Friday (e.g., Lk 24:21). Note too that the social networks of Jesus continued to operate for him after his death. Indeed, to judge from Acts 1:14, the previously unpersuaded family members become persuaded. An adequate explanation must be given for all these remarkable facts. Bearing these things in mind we turn to the so-called titles of Christ.

ENTITLED TO A NAME

Naming in antiquity was not very much like modern practices where a husband and wife gather together a list of names they like the sound of or family names they are partial to and then choose a moniker for their child. It was often and widely assumed in antiquity that a name, and perhaps especially a nickname or self-chosen form of identification, revealed something about someone's nature. Names were not mere distin-

---

[16]Indeed they were so bold as to proclaim him messiah in Jerusalem—the very place where there were numerous witnesses to his execution, which presumably should have scotched the rumor that he was more than an ordinary mortal.

[17]Note the suggestion in Mk 3:22 that Jesus is in league with the devil, that his social networks provide him power from a nefarious source, and in Jn 6:41-51 that Jesus is at best merely the son of Joseph, that he was not from God (cf. Jn 9:16).

guishing labels in antiquity. They were badges of honor or dishonor. And the exercise of naming established a social relationship of power flowing in a particular direction from one person to another (e.g., Mk 1:11; Mt 16:16-17). This process is different from title or honor recognition or from name calling in the pejorative sense (e.g., Jn 8:48). It needs to be seen then that the titles Son of man, Son of God, Lord and Christ are not names for Jesus or names that Jesus uses. Nor are they mere labels. In each case they are honor claims, and they are relational in character.

The first of these perhaps deserves the closest scrutiny. Whatever else one may wish to say about the endlessly debated phrase *bar enasha,* it is clear enough that it is not a proper name, nor is it a nickname, in Daniel 7 or in the Gospels. In Daniel 7 it is intended as a description, functioning as part of an analogy. Furthermore it says something about the person in question in his relationship to human beings. Like other such Semitic phrases that characterize using the phrase "son of" and then a qualifier, the qualifier is meant to inform us about something crucial or definitive that characterizes or shapes the person in question. For example, the phrase *Boanerges,* or sons of thunder, was meant to tell us something about the Zebedees that shaped or characterized them in their actions or attitudes or words, just as the phrases "sons of light" and "sons of darkness" in the Qumran literature indicate persons whose lives are charaterized by either one or the other of these qualities. The idea is that an outside force or group is shaping or defining a person's identity.

In Daniel 7 the phrase *bar enasha* must be exegeted in the larger context of what is suggested about the evil empires discussed in the previous chapters—namely, that they are beastly in character compared to this figure which comes into the presence of God. The one "like a son of man" has a human face and can truly represent human beings, particularly God's people, in the presence of God. He is representative of these human beings (hence he is said to be like them), and he represents them. He in turn is given tasks and dominion somewhat reminiscent of those given Adam (cf. Dan 7:14 to Gen 1:28).

Perhaps then the first question to be asked about Jesus' use of the phrase *bar enasha* of himself, especially when coupled with his regular pronouncements about God's dominion, is this—why did he most often choose these terms to identify himself instead of for instance the phrase "son of David"?[18] The latter would have more clearly had a messianic ring to it at least in some quarters. Perhaps the answer lies in the fact that Jesus believed that he represented humankind with a different vision of kingdom than that of the beastly kingdoms. God's dominion which Jesus would proclaim and seek to inaugurate would be a place where things dehumanizing would have no place and where even the least, last and lost would be able to be all they were meant to be. In other words, "Son of man" is a relational phrase, but it indicates that Jesus saw himself not as defined or characterized by humanness as opposed to divineness but rather, to judge from Daniel 7, by humanness as opposed to subhumanness or beastliness, especially in the form of the structured evil found in empires and their tyrannical rulers. To put it another way, the coming of God's dominion was about humanity gone right in the Son of man, as opposed to humanity gone beastly and wrong in Adam and his kin, or perhaps more nearly in Jesus' day in Caesar and his kin or in Herod and his. This is what God had promised to his oppressed people in Daniel 7.

The second phrase, "Son of God," will of course be more controversial, but it needs to be said that this is a phrase that the Synoptics all suggest Jesus first had applied to him by an outside source—namely, by a voice from heaven at his baptism (Mk 1:11 and par.).[19] This phrase is of course known to have messianic overtones from the discoveries in cave 4 at Qumran,[20] but here we are talking about the act of being named by a divine Power. Identity is being confirmed or established through this experience, and it is suggested that who Jesus is will perhaps best be revealed

---

[18]I am assuming, with most scholars, that Jesus did use the phrase "Son of man" of himself in various contexts and that in view of his proclamation of dominion it is likely that Dan 7 lies somewhere in the background of the use of this phrase by Jesus. On this see Witherington, *The Christology of Jesus,* pp. 238ff.

[19]The earlier Markan form of the text is crucial here, and makes clear that it is likely this was originally part of some sort of apocalyptic vision Jesus had at his baptism, not unlike the visions recorded in the book of Revelation. See Witherington, *The Christology of Jesus,* pp. 148-55.

[20]See J. A. Fitzmyer, *The Gospel of Luke 10-24* (New York: Doubleday, 1981), p. 347.

by the sort of relationship he has with God. It is in this light that the shorter phrase "the Son" or the use of the term *Abba* take on fresh meaning.

We are being told that if one wants to know who Jesus is one should contemplate how he relates to and names God and how as a basis of that he sees himself as being named by God. One is not Son of God in isolation but rather in constant relationship to the divine. It is this idea, rather than his being son of Joseph or Son of David, that characterized Jesus and how he viewed himself. Like other ancients he is named by others, and like other ancients he identifies himself by the group he sees himself representing. Yet for Jesus it is not finally gender, geography or ethnic generation that are the determinants but rather even more basic determinants both human and divine.

In many ways the scene we find in Mark 8:27-30 is a typical ancient naming story. Rather than Jesus telling his disciples who he is, he asks them what the word is on the street, so to speak. Having heard that answer he then asks the disciples directly what they think. Their response represented by Peter is said to be that they thought Jesus was God's Anointed One, that is, the person especially endued by God with power and mission to bring in God's reign among God's people. Once again this is not a case of Jesus making a claim and then responding to challenges. Jesus operates like other ancients and is told how he is viewed and then can concur or disagree or conclude the discussion. In the earliest form of this story in Mark, Jesus would appear not to disagree with the disciple's suggestion, but it is treated as a dangerous suggestion and apparently because of this is silenced. It is notable that it is this title that is closest to what seems to have appeared on the titulus at Jesus' death.

What would it have meant for Jesus to accept the acclamation that he was God's Anointed One, as he apparently did on this or some other occasion? It would mean that he recognized that his commission, his mission, his power, his authority came from God, and that he had certain eschatological tasks to perform for God and on behalf of God's people as a royal figure. It is telling that this term *mashiach,* which would more narrowly limit Jesus' scope to his relationship to Israel, is not his own preferred phrase of self-designation.[21] Yet he appears not to have simply rejected the suggestion that there was a certain appropriateness in claiming this relationship for Jesus.

Lastly, there is the term *Lord*. Apart from the fact that Jesus may have been called *mare* as a teacher or Jewish leader, indicating he was a respected figure, there is no suggestion in the Synoptics that Jesus was named this by others during his ministry with a meaning other than in the mundane sense of the term. It does, however, appear that Jesus may well have prompted such an exalted form of naming after he engaged in debate with other Jewish leaders about the significance of Psalm 110:1. Perhaps Jesus in this debate was suggesting that Davidic connections were not necessarily the most crucial issue when one is talking about one who is David's Lord (Mk 12:35-37 and par.). If this is so, it would comport with Jesus' efforts elsewhere to make clear that generation and geography should not be the final determinants of identity for someone such as this person that the Scriptures describe. In short, it would make clear that Jesus was acting as an ancient person and dealing with relational language in a way that his social world would find understandable. A great deal more could be said along these lines, but it will be appropriate to draw some conclusions at this point.

CONCLUSIONS: AND SO?

It is no accident that all the major titles used of Jesus in the Synoptics (Son of Man, Son of God, Christ, Lord) refer to relationships that Jesus was believed to have had and must be understood as relational in meaning and character. One can be a Son only in relationship to another or others, one can be an Anointed One only in relationship to an Anointer, and finally one can be a Lord only in relationship to some subjects. These titles attempt to tell us who Jesus was, not in isolation but in his social and religious relationships. The christological issue is framed in this fashion because of the social contours of the world out of which both Jesus and the Gospels came.

Whether we call it dyadic personality, as modern sociologists would, or group-formed identity, the christological discussions in the Gospels

---

[21]Note how in Mk 14:61-62 he does not reject the suggestion of the high priest, but he immediately shifts the discussion to his preferred form of self-identification—Son of Man.

clearly manifest a world where who a person was was largely determined by whose child one was, what group one was an indigenous part
of and what locale one lived in. Into this world where gender, generation and geography were major determinants of identity came Jesus,
who, at least in regard to the matter of generation and geography, seems
to have chosen to swim against the current. Then too he rejects various
of the basic assumptions about what roles are appropriate in Jewish society for men and women. This is not because he could even remotely
be thought of as being like a late-twentieth-century Western individual.
It is because Jesus chose a different sort of social network in which to
flesh out his identity, one where he would be primarily and properly
named by God and by his own disciples, and by himself rather than by
his parents, his home town folks or even his fellow male leaders in early
Judaism. It is the way Jesus modifies the social assumptions and networks of his day that reveals, more than any ordinary close scrutiny of
titles could, that Jesus stood out from the crowd, chose to create his own
community or family and thereby made at least implicit and indirect
claims about himself that were rightly interpreted by the earliest Christians as messianic or christological in character.

Jesus did not come on the scene of first-century Judaism to conform
to anyone's preconceived expectations about prophets, sages or messi-
ahs, much less to ours at the end of the twentieth century. He came to
make known something about God and something about humankind
and something about their interrelationship in the crucible of a volatile
environment in which proclamations about the intervening saving reign
of God were dangerous and could get one crucified because of what
such messages implied about one's own relationships of power to both
God and God's people. The names Jesus chose for himself as well as the
ones he accepted from others both divine and human are meant to help
us locate Jesus on the social map of Jewish messianic pretenders and
contenders. They distinguish Jesus from many other contemporary
claimants, but they also identify him with basic elements imbedded in
the Hebrew Scriptures as part of the hopes of God's people. The more
we learn about Jesus' social matrix, the more clearly the christological
questions seem to come into question.

What this greater clarity does not do is settle whether we likewise will name Jesus as the Evangelists did. It is always possible that one may become convinced that though there was a christological claim made by Jesus in the way he related to others (receiving and offering names), that in the end that claim was not justified. The truth about the historical issues does not settle whether we will conclude that the theological claims are also true.

Finally, whatever else we may say, it is clear enough from the recent sound and fury of the Third Quest for the Historical Jesus that the Western world is still a Jesus-haunted place, with many wishing to claim Jesus for their own causes and caucuses.[22] In our own social context a bit more light on the historical Jesus is always welcome, especially when the hysterical Jesus is the one who seems to appear most frequently in the Western media.

Perhaps *fides quaerens intellectum* is after all not such a bad mode of pursuing and perusing this issue of Jesus' names and claims, since we know very well there is no such thing as pure objectivity in such matters. This Anselmian model appears to be a sane and sober one which will direct our studies to the most secure results.

FOR FURTHER READING

Habermas, Gary R. *The Historical Jesus: Ancient Evidence for the Life of Christ.* Rev. ed. Joplin, Mo.: College Press, 1996.

Harris, Murray J. *Jesus As God: The New Testament Use of* Theos *in Reference to Jesus.* Grand Rapids, Mich.: Baker, 1992.

Kreeft, Peter. *Between Heaven and Hell.* Downers Grove, Ill.: InterVarsity Press, 1982.

Wilkins, Michael, and J. P. Moreland, eds. *Jesus Under Fire: Modern Scholarship Reinvents the Historical Jesus.* Grand Rapids, Mich.: Zondervan, 1995.

Witherington, Ben, III. *The Christology of Jesus.* Minneapolis: Fortress, 1990.

———. *The Jesus Quest: The Third Search for the Jew from Nazareth.* 2nd ed. Downers Grove, Ill.: InterVarsity Press, 1997.

---

[22]See Ben Witherington III, *The Jesus Quest: The Third Search for the Jew from Nazareth,* 2nd ed. (Downers Grove, Ill.: InterVarsity Press, 1997).

10

MIRACLES

Winfried Corduan

MIRACLES ARE NOT SUPPOSED TO HAPPEN.[1] THAT'S THE WHOLE POINT ABOUT miracles. If miracles were things that normally happened in the course of an average day—or even if they were just somewhat unusual events— any discussion of miracles would really be pointless. For believers and skeptics alike, a miracle is an event that leaves everyone speechless, try- ing to find some explanation other than supernatural intervention but not being able to do so. If the element of the inexplicable is missing, we do not have a miracle in the true sense of the word. To borrow a sen- tence from Charles Dickens, "This must be distinctly understood, or nothing wonderful can come of the story I am going to relate."[2] Any dis- cussion about miracles needs to begin by acknowledging that miracles are events that defy natural explanation. Otherwise, nothing wonderful can come of them.

As we go through our daily existence we predicate all we do and be- lieve on a basic uniformity. When we wake up in the morning we expect the world to be just as it was when we went to bed, and we presume that

---

[1]Some of the best discussions of miracles from a Christian point of view include the following: Francis J. Beckwith, *David Hume's Argument Against Miracles: A Critical Analysis* (Lanham, Md.: University Press of America, 1989); Colin Brown, *Miracles and the Critical Mind* (Grand Rapids, Mich.: Eerdmans, 1984); Norman L. Geisler, *Miracles and the Modern Mind* (Grand Rapids, Mich.: Baker, 1992); R. Douglas Geivett and Gary R. Habermas, *In Defense of Miracles* (Downers Grove, Ill.: InterVarsity Press, 1997); C. S. Lewis, *Miracles* (New York: Collier, 1947).

[2]Charles Dickens, *A Christmas Carol,* available in many editions. A recent critical text is posted at the Charles Dickens website: <www.lang.nagoya-u.ac.jp/~matsuoka/cgi-bin/carol/hmt/ carol-1.html>.

our circumstances, whether good or ill, will not have changed. We count on the food in our refrigerators to continue to nourish us and on the North Pole to have a colder climate than the equator. We feel justified in believing that the good things of life still are good, but we are also reconciled to the fact that the bad things of life—sickness, old age, death—cannot be staved off forever, and so we plan for that inevitable future.

Consequently, it should be in the very nature of any discussion of miracles that it must address a fundamental ambiguity. Clearly, a believer in miracles is committed to their possibility and reality, and this is the issue we will address in this chapter. Nevertheless, believers need not be gullible and usually aren't. Christian believers will be skeptical of reports of miracles occurring within the context of other religions, and many of them will even question reports of miraculous claims from within a Christian environment. For example, Princeton theologian B. B. Warfield devoted a lifetime of writing to defending the supernatural character of biblical Christianity;[3] yet he adamantly opposed the idea that there could have been any true miracles after the age of the apostles. "A debased superstition has fallen like a pall over entire communities and for ages has darkened their minds and cursed their whole life,"[4] he says of the portions of humanity that take an excessively (to him) supernatural view of life. Strong words for a Christian apologist.

And yet, despite the healthy skepticism that most people will naturally bring to miracles, it is also just as much the case that human beings will look for and embrace evidence of the supernatural. Not only does the majority practice some form of religion, many people who would otherwise deny any formal supernatural beliefs practice superstitions or look for some implicit supernatural assistance for their lives, such as horoscopes and lucky charms. It seems that we do not believe in supernatural agency lightly, but when we do we are firmly committed to it.

A CENTRAL ROLE

For Christians, miracles are an especially important aspect of their reli-

---

[3]See, for example, B. B. Warfield, "Christian Supernaturalism," in *Biblical and Theological Studies,* ed. Samuel G. Craig (Philadelphia: P&R, 1968), pp. 1-21.
[4]Ibid., p. 2.

gion, though not entirely for conventional reasons. For other religions, miraculous events tend to perform two important functions, both of which are also true for Christianity. First, a religion may contain stories of miracles performed by a special person, most likely the founder. For example, Zoroaster, the founder of Zoroastrianism, is said to have healed the horse of a king and thereby brought about the conversion of the king to his teachings. Or, in present-day Hinduism, the teacher Satya Sai Baba supposedly performs miracles of healing and the materialization of objects. In these cases, the miracles are a tool of authentication; they are intended to verify the claims of the person as having a particular special status, whether it be as prophet, God or whatever.

Furthermore, many other religions offer miracles for their adherents as an ongoing benefit of belonging to that religion. Muhammad, the founder of Islam, did not perform miracles,[5] but folk Islam has always been preoccupied with miracles and other supernatural manifestations, most frequently in association with Muslim saints and pilgrimages to their graves.

Christianity offers miracles as demonstrations of Christ's claims (Jn 20:30) and as possible answers to prayer (as illustrated with irony in Acts 12:6-17), but miracles are even more crucial, both in the Old and New Testament. The very nature of the religion depends on certain miraculous events having occurred. In most other religions miracles are merely an added attraction because only the teaching of the religion is what is centrally important about the religion, but Christianity is founded on the miraculous event of Christ's resurrection. The fact that neither Muhammad nor Buddha were miracle workers is not relevant to their respective religions since their religions consist of teachings which ultimately anyone can obey, even if they have never heard of their founders. But Christianity is based not just on the teachings of Christ but also on what he

---

[5]Muslims sometimes point to certain events as miraculous: Muhammad's night journey, the victory of the battle of Badr and the fact that Muhammad received and recited the Qur'an. My point here is not to quibble over definitions or over the validity of those events but to mention that they are not what we usually have in mind when we speak of miracles. Muhammad explained the absence of miracles by protesting that they were useless; unbelievers would reject the truth regardless of whether it came with miracles or not (Qur'an 3:183-84; 20:133; 30:58).

did, and at that point his miracles, particularly the resurrection, take center stage.

So, for Christianity, a discussion on the reality of miracles is not just
an excursus along a tangent; it reaches to the very lifeblood of the religion. What makes this truth so poignant is the fact that for many centuries there have been those who have called themselves Christians but
who have believed that Christianity could dispense with the supernatural. For instance, Gotthold Ephraim Lessing (1729-1781), in trying to
soften the blow of the skeptical writings of his day, tried to make the
case that even if one would have to eliminate all supernatural and miraculous elements from Christian doctrine, one could still have what he
called "true" Christianity, a religion that begins and ends with the exhortation to love one's neighbor. From a more biblical perspective, this is
clearly inadequate. But then again, many Christian Bible scholars already
come to their subject with presuppositions that eliminate miracles up
front. A Christian minister asks concerning the historicity of 1 and 2
Chronicles, "First, does Chronicles satisfy the standards of modern his-
tory-writing? When phrased in this manner, the answer is almost certainly negative. Chronicles relies on divine intervention and involve-
ment, assuming that God's activity is determinative for the course of
history; this fact alone would render it suspect in modern discussions of
history."[6] Thus, for that commentator, as for many others, his presupposition against the possibility of miracles already indicts the truth of the
Bible.

THE LOYAL OPPOSITION

We stated above that a healthy amount of incredulity concerning miracles is a positive human trait; we cannot just take people's word for all
they claim anyway, but certainly not when it comes to the supernatural.
A serious problem arises, however, when that skepticism becomes universal and when even inescapably documented miracles no longer get
their hearing. Obviously, people take a stand against miracles from var-

---

[6]Paul K. Hooker, *First and Second Chronicles,* Westminster Bible Companion (Louisville, Ky.:
Westminster John Knox, 2001), p. 12.

ious positions, and even from within their context they will have differing arguments as to why they believe that we should not believe in miracles. Let me mention three.

The naturalist. For our purposes, I'm going to bring together into
one category everyone who denies the supernatural altogether. Thus, a
true atheist, someone who does not accept the existence of God, would
certainly epitomize this category. But let us also include here anyone
else who denies supernatural events in the world, not just God's, but
those of lesser beings, such as spirits and angels, as well.

The deist. The deist, as we will define the term here, is someone who
accepts the existence of God but who rules out divine agency in the
world. Most importantly, the nature of deism is not just that God has not
performed any miracles, but that it would be against God's very nature to
do so. God has created a natural order, and it would be irrational, and
hence impossible, for him to break the order of nature that he has created.
Deism, then, does not differ dramatically from atheism on this point.[7]

The supernaturalist. Some people, particularly pantheists (who believe that all of reality is identical with God), believe that the fundamental nature of the universe is spiritual. Thus for them every event in the
world would be an instance of the supernatural, and it would not be
possible to distinguish miracles from other events in that kind of framework. Everything that happens is equally miraculous (or nonmiraculous,
if you will) since everything is brought about by spiritual beings.

In their own way, each of these three classes of people will have reasons against the validity of Christian miracle claims; as a group, I will
label them as "skeptic." Those who either accept the reality of at least
one specific miracle or accept that miracles are possible in general, I will
call "believer."

ENABLING

As we already suggested at the outset of this chapter, a big temptation
for the contemporary believer is to attempt to defend miracles by mak-

---

[7]See the thorough study by Cornelio Fabro, *God in Exile: Modern Atheism* (Westminster, Md.:
Newman Press, 1968).

ing them appear not-so-miraculous. In trying to get the skeptic to accept a particular miracle, the believer may let the supernatural air out of the event in the hope that it will thus be more plausible to the skeptic. The problem is, of course, that the more you tailor the explanation of the event to the skeptic's expectations, the more you may wind up conceding your case. A skeptic does not need to be convinced that unusual natural events can happen; he knows that already. A skeptic needs to understand that sometimes events are so unusual that we know that only God could have brought them about.

Let me give you a specific example. Many people do not believe the Old Testament story of how Jonah was swallowed by a big fish and stayed alive in it for three days. Bible critic Robert Pfeiffer asserts that it is not "an account of actual happenings," but "it is a fiction."[8] His reason is simple: "A man's survival for three days in the belly of a fish, or even a whale, which is the only marine animal of sufficient size, is physiologically improbable, to say the least, even if alleged modern parallels are taken into account."[9]

Pfeiffer will not believe the story because it apparently violates natural laws as he understands them. Now, one interesting aspect of his declaration is that he makes reference to "alleged modern parallels." It turns out that a number of writers defending the story of Jonah have made an effort to document that such things do, in fact, happen; there have supposedly been other cases of people being swallowed and preserved inside of big fish. For example, Gleason L. Archer mentions several such incidents[10] but then also attributes an antisupernatural bias to critics of the story. But if we try to defend the story on the basis of natural parallels, aren't we guilty of a vestigial antisupernaturalism ourselves?

My point is this: I do not believe that the case for the plausibility of the Jonah story is really enhanced by making it appear more like a natural event. The whole story focuses on the idea that it was God who sent

---

[8]Robert Pfeiffer, *Introduction to the Old Testament* (New York: Harper & Brothers, 1941), p. 587.

[9]Ibid., p. 588.

[10]Gleason L. Archer, *A Survey of Old Testament Introduction* (Chicago: Moody Press, 1964), pp. 302-3.

the fish, that it was God who preserved Jonah inside the fish for three days and that it was God who caused the fish to spew out Jonah after that time. There is little to be gained by showing to the skeptic some dubious reports of how supposedly something similar happened at other times and places without God's direct agency. To use contemporary psychological jargon, there is no need for the believer to be an enabler for the skeptic's antisupernatural addiction.

THIS IS NOT ICE SKATING

How would we feel about a sport in which the final outcomes were determined by a panel of judges chosen in advance for their support of a specific contestant? This would strike us as highly unfair, and we wouldn't stand for it, would we? Come to think of it, there is one sport like that; it's called Olympic ice skating, and every once in a while, when things get too far out of hand, the people in charge of it implement some modest cosmetic reforms. For the most part, though, we expect athletic contests to be carried out in such a way that all contestants begin with an equal chance at victory.

Unfortunately, many skeptics expect the debate on miracles to be carried on along the lines of Olympic figure skating; that is to say, they want to come to the discussion with an assured outcome in their favor. More specifically, they expect to be able to set the terms of the debate in such a way that the believer never has a reasonable shot at making his case. In a moment we are going to look at two examples of this strategy by the skeptic. For now, let me just switch analogies and look at the skeptic's demands in this way. Imagine that some ichthyological agnostic does not believe in fish and tells us:

> Okay, I will allow you to demonstrate to me that there are such things as fish and what the criteria are for recognizing them. As you do so, please keep in mind that I do not believe that there is such a thing as water, and that furthermore, even if I conceded hypothetically that there were, I could never accept that any living being could survive in it. But please—I'm an open-minded person—don't let me keep you from making your case, and I will be happy to give you a frank appraisal as to whether you succeeded or not.

In the same way, the skeptic has come to the believer in miracles and said:

> Okay, I will allow you to demonstrate to me that there are such things as miracles and what the criteria are for recognizing them. As you do so, please keep in mind that I do not believe that there is such a thing as any supernatural agency, and that furthermore, even if I conceded hypothetically that there were, I could never accept that we could actually recognize a miracle if it had happened. But please—I'm an open-minded person—don't let me keep you from making your case, and I will be happy to give you a frank appraisal as to whether you succeeded or not.

As backwards as this situation sounds, for about four hundred years this has been the position of the debate in Western philosophy. Not only have skeptics laid out what the terms are supposed to be, they have even convinced believers that unless they come to the debate on the skeptics' terms, they are not truly entitled to believe in their own miracles. But this is silly; why should those who have already declared their steadfast refusal ever to believe be the ones who set the terms for those who do?

THE RIGHT STARTING POINTS

Clearly the question of miracles has many starting points. It is one of the besetting maladies of philosophy that people who have made some great contributions have baptized their methodology as the one and only appropriate one—for example, *the* way of having knowledge or *the* way of making moral decisions. Then someone else would come along and show that maybe this particular method was not universal in scope after all—and declare that, therefore, there was no correct method whatsoever. Wouldn't it be more reasonable to say that different areas of life and philosophy may require different ways of approaching them? So it would seem to be the case for miracles. An important area of the technical exploration of the nature of miracles is, of course, the relationship of the allegedly miraculous to the laws of science, and we shall return to this point below. However, I think it is safe to say that most of the world's reports of miracles have been provided by people who would have had only a rudimentary grasp of what we would call the laws of science. If we want to define a miracle in terms of an anomaly of the laws of science, and sometimes it may be helpful to do so, keep in mind that we are actually redefining the concept into parameters that would have been foreign to the ones who were involved with or were reporting the miraculous event.

Similarly, sometimes it is helpful to analyze miracles from the standpoint of probability assessment, and again, we shall allude to this point some more in a little while. Still, to a believer in miracles, the improbability of the event is a given. Otherwise—to return to the *leitmotif* of this chapter—it would not be a miracle.

Undoubtedly, the most important aspect of the problem of miracles is the surrounding context of understanding. We have already made reference to the fact that both believers and skeptics come to the issue with various preconceptions; this is how people's minds work, and it does no good to deny it—it's simply a fact. However, in contrast to the great leap into relativism that has characterized philosophy over the last 150 years, there is no need to conclude that, therefore, people cannot communicate, let alone interact with each other rationally about philosophical concepts. Of course they can; if they could not, you would not be reading this chapter right now, consenting or disagreeing as you go along. Having said that, however, it is clear that on a topic such as miracles, the larger worldview a person brings to the issue is going to be of enormous consequence. To use myself as the example I know best, there is no question that the totality of my belief system, as well as my cultural heritage as a Christian, direct me to the acceptance of miracles; my background beliefs as a Christian theist, including the supernatural components, are what make miracles possible and knowable; whatever I say in the context of the nature of miracles is going to be colored by the goal of rational coherence for my worldview, which includes the reality of miracles.

But surely these qualifications apply to the skeptic as well. Let us say that the owner of the website "infidels.org" posted an essay in which he argued against the reality of miracles.[11] Clearly it is reasonable to assume

---

[11]As he in fact did. See Richard Carrier, "The Problem with Miracles: The Shaky Groundwork of Corduan and Purtill," <http://www.infidels.org/library/modern/richard_carrier/indef/3a.html>.

that the totality of his belief system, as well as his cultural heritage in the world of atheism, direct him to the rejection of miracles; his background beliefs as an atheist, including the rejection of the supernatural component of religious belief, are what makes miracles impossible and unknowable; whatever he says in the context of the nature of miracles is going to be colored by the goal of rational coherence for his worldview, which includes the unreality of miracles.

This observation is not intended as an *ad hominem* attack on the atheist or to relativize, personalize or trivialize the issues. But it is to indicate that much of the time—perhaps even most—the central issue is neither whether miracles have occurred nor whether miracles are even possible, but what one's worldview is. The confirmed antisupernatural atheist is not just within his rights. He is under an intellectual obligation to deny the reality of miracles in general and specific miraculous events in particular. However, and this is crucial for our point, he is not within his rights to assume the atheist standpoint as normative for anyone else or—if he wishes to engage in intellectual debate—to insulate his atheistic presuppositions from the discussion.

For the believer, miracles are usually a simple outgrowth of a worldview that is centered on a supernatural agency, most likely God. To focus on Christian theism in particular, the person who believes in God according to traditional Christian teaching accepts that there is a Being with infinite power and knowledge, who created the world and is moment by moment sustaining the universe with his power. For the person who holds this view, it is entirely obvious that God could, at any time he chose, act directly within the finite order that he himself created.

But that does not mean that God did act in such a way. The nature of theism makes miracles possible because it looks at God as a personal agent who is free to intervene in his created order, should he so desire. But this very nature also implies, then, that God is free not to intervene. God is not compelled to act in a miraculous manner, and believers are not obligated to accept each and every purported case of a miraculous event as real. Thus, for the person who is disposed toward accepting the reality of miracles, there continue to be ongoing concerns. For a specific

event, the believer still needs to know whether there is sufficient reason
to recognize it as a miracle. We will expand on this matter further below.

So we see that the issue of miracles represents a confluence of many
issues and concerns. Figure 10.1 illustrates the point. We will now address the skeptic's concerns a little more and then follow up with some
applications within the believer's circle.

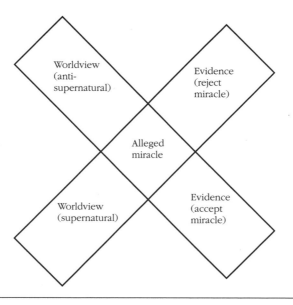

Figure 10.1

DAVID HUME'S "YEAH, RIGHT" ARGUMENT

There has been a lot of debate concerning miracles over the centuries.
Much of it has been simply a confrontation of dogmatic commitments,
whether it be from the skeptic's assertion that miracles just cannot happen or from the believer's demand that all authorized miracles must be
accepted as true as a matter of faith. Two lines of argument on the skeptic's side stand out, one going back to the eighteenth century and one
from the twentieth.

Perhaps the best-known argument against the reality of miracles
comes from the Scottish philosopher David Hume.[12] Among his many-

---

[12]The following argument is summarized from David Hume, *An Inquiry Concerning Human
Understanding* (1748; Indianapolis: Bobbs-Merrill, 1955), pp. 117-41.

faceted arguments, the most famous one focuses on the notion that even if miracles could theoretically occur, we could rationally never know that they did. Obviously, Hume was not saying that people cannot believe in miracles, because they clearly do, but his point was that reasonable people should not do so because the evidence in their favor can never be sufficient. With this argument, Hume believed that he had established "an everlasting check to all kinds of superstitious delusion, and consequently will be useful as long as the world endures."[13]

Imagine that I told you of an event that clearly violates a law of nature. Say I report to you that my cat just spoke to me in plain English, confirming his menu demands for the next week. What is your reaction going to be? Presumably, if you have a little common sense, you are not going to believe my story. In contemporary vernacular, the popular expression of disbelief is, "yeah, right." Cats can't speak English, and there is not much else to say about the matter except to figure out why I might be saying such a thing. I could be telling a deliberate lie for some peculiar reason; I could be trying to make a joke at my cat's expense; I could be hallucinating; I could even just be testing a silly example for a chapter on miracles. Whatever explanation we may want to settle on is going to be more plausible than that my cat spoke to me in English. The weight of probability goes to an alternative explanation.

But note that not every alternative is necessarily preferable. The "explanation" that what I see before me as my cat is actually my neighbor's dog, who disguised himself as my cat in order to speak to me, really compounds the implausibility. A reasonable person will weigh the probability of all the various alternatives and choose the one that affords the least absurdity. This is what Hume wanted us to see. Ultimately every claim to knowledge involves an assessment of probability, and the rational person will believe whatever is most probably true. In many cases, the probability of a claim is so low that there is no chance whatsoever of a sane person accepting it.

Let us shift to an example not quite as absurd as my cat speaking English. Say that I inform you that I just saw a man turn water into wine.

---

[13]Ibid., p. 118.

Assume additionally that you know me to be honest, sober and obser-vant, and that I manifest all of the signs we usually expect from people who believe their own story. In other words, the probability of my being deluded or my intentionally deceiving you is quite low. But something else is even lower, namely, the probability of someone actually turning water into wine. As a rational person you will have to make a decision. Which is more probable: that I might be making some kind of mistake in reporting this alleged miracle or that the laws of nature were actually violated by a water-to-wine transformation? For Hume, this is an easy choice. Water into wine—"yeah, right."

The upshot for Hume is that we should always follow this process of evaluating alternatives. Someone reports a miracle to us. We put the re-port on the scales of probability, and the laws of nature will always win out, as illustrated in figure 10.2.

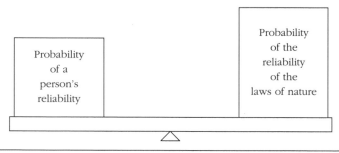

Figure 10.2

Regardless of how strong the reports about a violation of the laws of nature might be, a reasonable person will never believe that they were violated.

But you may already have noticed that this is really no argument at all. It is nothing more than an expression of a predisposition against mir-acles at all costs. Other than as a subjective preference, there is really no good reason why we should always choose to believe that a person gave an erroneous report. A statistical generalization, such as "we have never known the laws of nature to fail," is either false or question begging since that is precisely the issue in question. The theistically based be-liever does not say that the laws of nature do not take precedence in our

day-to-day lives; of course they do. However, he does claim that there
may be (and, in fact, have been) times when there is enough evidence
in favor of a miraculous event that a rational person should recognize
that the laws of nature have actually been superseded by divine agency.

ANTONY FLEW'S "I JUST KNOW IT" ARGUMENT

The second most celebrated argument against miracles looks somewhat
like a restatement of Hume's, but it actually takes us in a different direction.[14] Antony Flew is a twentieth-century skeptical philosopher who has
argued strenuously against various forms of religious belief. He may be
most famous for his thesis that Christians have allowed their language
about God to become meaningless because they do not allow any evidence to count against their claims about God.[15] Specifically, Flew al-
leges that Christians will continue to assert their belief that God loves
them as a father loves his children, even when there is so much evidence
in the world counting against God's love. The issue is not just that Christians have weighed the evidence and decided in favor of believing in the
love of God but that Christians will not even concede that there is any
evidence that could count against divine love. Whenever there is a challenge to their belief in God's love, they simply redefine the concept so
as to avoid having to deal with the possibility that maybe the loving God
in whom they believe does not exist. At least this is what Flew claims,
though, needless to say, there is quite a bit of debate on whether he is
right.

What there cannot be any debate about is that—ironically—this is the
exact strategy that Flew uses with regard to his denial of miracles. He is
particularly opposed to the idea that any historical account could ever
be a legitimate source for information on supernatural events. In contrast
to Hume's argument as we presented it above, Flew does not just question the reliability of testimonies to the miraculous; he asserts that it is

---

[14]The following argument is summarized from Antony Flew, *God and Philosophy* (New York:
Delta, 1966), pp. 140-58, and Antony Flew, "Miracles," in *The Encyclopedia of Philosophy,* ed.
by Paul Edwards (New York: Macmillan, 1967), pp. 346-53.

[15]Antony Flew, "Theology and Falsification," in *New Essays in Philosophical Theology,* ed. Antony Flew and Alasdair MacIntyre (London: SCM, 1955), p. 99.

fundamentally incorrect ever to accept any report of a miracle as true. According to Flew, it is contrary to the nature of science to make allowances for the supernatural, and historical reports should not be permitted to violate the nature of reality as science circumscribes it for us. According to Flew, that does not mean that science necessarily has the correct explanation for every historical event but that whatever the ultimate explanation may be for a specific event, it cannot be miraculous. Thus Flew makes the following astounding statement: "If ever we became able to say that some account of the ostensibly miraculous was indeed veridical, we can say it only because we now know that the occurrences reported were not miraculous at all."[16] Consequently, Flew's claim that no events are miraculous is completely unfalsifiable, and, just as he accuses the Christian in his defense of the love of God, it becomes a meaningless mantra. No evidence could conceivably count against his rejection of any event as miraculous. To use another piece of contemporary jargon, "he just knows it."

This attitude would, of course, result in an immediate victory for the antisupernaturalist, but only because he mounted his own platform to crown himself with laurels of his own plucking. Once evidence for the miraculous has been ruled out of court a priori, obviously it is impossible even to begin making an evidential case for miracles. A more plausible strategy would seem to be to allow the case for each specific miracle to rest on its own merits. If the historical support is insufficient, if the alleged eyewitness testimony is incompetent, or if there are plausible alternative explanations, then one should not invoke the supernatural. But a case against the supernatural that begins with a broad dismissal of the supernatural as its major premise is not terribly convincing.

How to Recognize a Miracle

In general, what would people do if they were confronted with the claim that a particular miracle has occurred? Let us ignore for the moment the reaction of those who are going to dismiss all claims to the supernatural as well as those who are simply ready to embrace various alleged mira-

---

[16]Flew, "Miracles," p. 352.

cle accounts (particularly those within the context of their own religion) as true. For those who bring a certain amount of critical thought to an event, it seems fair to delineate the following conditions.

There needs to be some kind of reasonable expectation that the event in question even should be considered to be a miracle. This prima facie presumption would separate the event from nonmiraculous occurrences. For example, if a man stepped out of a boat in the middle of a lake and immediately sank, there would be no presumption toward a miracle. But if he stepped out of the boat and proceeded to walk on the water, the idea of a miracle would at least be a contender among various explanations.

The event must be unusual enough to defy common explanations. In other words, it should present what we would consider to be either an impossibility or an extreme improbability. Generally, writers on the subject divide miracles into two classes, which often go by different names.

Class 1: violation, superseding or first-order miracles. These are events in which the basic nature of reality has been defied. For example, if I poured pure water into the gas tank of my car and the water instantaneously turned to gasoline, this event would qualify as a class 1 miracle.

Class 2: configuration, contingency, constellation or second-order miracles. These miracles do not appear to break any laws of nature per se, but they present us with a sequence of events that is so improbable as to be as astounding as an apparent violation of the laws of nature. An example of such a miracle could be a scenario in which a meteor hits an apartment building at two in the morning, but an hour earlier, for totally unrelated reasons, all seventy-three people living in that building decided to get up and go somewhere else.

The event in question has to occur in a framework directed toward the supernatural. This point could be understood as a sub-point under the first one (assuming a reasonable prima facie presumption), but it also specifies a very important additional requirement. In order to be thought of as a miracle, there should be some reason to associate the event with the supernatural. If a highly unusual event were to happen, and no one (neither the person who performed the action nor any of the witnesses) were making any reference to God or other supernatural agency, even

Antony Flew would be entitled to bypass a supernatural explanation.

Supernatural agency should be the most reasonable explanation for the event in question. Note that I am not saying that it should be the only explanation available, since it is always possible to concoct some explanation, no matter how far-fetched, as an alternative. Antony Flew's position of "I-just-know-it-can't-be-a-miracle-regardless-of-the-evidence" comes to mind. Nevertheless, when looking at the event, it should be such that reasonable people feel compelled to conclude that, contrary to their normal expectations, here is a genuine miracle.

The last point in particular highlights the fact that, even with a formal delineation of this sort, the ambiguity never goes away. There are bound to be many cases in which believers disagree as to whether an actual miracle occurred or not. But that ambiguity does not mean that it is impossible to identify a miracle. Some people believe that the victories of Joan of Arc were miracles; others do not. However, it is not necessary to have a foolproof deductive method for an evaluation of all such claims in order to be quite certain that certain other events, say the resurrection of Jesus Christ, were miracles.[17]

CLIMBING DOWN MOUNT CARMEL AND UP MOUNT CALVARY

Please note that I have not given the evidence for a specific miracle, and it is not in the purview of this chapter to do so. All I have hoped to have accomplished at this point is to show that despite the fact that claims for miracles should never be accepted lightly, there may be times when such a claim could turn out to be the most reasonable one.

---

[17]A common fallacy in debates such as this one consists of asserting that, since we do not have a method for accounting for everything, we cannot account for anything. If I do not have hard and fast criteria to classify every event as either a miracle or not a miracle, I cannot classify any event at all as miracle. But, of course, once the matter is stated in this way it is clear that this is not a reasonable demand. I may have fully adequate criteria to recognize most of the clear cases, even if there are some unresolved ones. I can know that the resurrection was a miracle, even if I am fuzzy on Joan of Arc. This fallacy is a subset of the larger problems that have come with the legacy of René Descartes, who left us the unfortunate idea that only a universal, unassailable method of knowledge (virtual omniscience) can qualify as knowledge at all. A more reasonable view would contend that we can know our multiplication tables to be true, even if we have not proved the Riemann hypothesis, and I can be quite sure that a lot of people died on the *Titanic,* even if I am unaware of their names and birthdates.

Now, let us skip ahead and ask ourselves: what if we have reasonably identified an event as miracle? What would that prove? The answer depends on the particular instance, of course, since miracles occur in different circumstances and seem to be intended to carry out different tasks. Within discussions of Christian apologetics, such as this one, miracles are expected to be evidence to lead people to belief in God, but in reality they hardly ever function this way. As a case in point, we read in Matthew's Gospel concerning Christ's return to his hometown of Nazareth, "And he did not do many miracles there because of their lack of faith" (Mt 13:58). Clearly faith was a precondition for the possibility for Christ to do miracles, not the intended outcome.

In general, it would seem to be fair to say that miracles usually are intended to reinforce some already established beliefs. For example, a miracle can demonstrate the love of God to someone who is being healed; in such a case probably no new belief is being created, but an already existing one is supported. Miracles can even take on a negative quality. Moses warned the people to be on guard against any future prophet who would lead the people into apostasy precisely because such a prophet's predictions would actually be fulfilled. He might predict a miracle, and "the sign or wonder of which he has spoken takes place" (Deut 13:2). Such a prophet, according to Mosaic law, should be executed because his miracles, though genuine, are an attestation of his false teachings. So, it would definitely be a mistake to think of miracles as having their only, or even primary, function in trying to convince an unbeliever to come to faith.

So, it would definitely be wrong to think of miracles as the chips in some huge wagering game among the great religions of the world. The resurrection turns out to be the biggest miracle, and so the religion with the resurrection (Christianity) wins. Obviously, some people do try to use the miracles of their religions in such a way, but it is contrary to the way in which miracles are usually seen within the religions themselves. Hume, the skeptic, thought that miracles served in such a corroborative capacity and that they cancelled themselves out since every religion seems to lay claim to similar supernatural events. "Every miracle, therefore, pretended to have been wrought in any of these religions . . . as its direct scope is to establish the particular system to which it is attributed, so has it the same force, though more indirectly, to overthrow every other system."[18]

Nevertheless, as we pointed out, miracles do not usually function as support pillars for entire religions.

Still, that does not mean that miracles can play no role in the personal formation of Christian belief. However, when they do so, it is a matter of an individual confronting the supernatural work of God. The apostle John says concerning the miracles of Christ he reported in his Gospel: "These are written that you may believe that Jesus is the Christ, the Son of God, and that by believing you may have life in his name" (Jn 20:31).

But what about what we said earlier concerning the resurrection of Christ? Did we not state early on in this chapter that the resurrection is central to Christianity, and that in fact this is what distinguishes it from other religions? Yes, we did, and let there be no doubt about it: Christ's resurrection is a huge miracle, based on extremely reliable sources and defying nonsupernatural explanations. But this is not its importance per se. It is important first of all because it happened. The resurrection is crucial to Christianity because the Son of God incarnate, having died for our sins, returned to life so that we may also receive eternal life. There may not be any bigger miracle, but it is not the magnitude of the miracle that matters so much as what God did in this event.

Belief in miracles is neither easy nor an end in itself. But, as we have seen, it is the transition that makes it possible for us to move from a general theistic worldview to a specific acceptance of what God has done in history on behalf of our redemption. A long time ago on Mount Carmel, the prophet Elijah held a contest with the prophets of Baal as to which god—Yahweh or Baal—could miraculously produce fire. Yahweh, of course, came through. However, such a contest is not at the heart of what miracles mean for the Christian. Much more importantly, it is because there is a God who does miracles that we can be sure of the salvation God provided for us on Mount Calvary.

---

[18]Hume, *Inquiry*, p. 129.

For Further Reading

Beckwith, Francis J. *David Hume's Argument Against Miracles: A Critical Analysis*. Lanham, Md.: University Press of America, 1989.

Brown, Colin. *Miracles and the Critical Mind*. Grand Rapids, Mich.: Eerdmans, 1984.

Geisler, Norman L. *Miracles and the Modern Mind*. Grand Rapids, Mich.: Baker, 1992.

Geivett, R. Douglas, and Gary R. Habermas, eds. *In Defense of Miracles*. Downers Grove, Ill.: InterVarsity Press, 1997.

Lewis, C. S. *Miracles*. New York: Collier, 1947.

Swinburne, Richard, ed. *Miracles*. Englewood Cliffs, N.J.: Prentice-Hall, 1989.

11

THE CASE FOR CHRIST'S RESURRECTION

Gary R. Habermas

THE CASE FOR THE RESURRECTION OF JESUS CHRIST IS CERTAINLY MULTIFACETED. Few New Testament topics involve more details or are treated so seriously by recent critical scholars. Due to the hundreds of studies on this topic, this chapter must frequently rely on a summarized format that simply lists some of the many conclusions that have emerged in contemporary research.

Throughout, we will cite chiefly those data to which the vast majority of recent researchers agree, regardless of their prior theological positions. Even more crucial is that these critical scholars agree with these data precisely because they are well supported on factual grounds, often for multiple reasons. I have argued the details for my conclusions elsewhere, as have others. So the sources cited in the notes will provide additional background information, argumentation, as well as other details for those who wish to consult them. The author is employing the results of his recent study of fourteen hundred sources on this subject, published since 1975 in German, French and English.

In addition to furnishing some of these summarized conclusions, I will concentrate in this chapter on just two major topics that are seldom discussed in detail. Both are crucial components in a historical case for the resurrection of Jesus Christ.

First, for a variety of reasons, it is the virtually unanimous conclusion of contemporary scholars that Jesus' early followers at least *thought* that they had seen appearances of the risen Jesus after his death. But how do we move from our certainty that the early disciples *believed* that they had seen appearances of Jesus to their *really* seeing Jesus? In other words, how do we move from their convictions to a historical resurrection? It is my contention that this is the single most crucial aspect of an argument for the historical resurrection appearances of Jesus.

Second, religious and political transformations are common in our world during recent decades. Whether one studies the history of communism, Muslim suicide strategies, missionary activity or particular news events such as Jonestown, David Koresh or the Heaven's Gate UFO group, it is increasingly obvious that many individuals, both Christians and non-Christians, are willing to give their lives for what they believe. So what makes the transformations of Jesus' disciples, even to the point of being willing to die for their faith, so unique? How can this aspect of early Christianity be such an important component of most arguments for the resurrection, if it is nowhere near unique?

THE DISCIPLES' EXPERIENCES OF THE RISEN JESUS

In contemporary studies of the historical Jesus, some items are supported by a broad scholarly consensus. That Jesus' proclamation of the kingdom of God was his central message and that Jesus died by crucifixion are two of the most readily agreed-upon events in Jesus' life.

Ranking with these two is the substantially unanimous verdict of contemporary critical scholars that Jesus' early disciples at least thought that they had seen the risen Jesus. Prominent historian E. P Sanders, who calls himself a liberal,[1] signifies this agreement. He declares that the "equally secure facts" include that Jesus' disciples "saw him (in what sense is not certain) after his death. . . . Thereafter his followers saw him."[2]

Support for the disciples' experiences. It is certainly noteworthy that the vast majority of scholars, representing many viewpoints, in spite of extensive disagreements in other areas, recognizes that the disciples

---

[1] E. P. Sanders, *Jesus and Judaism* (Philadelphia: Fortress, 1985), p. 324.
[2] E. P. Sanders, *The Historical Figure of Jesus* (London: Penguin, 1993), pp. 11, 13.

actually had real experiences of some sort. It seems equally clear that this recognition is due to the presence of a rather impressive number of strong reasons for holding this conclusion. Even a brief listing of these reasons may be instructive.

1. In contemporary critical studies, the apostle Paul is almost always thought to be the best witness among the New Testament writers. A former opponent of this message, Paul clearly points out that the risen Jesus appeared personally to him. Paul makes this claim more than once (1 Cor 9:1; 15:8; Gal 1:16). We also have corroboration of Paul's testimony from another New Testament author, who retells the story three times (Acts 9:1-8; 22:3-11; 26:9-18).

The data behind the fact of Paul's conversion from being an enemy of the church are recognized by all. But there needs to be a reason for this brilliant young scholar being convinced against his former beliefs and persecution of believers, as he explains (1 Cor 15:9; Gal 1:13-14; Phil 3:4-7). Paul's reason is very clear: he was persuaded that he had seen the risen Lord. Therefore Paul was obviously an eyewitness to his own experience. The scholarly consensus here is attested by Michael Martin, a philosophical atheist who admits: "However, we have only one contemporary eyewitness account of a postresurrection appearance of Jesus, namely Paul's."[3]

2. Beyond Paul's own experience, this apostle presents plenty of additional evidence for the claim that Jesus had appeared to his early followers. Essentially all critical scholars today agree that in 1 Corinthians 15:3-8, Paul records an ancient oral tradition(s) that summarizes the content of the Christian gospel. Jesus the Christ died for human sin, was buried and raised from the dead, afterwards appearing to both individuals as well as groups of witnesses. While Paul penned the words, he is clear that this material was not his own but that he had passed on to his listeners years before (1 Cor 15:1-2) what he had received from others, as the very heart of his message (1 Cor 15:3). If he were writing today, he might have footnoted his source! Thus this testimony is actually years earlier than the book of 1 Corinthians. Reginald Fuller indicates the

---

[3]Michael Martin, *The Case Against Christianity* (Philadelphia: Temple University Press), p. 81.

scholarly agreement here: "It is almost universally agreed today that Paul is here citing tradition."[4]

So Paul provides a straightforward explanation that he delivered to his audience what he had first received from others (1 Cor 15:3), which are the equivalent terms for passing rabbinic tradition to others (cf. 1 Cor 11:23). Besides this clear declaration of his actions, there are many other indications that this is exactly what happened. The sentence structure, diction, verbal parallelism, the threefold sequence of "and that," as well as the presence of several non-Pauline words, the proper names of Cephas (cf. Lk 24:34) and James, and indications that there may have been an Aramaic original all point clearly to this tradition being pre-Pauline. Critical scholars agree that Paul received it from others.[5]

The most popular view among scholars is that Paul first received this very early material when he visited Jerusalem just three years after his conversion. He visited Peter and James, the brother of Jesus (Gal 1:18-19), both of whom are listed as having seen the risen Jesus (1 Cor 15:5, 7).

Stronger evidence to support this conclusion comes from Paul's use of the verb *historēsai* in Galatians 1:18, which is usually not very helpfully translated into English. The Greek term indicates that Paul visited Peter for the purpose of investigating a particular subject. The immediate context reveals that subject: Paul's topic for discussion was ascertaining the nature of the gospel message (Gal 1:11—2:10). And Jesus' resurrection was the focus of the gospel message (1 Cor 15:3-4; Gal 1:11, 16). Without it, faith is vain (1 Cor 15:14, 17).

Critical scholars usually concede that this pre-Pauline tradition(s) originated at an exceptionally early date. For Ulrich Wilckens, this content "indubitably goes back to the oldest phase of all in the history of primitive Christianity."[6] Walter Kasper even thinks that this "ancient text" was

---

[4]Reginald Fuller, *The Formation of the Resurrection Narratives* (New York: Macmillan, 1980), p. 10.

[5]Of the dozens of scholarly publications here, the following are among the more helpful sources: Fuller, *The Formation of the Resurrection Narratives,* pp. 10-11; Pinchas Lapide, *The Resurrection of Jesus: A Jewish Perspective* (Minneapolis: Augsberg, 1983), pp. 97-99; John Kloppenborg, "An Analysis of the Pre-Pauline Formula in 1 Corinthians 15:3b-5 in Light of Some Recent Literature," *Catholic Biblical Quarterly* 40 (1978), pp. 351, 360; John P. Meier, *A Marginal Jew,* vol. 2, *Mentor, Message and Miracle* (New York: Doubleday, 1994), p.139; Sanders, *The Historical Figure of Jesus,* p. 277.

possibly "in use by the end of 30 A.D."[7]

Perhaps surprisingly, skeptics frequently even agree. Skeptic Gerd Lüdemann asserts that "the elements in the tradition are to be dated to the
first two years after the crucifixion of Jesus . . . not later than three years.
. . . *The formation of the appearance traditions mentioned in I Cor.15.3-
8 falls into the time between 30 and 33 C.E."*[8] Philosopher Thomas Sheehan thinks that this pre-Pauline formula "probably goes back to at least
32-34 C.E., that is, to within two to four years of the crucifixion."[9] Michael
Goulder holds that this resurrection report "goes back at least to what
Paul was taught when he was converted, a couple of years after the crucifixion."[10]

Other skeptics are often not shy about expressing their agreement.[11]
In fact, most of the critical scholars who date these events conclude that
Paul received this material within just a few years after Jesus' death, in
the early or mid 30s.[12] We will see how the existence and circumstances
at such an early date translate to additional eyewitness testimony besides Paul's.

3. Paul was exceptionally careful to ascertain the content of the gospel

---

[6]Ulrich Wilckens, *Resurrection: Biblical Testimony to the Resurrection: An Historical Examination and Explanation* (Edinburgh: St. Andrew Press, 1977), p. 2.

[7]Walter Kaspar, *Jesus the Christ,* trans. V. Green (Mahwah, N.J.: Paulist, 1976), p. 125.

[8]Gerd Lüdemann, *The Resurrection of Jesus,* trans. John Bowden (Minneapolis: Fortress, 1994),
p. 38 (Lüdemann's emphasis).

[9]Thomas Sheehan, *The First Coming: How the Kingdom of God Became Christianity* (New
York: Random, 1986), p. 118; cf. pp. 110-11.

[10]Michael Goulder, "The Baseless Fabric of a Vision," in *Resurrection Reconsidered,* ed. Gavin
D'Costa (Oxford: Oneworld, 1996), p. 48.

[11]For just a few examples, see Robert Funk, Roy W. Hoover and the Jesus Seminar, *The Five
Gospels* (New York: Macmillan, 1993), p. 24; Jack Kent, *The Psychological Origins of the Resurrection Myth* (London: Open Gate, 1999), pp. 16-17; A. J. M. Wedderburn, *Beyond Resurrection* (Peabody, Mass.: Hendrickson, 1999), p. 274 n. 265; G. A. Wells, *Did Jesus Exist?* (London: Pemberton, 1986), p. 30.

[12]Some of the other scholars who agree here include: Fuller, *The Formation of the Resurrection
Narratives,* pp. 10, 14, 48; Raymond Brown, *The Virginal Conception and Bodily Resurrection
of Jesus* (New York: Paulist, 1973), p. 81; J. A. Fitzmyer, "The Resurrection of Jesus Christ According to the New Testament," *The Month,* SNS, 20 (1987), p. 409; J. D. G. Dunn, *The Evidence for Jesus* (Louisville, Ky.: Westminster, 1985), p. 70; C. E. B. Cranfield, "The Resurrection
of Jesus Christ," *Expository Times* 101 (1990), p. 169; Peter Stuhlmacher, *Jesus of Nazareth—
Christ of Faith,* trans. Siegfried S. Shatzmann (Peabody, Mass.: Hendrickson, 1993), p. 8; Le-
ander E. Keck, *Who Is Jesus? History in Perfect Tense* (Columbia: University of South Carolina,
2000), p. 139; Meier, *A Marginal Jew,* vol. 2, *Mentor, Message and Miracle,* p. 139.

message, which centered on the resurrection. To do so, he made a second trip to Jerusalem specifically for the purpose of checking out his gospel preaching (Gal 2:1-10). Amazingly, he states his fear that perhaps he had been teaching the wrong message (Gal 2:2). Some think that Acts 15:1-35 describes an amazing third trip to Jerusalem to do the same.[13] Paul obviously desired to be absolutely positive of the gospel truth! Further, Paul was careful to ask his questions of the proper authorities—the chief apostles. In his initial trip, he met with Peter and James, the brother of Jesus (Gal 1:18-20). On the second occasion, he met with these same two men, plus the apostle John (Gal 2:9). Martin Hengel points out that "evidently the tradition of I Cor. 15.3 had been subjected to many tests" by Paul.[14]

It is easy to overlook the significance of these meetings. The four men who met together on the latter occasion were certainly the chief apostles in the early church, and each one had been an eyewitness of Jesus' resurrection appearances (1 Cor 15:5-7). Therefore, when Paul received their confirmation that his gospel was correct (Gal 2:9; cf. Acts 15:23-35), we have their assurance that Paul's message of Jesus' resurrection appearances agreed with their own experiences. Certainly, if they thought that Paul erred on the central fact of the gospel, this would have created grave problems, especially given the apostolic concern to insure doctrinal truth in the early church.

So Paul provides more than his own eyewitness testimony, as in (1) above. During his trips to inquire of the three senior apostles in Jerusalem, Paul passed their examination regarding his gospel proclamation. Their blessings assume their own eyewitness testimony concerning Jesus' resurrection appearances, since they had also experienced the risen Jesus. Here we are but one step removed from additional eyewitness testimony.

4. Not only did the other apostles confirm Paul's gospel message, but we also have the reverse testimony. After reporting a list of Jesus' resurrection appearances, Paul explains that he knew what the other apostles

---

[13]Others hold that the account in Acts 15 confirms the same meeting as that in Gal 2:1-10.

[14]Martin Hengel, *The Atonement: The Origins of the Doctrine in the New Testament,* trans. John Bowden (Philadelphia: Fortress, 1981), p. 38.

were preaching on this subject and that it was the same as his teaching about Jesus' appearances (1 Cor 15:11). Together, they proclaimed the risen Jesus (1 Cor 15:12, 15). So we have both the previous, more indirect apostolic confirmation of Paul's gospel message provided by the apostolic leadership, as well as Paul's firsthand, more direct approval of their resurrection message.

5. Insights into the earliest resurrection preaching are gleaned not only from the pre-Pauline report in 1 Corinthians 15. Other early creedal texts found in the New Testament also provide spotlights on the apostolic witness to the resurrection appearances. The book of Acts incorporates many of these early traditions, located in the sermons contained there.[15] Although not as unanimously as with the creed(s) in 1 Corinthians 15:3-8, a majority of critical scholars still hold that at least some of these snippets represent the earliest Christian gospel preaching.[16] Like other early traditions, they are identified by their brevity, lack of theological complexity, and because the structure, style and/or diction reflect language patterns other than the author's. Crucially for our purposes, the risen Jesus is the center of each of these traditions.

These Acts creeds could provide a window on the ancient world of apostolic preaching before a single New Testament book was written. John Drane thinks that these sermons in Acts are our "earliest evidence" for Jesus' resurrection and that this material "almost certainly goes back to the time immediately after the resurrection event is alleged to have taken place. . . . But there can be no doubt that in the first few chapters of Acts its author has preserved material from very early sources."[17] Ger-

---

[15]The condensed creedal segments are found within a number of the sermons in Acts: Acts 1:21-22; 2:22-36; 3:13-16; 4:8-10; 5:29-32; 10:39-43; 13:28-31; 17:1-3; 17:30-31; cf. Lk 24:34.

[16]For just a small sampling of these scholars, see Gerd Lüdemann, *Early Christianity According to the Traditions in Acts: A Commentary,* trans. John Bowden (Minneapolis: Fortress, 1989), pp. 47-49, 112-15; Hengel, *The Atonement,* p. 34; Pheme Perkins, *Resurrection: New Testament Witness and Contemporary Reflection* (Garden City, N.Y.: Doubleday, 1984), pp. 90, 228-31; Raymond E. Brown, *An Introduction to New Testament Christology* (Mahwah, N.J.: Paulist, 1994), pp. 112-13, 164; Fuller, *The Formation of the Resurrection Narratives,* pp. 44-45; Kloppenborg, p. 361; Johnson, *Living Jesus: Learning the Heart of the Gospel* (San Francisco: Harper Collins, 1999), p. 34; although older, two of the better studies are C. H. Dodd, *The Apostolic Preaching and Its Developments* (reprint, Grand Rapids, Mich.: Baker, 1980), pp. 17-31, and Max Wilcox, *The Semitisms of Acts* (Oxford: Clarendon, 1965), esp. pp. 79-80, 164-65.

[17]John Drane, *Introducing the New Testament* (San Francisco: Harper and Row, 1986), p. 99.

ald O'Collins concludes more specifically that Acts "incorporates resurrection formulae which stem from the thirties."[18]

6. We have been discussing the earliest apostolic witness to Jesus' resurrection appearances. It is seldom questioned by critical scholars that James, Jesus' brother, was an unbeliever and probably a skeptic during his brother's public ministry (Mk 3:21-35; Jn 7:5). Then, just a few years later, James is the pastor of the Jerusalem church, where Paul finds him when he went for his two visits (Gal 1:18-19; 2:1-10; cf. Acts 15:13-21). In between, the early pre-Pauline creed in 1 Corinthians 15:7 states that James met the risen Jesus. One can only imagine what transpired there!

While there may not seem at first look to be much textual data here, critical scholars find at least three major reasons for concluding that James was an unbeliever before he met the risen Jesus. John Meier states the case well. James's unbelief is attested by multiple independent sources.[19] Further, the criterion of coherence is satisfied in that Jesus frequently demanded that his disciples be willing to leave their family behind and follow him, even if it engendered their wrath, as it did with Jesus' own family. The criterion of embarrassment probably provides the strongest reason here, since it is highly unlikely that early church authors would make such potentially "deeply offensive" comments regarding both an esteemed leader as well as Jesus' own brother, unless they thought they were reporting facts.[20]

Fuller concludes that even if the pre-Pauline creed in 1 Corinthians 15:7 had never been recorded, "we should have to invent" an appearance to James to justify both his conversion as well as his promotion to the pastorate in Jerusalem, the largest of the early churches![21] The majority of scholars, including many skeptics, agree that James was converted by Jesus' appearance to him.[22]

---

[18]Gerald O'Collins, *Interpreting Jesus* (London: Geoffrey Chapman, 1983), pp. 109-10.

[19]The Jesus Seminar even thinks that two independent sources indicate that a teaching may be older than its source. See Funk, Hoover and the Jesus Seminar, *The Five Gospels*, p. 26.

[20]Meier, *A Marginal Jew*, vol. 2, *Mentor, Message and Miracle*, pp. 68-71.

[21]Fuller, *The Formation of the Resurrection Narratives*, p. 37.

[22]For instance, see Lüdemann, *The Resurrection of Jesus*, p. 109; Helmut Koester, *History & Literature of Early Christianity*, vol. 2 of *Introduction to the New Testament* (Philadelphia: For-

7. If Jesus' burial tomb was later found empty, this does not prove that a resurrection occurred. However, it adds some credibility to the disciples' claim to have seen the risen Jesus, since it both seriously complicates the search for a naturalistic hypothesis, as well as indicating that whatever happened most likely involved Jesus' body.

There are well over a dozen reasons supporting Jesus' empty tomb, only a few of which we will simply mention here. The Gospels are in complete agreement that women were the earliest witnesses to the empty tomb, a simply remarkable report since female testimony was generally disallowed in a law court for declarations on crucial topics. Thus, to fabricate this story with women as the central witnesses most likely would serve only to have the case dismissed without a hearing. This report only makes sense if it reflected what actually happened. Jerusalem is absolutely the last place on earth for Jesus' followers to proclaim that he had been raised, unless his grave was empty. Otherwise, a Sunday afternoon stroll would clearly indicate that the stone was still in place, revealing their erroneous message.

The empty tomb accounts are surprisingly attested by multiple sources, being found in almost every Gospel source. Ancient historian Paul Maier remarks, "Many facts from antiquity rest on just one ancient source, while two or three sources in agreement generally render the fact unimpeachable."[23]

The early pre-Pauline creed in 1 Corinthians 15:3-4 at least implies an empty tomb. The sequence involved in the triple "and that" phrases, especially for a Jew, intimates that if Jesus died, was buried, rose and appeared, then what had been living was placed in the ground and later emerged. In such a case, the tomb would have been vacated. What may be another early creed (Acts 13:29-31, 36-37) even more clearly indicates

---

tress, 1982), p. 84; John Shelby Spong, *The Easter Moment* (San Francisco: Harper and Row, 1987), p. 68; Wedderburn, *Beyond Resurrection,* p. 116; Funk, *Honest to Jesus* (San Francisco: Harper Collins, 1996), p. 33; Meier, *A Marginal Jew,* vol. 2, *Mentor, Message and Miracle,* pp. 70-71; Peter Stuhlmacher, "The Resurrection of Jesus and the Resurrection of the Dead," trans. Jonathan M. Whitlock, *Ex Auditu* 9 (1993), p. 49; E. P. Sanders, "But Did It Happen?" *The Spectator* 276 (1996), p. 17.

[23]Paul Maier, *In the Fulness of Time: A Historian Looks at Christmas, Easter and the Early Church* (San Francisco: Harper Collins, 1991), p. 197.

that Jesus was buried in a tomb, was raised and appeared.

Not only did the Jewish leaders not dispute the empty tomb, but their reported response even conceded it (Mt 28:11-15). So enemy attestation also supports the empty tomb.

While the empty tomb is not as unanimously held as are the other historical reasons that we have given for the disciples' experiences, most critical scholars still think that the tomb where Jesus was buried was later discovered to be empty.[24] J. D. G. Dunn firmly states: "I have to say quite forcefully: the probability is that the tomb was empty. As a matter of historical reconstruction, the weight of evidence points firmly to the conclusion." The alternative explanations are all worse.[25] Historian Michael Grant explains that "the historian . . . cannot justifiably deny the empty tomb" since normal historical criteria attest that, "the evidence is firm and plausible enough to necessitate the conclusion that the tomb was indeed found empty."[26]

8. Last, there is no question that the disciples' belief that they had actually seen Jesus after his death led to a radical transformation in their lives, even to the point of being willing to die for their faith. But since the question regarding the degree of the uniqueness here is the chief concern of the second section of this chapter, we will not belabor the point here.

We have listed eight different reasons that indicate why contemporary scholars almost without exception conclude that the disciples truly thought that Jesus had appeared alive to them after he had died on the cross. Paul's own eyewitness testimony, the exceptionally early date when he received the creed(s) recorded in 1 Corinthians 15:3-8, checking his own gospel message at least twice with the chief apostles who were also witnesses, and his knowledge of their eyewitness teaching on the resurrection appearances form a simply remarkable, interconnected

---

[24]My study of hundreds of scholarly sources on the resurrection, cited above, notes almost two dozen arguments for the empty tomb. About 75 percent of the surveyed scholars embrace one or more of the supporting arguments.

[25]Dunn, *The Evidence for Jesus*, p. 68.

[26]Michael Grant, *Jesus: An Historian's Review of the Gospels* (New York: Collier, 1992), p. 176. An excellent treatment of additional arguments for the empty tomb is William Lane Craig, "The Historicity of the Empty Tomb of Jesus," *New Testament Studies* 31 (1985): 39-67.

trail of evidence that is virtually unheard of in ancient documents. Eminent scholar Howard Clark Kee makes the astounding comment that Paul's research "can be critically examined and compared with other testimony from eyewitnesses of Jesus, just as one would evaluate evidence in a modern court or academic setting."[27]

Further, other early creedal witnesses such as those in Acts, the conversion of James the skeptic, the empty tomb and the disciples' transformation all provide support that the disciples were utterly convinced that they had seen the risen Jesus. Additional factors could be mentioned. For example, the centrality of the resurrection message in the early church provided ample opportunity for believers who were prepared to die for the message to repeatedly focus on its truth, but without refutation or recanting, as far as we know. And the Jewish leaders particularly had both a motive and the power to oppose a message that threatened their existence and came up empty-handed.[28]

No other hypothesis is even a viable rival to the conclusion that the early disciples at least thought that they had witnessed Jesus' appearances after he had died. But can we somehow move from the recognized historical fact that the disciples believed this to their actually having seen the risen Jesus? To make this move could well be the most crucial aspect of an historical argument for Jesus' resurrection appearances.

From conviction to event. Each of the eight reasons above points to the belief that Jesus was *seen* again after his death. In other words, the claim to which virtually all scholars agree is a *visual* claim. The disciples were sure that Jesus' person had impinged on their visual field. This is what Paul claimed. Peter agreed. So did Jesus' brother James. Further, the tomb was no longer occupied by his body. As a result, they were changed forever.

Even recent skeptical scholars agree. Koester asserts that "We are on

---

[27]Howard Clark Kee, *What Can We Know about Jesus?* (Cambridge: Cambridge University Press, 1990), pp. 1-2.

[28]For details on these two additional reasons, as well as much more information, including both factual and scholarly agreement, regarding the previous eight arguments, see Gary R. Habermas, *The Risen Jesus and Future Hope* (Lanham, Md.: Rowman and Littlefield, 2003), chap. 1.

much firmer ground with respect to the appearances of the risen Jesus and their effect." These appearances "cannot very well be questioned."[29] Bart Ehrman states that "we can say with complete certainty that some of his disciples at some later time insisted that he soon appeared to them. . . . Historians, of course, have no difficulty whatsoever speaking about the belief in Jesus' resurrection, since it is a matter of public record."[30] Traugott Holtz concludes that the disciples' "experience of resurrection . . . is in fact an undeniable historical event."[31] Lüdemann even reminds us that Paul's resurrection language is the language of real sight: "active sensual perception. . . . Paul is claiming a visual side to the appearance."[32] Moreover, Paul was teaching that Jesus appeared in his "transformed spiritual resurrection corporeality."[33]

It seems clear, then, that Jesus' disciples were utterly convinced that he had appeared to them after his death. It is granted by virtually all critical scholars because the data are extraordinarily strong. But how do we get from the disciples' resurrection *conviction* to the resurrection *event*, namely, to real appearances of the risen Jesus?

This may seem like a rather straightforward question, yet it can get a little slippery. Believers presumably would think that they were quite justified in their stance that reasons like those above establish their position. After all, each of the evidences points to a visual event that changed the disciples' lives, which they were utterly convinced was an appearance of their best friend.

Unbelievers would seemingly have to reply by severing the connection between what the disciples thought and what really happened. To do this, they might move in two directions, by indirectly or directly replying to a case like that which we have outlined here.

Initially, perhaps they might try an indirect maneuver by posing vari-

---

[29]Koester, *History and Literature*, p. 84.

[30]Bart Ehrman, *Jesus: Apocalyptic Prophet of the New Millennium* (New York: Oxford University Press, 1999), pp. 230-31.

[31]My translation of the German text in Traugott Holtz, "Kenntnis von Jesus und Kenntnis Jesu," *Theologische Literaturzeitung* 104 (1979), p. 10.

[32]Lüdemann, *The Resurrection of Jesus*, p. 50; cf. p. 37.

[33]Gerd Lüdemann, *What Really Happened to Jesus: A Historical Approach to the Resurrection*, with Alf Özen, trans. John Bowden (Louisville, Ky.: Westminster John Knox, 1995), p. 103.

ous a priori objections[34] that, whatever the data, Jesus was simply not raised from the dead. These sorts of miraculous events just do not occur in our world. These philosophical responses take us far beyond our study of the resurrection of Jesus, especially in that such objections are typically not concerned with this event at all. Usually, they make more general inquiries regarding the background information or the nature of the evidence, both areas where the resurrection excels.[35]

Or, another indirect move is to respond with the agnostic plea that we do not know what occurred. The disciples indeed believed that they saw Jesus, but we cannot determine a cause.

This fence-straddling approach is very difficult to maintain, since one must dodge many factual considerations, when just one might cause the thesis to topple. A few brief and general problems will have to suffice here. (1) The agnostic position smacks of rejecting the possibility of a resurrection before following the evidence to its conclusion or even re-senting that the discussion might lead to the truth of Christianity.[36] (2) To assert that we cannot discover a cause for the disciples' faith assumes its own burden of proof. But on what grounds should such an assertion be made?

More crucially, (3) we have plenty of evidence already to decide the case, *especially* since we used only those data that virtually all critical scholars accept. So critics must not reject or pull up short of the results that are indicated by their own research![37] (4) The objection often does not level complaints against this specific resurrection data, so believers

---

[34]It might be noted here that not all a priori questions are automatically ruled out as question begging. Some ask by various means if it is possible to postulate in advance a reason for questioning certain occurrences.

[35]For distinctions between various sorts of a priori arguments, along with a detailed response to several specific examples, see Gary R. Habermas and Michael Licona, *The Case for the Resurrection of Jesus* (Grand Rapids, Mich.: Kregel, 2004), chap. 9. For a more technical treatment, see Habermas, *The Risen Jesus and Future Hope,* esp. chap. 2.

[36]For details on how Jesus' resurrection and other relevant data lead to a case for the heart of Christianity, see Habermas, *The Risen Jesus and Future Hope,* chaps. 1-6. A more popular approach is detailed in Gary R. Habermas, "Evidential Apologetics," in *Five Views on Apologetics,* ed. Stephen B. Cowan (Grand Rapids, Mich.: Zondervan, 2000).

[37]For additional comments on how these methodological considerations used by critical scholars lead to the historicity of the resurrection, see esp. Habermas, *The Risen Jesus and Future Hope,* chap. 1.

are more than justified in holding their view in light of the many evidences for this event.

Our major methodology is applicable to this agnostic position. Throughout, we have used data that are recognized by virtually all scholars. These same minimal historical facts that even agnostics accept clearly indicate that more than an undefined something occurred to Jesus' disciples. We pointed out above that all the evidence supports a visual claim—the disciples thought they saw Jesus after his death. By failing to account viably for the majority of the recognized facts that even they generally accept, like the eight mentioned above, agnostics miss the cause of the disciples' experiences. But it is insufficient to simply stop there and refuse to investigate further. What they fail to explain may be precisely the data that are capable of establishing the resurrection appearances as the most likely explanation, as pointed out below. As Fuller asserts, what we know "therefore requires that the historian postulate some other event" besides the disciples' faith. We must ascertain "the cause of the Easter faith . . . outside of their belief."[38]

Precisely in order to address directly these facts, the more popular approach through the centuries has been to pose a naturalistic theory to account for the data. Such a move basically attempts to allow for historical facts where the evidence is the strongest, while veering off in a natural direction before getting to the punch line involving the resurrection. Here they need to propose an alternative scenario: "Jesus didn't really rise from the dead. What really happened was (fill in the blank)."

However, this is probably the most difficult method of all. In fact, when faced with this option, the vast majority of critical scholars opt out. They are often well aware that when an option is chosen, the weight of the known historical facts comes crashing down against their proposal. In fact, they are so well aware of this eventuality that only a few attempt it. Even among scholars, it is generally conceded that none of these options work.

For instance, Raymond E. Brown calls these theses "gratuitous charges."[39] Dunn concludes: "alternative interpretations of the data fail

---

[38]Fuller, *The Formation of the Resurrection Narratives,* pp. 169, 181.

to provide a more satisfactory explanation" than the resurrection.[40] Davis responds: "All of the alternative hypotheses with which I am familiar are historically weak; some are so weak that they collapse of their own weight once spelled out. . . . The alternative theories that have been proposed are not only weaker but far weaker at explaining the available historical evidence."[41] Robinson notes that "it is indeed very difficult to dismiss [Jesus' appearances] and still find a credible explanation."[42]

Given that the skeptic would have to account for the disciples being sure that they had seen the risen Jesus, the most popular naturalistic response (although still a real minority rejoinder) is to suggest that they saw hallucinations. A detailed critique is impossible here, but we can provide a list of some of the myriad problems with such a response.[43]

For example, (1) hallucinations are private experiences, while clearly we have strong reasons to assert that groups of people claimed to have seen Jesus. (2) The disciples' despair indicates that they were not in the proper frame of mind to see hallucinations. (3) Perhaps the most serious problem is that there were far too many different times, places and personalities involved in the appearances. To believe that with each of these varying persons and circumstances a separate hallucination occurred borders on credulity. (4) Further, on this view, Jesus' body should still have been located safely in the tomb! (5) Hallucinations very rarely transform lives, but we have no records of any of the eyewitnesses recanting their faith. Two huge problems are the conversions of both (6) Paul and (7) James, neither of whom had a desire to see Jesus. These are just a very few of the serious questions for this alternative view. All other proposed natural hypotheses have similarly been disproven.[44]

Now we are ready to state a general principle for moving from the dis-

---

[39] Brown, *An Introduction to New Testament Christology*, p. 163; cf. pp. 163-67.

[40] Dunn, *The Evidence for Jesus*, p. 76. Another more recent and similar testimony is that of N. T. Wright, "Christian Origins and the Resurrection of Jesus: The Resurrection of Jesus as a Historical Problem," *Sewanee Theological Review* 41 (1998): 118-22.

[41] Stephen T. Davis, "Is Belief in the Resurrection Rational?" *Philo* 2 (1999): 57-58.

[42] J. A. T. Robinson, *Can We Trust the New Testament?* (Grand Rapids, Mich.: Eerdmans, 1977), p. 124.

[43] For a treatment of the latest trends plus a detailed critique, see Gary R. Habermas, "Explaining Away Jesus' Resurrection: The Recent Revival of Hallucination Theories," *Christian Research Journal* 23 (2001), pp. 26-31, 47-49.

ciples' convictions to the historical resurrection appearances. The strong reasons for supporting the disciples' experiences of seeing Jesus, in conjunction with the failure of alternative theses, even by critical standards, indicates that by far the most likely scenario is that the disciples *actually* saw the risen Jesus. Further, the more thoroughly the natural hypotheses fail, the more likely are the historical resurrection appearances. To state this principle more briefly as a mock mathematical equation: given a reasonable explanation, the disciples' experiences plus the failure of alternatives equals the historical resurrection appearances of Jesus.

This follows because, due to the failure of alternatives, the impressive evidences that make the case for the disciples' experiences as strong as anything in the New Testament now become impressive evidences for the resurrection appearances themselves. In brief, the disciples' experiences are recognized for what they actually were: Jesus' postdeath appearances.

THE UNIQUENESS OF THE DISCIPLES' TRANSFORMATIONS

Today, many have been willing to die for their religious or even political convictions. From communists to Muslims to Christians, we are well-acquainted with examples. However, many throughout history have also propagated false beliefs. What separates Jesus' disciples from these latter cases? Is their transformation in any way unique?

Virtually no one disputes the disciples' radical transformations. Before Jesus died, his followers abandoned and even denied him.[45] In contrast, after the resurrection the remainder of their lives were undeniably and radically altered. They were willing to die for their faith, and many were martyred.[46] The disciples' metamorphoses are also visible from their eth-

---

[44]In "Explaining Away Jesus' Resurrection," I list nineteen different problems for various forms of the hallucination theory. For a readable treatment of many other potential naturalistic responses, see the more than one hundred pages devoted to the topic in Habermas and Licona, *The Case for the Resurrection of Jesus,* esp. chaps. 7-9.

[45]Some examples are found in Mt 26:56, 69-74; Mk 14:50, 66-72; Lk 22:55-72; Jn 18:25-27.

[46]See Acts 2:41-47; 4:1-4, 8-21, 29-31; 5:17-32, 40-42. For their willingness to die, see Jn 21:18-19; Acts 7:57-60; 12:1-3; 21:13; 25:11; Rom 14:8; 1 Cor 15:30-32; 2 Cor 4:7-14; 11:23-32; Phil 1:20-24; cf. 2 Pet 1:13-15. We have early references to the martyrdoms of Peter and Paul (Clement of Rome *Corinthians* 5) and two accounts of the martyrdom of James, the brother of Jesus (Josephus *Antiquities* 20:9:1; Hegesippus in Eusebius *Ecclesiastical History* 2:23). Eu-

ics, evangelism and other teachings, reflected throughout the New Testament. Extrabiblical sources, both secular and Christian, also attest to these changes.[47]

What is responsible for the changes in the disciples? The New Testament is unmistakably clear that Jesus' resurrection appearances were the intervening events, the catalyst between their confusion and exaltation. Critical scholars are in total agreement here. Ben Meyer states it clearly: "That it was the Easter experiences which affected [the disciples'] transformation is beyond reasonable doubt."[48] Hugo Staudinger agrees: "Only the appearances of Jesus brought about a new change of mood in them."[49] N. T. Wright declares: "the first generation of Christians . . . announced and celebrated the victory of Jesus over evil. . . . That was the basis of their remarkable joy."[50]

Admittedly, life conversions have happened for untrue causes. But I would assert that there is a *qualitative* difference between what occurred to the disciples and what we see today. Granted, there is the often-acknowledged precept that those who are willing to die for a cause genuinely believe in it. The disciples did suffer for their belief in a cause, like everyone else. But here the main similarities between the disciples and others stop.

Distinctly *unlike* the other cases, as we have seen in this chapter, the disciples died for more than being sold out to a cause. They willingly gave their lives *precisely because they were absolutely convinced that they had seen the risen Jesus*. In short, their transformations were not caused by an ideology, like the others, but their new outlook was expressly based on a personal experience—their profound conviction that

---

sebius records that James the brother of John, Peter and Paul all died for their faith (*Ecclesiastical History* 2:9, 25).

[47]Secular references appear in Tacitus (*Annals* 15.44), Josephus's disputed paragraph (*Antiquities* 18.3.3) and in Mara Bar-Serapion's letter to his son (located in the British Museum). Christian testimonies are recorded by Clement of Rome (*Corinthians* 42), Ignatius (*Smyrneans* 3) and *Barnabas* (5).

[48]Ben Meyer, *The Aims of Jesus* (London: SCM, 1979), p. 60.

[49]Hugo Staudinger, "The Resurrection of Jesus Christ as Saving Event and as 'Object' of Historical Research," *Scottish Journal of Theology* 36 (1983), p. 321.

[50]N. T. Wright, *Jesus and the Victory of God,* vol. 2 of *Christian Origins and the Question of God* (Minneapolis: Fortress, 1997), p. 659.

they had actually seen the risen Jesus.

Apart from their resurrection experiences, there would have been no transformations, for without this event their faith was vain (1 Cor. 15:14, 17). As Paul argues, they actually saw Jesus (1 Cor 15:1-11), and this is what confirmed their eternal life, for if Jesus was raised, so they would be raised (1 Cor 15:17-20). Death had no more sting for them (1 Cor 15:53-55). Peter similarly but surprisingly declares that because Jesus' resurrection secured heaven, even the serious struggles of life could be faced with rejoicing (1 Pet 1:3-7).

Think about it. If your eternity depended on Jesus being raised from the dead, which would you rather have—a strong conviction or your actually having seen the risen Jesus along with an even stronger conviction precisely because you did so? In other words, which circumstance would carry a greater conviction: your being convinced centuries later that you ought to follow someone's teachings, or simply the knowledge that you actually had been with that same person last night, however unusual the particulars? Now can you imagine the disciples' joy when they saw Jesus alive—face to face, gazing straight into his eyes? In that moment when they saw Jesus, heaven entered earth's realm and eternity burst upon them. After all, what is a resurrection appearance of Jesus? When the disciples saw the risen Jesus, they saw walking, talking, eternal life! No wonder they were assured of heaven![51]

So here is the chief difference between Jesus' disciples and others who hold religious convictions. In addition to their fortified convictions, the disciples had an evidenced experience that no one else ever has, before or since.[52] They saw heaven in the person of Jesus Christ. And although believers today have not seen Jesus (1 Pet 1:8), we have the next best thing—very powerful evidence that the disciples did!

CONCLUSION

I contend that the most crucial aspect of an argument for the historicity

---

[51]For an itemized argument from Jesus' resurrection to eternal life, see Habermas, *The Risen Jesus and Future Hope,* chaps. 1-7.

[52]Gary R. Habermas, "Resurrection Claims in Non-Christian Religions," *Religious Studies* 25 (1989):167-77.

of Jesus' resurrection is that the disciples were totally convinced that they had seen appearances of the risen Jesus. The community of critical scholars holds that these experiences are thoroughly historical. These same scholars nearly always recognize that natural alternative responses do not explain the data. Therefore, the impressive evidences that establish the disciples' experiences, especially in light of the failure of these alternatives, now become impressive evidences for the resurrection appearances themselves.

Further, that these appearances were the reason for the disciples' transformations separates them from other religious and political metamorphoses. That the disciples actually saw the risen Jesus bases their convictions of heaven on their foretaste of that reality, which they had personally witnessed. Excitingly, although they have not seen the resurrected Jesus, believers today have the next best thing—very powerful evidence that the disciples did! The argument is firm and heaven still follows!

FOR FURTHER READING

Craig, William Lane, and John Dominic Crossan. *Will the Real Jesus Please Stand Up?* Edited by Paul Copan. Grand Rapids, Mich.: Baker, 1998.

Craig, William Lane, and Gerd Lüdemann. *Jesus' Resurrection: Fact or Figment?* Edited by Paul Copan and Ronald Tacelli. Downers Grove, Ill.: InterVarsity Press, 2000.

Habermas, Gary R. *The Risen Jesus and Future Hope.* Lanham, Md.: Rowman & Littlefield, 2003.

———. *The Historical Jesus: Ancient Evidence for the Life of Christ.* Rev. ed. Joplin, Mo.: College Press, 1996.

Habermas, Gary R., and Michael Licona. *The Case for the Resurrection of Jesus.* Grand Rapids, Mich.: Kregel, 2004.

Wright, N. T. *The Resurrection of the Son of God.* Vol. 3 of *Christian Origins and the Question of God.* Minneapolis: Fortress, 2003.

PART 4

PHILOSOPHICAL AND CULTURAL CHALLENGES TO CHRISTIAN FAITH

J. P. Moreland

THE STRUCTURE OF THIS BOOK FOLLOWS A VERY CAREFULLY CRAFTED PROGRES-sion of ideas. In part 1 we tackled the whole question of faith and reason in order to defend the very practice of apologetics. Having given a rationale and some practical advice for its employment, parts 2 and 3 took on the task of providing a defense of the existence of God and the truth of Christianity. Again, the order is important. If monotheism is true, then it is clearly possible that God could perform miracles in human history and reveal himself in ways consistent with his reality as known from the creation itself and the arguments for his existence. So understood, the arguments of part 2 do not merely provide grounds for God's reality; they also provide some information about his nature (that he is wise, intelligent, good, powerful and excellent in all ways appropriate to being a person). Part 3 captured the search to see if God has in fact revealed himself in a special way, and the case for the New Testament's depiction of Christ and the credibility of miracles, especially the resurrection of the Lord Jesus, constitute the appropriate end of that search.

However, no case is complete if it considers only evidence in its favor, and the case for the Christian worldview is no exception to this rule. So in parts 4 and 5, we provide a statement and response to some important philosophical, cultural and religious challenges frequently raised against

Christianity or aspects of the Christian worldview. In this section, the focus is on philosophical and cultural challenges.

Chapter twelve jumps into the fire and addresses the most frequently raised objection to the Christian faith—the problem of evil. Ronald Nash begins his chapter on the problem of evil by admitting that most people see the problem as the most serious intellectual challenge for the Christian faith. According to Nash, there are times when the religious believer must assume the burden of proof, as when for example it might appear that a Christian has to offer arguments for the existence of God. In the case of the problem of evil, however, this clearly is a situation where opponents of Christianity have the obligation to offer arguments against the existence of God. Since the burden of proof in this case lies with the anti-theist, Nash argues, one task of the believer is to show that the existence of evil does not undermine the rationality of belief in God. As he does in many writings, Nash uses a worldview approach to deal with the problem of evil. After all, the problem of evil arises out of major elements of the Christian's approach to God. But the Christian worldview has more than enough resources to blunt the anti-theist's development of the theoretical problem of evil and the Christian's challenge to deal with the personal problem of evil.

A Christian worldview includes an immaterialist view of reality in this sense—God, angels (good and bad), and animal and human souls are spiritual and not physical realities. More specifically, the human being is made in the image of God, and this doctrine includes the immaterial nature of the human person so constituted in that image. And the Christian view of the afterlife requires a soul that survives in a disembodied intermediate state between death and the final resurrection. Yet today it is widely thought that belief in an immaterial soul has been scientifically discredited and a physicalist view of human beings is the only reasonable position. After clarifying some important concepts, in chapter thirteen J. P. Moreland presents arguments for the claim that both consciousness and the soul that contains it are immaterial, spiritual realities and not physical.

In chapter fourteen, Douglas Groothuis takes up the crucial topic of the existence and nature of truth, the value of logic and the postmodern challenge to these notions. Groothuis provides a skillful and timely critique of the basic ideas of secular postmodernism regarding truth, logic and language. He argues that these notions are generally hostile to the Christian worldview as well as intrinsically illogical and should be critiqued as part of the task of Christian apologetics. According to Groothuis, postmodernism has little if anything of value to offer Christian witness in the contemporary world.

While chapters twelve through fourteen respond to philosophical challenges to Christianity, chapters fifteen and sixteen turn to an examination of cultural challenges. In chapter fifteen, theologian Michael Bauman examines the concern that is often raised against Christians who seek to shape and influence our public life by suggesting policies and laws that take a particular moral point of view. It is usually expressed in the form of the crude assertion: you can't legislate morality! Bauman responds that it is not only permissible but that it is inescapable, that no matter which way the law goes it will legislate someone's moral point of view. Furthermore, those laws, for good or for ill, will help shape the character of the people under their authority.

Finally, in chapter sixteen, philosopher and legal scholar Francis Beckwith responds to what may be the most ferocious cultural attack currently waged against theism, namely, the attempt to silence critics of evolutionary theory in the public schools who sometimes argue for some sort of Intelligent Design (ID) theory of origins. Beckwith argues that it would not violate the U.S. Constitution if a school board or legislature either allowed or prescribed the teaching of ID, or nonreligious criticisms of evolution, in its public school science classrooms.

12

THE PROBLEM OF EVIL

Ronald H. Nash

THE MOST SERIOUS INTELLECTUAL OBSTACLE THAT STANDS BETWEEN MANY PEO-
ple and religious faith is the problem of evil. Because of the complexity
of issues that make up this problem, I will devote a considerable part of
the space available to me providing a map of the terrain through which
thoughtful people must journey in their quest for some kind of plausible
answer. The reason many people never find their way through this terrain is their failure to spend time preparing for the journey. The first step
in this process, I believe, is getting oriented to worldview thinking.

WORLDVIEW THINKING

Whether we know it or not—whether we like it or not—each of us has
a worldview. These worldviews function as interpretive conceptual
schemes to explain why we see the world as we do, why we often think
and act as we do. Competing worldviews often come into conflict. These
clashes may be as innocuous as a simple argument between people or
as serious as a war between two nations.

In its simplest terms, a worldview is a set of beliefs about the most
important issues in life. The philosophical systems of great thinkers such
as Plato and Aristotle were worldviews. Every mature rational human being, each reader of this book, has his or her own worldview just as surely
as Plato did. It seems sometimes that few have any idea what that worldview is or even that they have one. Yet achieving awareness of our
worldview is one of the most important things we can do to enhance

self-understanding. Insight into the worldviews of others is essential to an understanding of what makes them tick.

Implicit in all this is the additional point that these worldview beliefs should be logically consistent. A fancy term that can be useful here is *conceptual system,* by which I mean a pattern or arrangement of concepts (ideas). A worldview, then, is a conceptual system by which we consciously or unconsciously place or fit everything we believe and by which we interpret and judge reality.

Worldviews are double-edged swords. An inadequate conceptual system can, like improper eyeglasses, hinder our efforts to understand God, the world and ourselves. The right conceptual system can suddenly bring everything into proper focus. But the choice among competing worldviews involves a number of difficult questions. Because my own worldview is Christian theism, it will be convenient for me to illustrate several points in terms of my Christian commitment. That also seems fair since the religious worldview that is often thought to be compromised by the problem of evil is Christianity.

VIEWING CHRISTIANITY AS A WORLDVIEW

As Francis J. Beckwith pointed out in this book's introduction, instead of thinking of Christianity as a collection of theological bits and pieces to be believed or debated, Christians should approach their faith as a conceptual system, as a total world-and-life view. Naturally, this is true of any competing worldview be it one of the major theistic systems such as Judaism and Islam or a nontheistic religion such as Buddhism or Shinto or an antireligious system such as naturalism.[1] Once people understand that both Christianity and its adversaries in the world of ideas are worldviews, they will be in a better position to judge the relative merits of the total Christian system.[2]

The case for or against Christian theism should be made and evaluated in terms of total systems. Christianity is not simply a religion that

---

[1]By naturalism I mean what is described in other chapters of this book as metaphysical naturalism.

[2]Obviously, Christianity is more than a set of beliefs. More importantly, it is a relationship between the individual believer and God based upon those beliefs.

tells humans how they may be forgiven, however important this information is. Christianity is also a total world-and-life view. The Christian faith has important things to say about the whole of human life. Once Christians understand in a systematic way how the options to Christianity are also worldviews, they will be in a better position to justify their choice of Christianity rationally. The reason many people reject Christianity is not due to their problems with one or two isolated issues; it is the result of their anti-Christian conceptual system, which leads them to reject information and arguments that for believers provide support for the Christian worldview. Every worldview has questions it appears unable to answer satisfactorily. One might wish that all Christians were able effectively to defend their faith; therefore, our important task is to equip ourselves so that we are able to show detractors that the Christian worldview is superior rationally, morally and existentially[3] to any alternative system.

Still another reason for spending a little time unpacking elements of the Christian worldview is the fact that Christians should be faithful to what their worldview teaches about the problem of evil. When tempted to abandon their worldview, they need to understand the nature of the competing worldviews they might have to consider as a replacement for their current worldview.

THE MAJOR ELEMENTS OF A WORLDVIEW

A well-rounded worldview includes beliefs in at least five major areas: God, ultimate reality (metaphysics), knowledge (epistemology), ethics and humankind. My need to be brief allows me time to discuss only the first of these areas, God. Of course, the existence and nature of God are linked essentially to the major issue of this chapter, the problem of evil.

The existence and nature of God. The most important element of any worldview is what it says or does not say about God. Worldviews differ greatly on this matter. Does God exist? What is the nature of God?

---

[3]My use of the word *existentially* here has nothing to do with any of the forms of existential philosophy. I am referring to the fact that any worldview must be such that those who accept it intellectually can also live what they profess. Competing worldviews need to be tested both in the philosophy classroom and in the laboratory of life.

Is there only one true God? Is God a personal being, that is, is God the kind of being who can know, love and act? Or is God an impersonal force or power? Because of conflicting views about the nature of God, such systems as Buddhism, Hinduism, Shintoism and Zoroastrianism are not only different religions, they embrace different worldviews. Because Christianity, Judaism and Islam are examples of theism, conservative adherents of these religions hold to worldviews that have more in common than they do with dualistic, polytheistic and pantheistic systems.[4]

The Christian worldview is theistic in the sense that it believes in the existence of one supremely powerful and personal God. Theism differs from polytheism in its affirmation that there is only one God (Deut 6:4). It parts company with the various forms of pantheism by insisting that God is personal and must not be confused with the world that is his creation. Theism must also be distinguished from panentheism, the position that regards the world as an eternal being that God needs in much the same way a human soul needs a body. Theists also reject panentheistic attempts to limit God's power and knowledge, which have the effect of making the God of panentheism a finite being.[5] Other important attributes of God, such as his holiness, justice and love, are described in Scripture. Historical Christian theism is also trinitarian. The doctrine of the Trinity reflects the Christian conviction that the Father, the Son and the Holy Spirit are three distinct centers of consciousness sharing fully in the one divine nature and in the activities of the other persons of the Trinity.

What is the problem of evil? The problem of evil is grounded on the fact that a number of related and essential beliefs about God appear

---

[4]A dualistic system teaches the existence of two supreme beings; an example would be the ancient position known as Manichaeism. A polytheistic religion believes in many gods, while a pantheistic system tends to regard all of reality as divine in some sense.

[5]For a more complete discussion, see Ronald Nash, *The Concept of God* (Grand Rapids, Mich.: Zondervan, 1983). Panentheism can be thought of as a position somewhere between theism's belief in a personal, almighty, all-knowing God and the impersonal god of pantheism that is identical in some way with nature of the world order. While the god of panentheism is not identical with the world, this god and the world necessarily coexist eternally. Another basic feature of panentheism is the denial of the view that God can act as an efficient cause, a belief that precludes any belief in either creation or in such miracles as the incarnation or the resurrection.

to be incompatible with the evil we encounter in the world. Christians believe that God is totally good (omnibenevolent), all-knowing (omniscient) and all-powerful (omnipotent). Christians also believe that God created the world. The difficulties that these beliefs seem to engender with respect to evil look like this:

If God is good and loves all human beings, it is reasonable to believe that he wants to deliver the creatures he loves from evil and suffering.

If God is all-knowing, it is reasonable to believe that he knows how to deliver his creatures from evil and suffering.

If God is all-powerful, it is reasonable to believe that he is able to deliver his creatures from evil and suffering.

Given these claims, it seems to follow that God wants to eliminate evil, that God knows how to eliminate evil, and that God has the power to eliminate evil. But evil exists. In fact, great amounts of evil exist. Indeed, great amounts of apparently senseless and purposeless evil seem to exist. It seems reasonable to believe that God doesn't want to eliminate evil (thus casting doubt on his goodness) or doesn't know how to eliminate evil (raising questions about his knowledge) or lacks the power. In short, the existence of evil seems inconsistent with our belief in God's goodness or omniscience or power. Troubled by their reflection on these difficulties, many have found it easy to take the additional step and conclude that the existence of evil in the world makes it unlikely that God exists.

Thinking Christians appear to be stuck between a rock and a hard place. They cannot deny any of the factors that make up the problem of evil. They can hardly deny that the world God created contains large amounts of evil, much of it apparently gratuitous or meaningless. But as theists, these Christians must affirm their belief that this world with all its evil was created by a good, loving, omnipotent and omniscient God. The challenge for theists is to show that the existence of the evils we find in this world fit or are consistent with the Christian view of God and the world. In other words, we must explain how the conceptual system that is the Christian worldview is consistent with the evil we find in the world.

TWO KINDS OF EVIL

A good place to begin our downsizing of the problem of evil is rec-

ognizing the difference between two kinds of evil: moral evil and natural evil. Moral evil results from the choices and actions of human
beings. When the question *why* is asked about some moral evil, the
answer will include a reference to something that humans did or did
not do. Moral evil sometimes results when humans act, for example,
by shooting a gun. But moral evil may also occur as a result of human
inaction. Perhaps someone could have prevented the person from
getting the gun and didn't. So moral evil is evil brought about by human choices and actions; any other kind of evil is what we call natural evil. The class of natural evils includes such things as earth-
quakes, tornadoes and diseases not resulting from human choices.
Many wise people believe the two types of evil require different
kinds of answers.

The Theoretical Versus the Personal Problem of Evil

It is one thing to deal with evil on a purely theoretical or philosophical
level. It can be something quite different to encounter evil in a personal
way. Sitting in a philosophy classroom and thinking about the problem
of evil is obviously different from struggling with the news that a loved
one has just died in an automobile accident. At the moment when one
is being hammered existentially by some particular instance of evil, it is
easy to forget that some philosophical argument once seemed to suggest
answers as to why evil exists. When someone is troubled by aspects of
the theoretical or philosophical problem of evil, the assistance of a good
philosopher or apologist may help. But when we are confronted by the
personal problem of evil, what we may need is a wise and caring friend,
pastor or counselor.

The distinction between the theoretical and personal problems of evil
is relevant to events in the life of the Christian writer C. S. Lewis. One of
Lewis's more influential books, *The Problem of Pain,* offers his answers
to the theoretical problem of evil. I am one of many who believe there
are some very good arguments in that book. However, after Lewis met
and then married Joy Gresham, he learned the painful truth about the
personal problem of evil. His wife's eventual death from cancer after a

long period of suffering plunged Lewis into a time of doubt and depression. Now he was confronted by the personal problem of evil, and the philosophical arguments in his earlier book seemed to offer little help. After Joy's death, Lewis wrote a significantly different book titled *A Grief Observed*. It and *The Problem of Pain* should be read together to show what different steps must be taken to deal with both facets of the problem of evil.

EVIL AND TWO ALTERNATIVES TO THE CHRISTIAN WORLDVIEW

The problems that Christians appear to have with the evil in God's creation are supposed to drive Christians to abandon belief in the Christian God and turn to a different religious worldview such as dualism, pantheism or panentheism, or to an antireligious, materialistic and atheistic worldview known as naturalism. Limitations of space and time make it necessary to focus on only two of these alternatives, namely, religious dualism and metaphysical naturalism.[6]

Religious dualism. Religious dualism is a very old alternative to the Christian view of evil. In place of the one good God of historic Christian theism, many people have tried to explain evil in terms of two gods or supreme beings, one good and the other evil. According to this dualistic worldview, the good god (thought of in terms of Light) and the evil god (Darkness) are coeternal and coequal in power. Neither can defeat the other. The battle between Good and Evil has already been going on forever and will continue forever into the future.

Variations of this view can be found in the ancient Persian religion known as Zoroastrianism. Advocates of this religion can still be found in some areas of present-day Iran. Another manifestation of this kind of dualism occurred in a religious sect known as Manichaeanism. Augustine of North Africa held this view before his eventual conversion to Christianity. Large numbers of people in contemporary Christendom have

---

[6]One alternative to Christian theism that has gained much influence in recent years is the system known as panentheism or process theology. Because there is not time to cover this subject in this chapter, interested readers are directed to Nash, *The Concept of God*, or Ronald Nash, ed., *Process Theology* (Grand Rapids, Mich.: Baker, 1987).

been bitten by the dualistic bug. It should be noted that the being that
Christians call Satan or the devil is not a party to this kind of dualism.
Scripture clearly teaches that Satan is a created being and not an eternal
god whose power matches that of the Christian God.

There is a short, clear and powerful refutation of the kind of dualism
I have described. I will develop the argument in three steps.

Step 1: How do we know which God is the good one? Religious dualism
can be challenged by asking people how they know which of their two
gods is the good one. Of course, most people will reply that the god
who encourages humans to kill, steal, rape, lie and so on, is the evil god.
And, they will assure us, the god who commands us to love, tell the
truth, protect the innocent and so on, is the good god. But what is the
ground for such claims? Perhaps the god who commands us to kill, steal
and rape is the good god. One way to avoid absurdities like this is to
appeal to a standard that is higher or more ultimate than the gods of
Light and Darkness. Only if such a standard exists can we identify which
of the two gods is the good one.

Step 2: What is the content of the absolute standard? Unless there is an
absolute and objective standard by which we can judge dualism's two
candidates for god, there is no definitive way for humans to know which
god is the good one. But there seem to be two possibilities: the ultimate
standard might be Absolute Goodness or it might be Absolute Evil. Are
there compelling reasons that tip the scales in favor of one of these two
options? According to Lewis, there is a persuasive argument in favor of
the view that the ultimate standard in such a case must be Good rather
than Evil. Lewis argues that evil is always parasitic upon the good. As we
know, a parasite is an organism that survives by living in or off of a host
organism while contributing nothing to the survival of the host. Two examples of parasites are tapeworms and mistletoe.

In order for a parasite to grow and survive, it must prey upon a
healthy organism. The parasite needs its host; the host is not dependent
upon the parasite. Following this analogy, Lewis states that the Good is
primary and Evil is always a corruption of some prior good. It would be
odd to contend that the healthy human body is the parasite and the tape-
worm is the host. In the conflict between Good and Evil, Goodness is

prior, and Evil is the corruption of the Good. And so, Lewis contends, when we seek the ultimate standard to judge whether Light or Darkness is the good god, that standard must be the Absolute Good.

Step 3: Bad news for dualism. And so, we learn that dualism requires an appeal to one, monistic principle; without such an ultimate principle, we could never know which god is the good one. We also learn that the one, ultimate, monistic principle is Good. And once we recognize that there must be one ultimate Good that stands over the finite gods of Light and Darkness, it follows that neither of dualism's two gods can be God. Proper reflection about the two deities of dualism leads us to the existence of one absolutely good Being. To rescue dualism from absurdity, we must become believers in one good God. Since dualism turns out to be a logically self-defeating position, it obviously offers no help at all in human efforts to resolve the problem of evil.

AN ANTIRELIGIOUS ALTERNATIVE TO CHRISTIAN THEISM: NATURALISM

For much of the twentieth century, the worldview of naturalism has been the major antagonist of the Christian faith in nations like the United States. There is little doubt that naturalism is the preferred worldview of many who seek to use the problem of evil as a defeater[7] for the Christian worldview.

The central claim of metaphysical naturalism is that nothing exists outside the material, mechanistic (that is, nonpurposeful), natural order. My discussion will focus on naturalists who are what we call physicalists, people who insist that everything that exists can be reduced to physical or material entities. A naturalist believes that the physical universe is the sum total of all that is. In the famous words of Carl Sagan (1934-1996), "The universe is all that is, or ever was, or ever will be."

For a naturalist, the universe is analogous to a sealed box. Everything that happens inside the box (the natural order) is caused by or is explicable in terms of other things that exist within the box. Nothing, includ-

---

[7]In contemporary philosophic parlance, a defeater is an argument that functions for some person as a reason to reject a particular belief.

ing God, exists outside the box; therefore, nothing outside the box that we call the universe or cosmos or nature can have any causal effect within the box.

Philosopher Bertrand Russel summarized his view of naturalism in the following words:

> Brief and powerless is Man's life; on him and all his race the slow, sure doom falls pitiless and dark. Blind to good and evil, reckless of destruction, omnipotent matter rolls on its relentless way; for Man, condemned today to lose his dearest tomorrow, himself to pass through the gate of darkness, it remains only to cherish, ere yet the blow falls, the lofty thoughts that ennoble his little day.[8]

Naturalism and the Christian faith are natural opponents in the world of ideas. If one of them is true, the other must be false. Some people reject the Christian faith because they make a religious commitment to naturalism[9] and then find any further interest in Christianity logically impossible. Other people begin by rejecting Christianity for one reason or another and then naturally gravitate to naturalism.

Naturalism, good and evil. There is an obvious reason why naturalists do not believe in any objective good. Their worldview will not allow them to. "Good" and "evil" in a naturalistic universe cannot possibly refer to anything transcendent, anything that has standing outside of the box, the natural order of things. For this reason, many naturalists simply assert that what we call good and evil are merely subjective preferences. Other naturalists balk at this extreme view and find other grounds for treating good and evil as relative.

Few naturalists seem to realize how their relativistic approach to good and evil disqualifies them from being proponents of the problem of evil. Whenever they seek to raise problems for Christians by pointing to this or that instance of evil, they do so in terms that are not consistent with their naturalistic and relativistic understanding of things. For a naturalist,

---

[8]Bertrand Russell, *Mysticism and Logic* (London: Longmans, Green, 1925), p. 48.

[9]Some may find it difficult to understand the first clause in this sentence. A worldview choice regarding the existence or nonexistence of God is a religious choice that flows from the heart, the religious center of the person. See Ronald Nash, *Faith and Reason* (Grand Rapids, Mich.: Zondervan, 1988), pp. 28-29.

there cannot be any real, objective, transcendent standards of good and evil. The Christian worldview allows Christians to recognize the existence of real goods and real evils. The naturalistic worldview does not.

Even if Christians have their difficulties with the problem of evil, it ought to be obvious to fair witnesses of the debate that naturalists have difficulties with what could be called "the problem of goodness." Imagine yourself in Bertrand Russell's world. The cosmos is a closed box. The physical universe is all that exists. Outside the box, nothing exists—no God, no transcendent truths, no transcendent standards of good and evil, in other words, *nothing!* Here is another description of Russell's view of the world:

> That man is the product of causes which had no prevision of the end they were achieving; that his origin, his growth, his hopes and fears, his loves and his beliefs are but the outcome of accidental collocations of atoms; that no fire, no heroism, no intensity of thought and feeling, can preserve an individual life beyond the grave; that all the labours of the ages, all the devotion, all the inspiration, all the noonday brightness of human genius, are destined to extinction in the vast death of the solar system, and the whole temple of Man's achievement must inevitably be buried beneath the debris of a universe in ruins—all these things, if not quite beyond dispute, are yet so nearly certain, that no philosophy which rejects them can hope to stand. Only within the scaffolding of these truths, only on the firm foundation of the unyielding despair, can the soul's habitation henceforth be safely built.[10]

The Christian worldview provides a ground both for the existence of real goodness as well as for real evils. Naturalism can do neither.

TWO VERSIONS OF THE PROBLEM OF EVIL

Two major versions of the problem of evil exist.

The deductive version. What is often called the deductive version of the problem of evil aims to show that the existence of evil is logically inconsistent with one or more major tenets of the Christian faith. Proponents of the deductive version claim that a logical contradiction lurks at

---

[10]Russell, *Mysticism and Logic,* p. 47.

the very core of Christian theism. In a 1955 article, the British philosopher J. L. Mackie, at the time an advocate of this position, wrote, "It can be shown not that religious beliefs lack rational support, but that they are positively irrational, that the several parts of the essential theological doctrine are *inconsistent* with one another."[11] Since a contradictory set of beliefs is necessarily false, the deductive version of the problem of evil would—if sound—pose the most serious threat possible to Christian theism. It would mean that Christianity is not just possibly false, but necessarily false. Things can't get much worse than that.

The problem arises because of a supposed contradiction that lies in the following six propositions:

1. God exists.
2. God is omnipotent.
3. God is omniscient.
4. God is omnibenevolent.
5. God created the world.
6. The world contains evil.

Obviously this list lacks two contradictory propositions. While the list contains the proposition *the world contains evil,* the proponent of the deductive problem of evil must find a way to demonstrate that propositions 1 through 5 entail the claim that *the world does not contain evil.* That would then produce the desired contradiction, namely, the conjunction of *The world contains evil* and *The world does not contain evil.* In other words, the advocate of the deductive version must find a way to get from propositions 1 through 5 to a new proposition, namely,

7. The world does not contain evil.

If this can be done, then our set of Christian beliefs (1-7) would indeed have a problem; the set would be logically inconsistent and thus necessarily false.

However, in order to make their case, the critics must find another proposition that in conjunction with statements 1 through 5 would imply proposition 7, the claim that the world does not contain evil. Only by

---

[11]J. L. Mackie, "Evil and Omnipotence," in *The Philosophy of Religion,* ed. Basil Mitchell (London: Oxford University Press, 1970), p. 92. Mackie's article appeared originally in *Mind* 64 (1955).

supplying such a missing premise would the alleged contradiction become evident. While proponents of the deductive problem of evil tried every move possible, none of them succeeded. The new propositions they offered to educe the sought-for contradiction failed either because they were not true or because they were not claims that Christians embrace. For example, some anti-theists offered as the missing premise the claim that an omnipotent being can do absolutely anything, believing that when this proposition was added to our original list, it would entail proposition seven, the claim that the world does not contain evil. In this way, they sought to generate the contradiction that would presumably demonstrate that Christian theism does contain a logical inconsistency at its core.

But there was a major catch to this move. The claim that God can do absolutely anything is not true. Informed Christians have always recognized that an omnipotent being cannot do lots of things. For example, even the Bible declares that God cannot lie or swear by a being greater than himself. The end result of all the hoopla over the alleged contradiction existing at the heart of the Christian faith turned out this way: no proponent of the deductive problem of evil ever succeeded in supplying the missing proposition needed to reveal the presumed contradiction.[12]

Obviously, it is one thing to demonstrate that no one has discovered the required missing premise up to this point. But what about the future? Philosopher Alvin Plantinga has provided a procedure by which Christians can demonstrate the logical consistency of their set of beliefs.[13] This information demonstrates that no philosopher can ever do this in the future.

All that is required to prove our list of propositions is logically consistent (and thus forever immune to the possibility of being shown to be inconsistent) is to add a new proposition that is logically possible, which means simply that it does not describe a contradictory state of affairs. The new proposition must be consistent with the other propositions in the list, and, in conjunction with the other propositions, it must entail that evil ex-

---

[12]For a more detailed discussion of this issue, see Nash, *Faith and Reason,* chap. 13.
[13]See Alvin Plantinga, *God, Freedom and Evil* (Grand Rapids, Mich.: Eerdmans, 1974).

ists in the world. Plantinga's proposition is the claim that *God creates a world that now contains evil and has a good reason for doing so.*

Telescoping our earlier list to save space, our new list of Christian beliefs looks like this:

1. God exists, is omnipotent, omniscient, omnibenevolent, and created the world.
2. God created a world that now contains evil and had a good reason for doing so.
3. Therefore, the world contains evil.

Numbers 1 and 2 taken together do, of course, entail 3. Therefore, the propositions from our original list of Christian beliefs that now appear in number 1 are logically consistent with the existence of evil. The only relevant question regarding proposition 2 is whether it is possibly true. Obviously it is, since it is not logically false (is not a contradiction). Therefore, our original list of Christian beliefs is shown to be logically consistent, from which it follows that the deductive problem of evil has been answered. The existence of evil in the world cannot be used to demonstrate a logical inconsistency at the heart of the Christian faith.

My discussion of the deductive problem of evil has of necessity skipped over a number of details, some of them technical in nature. The interested reader is advised to examine these details in other publications, which are readily available.[14] But the point is clear. The existence of evil in the world does not create a logical problem for the Christian. Of course, it may still raise other sorts of problems, some of which will appear in the rest of this chapter. It is important to note that even Mackie, one of the fathers of the deductive problem of evil, conceded that his earlier position "does not, after all, show that the central doctrines of theism are logically inconsistent with one another."[15] Philosopher William Rowe, a frequent critic of Christian theism, admits, "Some philosophers have contended that the existence of evil is *logically inconsistent* with the existence of the theistic God. No one, I think, has succeeded in establishing such an extravagant claim. Indeed, there is a fairly

---

[14]See, for example, Nash, *Faith and Reason,* chap. 13.
[15]J. L. Mackie, *The Miracle of Theism* (Oxford: Clarendon Press, 1982), p. 154.

compelling argument for the view that the existence of evil is logically consistent with the theistic God."[16]

We may ask, "But why did God permit evil?" However, the relevant issue here is that such a reason need not be known or produced for the argument of this section of the chapter to succeed. The rules of modern logic make the strategy of this argument successful, whether or not we can identify God's reason. The point at the moment is that the claim that God has a reason for creating a world that now contains evil is logically possible. Since it is, the argument succeeds and the attempt to locate a contradiction at the heart of Christian theism fails.

As a final observation, we should note once again that nothing significant follows from the fact that Christians may admit they don't know God's reason for permitting evil. Some opponents of theism act as though such an admission implies that there is no reason. This hardly follows. In fact, all one could reasonably infer from the admission is that the Christian in question does not know everything. But that is hardly surprising news.

The inductive version. The shortcomings of the deductive problem of evil do not mean that opponents of Christian theism have given up on the problem of evil. It simply means that they have turned to a different way of formulating the problem. The move from the justly discredited deductive to an inductive form of the problem of evil is a shift from the strong claim that theism is logically and necessarily false to the more modest assertion that it is probably false. According to advocates of the inductive problem of evil, evil tips the scales of probability against theism; the existence of evil makes theistic belief improbable.

Most attempts to answer the inductive problem of evil are variations on one basic theme, namely, that God permits evil either to make possible some greater good or to avoid some greater evil. God, it is claimed, always has some reason for allowing evil. An instance of evil might be a test to strengthen character or punishment for some previous act of moral evil. What does seem likely is that no human knows what God's

---

[16]William L. Rowe, "The Problem of Evil and Some Varieties of Atheism," *American Philosophical Quarterly* 16 (1979), p. 335.

reason might be for any specific instance of evil.

The need to cover other subjects makes it necessary to cut off this discussion while there is still more to say.[17] For the next few pages, I will examine what appears to be the most powerful version of the inductive problem of evil, what many call the problem of gratuitous evil.

What if the world contains gratuitous evil, that is, truly senseless, mindless, irrational and meaningless evil? If this is so, the appeal to greater good would collapse and with it, apparently, would also fall the claim that God permits evil because it is a necessary condition for some greater good or the avoidance of some greater evil.

One version of the problem of gratuitous evil proceeds in the following way:

1. If God exists, then all evil has a justifying reason.

2. But it is not the case that all evil has a justifying reason.[18]

3. Therefore, God does not exist.

What can we say about this argument? To begin with, it is certainly valid; it conforms to the rules of formal logic. If the premises are true, then the conclusion is certainly true. But are the premises true? Suppose for now we concentrate only on the second premise, the claim that not all evil has a justifying reason. Several questions come to mind. For one thing, how can the critic of Christian theism know that premise 2 is true? And to get right to the heart of the matter, how could any human being know that gratuitous evil exists? Any sensitive and observant person must admit that many evils in the world appear to be gratuitous: accidents that strike people down in the prime of life, diseases that result in long periods of horrible suffering, birth defects, natural disasters that can suddenly kill hundreds of people and destroy the lives of survivors. But given the limitations of human knowledge, it is hard to see how any human being could actually *know* that some particular evil is totally senseless and purposeless. It seems, then, that the most any human can know is that some evils appear gratuitous. But of course such a claim in the place of premise 2 would not entail the conclusion that God does not exist.

---

[17]For a more complete discussion of the inductive problem of evil, see Nash, *Faith and Reason,* chap. 14.

[18]This premise is simply another way of saying that the world contains gratuitous evil.

Philosopher Jane Mary Trau has provided a different formulation of the problem of gratuitous evil. She writes:

> It seems that unless it can be shown that all cases of apparent gratuitous suffering are in fact not purposeless, it is most reasonable to believe that they are as they appear to be; and since it cannot be shown that they are in fact not purposeless, it is reasonable to believe that they are as they appear to be; since there appear to be such cases, it is more reasonable to believe that God does not exist.[19]

While this is an interesting argument, it raises at least two questions. The first and less serious question concerns the placement of the burden of proof in this matter. How did the theist suddenly get stuck with the burden of proof? After all, he was simply minding his own business as he went about the task of believing in God and living in the world. Suddenly he is told that unless he (the theist) can show that none of the evils in the world are gratuitous, belief in the existence of God must be judged to be unreasonable. But, we should remember, it is the atheist who is attempting to prove that God does not exist; in this case, the atheist is attempting to make his case for the nonexistence of God by pointing to the existence of gratuitous evil. Since the atheist is issuing the challenge, should not the burden of proof rest on his shoulders? Should not the atheist be the one required to show that there *is* gratuitous evil in the world? My point, of course, is that the atheist knows fully well that no human being can show that there is gratuitous evil in the world. So he simply adopts an attitude of philosophical imperialism, throws down the gauntlet and adds in passing, "By the way, I thought you should know that you also have the burden of proof in this matter." I am not trying to defend theism by default in the last paragraph. I am simply pointing out that it is not at all clear that the theist has the burden of proof in this matter.

But Trau's argument, as stated, suffers from still another problem, as she points out. The second premise of the argument involves an appeal

---

[19]Jane Mary Trau, "Fallacies in the Argument from Gratuitous Suffering," *The New Scholasticism* 60 (1986): 487-88. As we will see shortly, Trau only presents the argument; she does not accept it.

to ignorance, a common logical fallacy. Simply because the theist cannot prove that all evils in the world are not gratuitous, it hardly follows that some of them are. Indeed, Trau goes on to say,

> The most reasonable position to hold appears to be this: we cannot explain cases of apparently gratuitous suffering until we know whether or not they are indeed gratuitous. And this we can never claim unless we are sure as to the ontological status of God. Since we cannot prove or disprove His non-existence [via the argument from gratuitous evil], we must first prove or disprove His existence. Until that is accomplished we cannot know whether there are such cases.[20]

According to Trau, the one sure way of showing that the world does contain gratuitous evils is to prove that God does not exist. But it would then seem to follow that one cannot appeal to gratuitous evils while arguing against the existence of God—unless, that is, one is unconcerned about begging the question.

One final point is worth noting: what properties must a being possess in order to know that some evils really are gratuitous? It certainly appears as though one such property must be omniscience. It would seem then that the only kind of being who could know whether some gratuitous evils exist would be God. But if the only being who could know whether such evils exist is God, there surely are problems in arguing that the existence of gratuitous evils are a defeater for the existence of God.

THE CHRISTIAN WORLDVIEW AND EVIL

It is important to remember that the worldviews of millions of people deny the existence of evil, that affirm that such evils as pain and death are illusory. This is the case with non-Christian forms of pantheism as well as the bizarre theories of the American-born system known as Christian Science. Surely, fair people will agree that Christian theism deserves credit for not running away from the problem of evil. The remaining pages of this chapter offer some final observations about evil from the perspective of the Christian worldview.

---

[20]Ibid., p. 489.

Two kinds of good. The best way I know how to make the distinction before us is to use the terms *transcendent good* and *nontranscendent good*. I define a transcendent good as that good than which a greater good cannot be conceived. From the perspective of the Christian worldview, there can be no greater good than eternal fellowship with the God who made us, loves us and redeems us through the salvific work of Jesus Christ, the eternal Son of God. It should not be difficult to see that all other goods that humans seek are nontranscendent.

Two kinds of evil. Using the same terminology, then, we can think about transcendent and nontranscendent evils. Suppose we define a transcendent evil as that evil than which a greater evil cannot be conceived. From the perspective of the Christian worldview, that kind of transcendent evil would be losing one's soul and being forever separated from the source of love, righteousness and goodness of the God who created us and the universe in which we live. As horrible as many evils in the history of the world have been, the biblical worldview tells us that there is one transcendent evil that makes all other evils nontranscendent.

Romans 8:28. People who regard themselves as Christians ought to seek a better understanding of their worldview. That understanding requires them to know what their ultimate rule of faith and practice, the Christian Scriptures, have to say about their worldview. And finally they need to show that they have the strength to put the beliefs they profess into practice. One important passage in the New Testament that speaks to this point is Romans 8:28: "And we know that all things work together for good to those who love God, to those who are the called according to his purpose."[21]

Many of us know people who believe the verse reads like this: "All things work together for good, period." And because of this error, millions of people mistakenly think the promise in this verse applies to them. But the proper audience for this verse is the large company of people who not only love God but who are called according to God's

---

[21]Romans 8:28 NKJV. This is no place to quibble over the best translation to use in this case. The familiarity of the King James Version is worth retaining.

own purpose. The full understanding of who these people are requires a fairly competent grasp of the entire New Testament.

One more comment is needed. Does Romans 8:28 promise that everything works for good during the earthly existence of the people who are described in the latter part of the verse? Many competent expositors of the text think not. They believe the text reports that all things work together for good when viewed from the perspective of eternity. Then and only then, they suggest, will believers fully recognize how the trials and travail of the Christian pilgrimage in this life have worked together for good.

Romans 8:18. I trust it is clear that all I am doing here is explaining important teachings of the worldview that millions of people believe. It is worth remembering that this is the same worldview that most proponents of the problem of evil hope to show unreasonable. A companion text to Romans 8:28 is Romans 8:18, which says, "For I consider that the sufferings of this present time are not worthy to be compared with the glory which shall be revealed in us." Here the apostle Paul acknowledges the pain, grief and suffering that often afflict believers in this life. He implies that a day will come when believers can look back and say, "That was a really tough time in the life of my family. We cried a lot. We miss those who died before us. Those things really hurt. But when I am finally in the presence of the God who has always loved me, that earlier suffering just cannot be compared with the glory of what God has prepared for me."

Paul's points can be expressed in terms of my earlier distinctions between transcendent and nontranscendent goods and evils. Is he not saying that all of the sufferings he experienced, which finally ended in his being stoned to death, were nontranscendent evils? And when finally compared to his ultimate standing in the presence of the triune God, when he attains that transcendent good than which no greater good can be conceived, he will know that all things did work for good.

CONCLUSION

Do I believe that I have answered the problem of evil? I know better than to think I could or should do this for everyone. I began this chapter by noting that every reader will approach this issue from the perspective of a worldview, many of which arc incomplctc, confuscd and incohcrent. I explained my worldview and pointed out that many opponents of my worldview think the problem of evil is its greatest challenge. While I have admitted that I know no one who can explain every evil that occurs, it seems unreasonable to demand that people who share my worldview be able to do this. It is one thing to attack a worldview; it is far more demanding to offer a competing worldview such as naturalism or dualism or pantheism or panentheism that answers more questions and leaves fewer questions unanswered than the worldview of the Christian faith.

FOR FURTHER READING

Clark, Kelly James. *Return to Reason*. Grand Rapids, Mich.: Eerdmans, 1990.

Geisler, Norman L. *The Roots of Evil*. Grand Rapids, Mich.: Zondervan, 1978.

Nash, Ronald H. *Faith and Reason*. Grand Rapids, Mich.: Zondervan, 1988.

———. *Life's Ultimate Questions: An Introduction to Philosophy*. Grand Rapids, Mich.: Zondervan, 1999.

Plantinga, Alvin. *God, Freedom and Evil*. Grand Rapids, Mich.: Eerdmans, 1974.

Purtill, Richard L. *Reason to Believe*. Grand Rapids, Mich.: Eerdmans, 1974.

13

PHYSICALISM, NATURALISM AND THE NATURE OF HUMAN PERSONS

J. P. Moreland

AN ISSUE OF *TIME* MAGAZINE FEATURED AN ARTICLE DEFENDING STEM-CELL research on human embryos: "These [embryos] are microscopic groupings of a few differentiated cells. There is nothing human about them, except potential—and, if you choose to believe it, a soul."[1] This statement expresses a widely held opinion that when it comes to belief in the soul, you're on your own. There is no evidence one way or another. You must simply choose arbitrarily what you believe about the soul.

Nothing could be further from the truth. In reality, a very strong case can be offered for the view that consciousness and the soul are immaterial—not physical—realities. Thinking through this issue is not only a fascinating adventure, but for at least four reasons, it is a matter of considerable importance.

First, the Bible teaches that consciousness and the soul are immaterial. This is the most obvious reading of the biblical text. For example, in Matthew 10:28, Jesus recognizes body and soul as distinct entities (cf. Lk 12:4-5): "Do not be afraid of those who kill the body but are not able to kill the soul; rather, be afraid of the One who is able to destroy soul as well as body in hell."

Second, as the *Time* article implies, the reality of the soul is important

---

[1]Michael Kinsley, "If You Believe Embryos Are Humans . . . " *Time,* June 25, 2001, p. 80.

to various ethical issues that crucially involve an understanding of human persons. For example, is personhood—and therefore worth or dignity—defined by one's properly functioning body or brain? Or does it relate to something deeper—an enduring spiritual self—that remains even if mental functioning is lost?

Third, some argue that the Christian view of the afterlife requires a soul that survives in a disembodied intermediate state between death and the final resurrection, yet science has discredited belief in the soul.

Finally, some argue that finite minds provide evidence of a divine Mind as their creator. If we limit our options to theism and naturalism, it is hard to see how finite consciousness could result from the rearrangement of brute matter; it is easier to see how a conscious Being could produce finite consciousness. Prior to the appearance of consciousness, the universe contained nothing but aggregates of particles/waves standing in fields of forces. The emergence of consciousness seems to be a case of getting something from nothing. This radical discontinuity seems like a rupture in the natural world best explained by a spiritual Creator.

After clarifying some important concepts, this chapter will present arguments for the claim that both consciousness and the self that contains it are immaterial, spiritual realities and not physical. Property dualism is the view that consciousness is spiritual and not physical, and while substance dualism comes in different varieties, it will be used in this chapter to mean that the self is a spirit and not a physical object.

IMPORTANT PRELIMINARY CONCEPTS

Let's first clarify what is the nature of substances, properties and events. First, a *substance* is an entity like an acorn, a dog or an angel with at least three important features.

- *A substance is a particular, individual thing.*
- *A substance is a continuant*—it can change by gaining new properties and losing old ones, yet it remains the same thing throughout the change. An acorn can change colors, or an angel can change its thinking, and both are still the same thing.
- *Substances are basic, fundamental existents.* Substances are not in other things, nor are they had by other things. *Properties* are in

things and are had by them. The dog Fido is not in or had by something more basic than he. Rather, properties such as brownness (and parts) are in substances like Fido that have them.

Second, some examples of *properties* are brownness, triangularity and painfulness. There are two relevant features of properties.

- *Properties don't change.* When a leaf goes from green to red, the leaf changes but redness does not.

- *Properties can be in or had by other things.* Properties are in the things that have them. For example, redness is in the apple. When we are talking about a property, it makes sense to ask the question "What is it that has that property?" Substances have properties; properties are had by substances.

Finally, there are entities in the world called *events*. Examples of events are a flash of lightning or the having of a thought. Events are ongoing states or changes of states of substances. An event is the coming or going of a property in a substance at a particular time, or the continued possession of a property by a substance throughout a time.

An overview of physicalism and dualism. According to *physicalism,* a human being is merely a physical entity. The only things that exist are physical substances, properties and events. The human, therefore, is a physical substance—namely, a material brain or body. This physical substance has physical properties—a certain weight, volume, size, electrical activity, chemical composition, and so forth. There are also physical events that occur in the brain. When someone has an occasion of pain or an occurrence of a thought, physicalists hold that these are merely physical events that can be exhaustively described in physical language. One's conscious mental life of thoughts, emotions and pain is nothing but physical events in one's brain and nervous system.

What is *matter?* It is hard to define, but examples are easy to supply. Material objects are things like computers, carbon atoms and billiard balls.

Material properties are

- *publicly accessible* in the sense that no one person is better suited to have private access to a material property than anyone else;

- such that an object must be *either spatially located or extended* to be considered having material properties;
- such that when a strictly material object has physical properties, that object does not behave in a goal-oriented or purposeful (teleological) manner (i.e., it does not undergo change for the sake of some end or purpose—what Aristotle referred to as a "final cause").

Physical properties are the properties that one finds listed in chemistry or physics books. They are properties such as hardness; occupying and moving through space; having a certain shape; possessing certain chemical, electrical, magnetic and gravitational properties; having density and weight; and being breakable, pliable and elastic. A physical event would be the possession, coming or going of one or more of these properties by a physical substance (or among physical substances).

Another very crucial observation to make about material substances, properties and events is this: *No material entity presupposes or requires reference to consciousness for it to exist or be characterized.* You will search in vain through a physics or chemistry textbook to find consciousness included in any description of matter. A completely physical description of the world would not include any terms that make reference to or characterize the existence and nature of consciousness.

Dualists disagree with physicalists. According to dualists, genuinely mental entities are real. As with matter, it is hard to give a definition of mental entities. But examples of mental entities are easy to supply. There are at least five different kinds of mental properties/events. A *sensation* is a state of awareness or sentience, a mode of consciousness (e.g., a conscious awareness of sound, color or pain). Some sensations are experiences of things outside ourself like a tree or table. Others are awarenesses of other states within ourself like pains or itches. Emotions are a subclass of sensations and, as such, they are forms of awareness of things.

A *thought* is a mental content that can be expressed in an entire sentence and that exists only while it is being thought. Some thoughts logically imply other thoughts. For example, "All dogs are mammals" entails "This dog is a mammal." If the former is true, the latter must be true. A *belief* is a person's view, accepted to varying degrees of strength, of how things really are. If a person has a belief (e.g., that it is raining), then that belief serves as the basis for the person's tendency or readiness to act as if the thing believed were really so (e.g., the person gets an umbrella). At any given time, one can have many beliefs that are not currently being contemplated. A *desire* is a certain felt inclination to do, have or experience certain things. Desires are either conscious or such that they can be made conscious through certain activities, for example, through therapy. A *free choice* is an exercise of power, an endeavoring to do a certain thing, usually for the sake of some purpose or end.

Dualists argue that these five properties/states are examples of genuine mental—not physical—entities.

In addition to these differences between physicalists and dualists, there is also an intramural debate between *mere property dualists* and *substance dualists.*

Mere property dualists believe there are some physical substances that have only physical properties: for example, a billiard ball is hard and round. They also maintain that there are no mental *substances*. On the other hand, they contend there is *one* material substance that has both physical and mental properties—the brain. When I experience a pain, there is a certain physical property possessed by the brain (a C-fiber stimulation with chemical and electrical properties), and there is a certain mental property possessed by the brain (the pain itself with its felt quality). The brain is the possessor of all mental properties. I am not a mental self that has my thoughts and experiences. Rather, I am a brain and a series or bundle of successive experiences themselves. Moreover, mere property dualists claim that just as wetness is a real property that comes about with (or supervenes upon) a certain structure of water molecules, so mental properties arise from (or supervene upon) brain states.

In contrast with mere property dualism, *substance dualism* holds that the brain and the mind/soul are two distinct things: the brain is a physical thing that has physical properties, and the mind or soul is a mental substance that has mental properties. When I am in pain, the brain has certain physical properties (electrical, chemical), and the soul or self has certain mental properties (the conscious awareness of pain). The soul is the possessor of its experiences. It stands behind, over and above them and remains the same throughout my life. The soul and the brain can interact with each other, but they are different particulars with different properties. Substance dualists accept the existence of both mental properties and substances.

Identity, causation and correlation. It is time to turn to a topic that will explain our strategy for defending dualism: the nature of *identity*. The eighteenth-century philosopher and theologian Joseph Butler once remarked that *everything is itself and not something else.* This simple truth has profound implications. Suppose you want to know whether J. P. Moreland is Eileen Spiek's youngest son. If J. P. Moreland is identical to Eileen Spiek's youngest son (everything true of one is true of the other), then in reality, we are talking about one single thing: J. P. Moreland, who *is* Eileen Spiek's youngest son. However, if even one small thing is true of J. P. Moreland and *not* true of Eileen Spiek's youngest son, then these are two entirely different people. Furthermore, J. P. Moreland is identical to himself and not different from himself. So if J. P. Moreland is *not* identical to Eileen Spiek's youngest son, then in reality we must be talking about two things, not one.

This illustration suggests a truth about the nature of identity known as Leibniz's law of the indiscernibility of identicals: *If you've got two truly identical things, then there is only one thing you are talking about—not two—and any truth that applies to "one" applies to the "other."* This suggests a test for identity: If you could find one thing true of x that is not true of y, or vice versa, then x cannot be identical to y. Further, if you could find one thing that could possibly be true of x and not y (or vice versa), even if it isn't *actually* true, then x cannot be identical to y. If J. P. Moreland is 5' 8" tall, but Eileen Spiek's youngest son is 6' tall, then they are not the same thing. Further, if J. P. Moreland is 5' 8" and Eileen Spiek's youngest son is 5' 8", but it would be possible for J. P. to be 5' 9" while Eileen's youngest son were 5' 8", then they are not the same thing either.

What does this have to do with the mind-body problem? Simply this: Strict physicalists make the bold claim that alleged mental entities are really identical to physical entities—brain states, properties of the brain, overt bodily behavior and dispositions to behave. For example, pain is just the tendency to shout "Ouch!" when stuck by a pin, instead of pain being a certain mental feel. If physicalism is true, then everything true of the brain (and/or its properties/states) is true of the mind (and/or its properties/states) and vice versa. But if we can find just one thing true, or even possibly true of consciousness and the self that is not of the brain/body and its physical states, or vice versa, then dualism is established.

Keep in mind that the relation of identity is different from any other relation, for example, the relation of causation or constant connection. With regard to the relation of *causation,* it may be that brain events cause or are correlated with mental events or vice versa. But just because A causes B (or vice versa), or just because A and B are constantly correlated with each other, that does not mean that A is identical to B. Correlation is not the same thing as identity. Physicalism needs identity to make its case.

CONSCIOUSNESS AND PROPERTY DUALISM

Are properties such as being a thought or being a pain—and the events/ states composed of them (a pain or thinking event)—genuinely mental or physical? In this section, we will look at a case for property dualism— the view that conscious properties/events are mental and not physical.

Property dualists argue that mental states are in no sense physical since they possess five features that physical states don't have:

1. there is a raw qualitative feel or a "what it is like" to have a mental state such as a pain;

2. at least many mental states have intentionality—*of*ness or *about*ness —directed toward an object (a thought may be about the moon);

3. mental states are inner, private and immediate to the subject having them;

4. mental states require a subjective ontology—namely, mental states are necessarily owned by the first-person sentient subjects who have them (I own them; they are mine; they are directly accessible to me);

5. mental states fail to have crucial features (e.g., spatial extension,

location) that characterize physical states and, in general, cannot be described using physical language.

The dualist argues that once one gets an accurate description of consciousness, it becomes clear that mental properties/events are not identical to physical properties/events. Mental states are characterized by their intrinsic, subjective, inner, private, qualitative feel, made present to a subject by first-person introspection. In general, mental states have some or all of the following features, none of which is a physical feature of anything: Mental states like pains have an intrinsic, raw conscious feel. There is a "what it is like" to a pain. Most—if not all—mental states have intentionality, that is, they are of or *about* things. Mental states are inner, private and known by first-person, direct introspection. Any way one has of knowing about a physical entity is available to everyone else, including ways of knowing about one's brain. The examination of physical states and events is in principle publicly accessible. But a subject has a way of knowing about his own mental states not available to others— through introspection. He alone knows his own private mental states by first-person introspection. Mental states are made up of directly available—or self-presenting—properties. One can be aware of the external, physical world only by means of one's mental states, but one need not be aware of one's mental states by means of anything else. One is directly aware of them. For example, it is by way of a sensation of red that one is aware of an apple, but one is not aware of the sensation of red by way of another sensation. Mental states are necessarily owned by a subject, indeed, by the particular subject that has them. One's mental states could not have belonged to someone else. However, no physical state is necessarily owned, much less necessarily owned by a specific subject.

We can add other differences between mental and physical states to the list. Some sensations are vague (e.g., a sensation of an object may be fuzzy or vague), but no physical state is vague. Some sensations are pleasurable *or* unpleasurable, but nothing physical has these properties. A cut in the knee is, strictly speaking, not unpleasurable. It is the pain event caused by the cut that is unpleasurable. Mental states can have the property of familiarity (e.g., when a desk looks familiar to someone), but familiarity is not a feature of a physical state.

Since mental states have these features and physical states do not, mental states therefore are not identical to physical states.

THE IMMATERIAL SOUL

At least three arguments have been offered in the recent literature for some form of substance dualism.

Our basic awareness of the self. The first one focuses on one's basic awareness of the self. When we enter most deeply into ourselves, we become aware of a very basic fact presented to us: We are aware of our own self (ego, I, center of consciousness) as being distinct from our bodies and from any particular mental experience we have, and as being an uncomposed, spatially unextended center of consciousness. I simply have a basic, direct awareness of the fact that I am not identical to my body or my mental events; rather, I am the immaterial self that has a body and a conscious mental life.

An experiment may help convince you of this. Right now I am looking at a chair in my office. As I walk toward the chair, I experience a series of what are called phenomenological objects or chair representations. That is, I have several different chair experiences that replace one another in rapid succession. As I approach the chair, my chair sensations vary. If I pay attention, I am also aware of two more things. First, I do not simply experience a series of sense images of a chair. Rather, through self-awareness, I also experience the fact that it is I myself who has each chair experience. Each chair sensation produced at each angle of perspective has a perceiver who is I. An "I" accompanies each sense experience to produce a series of awarenesses—"I am experiencing a chair sense image now."

I am also aware of the basic fact that the same self that is currently having a fairly large chair experience (as my eyes come to within twelve inches of the chair) is the very same self as the one who had all of the other chair experiences preceding this current one. Through self-awareness, I am aware of the fact that I am an enduring I who was and is (and will be) present as the owner of all the experiences in the series.

These two facts—I am the owner of my experiences, and I am an enduring self—show that *I am not identical to my experiences*. I am the conscious thing that has them. I am also aware of myself as a simple, uncomposed and spatially unextended center of consciousness (I am "fully present" throughout my body; if my arm is cut off, I do not become four-fifths of a self). In short, I am a mental substance.

Unity and the first-person perspective. A complete physicalist description of the world would be one in which everything would be exhaustively described from a third-person point of view in terms of objects, properties, processes and their spatio-temporal locations. For example, a description of an apple in a room would go something like this: "There exists an object three feet from the south wall and two feet from the east wall, and that object has the property of being red, round, sweet, and so on."

The first-person point of view is the vantage point that I use to describe the world from my own perspective. Expressions of a first-person point of view utilize what are called *indexicals*—words like *I, here, now, there, then. Here* and *now* are *where* and *when* I am; *there* and *then* are *where* and *when* I am not. Indexicals explicitly or implicitly refer to one's self. "I" is the most basic indexical, and it refers to one's own self that one knows by acquaintance with one's own self in acts of self-awareness. I am immediately aware of my own self, and I know to whom "I" refers when I use it: It refers to me as the self-conscious, self-reflexive owner of my body and mental states.

According to physicalism, there are no fundamentally basic or intrinsic (irreducible), privileged first-person perspectives. Everything can be exhaustively described in an object language from a third-person perspective. A physicalist description of me would say, "There exists a body at a certain location that is five feet eight inches tall, weighs 160 pounds," and so forth. The property dualist would add a description of the properties possessed by that body, such as the body is feeling pain or thinking about lunch.

But no amount of third-person descriptions ("he," "she," "it") captures my own subjective, first-person ("I") acquaintance of my own self in acts of self-awareness. In fact, for any third-person description of me, it would always be an open question as to whether the person described in third-person terms was the same person as I am. I do not know my self *because* I know some third-person description of a set of mental and physical properties and also know that a certain person satisfies that description. I know myself as a self immediately through being acquainted with my own self in an act of self-awareness. I can express that self-awareness by using the term *I*.

I refers to my own substantial soul. It does not refer to any mental property or bundle of mental properties I am having, nor does it refer to any body described from a third-person perspective. *I* is a term that refers to something that exists, and *I* does not refer to any object or set of properties described from a third-person point of view. Rather, *I* refers to one's own self with which one is directly acquainted and which, through acts of self-awareness, one knows to be the substantial uncomposed possessor of one's mental states and one's body.

The modal argument. Thought experiments have rightly been central to debates about personal identity. For example, we are often invited to consider a situation in which two persons switch bodies, brains or personality traits or in which a person exists disembodied. In these thought experiments, someone argues in the following way: Because a certain state of affairs S (e.g., the disembodied existence of Smith) is conceivable, this provides justification for thinking that S is metaphysically (or really, actually) possible. Now if S is possible, then certain implications follow about what is or is not essential to personal identity (e.g., Smith is not essentially a body).

We all use conceiving as a test for possibility/impossibility throughout our lives. I know that life on other planets is possible (even if I think it is highly unlikely or downright false) because I can conceive it to be so. I am aware of what it is to be living and to be on earth, and I conceive no necessary connections between these two properties. I know square circles are impossible because it is inconceivable, given my knowledge of being square and being circular. To be sure, judgments that a state of affairs is possible/impossible grounded in conceivability are not infallible. They can be wrong. Still, they provide strong evidence for genuine possibility/impossibility. In light of this, I offer the following criterion:

For any entities *x* and *y*, if I have good grounds for believing I can conceive of *x* existing without *y* or vice versa, then I have good grounds for believing *x* is not essential or identical to *y* or vice versa.

Let us apply these insights about conceivability and possibility to the modal argument for substance dualism. The argument comes in many forms, but it may be fairly stated as follows:[2]

1. The law of identity: If *x* is identical to *y*, then whatever is true of *x* is true of *y* and vice versa.

2. I can strongly conceive of myself as existing disembodied.

3. If I can strongly conceive of some state of affairs S that S possibly obtains, then I have good grounds for believing of S that S is possible.

4. Therefore, I have good grounds for believing of myself that it is possible for me to exist and be disembodied.

5. If some entity *x* is such that it is possible for *x* to exist without *y*, then (i) *x* is not identical to *y* and (ii) *y* is not essential to *x*.

6. My body is not such that it is possible to exist disembodied, i.e., my body is essentially a body.

7. Therefore, I have good grounds for believing of myself that I am not identical to my body and that my physical body is not essential to me.

A parallel argument can be advanced in which the notions of a body and disembodiment are replaced with the notions of physical objects. So understood, the argument would imply the conclusion that I have good grounds for thinking that I am not identical to a physical particular nor is any physical particular essential to me. A parallel argument can also be developed to show that possessing the ultimate capacities of sensation, thought, belief, desire and volition are essential to me; that is, I am a substantial soul or mind.

I cannot undertake a full defense of the argument here, but it would be useful to a say a bit more regarding (2). There are a number of things about ourselves and our bodies of which we are aware that ground the conceivability expressed in (2). I am aware that I am unextended (I am

---

[2]Cf. Keith Yandell, "A Defense of Dualism," *Faith and Philosophy* 12 (October 1995): 548-66; Charles Taliaferro, "Animals, Brains and Spirits," *Faith and Philosophy* 12 (October 1995): 567-81.

"fully present" at each location in my body as Augustine claimed); I recognize that I am not a complex cluster of separable parts, nor am I the sort of thing that can be composed of physical parts. Rather, I am a basic unity of inseparable faculties (of mind, volitions, emotion, etc.) that sustains absolute sameness through change and that I am not capable of gradation (I cannot become two-thirds of a person).[3]

In near-death experiences, people report themselves to have been disembodied. They are not aware of having bodies in any sense. Rather, they are aware of themselves as unified egos that have sensations, thoughts, and so forth. Moreover, Christians who understand the biblical teaching that God and angels are bodiless spirits also understand by direct introspection that they are like God and angels by virtue of the following: (a) They are spirits with the same sorts of powers God and angels have but that they also have bodies. (b) The New Testament teaching on the intermediate state (between the body's death and its final resurrection) is intelligible in light of what they know about themselves and it implies that we will and, therefore, can exist temporarily without our bodies. In 2 Corinthians 12:1-4, Paul asserts that he, in the midst of a visionary experience, may actually have been disembodied. Surely part of the grounds for Paul's willingness to consider this a real possibility were (i) his own awareness of his nature through introspection, (ii) his recognition of his similarity to God and angels in this respect and (iii) his knowledge of biblical teaching.

All of the factors mentioned in the above paragraph imply that people can conceive of themselves as existing in a disembodied state, which provides grounds for thinking that this is a real possibility (even if it is false, though, of course, I do not think it is false). Thus, one cannot be one's body, nor is one's body essential to him.

CONCLUSION

In this chapter we have seen that the immaterial nature of consciousness

---

[3]In normal life, I may be focusing on speaking kindly and be unaware that I am scowling. In extreme cases (multiple personalities and split brains), I may be fragmented in my functioning or incapable of consciously and simultaneously attending to all of my mental states, but the various personalities and mental states are still all mine.

and the soul are important topics for Christians to defend, and we have looked at a case for dualism. Jesus once warned that we should fear those who can "destroy both soul and body in hell" (Mt 10:28). On another occasion he cautioned about being cavalier regarding forfeiting one's soul (Mt 16:24). Perhaps the first step in losing something is to stop believing it is real in the first place.

FOR FURTHER READING

Habermas, Gary R., and J. P. Moreland. *Beyond Death: Exploring the Evidence for Immortality*. Rev. ed. Eugene, Ore.: Wipf & Stock, 2004.

Hasker, William. *The Emergent Self*. Ithaca, N.Y.: Cornell University Press, 1999.

Lee, Patrick. *Abortion and Unborn Human Life*. Washington, D.C.: The Catholic University of America Press, 1996.

Machuga, Ric. *In Defense of the Soul: What It Means to Be Human*. Grand Rapids, Mich.: Brazos Press, 2002.

Moreland J. P., and Scott B. Rae. *Body and Soul: Human Nature and the Crisis in Ethics*. Downers Grove, Ill.: InterVarsity Press, 2000.

Swinburne, Richard. *The Evolution of the Soul*. 2nd ed. New York: Oxford University Press, 1997.

14

FACING THE CHALLENGE OF POSTMODERNISM

Douglas Groothuis

A MAN RECENTLY WROTE DENVER SEMINARY CONCERNED THAT OUR WEBPAGE mentions the seminary's mission to defend "absolute truth." This put off the prospective student. He thought that those who believe in absolute truth think they have all the answers and are not receptive to dialogue with others with whom they disagree. He had been influenced in his thinking by Brian McLaren's *A New Kind of Christian.*[1] This is not surprising, because McLaren's book is an apologetic for importing postmodernism into evangelical Christianity. A hearty emphasis on objective truth and traditional apologetic engagement are two of the book's main targets. This book received an Award of Merit in the category of Christian Living for the 2002 *Christianity Today* book awards.

McLaren provides a window into the corrosive effects of postmodernism in the church. He tells a story in which one character, Neo, speaks for a postmodern approach to Christianity. The narrative format makes the material more lively for those not inclined to read weightier treatises on postmodernism. It also allows the writer to insinuate and suggest controversial ideas through his spokesman without forthrightly stating these ideas. This book complements the postmodern approaches to theology and culture articulated by Christian writers such as Stanley Grenz, Leonard Sweet and Nancey Murphy (all mentioned in the footnotes), but

[1]Brian McLaren, *A New Kind of Christian: Two Friends on a Spiritual Journey* (San Francisco: Jossey-Bass, 2001).

without the academic air. There is little recognition of the profoundly un-biblical and irrational nature of postmodernism and the threat it poses to the articulation and defense of Christian truth. Nevertheless, many writers are claiming that since our society is postmodern (more pluralis-tic, less idealistic and less tolerant of absolute truth-claims), the church and apologetics must bend in this direction as well.

Postmodernism poses a great challenge to the enterprise of Christian apologetics, largely on account of its views of truth, rationality and lan-guage. Historically, defenders of the Christian worldview have argued that the biblical worldview is both objectively true and rational (Is 1:18; 1 Pet 3:15; Jude 3). It is derived from the Bible, which contains a true and ra-tional revelation in linguistic form (2 Tim 3:16-17). That is, apologetics en-deavors to show that biblical truth can be known to be true and that it can survive and thrive even when under intellectual attack (2 Cor 10:3-5). Apologetics is a command given to the church and cannot be ignored by faithful followers of Christ.[2] While many attempts to undermine Christian-ity argue that it is false or irrational, the postmodernists criticize Christian-ity for even claiming to be true, rational and knowable in a linguistic form. This is because postmodernism rejects notions of absolute truth and bind-ing rationality as well as the notion that language can unambiguously communicate matters of ultimate meaning. These claims need to be as-sessed and evaluated for the sake of Christian apologetics today.

This chapter cannot do justice to the multifaceted and often convo-luted variety of postmodernist theories. I will focus on avowedly secular postmodernists and respond to general trends in their philosophies. In a nutshell, postmodernism holds that truth is determined by various so-cial constructions that are devised for different purposes. Various cul-tures have their own "language games," which describe reality very dif-ferently. However, we cannot adjudicate which language game or which linguistic "map" correlates more correctly with reality, since we cannot get beyond our own cultural conditioning. There is no objective reality apart from our languages and concepts. To say we know the objective

---

[2]See Norman L. Geisler, "Apologetics, Need For," in *Baker Encyclopedia of Christian Apologet-ics,* ed. Norman L. Geisler (Grand Rapids, Mich.: Baker, 1999), pp. 37-41.

truth is to set up a "metanarrative" that is intrinsically oppressive and exploitative (Jean-François Lyotard). Various "interpretive communities" (Stanley Fish) determine their own truth. Texts, whether religious or otherwise, do not have any objective meaning; therefore they are neither true nor false in themselves but inherently unstable and ambiguous (Jacques Derrida). Truth is not a matter of statements corresponding to reality but of how various power structures define "truth" (Michel Foucault). Various communities use various "vocabularies," none of which is closer or farther away from objective truth, since objective truth does not exist (Richard Rorty).[3] There is no "God's eye view" of anything; therefore, there is no objective truth binding on everyone everywhere.

The postmodernist deconstruction of objective truth and rationality amounts to this: truth does not lodge in statements that correspond to reality. That modernist notion needs to be deconstructed or reduced to its true elements. Truth is a matter of perspective only; it is something that individuals and communities construct primarily through language. If this postmodernist view is accepted, objective truth is ruled out in principle. Truth dissolves into communities, ethnic groups, genders, power relationships and other contingent factors. No one metanarrative (or worldview) can rightly claim to be a true and rational account of reality. That would be arrogant and impossible. We are left with only "micronarratives" and "local knowledge." The idea of finding absolute, objective and universal truth is taken to be part of the failed "Enlightenment project," which was initiated by René Descartes and brought to an end by Friedrich Nietzsche's attack on its rationalistic pretenses.[4]

Against the postmodernists, the vast majority of philosophers have held to the correspondence theory of truth, which asserts that statements or beliefs are true only if they agree or match up with reality.[5] As Nor-

---

[3]For more detail on individual secular postmodernist thinkers, see Millard Erickson, *Truth or Consequences* (Downers Grove, Ill.: InterVarsity Press, 2001).

[4]Various postmodernists assign different figures as pivotal in the Enlightenment project (or modernism) and postmodernism, but these two thinkers are pivotal markers.

[5]See Douglas Groothuis, *Truth Decay: Defending Christianity Against the Challenges of Postmodernism* (Downers Grove, Ill.: InterVarsity Press, 2000), chap. 4; Norman L. Geisler, "Truth, Nature of," in *Baker Encyclopedia of Christian Apologetics,* ed. Norman L. Geisler (Grand Rapids, Mich.: Baker, 1999), pp. 741-45.

man L. Geisler writes, "There may be many different ways to *defend* different truth claims, but there is really only one proper way to *define* truth, namely as correspondence."[6] Various groups may take different things to be true, but truth itself is unified and cannot be contradictory. Therefore, what is true does not depend on individual or collective opinion, tradition or perspective. Furthermore, philosophers—both East and West—have worked within a basic logical framework, which they did not take to be culturally contingent. We will discover some of the logical problems in denying truth as correspondence (or as objective) below. But even logic itself is being attacked by some postmodernist thinkers who claim that logic is merely the result of cultural factors.

THE LOGIC OF TRUTH

Postmodernist claims to the contrary, logic is not the product of white, male and totalitarian thinking. Logic is, rather, indispensable for all rational analysis, for the testing of truth-claims. Without logic, we are left mute and muzzled concerning reality.

The logic of truth is the logic of the law of noncontradiction. First codified but not invented by Aristotle, this law states, "Nothing can both be and not be at the same time in the same respect." Nothing can possess incompatible properties; that is, nothing can be what it is not. For example, Jesus cannot be both sinless and sinful. If there is exactly one God, there cannot be many gods. This logical principle is not the unique possession of Christianity. It is a truth of all creation and how God ordained us to think. Despite what some benighted theologians have claimed, Christian faith does not require that we somehow transcend this law of logic. God is consistent and cannot lie (Heb 6:18). God cannot deny himself or assert what is false; nor can he make something both true and false in the same way at the same time.

Those who claim that this basic principle of thought is false must assert this principle in order to deny it. In so doing, they make a mockery out of all thought, language and the very notion of truth. Consider the statement: "The law of noncontradiction is false." For this statement itself

---

[6]Geisler, "Truth, the Nature of," p. 745.

to be true, it must contradict its opposite (that the law of noncontradiction is true). But in so doing, it must affirm the duality of truth and falsity—which is the very thing that the law of noncontradiction itself requires. This is how God made us to think—to think in accord with reality. Postmodernists who assert that logical principles are merely social and historical constructs nevertheless often accuse their critics of culpable falsehood and thus assert the law of noncontradiction.[7]

The law of noncontradiction combined with the specificity of Christian truth and the high stakes involved in choosing whether to believe in Christ means that truth for the Christian is confrontational. When Paul beheld the idolatry of Athens, he was "greatly distressed" and "so he reasoned in the synagogue with the Jews and the God-fearing Greeks" (Acts 17:17). This apologetic spirit eventually led to his famous Mars Hill apologetics address. While the postmodern world beholds the great welter of lifestyles, trends and facades and can only utter "whatever" with a smirk and a slouch, the followers of "the Way" (Acts 11:26) must defend "the faith that was once for all entrusted to the saints" (Jude 3).

Anthropologist Ernest Gellner, a secular critic of postmodernism, pays tribute to biblical monotheism when he says that the Enlightenment emphasis on "the uniqueness of truth" and the hope of discovering nature's objective secrets is rooted in monotheism's avoidance of "the facile self-deception of universal relativism."[8] He further sharpens his analysis by claiming this connection between the singularity and supremacy of God with a fundamental logical principle closely related to the law of noncontradiction.

> It was a jealous Jehovah who really taught mankind the Law of Excluded Middle: Greek formalization of logic (and geometry and grammar) probably would not have been sufficient on its own. Without a strong religious impulse toward a single orderly world, and the consequent avoidance of opportunist, manipulative incoherence, the cognitive miracle [of the Enlightenment] would probably not have occurred.[9]

---

[7]On this, see Groothuis, *Truth Decay,* pp. 232-33.
[8]Ernest Gellner, *Postmodernism, Reason, and Religion* (New York: Routledge, 1992), p. 95.
[9]Ibid., pp. 95-96.

The law of excluded middle trades on the same essential insight as the law of noncontradiction by stating that any factual statement and its denial cannot both be true. Either Jehovah is Lord or he is not Lord. There is no middle option. Jesus assumes this principle when he warns that "no one can serve two masters. Either he will hate the one and love the other, or he will be devoted to the one and despise the other. You cannot serve both God and Money" (Mt 6:24).

These essential logical principles—and many more—are the necessary tools for fruitful work in apologetics, philosophy and all rational thought. To relativize or ignore them is to welcome irrationality and court intellectual suicide.[10] These principles should be part of the foundation of our knowledge.[11]

THE BIBLICAL VIEW OF TRUTH

In order to counter effectively the postmodernist attack on truth, the Christian apologist should master the biblical understanding of truth. The Scriptures use the Hebrew and Greek words for truth and its derivatives repeatedly and without embarrassment. The meaning of the Hebrew term *emet,* which is at the root of the great majority of the Hebrew words related to truth, involves the ideas of support or stability. From this root flows the twofold notion of truth as faithfulness and conformity to fact.[12]

God is true or faithful to his word and in his activities and attitudes; God is the God of truth. So David prays, "Into your hands I commit my spirit; redeem me, O LORD, the God of truth" (Ps 31:5; see 2 Chron 15:3). Through Isaiah, God declares, "I, the LORD, speak the truth; I declare what is right" (Is 45:19).

The Hebrew *emet* can also represent "that which is conformed to reality in contrast to anything that would be erroneous or deceitful."[13] In

---

[10]For an introduction to logic, see Norman L. Geisler and Ronald M. Brooks, *Come Let Us Reason: An Introduction to Logical Thinking* (Grand Rapids, Mich.: Baker, 1990).

[11]See Norman L. Geisler, "Foundationalism," in *Baker Encyclopedia of Christian Apologetics,* ed. Norman L. Geisler (Grand Rapids, Mich.: Baker, 1999), pp. 259-60.

[12]Roger Nicole, "The Biblical Concept of Truth," in *Scripture and Truth,* ed. D. A. Carson and John D. Woodbridge (Grand Rapids, Mich.: Zondervan, 1983), p. 290.

[13]Ibid.

several passages, "If it is true" means, "If the charge is substantiated" (Is
43:9; Deut 13:14; 17:4). Many biblical texts include statements such as
"speaking the truth" (Prov 8:7; Jer 9:5) or "giving a true message" (Dan
10:1) or a "true vision" (Dan 8:26). *Emet* can also connote "what is authentic, reliable, or simply 'right,' " such as "true justice" (Zech 7:9) or as
in swearing in a "truthful, just and righteous way" (Jer 4:2). Roger Nicole
explains that faithfulness and conformity to fact are

> converging lines of meaning [for the concept of truth] in the Old Testa-
> ment. Neither is reducible to the other, yet they are not mutually conflict-
> ing. It is because truth is conformity to fact that confidence may be placed
> in it or in the one who asserts it, and it is because a person is faithful that
> he or she would be careful to make statements that are true.[14]

There is no indication that in the Hebrew Bible truth is another word
for belief or mere social custom, since beliefs can be false and customs
may be opposed to God's will. Jeremiah attacked the falsehood and un-
faithfulness of his people when he said, "How can you say, 'We are wise,
for we have the law of the LORD,' when actually the lying pen of the
scribes has handled it falsely?" (Jer 8:8 NIV). Nicole notes that "the clear
and insistent witness of the Old Testament in condemnation of all lies
and deceit reinforces its strong commendation of *emet* as faithfulness
and veracity."[15]

Although some scholars have asserted a great difference between the
Hebrew and Greek notions of truth, the Greek New Testament's understanding of truth is consistent with that of the Hebrew Scriptures. The
New Testament word *alētheia* and its derivations retain the Hebrew idea
of "conformity to fact" expressed in *emet*. According to Nicole, "The primary New Testament emphasis is clearly on truth as conformity to reality
and opposition to lies and errors."[16]

Both the Hebrew Scriptures and the New Testament draw a clear contrast between truth and error. John warns of distinguishing the "Spirit of
truth and the spirit of falsehood" (1 Jn 4:6). Paul says that those who

---

[14]Ibid., p. 291.
[15]Ibid., p. 292.
[16]Ibid., p. 293.

deny the reality of the God behind creation "suppress the truth by their wickedness" (Rom 1:18). Before Pilate, Jesus divided the field into truth and error: "For this reason, I was born, and for this I came into the world, to testify to the truth. Everyone on the side of truth listens to me" (Jn 18:37).

This biblical conception of truth as fidelity to objective fact also involves the claims that God's revealed truth is absolute as well. It is invariant and without exception or exemption. Neither is it relative, shifting or revisable. A classic text on the absoluteness of truth is Jesus' uncompromising statement, "I am the way and the truth and the life. No one comes to the Father except through me" (Jn 14:6). There is no exception or exemption from this claim: there is but one way to the Father, Jesus himself.

The truth of the gospel is not subject to any human veto or democratic procedures. This claim does not mean that Christians claim to have absolute knowledge about God. It simply means that God has revealed his one way of salvation through Christ and made this known in history and as recorded in Scripture and as illuminated by the Holy Spirit. Those who know Jesus as Lord confess his absoluteness, not their own. We can know this truth and testify to it only in light of God's grace because it is only by grace that grace can be known. Postmodernists to the contrary, the biblical metanarrative does not lead to oppression and arrogance because it centers on the revelation of a good, loving and holy God who has commissioned his people to communicate the absolute claims of the gospel in humility and love.

Moreover, God's revealed truth is universal. To be universal means to apply everywhere, to engage everything and to exclude nothing. The gospel message and the moral law of God is not circumscribed or restricted by cultural conditions. When Peter preached before the Jewish religious authorities, he declared in clear terms concerning Jesus of Nazareth: "Salvation is found in no one else, for there is no other name given under heaven by which we must we saved" (Acts 4:12; see also 1 Tim 2:5-6). This, of course, is a direct spiritual and intellectual challenge to every other religion and philosophy on the planet (see also Acts 17:30).

A survey of the biblical view of truth can not do justice to the richness of the words employed in a wide diversity of contexts. Nevertheless, it should be clear that the biblical view of truth collides with postmodernist notions of the social construction of reality and the relativity of truth. Nicole concludes that "the biblical view of truth *(emet-alētheia)* is like a rope with several intertwined strands"; it *"involves factuality, faithfulness, and completeness."*[17] The Bible does not present truth as a cultural creation of the ancient Jews or the early Christians. They received truth from the God who speaks truth to his creatures, and they were expected by this God to conform themselves to this truth. With his basis in revealed truth, the defender of the faith can work to challenge false philosophies pitted against the Christian worldview (2 Cor 10:3-5; Col 2:8-10).

Problems with Postmodernism: Truth, Language and Ethics

Secular postmodernist philosophies come in various forms, but they all attempt to undermine the rich biblical concept of truth. However, they are subject to several criticisms. First, postmodern pronouncements on truth often contradict themselves. These pronouncements claim to be applicable to reality itself, not merely to their own language game or constructed map; yet this is just what postmodernists themselves claim cannot be done. They have painted themselves into a linguistic corner in which they are silenced from affirming anything objectively real. Consider this statement:

> All "truth" is a social construction of language, and nothing more. It cannot orient us to any objective reality outside a system of discourse.

This statement makes a claim about objective reality. It refers to all truth and says that it is nothing but a contingent construction that cannot connect us to objective reality at all. This claim includes the statement itself in its description or range of reference. Therefore, the postmodernist statement about truth is merely a social construction—and nothing more. But if it is, then the statement itself cannot be true to reality. Therefore, it is false. Put another way, the statement sets up conditions that it cannot fulfill.

---

[17]Ibid.; emphasis in the original.

NIETZSCHE'S PERSPECTIVISM: MANY ANGLES, NO TRUTH

This point of philosophical failure can be illustrated also by Nietzsche's philosophy of perspectivism, which has significantly shaped many postmodernist approaches to truth. He claimed that there are no facts but only interpretations (or constructions) created according to one's particular needs to enhance one's life, what he called "the will to power." There is "no true world," only "a perspectival appearance whose origin lies in us."[18] Everything is a matter of relative and pragmatic perspective, with no method by which to adjudicate between perspectives rationally in order to discern an objective truth true for everyone. Nietzsche claims: "There are many kinds of eyes. Even the sphinx has eyes—and consequently there are many kinds of 'truths,' and consequently there is no truth."[19]

But Nietzsche put this forward as an account of the human situation, as an explanation for human knowing, being and acting. Still, if Nietzsche's own view is nothing but a relative perspective whose origin lay in himself only, and not a fact of the matter, his own view cannot successfully describe the lay of the land. It summarily executes itself, however poetically or passionately enunciated. Moreover, Nietzsche condemns many other views as flatly false, including all nonperspectivist views. Consider this condemnation: "In Christianity neither morality nor religion has even a single point of contract with reality."[20] Nietzsche implicitly claims that this statement against Christianity corresponds to reality and directly claims that Christian truth-claims fail to correspond to reality. Hence Nietzsche reverts to a view of truth he elsewhere earnestly denies. But no zeal can make contradictions come true.

We all have different perspectives to some degree (which can be biased, prejudiced, ignorant, arrogant, and so on), but perspectives do not determine truth. They can, however, affect our sense of what is true. A perspective may be partially true, largely true or mostly false, but its worth is gauged by its truth. A perspective in itself does not establish

---

[18]Friedrich Nietzsche, *The Will to Power,* ed. Walter Kaufmann (New York: Vintage Press, 1967) #15, pp. 14-15.
[19]Ibid., #540, p. 291.
[20]Friedrich Nietzsche, *The Antichrist,* in *The Portable Nietzsche,* ed. Walter Kaufmann (New York: Viking Press), p. 581.

truth; it is a perspective on or about something else—something outside of itself. One has a perspective, but it refers to reality, either successfully (by being true) or unsuccessfully (by being false). Perspectivism reduces to a kind of collective autism: everyone has a perspective, no one has the truth—and that's the truth.

Postmodernist constructivism or perspectivism also renders the concept of lying impossible. One lies when one affirms the opposite of what one takes to be true: either affirming what should be denied or denying what should be affirmed, given the facts of the matter. However, if everything is a matter of interpretation or perspective all the way down, there are no bedrock facts at all—no facts to relay and no facts to obscure. One creates all the reality we can ever "know." Lies become nonexistent because they are impossible. This is so radically counter-intuitive as to be absurd. Lies, lying and liars have existed, do exist and will exist—and in abundance. Perjury is still a crime, as is defamation of character, libel, slander and the obstruction of justice. The commandment not to bear false witness against one's neighbor (Ex 20:16) is still broken, even in postmodern times.

POSTMODERN CONFUSIONS ON TRUTH IN LANGUAGE

The common postmodernist account of truth is based on several confusions about the nature of language in relation to truth. Truth, it is claimed, is not established by anything outside of the mind or the culture that shapes beliefs. The word *truth* is simply a contingent creation of language, which has various uses in various cultures. It expresses certain purposes, customs, emotions and values, but it cannot be said to represent or mirror reality itself. Our access to the territory of reality is through our language, which acts as a map. But we cannot check the map against the territory, since we can know nothing outside our language. Thus language becomes a kind of prison of signifiers that can never connect with the signified outside of itself. In other words, when language attempts to refer to anything beyond language itself, it must fail.[21]

---

[21]See Jim Leffel, "Our New Challenge: Postmodernism," in *The Death of Truth,* ed. Dennis Mac-Callum (Minneapolis: Bethany House, 1996), pp. 38-39.

The sheer fact that finite, previously earth-bound human beings could construct manned space vehicles that travel to the moon and back reveals that the sophisticated mathematical formulations required for the successful navigation of space corresponded to the territory where no one had gone before. The map was a proper guide to the territory because it objectively fit the territory. In other words, the mathematical equations and the language related to their implementation (the signifiers) connected to the objective realities of outer space (the signified).

In addition to the above notions about language, postmodernists often argue that the semantics (word meanings) and syntax (grammatical structure) of human languages are contingent and ultimately arbitrary. They are merely social constructions. Humans have many differing languages, and translations between languages are often difficult. Moreover, the way people understand reality is dependent on the nature of their languages. These observations have led postmodernists to take languages to be self-enclosed and self-referential systems.

However, as contemporary philosopher John Searle has noted, this argument commits a basic fallacy. Any number of words can be used to name a dog, a tree or a philosophy. In one sense, this is arbitrary; the semantics could be different. There is nothing in the nature of what we call a dog that demands it be called a dog (or any of the other English words for canines). This is true as well for trees, philosophies, music, and so forth. Yet this has no bearing on the effectiveness of the use of words in designating the reality to which they refer. The words, however varied in different languages, when used in propositions still have an irreducibly referential function; they point to things outside of themselves. To put it another way, words (or signifiers) in declarative sentences have an extralinguistic focus (the signified). As Searle puts it, "From the fact that a *description* can only be made relative to a set of linguistic categories, it does not follow that the *facts/states of affairs/, etc., described* can only *exist* relative to a set of categories."[22] How we apply the terms *cat, kilogram, canyon* or whatever is contingent on various languages.

---

[22]John Searle, *The Construction of Social Reality* (New York: Free Press, 1995), p. 166; emphasis in the original.

We arbitrarily define the word "cat" in such and such a way; and only relative to such and such definitions can we say, "That's a cat." But once we have made the definitions and once we have applied the concepts relative to the system of definitions, whether or not something satisfies our definition is no longer arbitrary or relative. That we use the word "cat" the way we do is up to us; that there is an object that exists independently of that use, and satisfies that use, is a plain matter of (absolute, intrinsic, mind-independent) fact.[23]

The postmodernists have confused the relativity of term selection (semantic variation) with an inability of language to represent truly objective reality at all. This is like saying that because we can drive any number of kinds of cars, trucks, bicycles or motorcycles, we can never arrive at the same destination. Semantic and syntactical differences do not annul the ability of language to refer to realities outside of itself. We do not create different worlds through our languages as the postmodernists would have it, but we do use varying descriptions of the actual world, which may correspond or fail to correspond to the world that is there.[24]

From another angle, the postmodernist idea that language defines thought is highly suspect. There are empirical counterexamples to this claim, as noted epistemologist Alvin Goldman observes. Babies have been shown to possess logical categories before they speak or understand any language. Adults can solve certain kinds of tasks by employing concepts without words. Moreover, people frequently have the sense that the words they have used to express something were not quite right. Therefore, what they intended to say is different from what was said. Yet this would be impossible if thought was exhausted by language. Therefore, thought is not exhausted by language.[25] "In short, postmodernists need to moderate their claim that language is the great determiner of thought, for that unqualified view is simply false."[26]

---

[23]Ibid.
[24]Ibid.
[25]Alvin Goldman, *Knowledge in a Social World* (New York: Oxford University Press, 1999), pp. 18-19.
[26]Ibid., p. 19.

ETHICAL QUANDARIES

Right-thinking people judge certain acts—such as racism, rape, child abuse and terrorism—as objectively evil, and not as merely relative social constructions. If such assessments are correct, then the postmodern view cannot be sustained. Postmodernism emphasizes the diversity of truth-claims, particularly in pluralistic settings, but it provides no key to test these claims against reality. Instead, it succumbs to a kind of intellectual indifference. Truth is what you make it, nothing more. Yet the despicable terrorist crimes of September 11, 2001, jostled even the secular *New York Times* into questioning some assumptions. On September 22, 2001, it ran an editorial by Edward Rothstein, who wrote that "cataclysms not only cast shadows over human victims but can also shake the foundations of intellectual life." He opines that the events of September 11 challenged the perspective of postmodernism, which denies that "truth and ethical judgment have any objective validity."

> But such assertions seem peculiar when trying to account for the recent attack. The destruction seems to cry out for a transcendent ethical perspective. Even mild relativism seems troubling by contrast.[27]

"A transcendent ethical perspective" hints at the will of God, but the article doesn't go that far. Nevertheless, it exposes an Achilles heel of postmodernism.

Postmodernists have difficulty in living out their denial that moral statements can be objectively true. While Foucault attacked objective standards of ethics as constructions used to support oppressive systems, he nevertheless had to rely on some standard independent of society itself to make these judgments.[28] Foucault, like so many postmodernists, is operating on borrowed capital, which he can never repay, given the impoverishment of his worldview. Ironically, Foucault himself worked for prison reform, taking the penal system of his day to be unjust.[29]

---

[27] Edward Rothstein, "Attacks on U.S. Challenge Postmodern True Believers," *New York Times*, September 22, 2001.

[28] See William C. Placher, *Unapologetic Theology: A Christian Voice in a Pluralistic Conversation* (Louisville, Ky.: Westminster John Knox, 1989), p. 94.

[29] Gary Gutting, "Michel Foucault," in *Routledge Encyclopedia of Philosophy*, ed. Edward Craig (New York: Routledge, 1998), 3:709.

As an anarchist, Foucault made the individual's freedom to maximize pleasure the highest good and was fearful that "society constitutes a conspiracy to stifle one's own longings for self-expression." He even "agonized profoundly over the question of whether rape should be regulated by penal justice" because he thought that law equaled oppression, and lawlessness meant freedom.[30] His final writings made clear his ethical concern to liberate "human beings from contingent conceptual constraints masked as unsurpassable a priori limits" in order to lay out "alternative forms of existence."[31]

The logic of Foucault's presuppositions forced him to wrestle with a proposition that is self-evident: rape is immoral violence and exploitation of the highest magnitude. Without an objective moral order, such judgments are void. Yet Foucault contradicts himself by granting some kind of individual rights to pleasurable self-expression, some goodness in the liberation of the marginalized. This claim has no foundation, however, since "man" is, according to Foucault, only a "recent invention" during "European culture since the sixteenth century."[32] To all those "who still ask themselves question about what man is in his essence," Foucault responds, "we can answer only with a philosophical laugh."[33] Foucault would have, therefore, no ethical standard beyond the contemporary social constructions of what humans are on which to base any ethical criticism. When God is eliminated, humanity is annulled, and ethics is eroded. Only madness and anarchy remain (Prov 8:36).

Conclusion: Leaving Postmodernism Behind

Postmodernism has many facets that I have not explored.[34] However, the central postmodernist accounts of truth, rationality, language and ethics need to be understood and critiqued by Christian apologists, since these

---

[30]Ronald Beiner, "Foucault's Hyper Liberalism," *Critical Review* (summer 1995): 353-54.

[31]Gary Gutting, "Michel Foucault," in *The Cambridge Dictionary of Philosophy,* ed. Robert Audi (New York: Cambridge University Press, 1995), p. 276.

[32]Michel Foucault, *The Order of Things: An Archeology of the Human Sciences* (New York: Random House-Pantheon, 1971), pp. 386-87.

[33]Ibid., p. 343.

[34]For more on postmodernism, see Groothuis, *Truth Decay.* Much of the material in this chapter was adapted from *Truth Decay.*

ideas generally stand in stark contrast to the fundamentals of a Christian worldview (Col 2:8). Some argue that the postmodern emphasis on the finitude and culture-bound nature of all knowledge claims is a fitting rebuke to the pretensions of rationalism and fits well with the biblical account of humans as limited and sinful knowers. While Paul says we "see but a poor reflection," we can see something. While we "know in part," we can know something (1 Cor 13:11-12).

Postmodernism's rejection of the classical and biblical views of truth, rationality and language is not a fitting tonic to intellectual arrogance. Instead it shackles the intellect in a prison with no windows open to objective reality. While Christian witness must be savvy concerning the realities of the postmodern condition in order to make the historic Christian message understandable and pertinent to denizens of the contemporary world, this does not mean that we should become postmodernists in the process.

FOR FURTHER READING

Anderson, Walter Truett, ed. *The Truth About Truth: Deconfusing and Reconstructing the Postmodern World*. New York: G. P. Putnam's Sons, 1995.

Beckwith, Francis J., and Gregory P. Koukl. *Relativism: Feet Firmly Planted in Mid-Air*. Grand Rapids, Mich.: Baker, 1998.

Erickson, Millard. *Truth or Consequences: The Promise and Perils of Postmodernism*. Downers Grove, Ill.: InterVarsity Press, 2001.

Groothuis, Douglas. *Truth Decay: Defending Christianity Against the Challenges of Postmodernism*. Downers Grove, Ill.: InterVarsity Press, 2000.

MacCallum, Dennis, ed. *The Death of Truth*. Minneapolis: Bethany House, 1996.

Veith, Gene Edward. *Postmodern Times*. Wheaton, Ill.: Crossway, 1994.

15

LEGISLATING MORALITY

Michael Bauman

MANY CHRISTIANS WANT TO SHAPE THE POLITICAL AND SOCIAL INSTITUTIONS of their communities by helping to pass or keep in place laws and ordinances that are intended to protect notions that are central to preserving civil society. These notions include the intrinsic dignity of each human person (before and after birth), the sanctity of marriage (between one man and one woman) and the primacy of the family. Those who do not believe that these notions should be reflected in our laws typically reply that Christians and their allies in other faith traditions have no right to legislate morality.

The constant or determined repetition of an error does not make it true. Errors are errors regardless of either their prevalence or the persistence of those who advance them. Indeed, given the egregious foolishness of some of our most widespread beliefs in the recent past, the great popularity or predominance of a notion sometimes is enough to raise suspicions about its truthfulness. We moderns too eagerly and too often live our lives on the basis of insupportable, indefensible, half-true truisms that cannot stand up to close analysis. The assertion that you cannot legislate morality is just such a notion. No matter how often one hears that you cannot legislate morality, the truth is that you can legislate nothing else.

All laws, whether prescriptive or prohibitive, legislate morality. All laws, regardless of their content or their intent, arise from a system of values, from a belief that some things are right and others wrong, that some things are good and others bad, that some things are better and others worse. In the formulation and enforcement of law, the question is never whether or not morality will be legislated but which one. That question is fundamentally important because not all systems of morality are created equal. Some are wise, others foolish. Few are still in their first incarnation, nearly all having been enshrined as law at some time or place, often with predictable results. For better or worse, every piece of legislation touches directly or indirectly on moral issues or is based on moral judgments and evaluations concerning what it is we want or ought to be, what it is we want or ought to produce and preserve.

When, for example, the founding fathers drafted the original U.S. Constitution, they did so on the basis of competing belief systems, on the basis of competing assertions of right and wrong, which they endeavored to build into the Constitution. One or more of those belief systems permitted slavery; others did not. No side in the slavery debate at the Constitutional Convention argued that you could not legislate morality. That notion they all recognized as balderdash. They knew that indeed you could legislate morality, and they intended for that legislated morality to be theirs.

Nor did any side in the struggle to legislate morality at our nation's founding say to its opponents that trying to legislate morality was a breach of the wall of separation between church and state. Morality, after all, is not a church. They would have laughed at the confusion of mind revealed in one who thought that separating church from state meant separating morality from law. They wanted the nation to be moral. They wanted its laws to be just. But they did not want to give any one church a national legal advantage over the others. They did not want the nation to be Presbyterian, Baptist or Roman Catholic, which is a far different issue from whether or not to have ethics-driven law. Under the Constitution the founders drafted, all persons are free to follow and to worship God. The founders enshrined freedom of religion, not freedom from religion. In seeking to avoid a state-established church, they were not thereby establishing secularism or separating law from morality.

More fundamentally, the very fact that the founders were creating a new Constitution for their fledgling nation arose from the fact that they understood the actions of King George to be morally evil, to be politically unjust. They all knew quite well that morality belonged in politics, in fact that politics was simply morality applied to the public square, to the public's business.

The founders sought to establish what they called an ordered liberty. The order they sought was provided in part by the morality they intended to enshrine in law. By seeking ordered liberty, the founders were not seeking anything new or unprecedented in political thought or in political history. They well knew from reading the ancient works of Aristotle, for example, that morality encoded in civil law helped to provide order because law inescapably has a teaching function, or pedagogical effect: law teaches the citizens what is right and good, and it punishes those who cannot or will not learn that lesson, or at least act as if they had.

To make the point from a different angle, when we pass laws that require drivers to drive their vehicles at 20 miles per hour or less in school zones, we do so because we have a value system that rightly puts greater worth in human life than in vehicular speed. That valuation is a moral judgment. That moral valuation we properly and wisely seek to translate into binding and enforceable law. We propose and pass such laws because we think it wrong for drivers recklessly to endanger the lives of defenseless children, who lack the experience, foresight and physical dexterity to keep themselves out of harm's way on the streets. Drivers who do not do as the law requires, we punish. No one, in the face of such proposed legislation, says to the local authorities that those authorities have no right to impose their morality on others, even though that is precisely what such laws do. Much less does anyone seriously argue that to propose such values-laden laws is an effort to tear down the wall of separation between church and state.

Those objections are not raised because the laws in question are laws with which all serious-minded citizens are in agreement. That these laws are morals-based, or values-driven, creates no problem for those who find the laws agreeable. Rather, people tend to complain that laws are morals-based only when the law in question is based upon a moral valuation with which they disagree. But to be consistent, those who object to morals-based laws would have to raise the same objection to all laws whatever, including the laws they support. But they do not. They never do. When their own morals are encoded in law, they raise not even the faintest whimper of protest. Yet when laws are passed that they dislike, they say almost nothing else. They seem to want a sword that will cut only others, never themselves. But any sword of objection sharp enough to cut Jack is sharp enough to cut John as well, even though John might not like it.

Legislating morality, in other words, is not an option; it is a necessity, an inevitability. Justice, equity, fairness—those characteristics that all thoughtful citizens want from their government and upon which they think government and its laws ought to be predicated—these are all moral categories. We outlaw slavery, theft, murder, fraud, deceit, rape, and so on, precisely because they are immoral and we want them stopped or at least radically curtailed. We propose, pass and enforce these morals-based laws specifically toward that end, and in so doing we are right.

Let me make the point more explicitly: When it comes to prohibiting sexual harassment or sexual discrimination in the marketplace, feminists do not complain that the proposed legislation attempts to enshrine morality in the civil or penal code, even though it most definitely does. No serious feminist has ever sought to undo or to oppose such legislation because it was based on a system of morals. Feminists complain about legislating morality only when it comes to outlawing abortion. They object to legislating morality only when the morality in question is one from which they dissent. When the law in question encodes a morality they support, their objection to morals-driven law disappears.

By the same token, when a civil rights leader supports affirmative action laws and opposes the Jim Crow legislation of the old South, both that leader's support and opposition are based upon the moral judgment that all persons are created equal and ought therefore to be treated equally under the law. That civil rights leader cannot then turn around and say to someone else, pro-life advocates for instance, that they are

imposing their morality on others because the pro-life advocates are doing exactly what the civil rights advocate is doing, and on precisely the
same basis, namely, upholding the dignity and worth of every human
being. Like the civil rights advocate, the pro-life advocates are affirming
the obligation of a just nation to insure that all persons enjoy equal protection under the law.

Sometimes those who resist legislating morality do so not because
they object to the morality being legislated but because they value freedom and wish to defend it. They seem not to understand, however, that
their allegedly morals-free proposals will be the death of the freedom
they value, not its protection. Without the guidance and constraint of
morally informed law, liberty degenerates into mere license, which is not
the same as political freedom. One simply cannot reject moral authority
and yet live in an orderly world. When you banish morality from the
public square, you give birth to an outlaw culture, not to freedom. To
live outside the moral law, to live without the wisdom of the ages and
of God, is to court slavery and death. Because human nature is what it
is, without great volumes of enforceable law political freedom is short-
lived and finally impossible. Indeed, without great volumes of enforceable law, chaos—not freedom—always results. Authentic political freedom, if it is to remain true to itself and avoid the excesses of license,
must be exercised according to the dictates of truth and virtue, never the
other way round. Freedom must be limited by the demands of justice,
of morality. The most important consideration regarding any action is
not "Is it free?" but "Is it good?"

Make no mistake, legislating morality is not only inescapable, it
works. The proof that laws change behavior is widely known and not
far to find: Almost no one in the South today argues that slavery is moral,
even though many of their grandparents and great-grandparents thought
it was and, as a result, owned other human beings as property. What
stands between today's southern Americans and their slave-owning an-
cestors is morals-based law, specifically the Thirteenth Amendment and
the civil rights laws of the 1960s and later, all of which helped radically
to reshape the behavior and beliefs of those who grew up in their wake.
Similarly, before Prohibition the average annual consumption of alcohol

in America was nearly three gallons per person. After Prohibition that number fell to slightly less than one gallon. In fact, alcohol consumption did not return to pre-Prohibition levels in America for nearly forty years. By the same token, before the Supreme Court legalized abortion in 1973, about 100,000 abortions were performed in the United States annually. After *Roe v. Wade,* however, the number rose to between 1.2 and 1.5 million a year. In short, whether the laws in question are good or bad, law has an effect. The morality in the law, whatever it might be, tends to become the morality of the people. Law is always a tutor to morals and a shaper of national character, both for good and ill.

To digress: While legislating morality is an inevitability, I am not saying anything so silly as that all sins ought to be made crimes. No government could effectively enforce laws against lustful thoughts, gluttony or so-called white lies, even though such activities are sinful. And if somehow the impossibility of enforcing such laws were overcome, the immediate result would not be less lust, for instance, but rather the overcrowding of penal facilities on an unimaginable scale.

Back to the point: When people object to legislating morality, they fail to recognize or to remember that their own understanding of morality is the impulse behind the laws they themselves propose and defend. It is also the impulse behind their opposition to other laws. Yet, despite their inescapable dependence upon their own moral code when designing, proposing or opposing laws, they seek to deny that same moral impulse to others who wish to be heard, who wish to have their own ideas taken seriously, who wish to have their own beliefs and values prevail. But you must not withhold from others in the public square what you wish to make use of yourself. If you would banish the moral basis of the laws proposed by your political opponents, you must banish it from your own. But no one does, and no one can.

Furthermore, if you object to legislating morality, you could not, for that very reason, raise any effective moral objection to execution as a punishment for jaywalking or decapitation for tax evasion or speeding. Your objection to such penal atrocities and to the laws that permit or require them is a moral objection, which you say ought to be banished from law.

Because law is not a substitute for parental authority but is a complement to it, one must not argue (as some do) that moral education is the function of parents only and not therefore of the state. Because parents teach morality does not mean that law does not or must not. Parents and law share at least this: They function inescapably as moral educators, whether for good or evil. In cases where parents fail to perform this task wisely or well—a not uncommon occurrence—law must function in this capacity all the more. Similarly, the fact that morality is meant to be implemented by individuals does not mean that there must be no public morality, no civil, social or legal standards of conduct, as if because morality has a personal dimension, it can have no social or political dimension, or as if the existence of personal morality meant that there ought to be no public morality.

But the case for morals-based law rests on a wider and more profound basis than the internal contradictions of those who oppose legislating morality and the impossibility of doing as they insist. Those who wish to banish ethical considerations from legal affairs forget that civilizations are not founded on considerations of mere personal comfort and pleasure, or on science and technology, or even on self-gratification and self-preservation, but on virtue—both public and private. The good society, in other words, depends for its preservation and well-being on the character of its people, on the virtues that accompany, perhaps even define, good citizenship. Only on the foundation of courage, of self-control and self-denial can a good society be founded and continued. But these civic virtues are not natural to us. We are not born into the world as good and competent citizens. The civic virtues and public responsibilities that define good citizenship must be acquired; they must be learned. In that sense, we all enter this world unequipped by natural endowment for effective citizenship and for self-government, which is why one of the oldest political insights available to us is that which insists that we are always only one generation from barbarism, that every newly-born generation needs to be civilized, or culturally housebroken, as it were. Those necessary but unnatural social skills and civic virtues require nurture and guidance for their growth, even for their existence. Consequently, moral education is a prerequisite for a sound and flourishing civil society. This moral nurture, this aid to character formation, the laws of a nation help to provide by setting before the citizenry examples of acceptable behavior and incentives toward adopting that behavior as one's own. But law divorced from morality, law that poses as morally agnostic, cannot accomplish that task. Instead, morally evacuated law teaches the citizens that moral conduct is not necessary, either for their own happiness or for the establishment and continuation of a good society and civil order.

In short, the rule of law is necessary to a civil society, and a just rule of law requires adherence to a strict moral code. Perhaps an analogy will serve to clarify the point: Computer programmers often employ the acronym *gigo,* derived from the first letter of the words "garbage in, garbage out," a phrase warning those programmers that no bad program yields good results. You get back from the computer results that reflect the worth of the program it employs. And farmers likewise understand that you could not reasonably expect to gather a harvest of corn from a field planted with beans. You reap what you sow; you harvest what you plant—a principle that applies to law and to culture as well as to farmers and programmers. Only a legal code counseled by virtue and rooted in goodness can yield civil justice. Justice is not the harvest of a legal system into which it was never planted. Moral outcomes are not to be expected from a legal system into which it was never programmed, never cultivated. Except by the happiest of chances, moral results—in other words, just results—do not grow from the legal field in which those seeds were never planted. If you neglect to plant morality in the legal code, you must not expect to harvest it in court, or in the character of those citizens whose moral nurture is shaped partly by the laws of the society in which they are raised.

One of the most distressing facts about the United States today, therefore, is that it is now undergoing a deliberate deflation of traditional ideals and values, both in the culture in general and in the law in particular. It is enduring what Gertrude Himmelfarb called the de-moralization of society, or what George Will described as the slow-motion barbarization of America, in the wake of which politics and life have become impoverished, coarsened and tawdry. This disaster we deliberately and foolishly inflict upon ourselves by insisting, in the face of history and of clear thinking, that we ought not to legislate morality, and that governing and government have no effect upon the character of the nation and the persons who constitute it.

Given the penchant we all have for self-seeking and for personal satisfaction, things for which we are sometimes sorely tempted to sacrifice almost anything, in our moments of honest self-reflection we know that we would alter both the government and the law to suit our whims and desires, however perverted they might be, had we the opportunity to do so. Only enforceable laws based on unchanging morality can obviate this threat. Civil society requires morality from its legal code for its very existence and continuance because our natural character does not suffice to constrain us. We must never forget what thinkers as divergent as Burke and Rousseau knew: the act of establishing a civil society is identical with that of establishing a binding morality, something a morally agnostic legal code is impotent to help produce.

Government does not exist simply to make possible whatever delights and advantages its citizens might happen to prefer at any given moment, whether privately or collectively. If some types of pleasure are better and more socially and morally suitable than others, then one of the purposes of government is to help educate the citizenry to pursue the higher pleasures rather than their lower or more base alternatives. Moral education, one of the functions of law, helps make those right thinking and right choosing citizens—and the culture they desire and seek to preserve—more likely. Good societies, in other words, depend for their existence upon good and decent people. Good and decent people do not simply happen. They are nurtured, and one of the institutions that helps to nurture them best is well-formed, morally responsible law. Public institutions, like law and law enforcement, need to be concerned with the bridling of egoistic motives and actions. If they are not, something worse than chaos ensues, namely, cultural perversity and moral decay.

Put differently, political questions are moral questions. For example, every government asks and answers, whether knowingly or not, "What things in life are worth having and preserving, and at what price to the nation, to the community, to the people?" Public policy issues are simply the political and economic application in the present of the enduring moral questions. In the public square and in the marketplace, our public policies are our appropriation of and approximation of the permanent things. To form wise public policy, and the system of laws under which it is best pursued and applied, requires not a flight from morality but a resort to it, a resort to prudence, which is by no means the same thing as a legally encoded moral agnosticism.

Law and morality share this burden: both serve the function of governor—morality for those with self-control and self-restraint, law for those without it. That is, morality and law are like the two banks of a river, the river in this case being human action and the passions and desires that drive it. The banks of a river run roughly parallel: where one turns left or right the other tends to do the same. If they did not, the river would become a swamp—putrid, fetid and stagnant. Law and morality, like the banks of a river, ought to move in roughly the same direction in order to help curb the defects in human nature. If they do not, human action and human society quickly become a swamp, a morass of polymorphic perversity, something that always occurs in the absence of public virtue and the enforceable law that upholds and nurtures it. To protect us from the moral and cultural swamp that threatens to engulf us, law must take its cue from morality.

Well-framed law helps us make the best use of our freedom by teaching us to avoid both excess and deficiency. Without the pedagogy of law, we are deprived of one of our best and potentially wisest instructors and are thereby vastly impoverished, both individually and corporately. Those who are frightened by the moral pedagogy of law seem not to understand that human beings can be oppressed by an excess of freedom, which is another name for licentiousness. Good law leaves room for liberty, not for license. Good law helps curb human excess, while morality helps curb the law. What a bridle is to the horse, law is to human nature. And what law is to human nature, morality is to law. Law helps regulate the people; morality helps regulate the law. In that light, some of those who object to morals-based law seem not to appreciate the great cultural and moral value of shame, of guilt, and of the proper fear of just punishment.

Morally sound law helps us to distinguish right from wrong, innocence from guilt, and justice from injustice. But if the law from which
we learn is not rooted in true morality, what we learn is misshapen, misguided and misleading, because law always teaches. In such cases it
teaches error. Put differently, ideas have consequences, and bad ideas
have bad ones. The bad ideas encoded in supposedly morals-free law
are corrosive of virtue, of duty, of civility and of human fulfillment. One
of the disastrous effects of allegedly morals-free legislation is that it tends
to produce deep and widespread doubt in persons across the culture
about what is right and what is wrong, which leaves only a resort to
power as a way out of our moral dilemmas. In a moral vacuum power
and doubt rule all. Doubt makes us unsure of ourselves and of our beliefs; power makes those who have it despotic over those who do not.
Without morality in law, we know less well and less surely what is right,
and if we are ignorant about what is right and wrong, we can raise no
compelling argument against evil, or even know it when we see it. Our
ignorance makes it so.

Government and governing involve questions of value, questions
about what is good and what is good for us, as well as what is evil and
what will do us harm. To instruct us regarding the good, to lead us toward it and to protect us from evil—whether our own or someone
else's—are all part of the function of law. But those who wish to exile
virtue from the legal code, who wish to banish virtue from law and to
render legislation a morality-free zone set these important and valuable
functions of law at naught. Were those persons to succeed, both they
and we would suffer incalculable harm, having had one of our most useful moral educators shut down, censored as it were. They would stop
the moral voice of law and in so doing would silence one of our most
valuable instructors of civic virtue and thereby destroy one of our most
effective guides to prudent social behavior and to the blessings that attend it.

All cultures are rooted in, and are expressions of, deeply held values.
Cultures are the historical outworking of those values, the historical human consequences of those values, values that sometimes lead to compassion, beauty, war, deprivation, heroism or degeneration. Law is a

function of culture—all cultures have law—which means that law is a function of values, of morality. Law without values is cultural suicide, which is what those who wish to separate the one from the other are going to produce, whether they wish to do so or not.

In our age of increasingly complex moral problems, where technological advances outstrip our moral growth and understanding, we must do our level best to cultivate the wisest persons, the noblest motives and the highest actions of which we are capable. To do so, we must make far better use of the law as tutor, as moral ennobler. We must remind ourselves repeatedly that the best habitat in which to raise ennobled citizens is a well-ordered society, one in which law is rooted in morality. We must not forget that law is an expression of, and a shaper of, the conscience of a nation. Consequently, the nearsighted and misguided movement to separate law from morality is as dangerous as it is impossible. Both for nations and for us as individuals, our character is our future. Morality is destiny.

FOR FURTHER READING

Arkes, Hadley. *First Things: An Inquiry into the First Principles of Morals and Justice*. Princeton, N.J.: Princeton University Press, 1986.

―――. *Natural Rights and the Right to Choose*. New York: Cambridge University Press, 2002.

Beckwith, Francis J., and Gregory P. Koukl. *Relativism: Feet Firmly Planted in Mid-Air*. Grand Rapids, Mich.: Baker, 1998.

Geisler, Norman L., and Frank S. Turek. *Legislating Morality: Is It Wise? Is It Legal? Is It Possible?* Minneapolis: Bethany House, 1999.

George, Robert P. *The Clash of Orthodoxies: Law, Morality and Religion in Crisis*. Willmington, Del.: ISI Books, 2001.

―――. *Making Men Moral: Civil Liberties and Public Morality*. New York: Oxford University Press, 1993.

16

DARWIN, DESIGN AND THE PUBLIC SCHOOLS

Francis J. Beckwith

ONE OF THE GREAT CULTURAL CONFLICTS IN AMERICAN HISTORY HAS BEEN over the teaching of evolution in public school science classes. Many Christians have objected to the teaching of evolution on the grounds that evolutionary theory is really a form of atheism and that public schools should not teach atheism as "the truth" because, according to several well-known Supreme Court opinions, the teaching of irreligion as a state orthodoxy violates the Constitution as much as teaching any religion as a state orthodoxy.[1] In order to create a fair public school curriculum, many Christians (often joined by like-minded citizens from other faiths such as Islam and Judaism) have supported legislation in their individual states that would require that their schools offer lesson plans that are balanced. Several federal courts, including the U.S. Supreme Court, have struck down these statutes as unconstitutional because they violate the clause of the First Amendment that forbids the government from establishing a religion (aka "the establishment clause").

In what was perhaps the most colorful of these cases, *McLean v. Arkansas* (1982),[2] Norman L. Geisler testified as an expert witness for the state of Arkansas, which passed a law requiring that the students in its

---

[1]The U.S. Supreme Court writes in *Epperson v. Arkansas,* 393 U.S. 97, 105 (1968): "[T]his Court said in Keyishian v. Board of Regents [385 U.S. 589, 603 (1967)], the First Amendment 'does not tolerate laws that cast a pall of orthodoxy over the classroom.' "

[2]*McLean v. Arkansas Board of Education,* 529 F. Supp. 1255 (1982).

public schools be offered a balanced approach on the question of evolution. This balance would include the teaching of creationism. In a
book that was released five years after *McLean,* Geisler (with coauthor
J. Kerby Anderson) would suggest a way to understand this debate that
was a forerunner of what would later be called the Intelligent Design
(ID) movement.[3]

Although the U.S. Supreme Court has dealt specifically with state laws
that either forbade evolution (*Epperson v. Arkansas* [1968]) or required
balanced treatment between evolution and creationism (*Edwards v.
Aguillard* [1987]),[4] it has never addressed directly the question of
whether a public school or teacher could offer scientific criticisms of,
and alternatives to, evolution that are not derived from religious literature but still lend support to a theological worldview. In this chapter, I
argue that the presentation of arguments for one of these points of view,
ID theory, in a public school science classroom does not violate the U.S.
Constitution.

There are several reasons why this issue should be important to Christian citizens. First, evolution, as it is widely understood in the professional
literature (see below), presupposes that only naturalistic accounts of natural phenomena count as science. But naturalism is a philosophical point
of view that holds that the natural universe is all that exists and all the entities in it can be accounted for by strictly material processes without resorting to any designer, Creator or nonmaterial entity as an explanation or
cause for either any aspect of the natural universe or the universe as a
whole. Thus, if science is the paradigm of knowledge, as is widely held
in our culture, and it presupposes naturalism, then naturalism is the only
worldview for which one can have knowledge. But if a public school science curriclum offers exclusively a naturalistic point of view, it is in fact
instructing the school's students that claims of knowledge outside of naturalistic science are not really knowledge. This sends the message to the
nation's citizens that non-naturalistic claims—whether in ethics, theology
or traditional metaphysics—are simply matters of opinion and/or subjec-

---

[3]Norman L. Geisler and J. Kerby Anderson, *Origin Science: A Proposal for the Creation-Evolution Controversy* (Grand Rapids, Mich.: Baker, 1987).
[4]*Edwards v. Aguillard,* 482 U.S. 578 (1987).

tive preference. This makes it more difficult for Christian (or even broadly religious) truth-claims to be taken seriously in the wider culture, because a naturalistic bias grants people the intellectual permission to reject non-naturalist truth-claims a priori without examining the arguments and evidence for their truth.

Second, although Christians should not be employing the resources of the state to coerce people to become Christians, naturalists should not do the same in order to advance the cause of naturalism. Thus, if a state were to permit or require its public school science teachers to explore in the classroom scientific alternatives to, and criticisms of, evolution, its schools would better reflect the wide disagreement over the nature of science, knowledge and metaphysics that pervades the worlds of philosophy and the philosophy of science. Right now students are given the false impression that naturalism is the only intellectually respectable view, and because alternatives to naturalistic science are dismissed as religious regardless of the quality of the arguments for them, naturalism also wins by default.

The purpose of this chapter is not to offer an argument for an aspect of Christian doctrine (e.g., the existence of God, Christ's resurrection) but rather to explore a cultural impediment to belief that has become part of the wider intellectual culture as a result of what has been taught in its publicly funded institutions. I will first define the terms *creationism, evolution* and *intelligent design* and then make the argument that ID may be taught in public school science classes without violating the establishment clause. Of course, whether ID *should* be taught is another matter altogether, one that falls outside the scope of this chapter. However, it seems to me that at minimum there should be some aspect of public school curriculum—whether inside or outside the science classroom—by which teachers may instruct their students that naturalism (or materialism) is as much a worldview as theism and that a scientist's preference for one or the other is driven by philosophical considerations, which may be rigorously defended and held by trained philosophers but are nevertheless not the result of the deliverances of science per se.

Important Terms

Creationism. Creationism, as understood by the courts, is synonymous with *young-earth creationism*. This view, according to Phillip E. Johnson, is associated with the "term 'creation-science,' as used in the Louisiana law [in the *Edwards* case], [and] is commonly understood to refer to a movement of Christian fundamentalists based upon an extremely literal interpretation of the Bible." "Creation-scientists," writes Johnson, "do not merely insist that life was *created;* they insist that the job was completed in six days no more than ten thousand years ago, and that all evolution since that time has involved trivial modifications rather than basic changes. . . . [Young-earth creationism] attributes the existence of fossils to Noah's flood."[5]

The statutes struck down as unconstitutional by the Supreme Court in *Edwards* and by a federal district court in *McLean* had this type of creationism in mind. Thus "creationism" refers exclusively to this point of view.

Evolution. "Evolution" can mean different things. Sometimes it is used as a synonym for Darwinism, both the theory defended by Charles Darwin (1809-1882) in his *On the Origin of Species* as well as the subsequent refinements of Darwin's theory. Arguing from what he observed occurs when domestic breeders engage in selection, Darwin offered *natural selection* as the engine by which living organisms adapt, survive and acquire new characteristics and pass them on to their offspring:

Owing to this struggle, variations, however slight and from whatever cause proceeding, if they be in any degree profitable to an individual of any species, in its infinitely complex relations to other organic beings and to external nature, will tend to the preservation of that individual, and will generally be inherited by the offspring. The offspring, also, will thus have a better chance of surviving, for, of the many individuals of any species which are periodically born, but a small number can survive. I have called this principle, by which each slight variation, if useful, is preserved by the term of Natural Selection, in order to mark its relation to man's power of selection. We have seen that man by selection can certainly produce great results, and can adapt organic beings to his own uses, through the accumulation of slight but useful variations, given to him by the hand of Nature. But Natural Selection, as we shall hereafter see, is a power inces-

---

[5]Phillip E. Johnson, *Darwin on Trial* (Chicago: Regnery/Gateway, 1991), p. 4.

santly ready for action, and is as immeasurably superior to man's feeble efforts, as the works of Nature are to those of Art.[6]

No one, not even hard-line creationists, deny this sort of evolution, if all that it means is that biological species adapt over time to changing environments and pass on those adaptations genetically to their offspring. This is typically called *microevolution*. This should be distinguished from *macroevolution,* the view that the complex diversity of living things in our world, through small, incremental and beneficial mutations over long eons of time, are all the result of one bacterial cell. That is, all living beings share a common ancestor, giving the appearance of being designed, though in reality engineered, by the unintelligent forces of natural selection.

The notion of common descent is fundamental to evolution even if Darwinian and neo-Darwinian accounts of this descent are replaced or supplemented by another theory (e.g., punctuated equilibrium). This is why Antony Flew correctly points out that "it is wrong to identify either the Darwinism of *On the Origin of Species* or Neo-Darwinism with biological evolution without prefix or suffix. That to which any account of the evolution of species is necessarily opposed is any doctrine of their immutability, combined, presumably, with the claim that they were, whether simultaneously or successively, specially created by *ad hoc* agency."[7]

Evolution is more than a theory applicable to biology and biochemistry. It also asserts that the bacterial cell from which all life arose sprung from inorganic matter. According to Douglas J. Futuyama, "we will almost certainly never have direct fossil evidence that living molecular structures evolved from nonliving precursors. Such molecules surely could not have been preserved without degradation." Nevertheless, "a combination of geochemical evidence and laboratory experiment shows that such evolution is not only plausible but almost undeniable."[8] More-

---

[6]Charles Darwin, *The Origin of Species,* a facsimile of the 1st ed. (1859), intro. by Ernst Mayr (Cambridge, Mass.: Harvard University Press, 1964), p. 61.

[7]Antony Flew, *Darwinian Evolution,* 2nd ed. (New Brunswick, N.J.: Transaction Books, 1997), p. 42.

[8]Douglas J. Futuyama, *Science on Trial: The Case for Evolution* (New York: Pantheon Books, 1983), p. 95.

over, inorganic matter, indeed the matter of the entire universe, is said to have resulted from an initial explosion called the big bang, an event that occurred over fifteen billion years ago.[9] Thus evolution is a grand materialist explanation for the diversity and apparent design of entities that make up what we call nature, including both organic and inorganic entities.[10] George Gaylord Simpson explains the "meaning of evolution":

> Although many details remain to be worked out, it is already evident that all the objective phenomena of the history of life can be explained in purely naturalistic or, in a proper sense of the sometimes abused word, materialistic factors. . . . Man is the result of a purposeless and natural process that did not have him in mind.[11]

Thus evolution, as understood in the professional literature, is *naturalistic* evolution, the view that the entire universe and all the entities in it can be accounted for by strictly material processes without resorting to any designer, Creator or nonmaterial entity or agent as an explanation for either any aspect of the natural universe or the universe as a whole. Therefore, to say that evolution is true is to say that naturalism (or materialism) as a worldview is true, for the former entails the latter, for the latter is a necessary condition of the former. Consequently, to challenge that necessary condition—by appealing to something even as modest as Intelligent Design—poses a threat to the materialist edifice. That is, naturalistic evolution provides an answer to the very same question ID provides an answer: What is the origin of apparent design in biological organisms and/or other aspects of the natural universe and/or the universe as a whole? Evolution answers the question by appealing to the forces of unguided matter (and/or energy), the latter to intelligent agency.

Intelligent Design (ID). Intelligent Design is a research program embraced by a small though growing platoon of academics who maintain that intelligent agency, as an aspect of scientific theory-making, has more explanatory power in accounting for the specified, and sometimes

---

[9]See Monroe W. Strickberger, *Evolution,* 3rd ed. (Sudbury, Mass.: Jones & Bartlett, 2000), p. 76.
[10]See ibid., chaps. 1-25.
[11]George Gaylord Simpson, *The Meaning of Evolution: A Study of the History of Life and of Its Significance for Man,* rev. ed. (New Haven, Conn.: Yale University Press, 1967), p. 279.

irreducible, complexity of some physical systems, including biological entities and/or the existence of the universe as a whole, than the blind forces of unguided matter.

We will look at two aspects of ID that are relevant to this chapter's purpose: the case against methodological naturalism and the case for Intelligent Design. Because the literature supporting ID is sophisticated, vast and growing, my presentation of its case will be cursory. For a more detailed presentation, see chapter five, authored by design advocate William A. Dembski.

THE CASE AGAINST METHODOLOGICAL NATURALISM

ID proponents maintain that there is a fundamental reason why evolution seems to most scholars to be the only real legitimate explanation for the origin of the universe and life: a prior commitment to methodological naturalism (MN), "the view that science must be restricted solely to undirected natural processes."[12] According to Johnson, "A methodological naturalist defines science as the search for the best naturalistic theories. A theory would not be naturalistic if it left something out (such as the existence of genetic information or consciousness) to be explained by a supernatural cause."[13] Thus, according to design theorists, once one defines science as a discipline that allows only naturalistic explanations, and if one maintains that science is the only field that provides truth on the question of origins, then evolution (not necessarily Darwinism) must be true even if there are many unanswered questions that seem incapable of being adequately addressed under the evolutionary paradigm.

Thus, the real question, according to design theorists, is whether their arguments for ID work, not whether ID conflicts with MN. After all, if the ID arguments work and they conflict with MN, then one may conclude that MN is not a necessary precondition of natural science and cannot be employed to exclude positions contrary to it.

---

[12]William A. Dembski, *Intelligent Design: The Bridge Between Science and Theology* (Downers Grove, Ill.: InterVarsity Press, 1999), p. 119.

[13]Phillip E. Johnson, *Reason in the Balance: The Case Against Naturalism in Science, Law and Education* (Downers Grove, Ill.: InterVarsity Press, 1986), p. 208.

THE CASE FOR INTELLIGENT DESIGN

At the core of the ID research program is its criteria by which its proponents claim they can detect or falsify design. One such criterion is proposed by Dembski, which he defends in chapter five. He proposes an explanatory filter in order to detect specified complexity (SC), something that we recognize in many fields as evidence of intelligent agency, for example, "forensic science, intellectual property law, insurance claims investigation, cryptography, and random number generation."[14] Thus, what Dembski is suggesting is not something unknown to the world of science. Rather what he is proposing is that we extend these insights, which have proved so fruitful in other fields, to the world of the natural sciences.

Why specified complexity? According to Dembski, "Whenever we infer design, we must establish three things—*contingency, complexity* and *specification*. Contingency, by which we mean that an event was one of several possibilities, ensures that the object is not the result of an automatic and hence unintelligent process." In other words, an event that is not contingent is one that can be completely accounted for by natural law (or an algorithm). To cite an example, a salt crystal "results from forces of chemical necessity that can be described by the laws of chemistry. A setting of silverware is not."[15] The place setting is contingent, for there are no laws of chemistry or physics that direct the knife and spoon to the right side of the plate and the fork to the left. In other words, a contingent event cannot be reduced to natural law.

"Complexity," writes Dembski, "ensures that the object in question is not so simple that it can readily be explained by chance." For Dembski, "complexity . . . is a form of probability." For example, the improbability of opening a combination lock by chance depends on the complexity of the mechanism. As the lock mechanism increases in complexity, the greater the improbability that one will be able to open the lock by

---

[14]William A. Dembski, "Reinstating Design Within Science," *Rhetoric and Public Affairs* 1, no. 4 (1998), p. 506.

[15]William A. Dembski in *Science and Evidence for Design in the Universe* by Michael J. Behe, William A. Dembski and Stephen C. Meyer, The Proceedings of the Wethersfield Institute, vol. 9 (San Francisco: Ignatius Press, 2000), pp. 25, 26.

chance. Therefore, "the greater the complexity, the smaller the probability. Thus to determine whether something is sufficiently complex to warrant a design inference is to determine whether it has sufficiently small probability."[16] Nevertheless, complexity by itself may not be design. For example, a random selection of one thousand symbols (rtvwix%*<3q498d . . .) and the result of a thousand coin flips are complex and improbable but can be explained by randomness or chance. This is why specification is essential.

"Specification ensures that this object exhibits the type of pattern that is the trademark of intelligence."[17] Specificity by itself may not be design. For example, redundant order, such as the beating of a pulsar or the earth's orbiting of the sun every 365 days, can be explained by law and necessity. However, if specification is combined with complexity, a design inference may be warranted. Dembski offers an example from one area of science, the Search for Extra-Terrestrial Intelligence (SETI). SETI researchers, in their attempt to detect intelligence outside earth, have developed a filter that has certain preset patterns so that it may discard radio waves that do not exhibit specified complexity. In the novel (authored by Carl Sagan) and movie versions of *Contact,* SETI researchers detect extraterrestrial intelligence when they discover a sequence of beats and pauses that correspond to the prime numbers from 2 to 101.[18]

Dembski makes a distinction between *specification* and *fabrication.* The latter occurs when one infers a pattern ad hoc after the fact even though chance and necessity may account for the pattern. For example,[19] suppose a hurricane moves through my neighborhood, destroying four out of the seven homes on my street, and the three homes not destroyed are owned by me and my two brothers. Moreover, my brothers and I own the second, fourth and sixth homes on the block, which means that the hurricane destroyed only the odd-numbered homes. Suppose I were to infer from this pattern either that the hurricane intentionally spared the property of the Beckwith boys and/or that the hurricane did not like

---

[16]Ibid, pp. 25-26, 27.
[17]Dembski, "Reinstating Design," p. 508.
[18]Ibid, pp. 507-9.
[19]This is my example, not Dembski's.

odd-numbered homes on my block. This design inference would not be warranted, since the pattern may be adequately accounted for by chance and necessity and thus is ad hoc. But the pattern detected by the SETI researchers in *Contact* is not a fabrication. It is an instance of specified complexity because it is not only highly complex and improbable but also has specification, a pattern that is independent of, or detachable from, the event it explains. That is to say, the pattern is one that is not derived exclusively from the event—as is the ad hoc pattern read back into the hurricane example—but one we could construct even if we did not know which one of the possible events would occur. Thus, my winning the lottery with eight randomly selected numbers, though the outcome of a highly complex process with a result that is antecedently improbable, is not detachable, for it does not exhibit a specified pattern. But the pattern of the message from space in *Contact* is detachable, for our background knowledge (or side information, as Dembski calls it)[20] about binary arithmetic provides us the resources by which we can construct this pattern independent of the message itself. As a researcher in the movie *Contact* exclaimed, "This isn't noise, this has structure."[21] In other words, the message is not merely complex with an improbable random pattern but has "structure," a pattern that one could have constructed independent of the message itself, as the SETI researchers evidently assumed when they constructed their pre-set patterns in a way that would not discard patterns that exhibited SC. According to Dembski, "this distinction between specifications and fabrications can be made with full statistical rigor."[22]

There are several ways in which design theorists employ Dembski's filter in order to detect design in nature. We will look at two: the irreducible complexity of certain biological systems and the fine-tuning of the universe for the existence of life.

Irreducible complexity of certain biological systems. Michael Behe takes seriously Darwin's claim that "if it could be demonstrated that

---

[20]See Dembski in *Science and Evidence for Design in the Universe*, pp. 47-51 n. 17.
[21]Quoted in Dembski, "Reinstating Design," p. 509.
[22]Ibid., p. 510, citing William A. Dembski, *The Design Inference: Eliminating Chance Through Small Probabilities* (New York: Cambridge University Press, 1998), chap. 5.

any complex organ existed which could not possibly have been formed by numerous, successive, slight modifications, my theory would absolutely break down."[23] Thus a system that is irreducibly complex (IC) is a serious challenge to the explanatory power of Darwin's theory of natural selection. Behe defines an IC system as "a single system of several well-matched, interacting parts that contribute to the basic function, wherein the removal of any one of the parts causes the system to effectively cease functioning."[24] A mechanical mousetrap is an example of such a system. Writes Behe:

> The mousetraps my family uses consist of a number of parts . . . : (1) a flat wooden platform to act as a base; (2) a metal hammer, which does the actual job of crushing the mouse; (3) a wire spring with extended ends to press against the platform and the hammer when the trap is charged; (4) a sensitive catch which releases when slight pressure is applied; and (5) a metal bar that connects to the catch and holds the hammer back when the trap is charged. (There are also assorted staples to hold the system together).[25]

The trap will not function if any one of its parts is removed. Because an IC system has no function until all its parts are in place, it cannot be accounted for by gradual changes over time, for according to natural selection a biological entity must have some function so that it may exist, change and pass that change on to its progeny. But with IC systems, there can be no functioning intermediate forms that have yet to acquire the requisite parts, for IC systems are irreducible and cannot be the legacy of intermediate forms. Thus, as Behe points out, "If there is no function, selection has nothing to work on, and Darwinian evolution is thwarted."[26]

---

[23]Charles Darwin, *The Origin of Species,* 6th ed. (1872), p. 154, as quoted in Michael Behe, "Intelligent Design as an Alternative Explanation for the Existence of Biomolecular Machines," *Rhetoric and Public Affairs* 1, no. 4 (1998), p. 566.

[24]Michael Behe, *Darwin's Black Box: The Biochemical Challenge to Evolution* (New York: Free Press, 1996), p. 39.

[25]Ibid., p. 42.

[26]Behe, "Intelligent Design," p. 567. There is controversy surrounding Behe's mousetrap example. For a response to these critiques as well as a fine-tuning of Behe's case, see William A. Dembski, *No Free Lunch: Why Specified Complexity Cannot Be Purchased Without Intelligence* (Lanham, Md.: Rowman & Littlefield, 2002), pp. 256-67, 279-89.

Behe cites a number of examples of irreducibly complex biological systems including those contained within the cell. One of the cell's molecular machines is the cilium.[27] Behe explains that in order for the cilium to work a number of components are needed. Writes Behe:

> Ciliary motion certainly requires microtubles; otherwise, there would be no strands to slide. Additionally, it requires a motor, or else microtubles of the cilium would lie stiff and motionless. Furthermore, it requires linkers to tug on neighboring strands, converting the sliding motion into a bending motion, and preventing the structure from falling apart. All of these parts are required to perform one function: ciliary motion. Just as the mousetrap does not work unless all of its constituent parts are present, ciliary motion simply does not exist in the absence of microtubles, connectors, and motors. Therefore we can conclude that the cilium is irreducibly complex—an enormous monkey wrench thrown into its presumed gradual, Darwinian evolution.[28]

According to Behe, reviewers of his book *Darwin's Black Box* "admit[ted] the current lack of Darwinian explanations," even though most "expressed confidence that in the future such explanations will be found."[29]

Behe does not share this optimism. Rather, he argues that the data are more consistent with an ID explanation. He suggests this explanation not from ignorance but because he maintains that we do have legitimate criteria by which to detect design (e.g., SC) and that an IC system exhibits the characteristics these criteria are meant to detect. It is contingent (i.e., it is one of many possibilities; Darwinian algorithms cannot account for it), complex (i.e., it involves numerous systems, subsystems and parts) and specified (i.e., patterns of biological systems and subsystems a capable intelligence would have constructed if it intended to bring about certain functions in an organism).

The fine tuning of the universe for the existence of human life.

---

[27] In addition to the cilium, Behe includes the bacterial flagellum, the mechanism of blood clotting, vesicular transport and immune systems as examples of irreducibly complex biological systems.

[28] Behe, *Darwin's Black Box,* pp. 64-65.

[29] Behe, "Intelligent Design," p. 569.

In the 1960s some physicists began making the observation that our universe appears to have been fine-tuned for the existence of human life.[30] During the 1980s and 1990s a number of works assessed this "anthropic coincidence" in differing ways.[31] According to Stephen C. Meyer, these scientists "discovered that the existence of life in the universe depends upon a highly improbable but precise balance of physical factors. The constants of physics, the initial conditions of the universe, and many other of its features appear delicately balanced to allow for the possibility of life."[32] Any negligible modification in these constants would have made human life impossible. For example, there would have been no life in the universe if the rate of the universe's expansion had been faster or slower, the strength of gravitational attraction had been stronger or weaker or Planck's constant had had a different value.[33] These, of course, are not the only characteristics of the universe that had to be in place to make life possible. In 1998 astrophysicist and design advocate Hugh Ross estimated that there are "twenty-nine characteristics of the universe that must be fine-tuned for any kind of physical life to be possible" and that our solar system has forty-five characteristics that are necessary for human life to arise in it.[34] Given the individual and collective probabilities for these characteristics to all arise by chance with precisely the correct values to make human life possible, Ross estimates that there is "[m]uch less than 1 chance in one hundred billion trillion trillion trillion [that there] exists. . . even one" planet on which life "would occur anywhere in the universe."[35] This is why a Nobel laureate in physics, Arno Penzias, writes that "astronomy leads us to a unique event, a universe which was created out of nothing, and delicately balanced to provide exactly the conditions required to support life. In the absence of an

---

[30]Karl Giberson, "The Anthropic Principle: A Postmodern Creation Myth?" *Journal of Interdisciplinary Studies* 9 (1997).

[31]See, for example, John Barrow and Frank Tipler, *The Anthropic Cosmological Principle* (Oxford: Clarendon Press, 1988); John Leslie, *Universes* (New York: Routledge, 1989); and Paul Davies, *The Accidental Universe* (Cambridge: Cambridge University Press, 1982).

[32]Stephen C. Meyer in *Science and Evidence for Design,* pp. 56-57.

[33]Ibid., p. 57.

[34]Hugh Ross, "Big Bang Refined by Fire," in *Mere Creation: Science, Faith and Intelligent Design,* ed. William A. Dembski (Downers Grove, Ill.: InterVarsity Press, 1998), p. 372.

[35]Ross, "Big Bang Refined by Fire," p. 381.

absurdly improbable accident, the observations of modern science seem to suggest an underlying, one might say, supernatural plan."[36]

ID advocates have applied Dembski's explanatory filter to this phenomenon.[37] According to some design theorists, the fine-tuning of the universe for the possibility of human life exhibits the characteristics of specified complexity and thus can be attributed to an intelligent agent. For it is contingent (i.e., it is one of many possibilities), complex (i.e., it is a highly improbable arrangement of independent variables) and specified (i.e., it is a cosmological pattern a capable intelligence could have constructed if it intended to make the universe conducive to the arising of human life).

ID AND THE EDWARDS STANDARD

If the Supreme Court were to assess a law that permitted or required the teaching of ID in the public schools, it would likely employ the test it set down in *Edwards,* the case that set the standard by which public school curricula on origins should be evaluated.

The Louisiana statute assessed in *Edwards* was struck down for four reasons: (1) its historical continuity with the *Scopes* trial and the creation-evolution debate, (2) its textual connection to the Genesis-inspired statutes struck down in previous federal court cases, (3) the religious motivation of its supporters and (4) its illegitimate means (e.g., advancing religion, limiting what teachers may teach) to achieve appropriate state ends (e.g., academic freedom), though the court concluded that the statute's purported purpose or end was "a sham,"[38] and thus the statute had no real secular purpose. Thus the court concluded that the Louisiana statute's only purpose was to advance religion and thus violated the establishment clause of the Constitution.

Reasons 1 and 2. Concerning reasons 1 and 2, ID is neither historically connected to the *Scopes* trial, nor is its literature replete, as is creationist literature, with science and recommended curricula that are

---

[36]Quoted in Walter L. Bradley, "Designed or Designoid," in *Mere Creation,* p. 40, quoting from D. L. Brock, *Our Universe: Accident or Design?* (Wits, South Africa: Star Watch, 1992), n. p.

[37]See, for example, Meyer in *Science and Evidence for Design,* pp. 56-66.

[38]*Edwards,* 482 U.S., p. 587.

transparently derived directly from the book of Genesis.

However, Jay Wexler argues that because ID has some historical connection to the creation/evolution controversy, it would not pass the *Edwards* standard.[39] But that would make the genetic fallacy[40] a principle of constitutional jurisprudence. After all, if an historical connection of any sort, no matter how distant or loose, is sufficient to prohibit the teaching of a subject, then perhaps astronomy and chemistry ought to be prohibited from public school classrooms since they have their historical origin in the religiously oriented practices of astrology and alchemy.

The court's historical problem with the creationism curriculum required in the statute struck down in *Edwards* was its transparent connection to the book of Genesis and the contents of previously repudiated statutes in *Epperson* and *McLean*. The courts in these cases were asking the question, How closely does the curricular content required by the statute parallel the creation story in Genesis, and/or is the curricular content prohibited by the statute proscribed because it is inconsistent with the creation story in Genesis? Therefore, if there are no essential differences between ID and creationism, the teaching of ID in public schools would not pass constitutional muster. ID can be summarized in the following way:

(A) If an apparently designed entity exhibits specified complexity (SC), one is warranted in inferring that the entity is the result of an intelligent agent.

(B) SC can be reliably detected by an explanatory filter.

(C) The irreducible complexity of some biological systems and the fine-tuning of the universe for the existence of life are instances of specified complexity.

(D) Presupposing methodological naturalism (MN) and relying exclusively on its resources (i.e., chance and necessity) cannot account

---

[39]Jay D. Wexler, "Of Pandas, People and the First Amendment: The Constitutionality of Teaching Intelligent Design in the Public Schools," *Stanford Law Review* (1997), p. 465.

[40]The genetic fallacy occurs when the origin of a viewpoint or argument rather than its merits is employed to dismiss it out of hand.

for SC in the instances listed in (C).

(E) Thus one cannot exclude ID from serious consideration because it is inconsistent with an a priori commitment to MN.

(F) Therefore, given (A) through (E), ID best accounts for the irreducible complexity of some biological systems and the fine-tuning of the universe for life.

No doubt ID has implications for the veracity of evolution: if its arguments work, then ID is a defeater to evolution (as defined earlier in this essay). But such arguments propose conclusions whose premises do not contain the book of Genesis and its tenets as explicit or implicit propositions. These premises and their propositions, unlike the ones of creationism, are not derived from, nor are they grounded in, any particular religion's interpretation of its special revelation. They are, rather, the result of empirical facts (e.g., the structure of the cell), well-grounded conceptual notions (e.g., SC, IC) and critical reflection. These subsequently serve as the basis from which one may infer that an intelligent agent is likely responsible for the existence of certain apparently natural phenomena. Granted, the conclusions inferred by these premises may be consistent with, and lend support to, a tenet or tenets of a particular belief system. But that in itself would not make ID ipso facto creationism or even constitutionally suspect. After all, the big bang theory, the most widely accepted theory of the universe's origin, is more consistent with, and lends support to, theism in comparison to other metaphysical rivals such as atheism.[41] ID is not creationism.

Reasons 3 and 4. In order to address the concerns of reasons 3 and 4 of the *Edwards* standard, any government body that sought to require or permit ID to be taught in its public schools would have to justify it by appealing to secular reasons. The following are four possible secular reasons such a body could employ.

1. The endorsement test. In *Lynch v. Donnelly* (1984), Justice Sandra Day O'Connor proposed an endorsement test by which the court may

---

[41]See, for example, William Lane Craig and Quentin Smith, *Theism, Atheism and Big Bang Cosmology* (New York: Oxford University Press, 1993).

assess alleged trangressions of the establishment clause. According to this test, if a government action creates a perception that it is either endorsing or disfavoring a religion, the action is unconstitutional. The concern of this test is whether the disputed activity suggests "a message to nonadherents that they are outsiders, not full members of the political community, and an accompanying message to adherents that they are insiders, favored members of the political community."[42]

That is, if a particular curriculum gives the impression that a certain disputed, irreligious point of view is favored—in this case, evolution and materialism—the state can argue that in order to erase that perception, a statute requiring or permitting the teaching of ID is necessary.

2. The neutrality test. The Supreme Court in *Epperson* writes that the "government . . . must be neutral in matters of religious theory, doctrine, and practice. It may not be hostile to any religion or to the advocacy of nonreligion; and it may not aid, foster, or promote one religion or religious theory against another or even against the militant opposite. The First Amendment mandates governmental neutrality between religion and religion, and between religion and nonreligion."[43] Thus an ID statute could be justified on the basis of neutrality by arguing that to teach only one theory of origins (evolution)—that presupposes a controversial epistemology (methodological naturalism), entails a controversial metaphysics (materialism) and is antithetical to traditional religious belief—the state is in fact advocating, aiding, fostering and promoting irreligion, which it is constitutionally forbidden from doing. The state is not merely teaching what some religious people find antagonistic or offensive to their faith, which would not be unconstitutional. Rather, it is promoting a point of view—a metaphysical perspective—"that occupies in the life of its possessor a place parallel to that filled by" traditional belief in God.[44]

Perhaps this is why Justice Hugo Black, in his *Epperson* concurrence, raised the question: "If the theory [of evolution] is considered anti-religious, as the Court indicates, how can the State be bound by the Federal

---

[42]*Lynch v. Donnelly*, 465 U.S. 668, 688 (1984) (O'Connor, J., concurring).
[43]*Epperson*, 393 U.S. 103-4.
[44]*United States v. Seeger*, 380 U.S. 163, 176 (1965).

Constitution to permit its teachers to advocate such an 'anti-religious' doctrine to schoolchildren?" According to Justice Black, "this issue presents problems under the Establishment Clause far more troublesome than are discussed in the Court's opinion," for "the very cases cited by the Court as supporting its conclusion that the State must be neutral" assert that the state should not favor "one religious or anti-religious view over another."[45]

Thus, when government schools, whose attendance is generally compulsory, delve into matters epistemological and metaphysical—matters that touch on the scope of human knowledge, the ultimate nature of things and who and what we are—and imply or affirm an orthodox position on such matters,[46] they violate what the court maintains is a fundamental liberty.

3. Exposing students to new and important scholarship. A state could appeal to the importance of exposing students to reputable scholarship that critiques evolution. The *Edwards* court maintains that its holding does "not imply that the legislature could never require that scientific critiques of prevailing scientific theories be taught." The court asserts that "teaching a variety of scientific theories about the origins of humankind to schoolchildren might be validly done with the clear secular intent of enhancing the effectiveness of science instruction."[47] In addition, the court points out, with apparent approval, that the Balanced-Treatment Act it struck down in *Edwards* was unnecessary because Louisiana already did not prohibit teachers from introducing students to alternative points of view.[48]

ID proponents have had their works published by prestigious presses[49] and in academic journals,[50] have aired their views among critics

---

[45]*Epperson,* 393 U.S., 113 (Black, J., concurring)
[46]The court writes in *Epperson* (93 U.S., 105): "[T]his Court said in *Keyishian v. Board of Regents* [385 U.S., 589, 603 (1967)], the First Amendment 'does not tolerate laws that cast a pall of orthodoxy over the classroom.'"
[47]*Edwards,* 482 U.S., 593, 594.
[48]Ibid., 587.
[49]See, for example, Dembski, *The Design Inference;* Paul A. Nelson, *On Common Descent,* Evolutionary Monograph Series (Chicago: University of Chicago Press, forthcoming); Del Ratzsch, *Nature, Science, and Design: The Status of Design in Natural Science,* Philosophy and Biology Series (Albany: State University of New York Press, 2001); Craig and Smith, *Theism, Atheism and Big Bang Cosmology;* John A. Campbell and Stephen C. Meyer, eds., *Darwinism, Design and Public Education* (East Lansing: Michigan State University Press, 2003); William A. Demb-

in the corridors of major universities and other institutions,[51] and have been recognized by leading periodicals, both academic and nonacademic.[52]

---

ski and Michael Ruse, eds., *Debating Design: From Darwin to DNA* (New York: Cambridge University Press, 2004); and William Lane Craig and J. P. Moreland, eds., *Naturalism: A Critical Analysis* (New York: Routledge, 2000).

[50]See, for example, Michael J. Behe, "Self-Organization and Irreducibly Complex Systems: A Reply to Shanks and Joplin," *Philosophy of Science* 6 (2000); Paul A. Nelson, "Is 'Intelligent Design' Unavoidable—Even by Howard Van Till? A Response," *Zygon* 34 (1999); William A. Dembski and Stephen C. Meyer, "Fruitful Interchange or Polite Chitchat? The Dialogue Between Science and Theology," *Zygon* 33 (1998); William A. Dembski, "Randomness by Design," *Nous* 25 (1991); William Lane Craig, "Barrow and Tipler on the Anthropic Principle vs. Divine Design," *British Journal for the Philosophy of Science* 39 (1989); William Lane Craig, "God, Creation and Mr. Davies," *British Journal for the Philosophy of Science* 37 (1986); John Leslie, "Anthropic Principle, World Ensemble, Design," *American Philosophical Quarterly* 19 (1982).

Because ID's project strikes at the philosophical core of evolutionary theory—its unchallenged epistemological and metaphysical presuppositions—ID proponents have published most of their pro-ID essays in peer-reviewed periodicals that specialize in the philosophy of science or in peer-reviewed anthologies produced by respected university presses. In addition, as shown in the previous note, ID proponents have made significant inroads in publishing peer-reviewed monographs with prestigious presses. The ID movement has found more success in these venues than in traditional scientific journals, for the latter typically do not have reviewers and editors adequately trained to assess the soundness of arguments—both empirical and philosophical—that challenge the core presuppositions of an entrenched paradigm. However, design theorists' publication in biology peer-reviewed journals is thin, and cannot be entirely attributed to hostile editorial boards who want to suppress ID (though that sometimes is the case).

For a nice assessment of peer-review journals and their relevance to the ID movement, see Frank J. Tipler, "Refereed Journals: Do They Insure Quality or Enforce Orthodoxy?" in *Uncommon Dissent: Intellectuals Who Find Darwinism Unconvincing,* ed. William A. Dembski (Wilmington, Del.: ISI Books, 2004).

[51]In 2000 Baylor University (The Nature of Nature: An Interdisciplinary Conference on the Role of Naturalism in Science, Baylor University, April 12-15, 2000) and Yale University (Science and the Evidence for Design in the Universe, Yale University, November 2-4, 2000) hosted major conferences on ID. The American Museum of Natural History (New York City) in April 2002 presented as part of its lecture series a public discussion entitled "Evolution or Intelligent Design?: Examining the Intelligent Design Issue" <www.amnh.org/programs/lectures/index.html?src=p_h#> April 23, 2002.

[52]See, for example, James Glanz, "Biologists Face a New Theory of Life's Origins," *New York Times* (April 8, 2001), pp. 1, 18; Teresa Watanabe, "Enlisting Science to Find the Fingerprints of a Creator," *Los Angeles Times* (March 25, 2001), available at <www.arn.org/docs/news/fingerprints032501.htm> (July 4, 2002); Beth McMurtrie, "Darwinism Under Attack," *Chronicle of Higher Education* (December 21, 2001), available at <http://chronicle.com/free/v48/i17/17a00801.htm> (March 15, 2002); Brian Fitelson, Christopher Stephens and Elliot Sober, "How Not to Detect Design," *Philosophy of Science* 66, no. 3 (1999); Neil W. Blackstone, "Argumentum Ad Ignorantam," *Quarterly Review of Biology* 72 (1997); J. A. Coyne, "God in the Details," *Nature* 383 (1996); and Robert Dorit, review of *Darwin's Black Box* by Michael Behe, *American Scientist* 85, no. 5 (1997), available at <http://www.sigmaxi.org/amsci/amsci/bookshelf/leads97/darwin97%2D09.html> (March 25, 2002).

4. Furthering and protecting academic freedom. A state could also make the argument that an ID statute enhances and protects the academic freedom of teachers and students who may suffer marginalization, hostility and public ridicule because of their support of ID and/or doubts about the veracity of the evolutionary paradigm. This is not as farfetched as one may think. Consider just one example.

In 1999, a Burlington, Washington, high school biology teacher, Roger DeHart, was instructed by his superiors, as a result of a student complaint filed by the American Civil Liberties Union (ACLU), to "drop references to design and stick to the textbook." In 2001, "DeHart was told he could not even introduce materials questioning Darwin's theories," something he had been doing for over nine years until the 1999 incident. Although no one disputes that DeHart taught the required curriculum correctly, and although he never mentioned God, he nevertheless was accused of the Socratic transgression of encouraging his pupils to think deeply and thoughtfully about the philosophical implications that flow from the Darwinian paradigm. According to a report in the *Los Angeles Times,* DeHart "dissected such scientific topics as bacterial flagella, fossil records and embryonic development. Examine the evidence, he told the students, and ponder the Big Question: Is life the result of random, meaningless events? Or was it designed by an intelligent force?"[53]

The Supreme Court has affirmed that a teacher engages in protected speech under the rubric of academic freedom (and thus the First Amendment) when she brings into the classroom relevant material that is supplementary to the curriculum (and not a violation of any other legal duties) and she has adequately fulfilled all of her curricular obligations.[54] Given that, it seems to me that any government body that passed legislation to protect the academic freedom of teachers and students to discuss in the classroom scientific alternatives to evolution, including design theory, would simply be affirming what is already a fixed point in constitutional law.

---

[53]Watanabe, "Enlisting Science."

[54]See David K. DeWolf, "Academic Freedom After *Edwards,*" *Regent University Law Review* 13, no. 2 (2000-2001): 480-81.

CONCLUSION

In a society of contrary and contradictory religious and philosophical points of view, the law must address, with fairness and consistency, how public schools ought to deal with the question of teaching origins without violating both the deliverances of science and the rights of the nation's citizens. The infusion of Intelligent Design into this debate has changed the legal landscape significantly. Unlike the creationism repudiated by the federal courts, ID cannot be dismissed as merely a transparent attempt on the part of religious people to force the teachings of Genesis in the public schools.

FOR FURTHER READING

Beckwith, Francis J. *Law, Darwinism and Public Education: The Establishment Clause and the Challenge of Intelligent Design.* Lanham, Md.: Rowman & Littlefield, 2003.

DeWolf, David K. "Academic Freedom After *Edwards.*" *Regent University Law Review* 13, no. 2 (2000-2001): 480-81.

DeWolf, David K., Stephen C. Meyer and Mark Edward DeForrest. "Teaching the Controversy: Science, or Religion or Speech?" *Utah Law Review* (2000).

Geisler, Norman L., A. F. Brooke II and Mark J. Keough. *Creator in the Courtroom: Scopes II.* Milford, Mich.: Mott Media, 1982.

Greenawalt, Kent. "Establishing Religious Ideas: Evolution, Creationism and Intelligent Design." *Notre Dame Journal of Law, Ethics and Public Policy* 17, no. 2 (2003).

House, H. Wayne. "Darwinism and the Law: Can Non-Naturalistic Scientific Theories Survive Constitutional Challenge?" *Regent University Law Review* 13, no. 2 (2000-2001).

PART 5

RELIGIOUS CHALLENGES TO CHRISTIAN FAITH

Francis J. Beckwith

CHRISTIANITY IS NOT THE ONLY RELIGION IN THE WORLD. THERE ARE SEVERAL major religions, thousands of offshoots of those faiths and literally tens of thousands of branches of those offshoots as well as small new religions that are found everywhere from large western cities to the jungles of Africa and South America. Like many of these faiths, Christianity claims that its central doctrines including the deeper philosophical implications of those doctrines are true descriptions of the nature and order of things. However, many people, especially well-educated American liberals, believe that theological claims, Christian or not, are subjective matters of private opinion and not much different from other matters of taste such as one's preferences for certain music, foods or sexual practices. Hence some people are deeply troubled by Christians who attempt to convert believers from other religions. In the minds of these people, such attempts are no different than trying to convince another that his preference for butter pecan ice cream or brunettes is wrong. Consider the example of the Southern Baptist Convention (SBC), the largest Protestant denomination in the United States.

In late 1999 there arose a controversy concerning the effort of the SBC to evangelize Jews, Muslims and Hindus in the summer of 2000 in conjunction with its meeting in Chicago. The SBC planned to bring 100,000 missionaries for the task. But this did not sit well with some local religious leaders. According to a story in the *Chicago Tribune,* "The Council of Religious Leaders of Metropolitan Chicago, representing the Catholic Archdiocese of Chicago and 39 other major Christian and Jewish institutions, sent a letter Saturday [Nov. 27, 1999] warning that the high-profile evangelical blitz proposed by the Southern Baptists in June would poison interfaith relations and indirectly contribute to violence."[1]

The letter states that "while we are confident that your volunteers would come with entirely peaceful intentions, a campaign of the nature and scope you envision could contribute to a climate conducive to hate crimes."[2] Although the letter acknowledges the Baptists' constitutional right to religious expression, "it cites last July's [1999] shooting of six Jews in West Rogers Park and vandalism of a mosque in Villa Park in May as evidence of the vulnerability of people targeted because of their faith."[3] It is interesting to note that the council did not tease out its own logic and conclude that perhaps its call for Southern Baptist self-censorship while connecting a time-honored Christian practice (i.e., evangelism) to vandalism and battery could itself "contribute to a climate conducive to hate crimes" and result in the Baptists being victims.

The council is not claiming that Christian doctrine is false, but rather it is claiming that religious beliefs are not legitimate claims to knowledge at all. So, it is not that the Southern Baptists are mistaken about the truth of Christianity; rather they are mistaken about the nature of religion. For if the council truly believed that religious doctrines, and Christian truth claims in particular, are claims to real knowledge, they would have not relied on demagoguery and scare tactics to make their point. In other words, the Southern Baptists are dangerous not because Christianity is false and they believe it is true but because they really believe that Christianity is true and they believe that other people from contrary religious traditions should become Christians as well. This is why Bishop C. Joseph Sprague of United Methodist Church's Northern Illinois Conference said of the Southern Baptists' plans for evangelism in Chicago: "I'm al-

---

[1]Steve Kloehn, "Clergy Ask Baptists to Rethink Area Blitz," *The Chicago Tribune* (November 28, 1999) at <www.chicagotribune.com/news/metro/chicago/article/0,2669,ART-38638,FF.html> (November 28, 1999).
[2]Council letter as quoted in ibid.
[3]Kloehn, "Clergy Ask Baptists to Rethink Area Blitz."

ways fearful when we in the Christian community move beyond the rightful claim that Jesus is decisive for us, to the presupposition that non-Christians . . . are outside God's plan of salvation. That smacks of a kind of non-Jesus-like arrogance."[4] Of course, if Jesus' disciples had followed the bishop's advice rather than their Lord's Great Commission, there would have been no church and hence no Methodist bishops calling for the revocation of the Great Commission.

But the council's letter is itself a form of evangelism for its own view of the nature of theological knowledge. For the council is suggesting that the Southern Baptists, the letter's target, abandon their religious tradition and embrace the council's subjectivist view of religious truth. Just as the Southern Baptists hope that non-Christians are converted to what Christians believe is true about God and religion, the Chicago clergy hope that the Southern Baptists are converted to what they believe is true about theological knowledge, namely, subjectivism. Thus even those who claim, like the Chicago clergy, that it is wrong to believe that one's religion is true and others false, believe that their own view of religion—that it is wrong to believe that one's religion is true and others false—is in fact true.

Consequently, there is no way to soft pedal the fact that religious claims—whether about the content and truth of one's own faith or about the nature of religious truth claims in general—are serious claims about a cluster of deep human concerns including the nature of reality, what we can know and the essence of human beings and their relationship to the transcendent. In this part of the book our contributors cover four important religious challenges to the Christian worldview: religious pluralism, eastern religious thought, Mormonism and Islam. The first concerns the question of Christian truth—and the belief on the part of most Christians that Jesus is the only way to salvation—in light of the wide diversity of religions in the world. The other three chapters deal with actual religious alternatives to Christianity, two of which—Mormonism and Islam—claim to be the true consummation of Christianity. Mormonism has experienced unprecedented growth, "from 6 members at its founding in

---

[4]Ibid.

1830 to over 11 million [as of 2002]."[5] Islam, due to the horrific events of September 11, 2001, has shown the Western world, and the Christian church in particular, that it must be addressed as a serious contender to the biblical faith on which Western liberal democracies first grounded their political principles.[6]

---

[5]Carl Mosser, "When the Saints Go Marching In: The New Mormon Challenge for World Missions, Apologetics and Theology," in *The New Mormon Challenge: Responding to the Latest Defenses of a Fast-Growing Movement,* ed. Francis J. Beckwith, Carl Mosser and Paul Owen (Grand Rapids, Mich.: Zondervan, 2002), p. 60.

[6]See, for example, John Locke, *Two Treatises of Government,* a critical edition with an intro and apparatus criticus by Peter Laslett (New York: Cambridge University Press, 1960).

17

RELIGIOUS PLURALISM AND CHRISTIAN EXCLUSIVISM

David K. Clark

TODAY'S SUPERMARKET OF RELIGIOUS IDEAS OVERFLOWS WITH ENTICING PRODUCTS. It offers intellectual shoppers countless religious options—everything from agnosticism to Zen. But which product is a *Consumers Digest* "Best Buy"? Is it crucial for a wise spiritual consumer to buy into the one right religion? Or should he feel free to select any religion at all?

Many today say that every religion is right. But my claim is that wisdom does not lie with the easy assumption that all the world faiths lead to God. That idea is fashionable, and it's initially attractive. But it runs into a buzzsaw of rational difficulties. Wisdom encourages a more difficult challenge: finding the one true pathway to God. This seems daunting at first, but it's more fulfilling in the end.

GETTING THE CONCEPTS CLEAR

Consumers enjoy complete freedom of choice. A television buyer can select either Sony or Magnavox; both produce solid televisions. All choices are good ones. Similarly, in religion, people assume that many religious roads lead to spiritual life. All faiths produce solid spiritual benefits; all are good choices. Someone who adopts this consumerist stance, whether or not she actually practices any religion, is a religious pluralist.

It's easy to confuse the concept of religious pluralism with ideas from two different categories. Some use the word *pluralism* for these categories. In the first category, "pluralism" denotes a factual claim. Factual claims are assertions about the way things are. For instance, a statement about the current population of Minnesota is a factual assertion. Some factual claims tell us that people believe different ideas. For example, political pluralism can mean that people embrace different political views. Some people are Republicans; others are Democrats. Cultural pluralism can mean that various individuals identify with different cultures. These are both obviously true.

Similarly, some use the phrase "religious pluralism" to designate the factual claim that various people follow different religions. This isn't how I'm using this phrase. I call this religious variety. The assertion that people do follow different religions is undeniable. It's uncontroversial. But the fact of religious variety differs from the theory of religious pluralism.

In the second category, "pluralism" names certain legal realities. These are statements about the rights people possess. People have the legal right (in the West) to adopt whatever views they choose. In this sense, political pluralism means it's legal to adopt either libertarianism or socialism. It's illegal to promote revolution. Beyond that, no law dictates any particular political view.

Likewise, "religious pluralism" could mean (in this legal sense) people have the right to adopt any religion—or none at all. This is religious freedom. Religious freedom is a constitutional guarantee of the right for citizens to practice the religion of their choice without interference. Religious freedom is not a factual claim describing what people actually do. It's a legal reality denoting what people *may* do. Unlike religious pluralism, religious freedom is uncontroversial in the West.

The concept "religious pluralism" doesn't fit in either of these categories. It's neither a factual claim nor a legal claim. It's a *philosophical* theory about religion.

Religious pluralism states:

a. Any (or perhaps all) religions lead to God or salvation. Following any religious path enables believers to reach the religious goal.

Religious pluralism, precisely speaking, is not a religious idea. There's a difference between a thing and theories about that thing. For example, suppose one Friday night, you decide to take in a movie. You search the Internet. A movie reviewer recommends a certain flick. So you head to the theater, pay eight dollars and enjoy the film. Now there's a difference between reading the review and watching the movie. The review is *about* the movie. The movie (obviously) *is* the movie. And it's the same way with philosophical theories. Holding a theory about religion differs from practicing a religion. Considering an idea about religion isn't the same as being religious.

A contrary view to pluralism is this: only one of the items offered for sale in the marketplace of religious ideas will actually deliver as promised. Not all choices are good choices. One religious path leads to God, but others don't. So let the spiritual buyer beware. A person who holds this view, whether or not he follows any religion, is a religious exclusivist.

Religious exclusivism says:

b. Only one true religion leads to God. Attaining the spiritual goal requires a believer to find and follow the one true faith, for other religious paths will not *lead to the spiritual goal.*

Now here's a critical point: exclusivism doesn't negate any factual claims or legal rights mentioned above. Why is that important? If religious exclusivism required that religious variety is false (obviously it's true), that would show exclusivism false. But exclusivism doesn't deny religious variety. And if religious exclusivism implied that religious freedom is a wrong value (obviously it's a good value), that would also count against exclusivism. But again, exclusivism doesn't reject religious freedom. Religious exclusivists feel no logical pressure to reject either religious variety or religious freedom. In fact, most exclusivists in the West happily accept them. Exclusivism requires the denial only of pluralism.

Interestingly, someone could hold to religious exclusivism and still not practice any religion. For instance, Vladimir believes that of all the world faiths, only Christianity really leads to spiritual benefit. (He's an exclusivist.) But he thinks to himself, "I know that Christianity is the true faith. But it's too costly. I know Christianity is the pathway to God, but it demands giving up betting on horses. I love horseracing! I choose not to practice any faith—at least not for now." (Vlad's irreligious.)

More generally, adopting pluralism or exclusivism is just different from practicing a religion. If Suzanne is convinced by arguments that she should abandon pluralism and believe exclusivism, then she'd change her philosophical idea. But that wouldn't necessarily mean changing religions. If she was a convinced Muslim before her philosophical conversion, she might remain one after. Conversely, if Juan's life is in a shambles, he might start Zen meditation, even though he's unsure about the arguments between pluralism and exclusivism. He might think it best to go ahead and do his meditation. He could come back at a later time to the questions of this chapter.

Those who discuss pluralism and exclusivism often mention a third position called religious inclusivism. Because inclusivism shares some ideas with pluralism and others with exclusivism, it stands halfway between pluralism and exclusivism. At the core, inclusivism says (with exclusivism) that only one religion is really genuine. It asserts (with pluralism) that people who follow many different religions can still be saved. While this sounds to some like the best of both worlds, I believe it's an unstable compound. It's worthy of discussion, but it reduces either to a modified exclusivism or an amended pluralism. So I focus this chapter on the exclusivism/pluralism debate.

Separating the Truth Question from the Salvation Question

Although we're getting the concept of religious pluralism into focus, we must straighten out one more issue. Different scholars use the categories of exclusivism, inclusivism and pluralism to answer two very distinct questions. I call these the truth question and the salvation question.

The truth question asks

c. *Which religion's teachings are true?*

When answering the truth question, pluralism asserts that all religions teach truth, and exclusivism claims that only one religion teaches truth.

But this is too vague. Obviously, all religions teach lots of things. Very probably, all religions teach some true things and some false things. So the truth question zeroes in on the most logically central questions, like What is the most basic metaphysical reality? What is the fundamental human religious problem? And what is the solution to that problem?

Let's call a religion deeply true if it gets the right answers to these very central questions. For instance, Christianity says that the most basic reality is the Creator God (the Trinity). The deepest human problem is human moral failure (sin). Sin drives people far from God. The solution (salvation) is moral forgiveness through the death of Jesus. By the Spirit's power, a believer receives this forgiveness as a gift. The gift of salvation places people in relationship with God. Now if these ideas really are true, then Christianity is deeply true. Even though every religion agrees with Christianity on some issues, they all contradict Christianity on these core questions. Since the various religions have rather different teachings on these central questions, only one religion could be deeply true.

Notice a couple of things about the truth question. First, those who follow a religion that's deeply true aren't necessarily right about everything. If Christianity is deeply true, that doesn't mean Christians have only true beliefs. Christians believe a thousand other things. Some of those thousand other beliefs are probably false. But if exclusivism is about the truth question and Christianity is deeply true, then exclusivism just means that the most central Christian teachings are true.

Second, even if exclusivism is about the truth question and only one religion is deeply true, other religions teach many true things. Examples are easy to find. If Christianity is deeply true, Buddhists are right that suffering is universal. Muslims are right to believe in one God. Hindus are right that Ultimate is infinite. Jews are right that God spoke through the Hebrew prophets. So exclusivism regarding the truth question means that only one religion is right on the most central of religious questions. It doesn't mean either that this one religion is right about everything, or that all other religions are wrong about everything.

In contrast to the truth question, the salvation question inquires

d. Which religions lead to God?

When answering the salvation question, pluralism asserts that following any religion leads to the religious goal, and exclusivism says that only practicing the true religion leads to the religious goal.

Many people today argue the central issue of religion is the salvation question. They often say that religion doesn't work with the usual kind of truth that describes the real world. That kind of truth is where statements describe a real world outside language. The statement "Kevin Garnett is a very tall basketball player" is true because and only because K. G. is nearly seven feet tall and plays in the NBA. If this kind of truth is relevant to religion, then assertions like "People matter to God" are true because and only because an actually existing God actually loves actually existing people.

But many people want religious teachings to perform some job other than describing reality. They say that religion doesn't literally speak about ultimate reality, the human condition and the spiritual path to life. Religious truth isn't about what's really true; it's about what's useful. For instance, some might claim that "God loves me" is true, but also that it's not true in the same way that "Mom loves me" is true. "God loves me" is true perhaps, in the sense that believing it gives me more courage to face life. The key is not that a real God really loves me. The key is that I believe God loves me. Believing this produces benefits.

This might seem odd, but some contemporary people think this approach provides a significant benefit. If religious beliefs like "God loves me" aren't supposed to be true but only beneficial, then there's no reason to argue about the truth values of religious beliefs. There's no reason to feel pressure to find the truth about religion. It's possible to respect the fact that others don't gain courage from believing "God loves me." Some find Zen meditation brings tranquility; others notice Jewish rituals pulling their families together. Everyone could respect everyone else's choice. All arrogance would disappear. Conflict would fade. Stressing the salvation question and evading the truth question seem to produce real social benefits.

The desire to tolerate others and avoid arrogance makes the truth question nettlesome and the salvation question appealing. If we could just agree that religions are just different paths to God, the pressure would dissipate. We could be religious consumers. I like Chryslers; he likes Buicks. I like Christianity; he likes Buddhism. Is religious exclusivism a good position to hold in light of pluralism's apparent advantage?

EVALUATING CRITIQUES OF RELIGIOUS EXCLUSIVISM

For people accustomed to thinking like consumers, religious exclusivism quickly draws many criticisms. We should examine them carefully. First, as I said above, some argue that religious exclusivism leads to arrogance and intolerance (and these are bad). If someone asserts that his religion is ultimately true, people say he's arrogant. If he argues other religions are wrong, he's intolerant. By definition, religious exclusivists think their religion is right and others are wrong. So clearly, exclusivists are guilty as charged. With so many different views to choose from, who can say who's right?

But this objection is as faulty as it is popular. For one thing, it overlooks a critical point. Sooner or later, everyone claims that some ideas are true. Let's say that Jane believes all religions lead to God. John believes that only Islam leads to God. Jane raises this objection: "John, you say all those other religions are wrong. You're arrogant to think you're right, and intolerant of others. How do you know you've got it right?" What Jane overlooks here is that she's making truth claims too. John maintains Islam is the one true religion. Jane insists pluralism is the one true philosophy. Playing Jane's game, John could respond, "Jane, you're saying that everyone who thinks she has the one true religion is wrong, for there is no one true religion. But you arrogantly think you're right as regards pluralism, and by *your* definition, you're intolerant of exclusivists. How do you know you're right about this?"

If the simple fact that someone believes she has the truth automatically means she's arrogant and intolerant, then everyone is arrogant and intolerant. All of us hold the views we do because we think we're right! (Why else would we adopt them?) But it's absurd to say everyone is arrogant. Conviction—holding our views because we think we're right—is not equivalent to arrogance and intolerance.

For another thing, this stance misunderstands arrogance and intolerance. These concepts don't describe whether a person disagrees with others. Everyone does that! These words describe how he disagrees. Some exclusivists certainly are arrogant and intolerant. But exclusivism doesn't necessarily lead to these evils. In fact, many Christian exclusivists show great respect. In religious discussions they say, "I believe that God created all things and loves all people. He wants everyone to love him. And he's made restored love relationship possible through Jesus Christ. That's what I think. But I'm interested in what you believe. Please share your view with me." How could you say such a person is arrogant or intolerant?

Second, some say religious exclusivism is fundamentally violent. Those who use violence to force compliance begin by thinking they're absolutely right. History shows that when people think they're right, they stop at nothing to force agreement. The Inquisition, for example, used terror tactics to require submission. Exclusivism spawns arrogance, and arrogance leads to violence. Essentially, this critique ratchets up the previous objection.

Before I respond, I need to make an admission. Historically, some supposed Christians did use force to promote their agenda. I confess this fact candidly. (I refuse to overstate it.) I believe using power to force religious compliance is not only completely fruitless (people believe as they will in their hearts) but fundamentally contrary to the Spirit of Jesus.

Now to respond. Although violent people are arrogant, the point fails as a criticism against exclusivism. For one thing, it commits a common fallacy. Those who violently force others to conform to their views do typically believe exclusivism. But this doesn't even hint that those who believe in exclusivism will use terror against others. This is a logical fallacy. If John is a father, he's a male. This doesn't prove that if John's a male, he's a father. If all *A* is *B*, it doesn't follow that all *B* is *A*.

For another, notice this: the rejection of violence actually requires commitment to truth. (Remember, today's common intuition is that anyone who believes he has the truth is arrogant and violent.) The idea—arrogance and violence are evil—is claimed as truth. The moral rules—combat arrogance and prevent violence—are moral truths. The critics' assumption that they possess the truth about these moral values usually lies hidden (to themselves). Now I completely accept these values. The difficulty arises for the critic, however, who argues against someone else's conviction on that grounds that holding convictions breeds violence. The critic's argument depends on his own deep moral conviction, and so his stance succumbs to his own complaint.

It's not commitment to truth that causes violence. Those who genuinely respect truth, as opposed to those who use so-called truth to further political agendas, know that power is subject to truth. This is precisely why a free and unbiased press promotes political liberty and propaganda doesn't. Rather the denial of truth triggers violence. What history actually teaches is this: when powerful people falsely believe they're entitled to ignore real, publicly tested truth and to snub the moral truth others live by, violence escalates. By contrast, Christianity is about the Prince of Peace who instructed his followers to turn the other cheek and love their enemies. Anyone who spreads this message by violent means distorts the gospel of Jesus beyond all recognition.

Third, some complain that religious exclusivism is profoundly unfair to any who happen to miss the one true message. If people fail to hear about the one true faith, obviously they can't practice it. And if they can't practice the true faith, they can't receive salvation. This leaves people with no chance at salvation through no fault of their own. This is simply unjust. With Christianity, what about people who lived before Jesus? Or cultures where Jesus is unknown? Or people who can't understand the Christian message—like very young children?

Exclusivists offer many responses. For one thing, many qualifications fit with exclusivism. Some say God gives special grace to children or others who can't understand a religious message. Others say that God knows every person who would respond and ensures that all people who would believe have a chance to believe.

For a Christian, this objection is difficult because we just don't know all that God will do for people who don't know about Jesus. But we do know about the character and the intentions of God. Regarding God's character, among God's essential attributes are justice (intense opposition to evil) and grace (passionate love for people). Regarding his intentions, a deep divine passion is to rescue all people. If we start with what we know, we can gain confidence. Somehow—it's speculation to say exactly how—God is at work to draw all people to himself.

One reasonable scenario is that God will give all people the opportunity to receive salvation. How God will do this is partly clear and partly hidden. The clear part is that God has instructed Christians to offer to others the opportunity to receive the gift of salvation. The less clear part is what God is doing behind the scenes. If God's character and intentions are as the Bible says, I surmise God is doing far more than we know.

So, on the one hand, it would be arrogant for Christians to presuppose
and mistaken for critics to assume that God's entire effort is limited to
what human beings do. On the other hand, it would be irresponsible for
Christians to conclude they may shirk their duty to share the message of
Jesus just because God works in unexpected ways behind the scenes to
bring his love to the world.

As I said, we don't know all God's ways. As a Christian, I say some
things (like my responsibility to humbly share Jesus with others) are
clear and nonnegotiable. But others are less clear. To answer the third
charge against Christian exclusivism, however, it's enough to know that
God will both conquer evil and draw all repentant people to himself. Remember, the point here is to answer an objection, not to give a full account of the unknown. The objection is that exclusivism is unfair to
those who have no chance for salvation because, humanly speaking,
they haven't heard that message. But I believe God will give the chance
to all. We don't know how this works. If God is committed to drawing
all people to himself, then the objection doesn't hold against Christian
exclusivism. We can reasonably infer, given God's commitment to overcome evil, his longing that all people love him, and his infinite resource-
fulness, that his plan is fair. Abraham once asked rhetorically, "Will not
the God of all the earth do what is right?" We don't know exactly how,
but we have confidence he will.

EVALUATING RELIGIOUS PLURALISM

Objections to exclusivism don't carry the freight. Even so, someone
could say that religious pluralism is superior because it's more open-
minded. But I have a surprising claim: pluralism is more subtly narrow-
minded than exclusivism. Why? Let me describe several forms of pluralism I've run across.

First, one form of pluralism interprets all religions as true in that they
produce valuable results. This view, as I said above, actually means that
religions are useful, not true. Religious claims (like "Yahweh is the Creator") are not literally true (like "St. Paul is the capital of Minnesota").
But believing them generates benefits. So religions are useful fictions.

Here's an illustration. A pluralist I once debated said that most major religions are good because they produce emotionally mature, socially adapted citizens (which any society needs). So the various faiths—Islam, Christianity and Buddhism—are valuable because they develop good people. I said in return that traditional Christianity doesn't merely produce good citizens in this world, although empirical evidence shows it does do this. The real point of Christian faith is to activate a spiritual relationship with God, beginning in this world and continuing in the next. In response, my friend said there is no afterlife. His comment entails that the Christianity I embrace is not true.

Notice what happened: my friend began by offering the attractive thesis that all religions are true. But truth, it turned out, doesn't mean literally true but merely useful. When I asked him whether my faith—a faith that billions of Christians have followed for centuries—is deeply true, he said it isn't. Now he could be right. Maybe billions of Christians are wrong. I can accept that. What I can't accept, because it seems deeply confused, is this combination of claims: my faith is literally false, my faith is useful to society, and he's open-minded because he thinks all the world's religions are true. I'd rather he admit he thinks my faith, as I hold it, is just plain false. But here's the rub: that honest admission would involve abandoning pluralism.

Second, another form of pluralism accepts the truth of all religions, but only after they are properly interpreted. A man I heard used a husk and kernel analogy. The husk on the outside (each religion's doctrinal teachings) differs among faiths. But the kernel inside (the deeper meaning) is identical. At the level of deeper meaning, all religions agree and are true.

But again, this subtly disrespects real religions. This man claimed to agree with all faiths. But when he spoke of any particular faith, he labeled the ideas he accepts as kernel and those he rejects as husk. So he edited my faith. He classified the teachings he accepts under the deeper-meaning-of-all-religion. He grouped the leftovers as husk. It turned out the deeper-meaning-of-all-religion is what he believed all along.

Now this just doesn't take my faith seriously. He said he agrees with my religion, but in fact he accepts an edited version of my faith—which ends up looking just like his faith. Then, on the grounds that his faith and his edited version of my faith look the same, he said all religions are identical. And he took credit for being open-minded. I, apparently, am narrow-minded. I felt as though I've been colonized by an imperialist power. He rejected my faith as I hold it. Then he reinterpreted it so it says what he believes and claimed we're on the same page. We're not on the same page. We hold different religions. And we should honestly acknowledge that. Again this would involve denying pluralism.

Third, another form of pluralism says that God is completely infinite and therefore unknowable. (This form of pluralism uses the phrase "Ultimate Reality," which is supposedly more neutral, but I'll use the word *God*.) Whenever we use concepts to describe some object, we say both what the object is and what it's not. So applying concepts to an object always limits the object. But God is not limited. He (or It) is infinite. So no concept really applies. This stance honestly acknowledges that all religious concepts are equally far from God (or equally close—it's the same thing). So the concepts *good* and *lampshade* are equal in their appropriateness or inappropriateness to God. Yet this view interprets all the religious experiences in the various religions as real encounters with God. We can't know anything of Reality, but we can experience it.

A full response to this deftly defended stance could fill a book. Let me briefly mention four points. For one thing, many real religions do assert that certain concepts do properly apply to God. (Many say "love" properly applies to God but "terrorist" doesn't.) So in denying this, pluralism implies yet again not that all religions are true but many are literally false. Once more, pluralism fails to take real religions seriously. In addition, if no concepts apply to God, how can we know that the object of religious experience is good and not evil? Good and evil are concepts. If they're equally appropriate/inappropriate to God, how do we know we're encountering God and not a demon? If no concepts apply, then no concepts apply, and we're ignorant of whatever it is we're supposedly experiencing. Further, for this reason, pluralists of this stripe often whisper what God is really like. That is, the temptation to break the rule against applying concepts to God is nearly irresistible. Indeed, just speaking about Ultimate Reality (as these pluralists say) applies the concepts *ultimate* and *real* to God. This seems inconsistent. Finally, why worship a God when we can't apply concepts like goodness, interest in us or ability to overcome evil to that God? Isn't it morally repulsive to worship something as ultimate and good when we have no way to know whether that thing really is ultimate and good?

I've focused on our topic by emphasizing the truth question. But pluralists want to focus on the salvation question. By ignoring the truth question, they can push aside pesky differences in truth claims. They can focus on the spiritual quest. But what's that? It's getting in touch with God. But what is God like? Is it personal (Islam) or impersonal (Buddhism)? It's overcome the human predicament. But what is that? Is it ignorance (Hinduism) or moral failure (Judaism)? It's pursuing spiritual life. And what is that? Is it a love relationship (Christianity) or a metaphysical absorption (Hinduism)? Is it finding our truest selves (Christianity) or extinguishing our truest selves (Buddhism)? These truth questions are unavoidable.

Saying that all religions help us achieve the spiritual quest is too vague. What is the truth about that spiritual quest? What is the true Summum Bonum—the Greatest Good? Religious analyses contradict. But getting the analysis right is important, for every practice depends on the truth of analysis. Should I take antacid or chemotherapy for my stomach pain? That depends on a truth question: Do I have heartburn or stomach cancer? Should I become a good citizen for today's society, as my pluralist friend encourages, or should I also prepare for the afterlife? That depends on a truth question. The truth question is unavoidable.

Those who try to focus only on the salvation question in fact assume background answers to truth questions. (And often, these unstated assumptions deny traditional Christianity.) It's unreasonable to say that all the religions are true paths to the spiritual quest, meaning that every religion is a true path to whatever that religion defines as the spiritual quest. There's just too much variation on the truth question. Saying that all religions have it right, even though they're all literally false, creates rational tension. I submit that people who claim every religion is true paint themselves into a corner. In the end they will tend to believe their own religion is deeply true, and that other faiths are true to the degree they agree with theirs. And that, of course, is not pluralism.

EXPLAINING CHRISTIAN EXCLUSIVISM

So far I've tried to answer criticisms against religious exclusivism, showing how several forms of pluralism fail to take real religions—religions
as they are actually believed and practiced—with any seriousness. I now
offer a positive explanation of religious exclusivism. But I'm not really
interested in religious exclusivism. I will discuss specifically Christian exclusivism.

Christian exclusivism includes at least two ideas. First, you find spiritual life by trusting in God and following Jesus Christ through the Holy
Spirit. Second, you do not find spiritual life on the strength of other religions. Actually, I can go farther. Christian exclusivism (as I hold it) says
that you won't find spiritual life by practicing any religion. No religion
leads to God, in my view. And that's why I'm not as interested in generic
religious exclusivism. Only following Jesus, by the Holy Spirit's power,
leads to God. And that's not religion.

Let me explain. Much religion is a variation on the following theme:
we have done bad things, and we suffer the results; we must do good
things to counteract those bad things. This treats religion as contract. In
a contract, a person enters a fee-for-service arrangement. He expects to
pay a fee and to gain some benefit. I sign a contract to have Drawbridge
Painting paint my house. I want a good paint job out of the deal. Drawbridge Painting wants my money. Neither is looking for a long-term love
relationship. Both would like to negotiate the price. I want a lower fee
but everything painted. Drawbridge Painting wants either a higher price
or to leave the window trim unpainted. Both sides have expectations. If
Drawbridge Painting doesn't paint, then I don't pay. The two parties care
only that the job is done well and the bill paid on time.

Contractual religiosity follows this pattern. People enter a fee-for-service arrangement with God. The human gives money, does religious rituals and believes religious ideas. In return, she expects protection, help,
good fortune, a sense of meaning in life and rescue from punishment in
the next life. The believer isn't thinking in terms of a long-term love relationship. He wants to negotiate the price down. If he can get a heavenly reward for himself and his family, but he only has to attend religious rituals twice a year rather than once a week, that's good—like

getting a great paint job at one tenth the price. If the believer has certain expectations of God and God doesn't meet expectations, then the contract is broken. Then the believer is freed of his obligation. A believer like this doesn't really care what happens to God. His question is, what can God do for me?

Most religions, I submit, are variations on this theme. The differences lie in the specifics. The Christian faith, however, is fundamentally not contractual. I don't follow Christ as a way of earning spiritual reimbursement. I enter into what the Bible calls covenant. A covenant is a mutual, faithful, long-term, love relationship. The key is not the benefits I receive but simply being in relationship. I just love, and I'm loved in return. The love is an unearned gift. I don't love to get something—least of all love as an earned stipend. I just give my life, trusting in the other. And the other does the same. In this trustful and faithful relationship I find the deepest intimacy of love. I don't control the relationship (as in contract). I must give myself in trust to the other. As Jesus said, if I lose my life, I find it. The result is a relationship with God through Christ that the Bible calls eternal life. It's what God created me for.

This differs radically from religion. In contractual religion, I live a good life in order to fulfill my half of the bargain and to gain benefits (either health and happiness in this life or heavenly reward in the next). In covenantal relationship, I live a good life because I'm responding faithfully to the gift of love. Like a groom who remains faithful to his bride, I follow God's will not to gain his love but because he first loved me. This is relevant to our topic—Christian exclusivism and religious pluralism—precisely because pluralism routinely garbles this Christian invitation to love relationship with God. Pluralism transmutes it into something unrecognizable. Christianity is not a series of practices I perform either to become a good citizen in America or to win rewards in heaven.

In the end, it's unreasonable to say that both contractual religiosity (which produces good people for this world) and covenantal faith (which invites us into a love relationship with the Creator for eternity) are the ultimate truth about life. These two visions of life are so different that only one can be true. (My pluralist friend reluctantly agreed.) That claim, plus the belief that following Jesus is the path to life, is, as I said, the essence of Christian exclusivism.

What about the major motive for moving to pluralism—combating arrogance and intolerance? Holding a view as true doesn't automatically make someone intolerant. (Remember, if believing a view—and denying its opposite—automatically makes a person arrogant, then pluralists who accept pluralism and reject exclusivism are automatically arrogant.) Arrogance and intolerance, as I said, are about how we hold our convictions. Everyone holds some convictions, and that requires denying opposite convictions. A person can hold her views confidently and yet humbly—Christian exclusivism demands that. We can believe we've found the truth. But we completely agree arrogance and intolerance are evil. So we practice humility. We say, "This is how I see it. I've thought about this, and I have some reasons for thinking as I do. But I'd like to know how you see it. What are your reasons? Let's examine all the reasons together."

This commitment to honest dialogue with others is both confident and humble. Because I'm firm in what I believe, I'm confident enough not to attack others out of insecurity. Confidence allows listening with respect. Fundamentally, arrogance and intolerance don't arise out of conviction but out of insecurity and fear. The solution to intolerance, then, is not a denial of conviction. Where there is no commitment to truth, power gains the upper hand. This is the essence of political correctness. Power reigns over truth. Those in power deem certain views acceptable not because of their rational merits but because of political advantage. If I hold the "right" view, I'm rewarded; if I hold the "wrong" view, I'm punished. But this has nothing to do with honest inquiry and genuine evidence. It's about those in power enforcing respectable views. Christian exclusivists committed to the reasonableness of truth and satisfied by the love of Christ can show true humility. If we're content in Christ's grace, we're secure in him. We don't feel threatened by difference. We can engage alternative views, neither cowering in fear nor exploding in aggression. We can bring a non-anxious presence into relational conversation with others because we are beloved by God. This is the Way of Jesus.

CONCLUSION

I began with a consumer metaphor. Consumerism pervades Western culture of the twenty-first century, and it shapes how many think about everything, including religion. A consumer wants lots of options. Not so a bride. A bride feels that having one special person who gives himself in deep, dedicated love relationship is far better than multiple options. A Christian exclusivist isn't a religious consumer. A Christian is like the bride, satisfied to know and love her groom—and to be known by and loved by her groom. This intimate love relationship with the Creator is what Christian exclusivists believe God offers through Jesus.

FOR FURTHER READING

Adler, Mortimer. *Truth in Religion: The Plurality of Religions and the Unity of Truth: An Essay in the Philosophy of Religion.* New York: Macmillan, 1990.

Copan, Paul. *That's Just Your Interpretation.* Grand Rapids, Mich.: Baker, 2001.

———. *True for You, but Not True for Me.* Grand Rapids, Mich.: Baker, 1998.

Nash, Ronald H. *Is Jesus the Only Savior?* Grand Rapids, Mich.: Zondervan, 1994.

Netland, Harold A. *Encountering Religious Pluralism: The Challenge to Christian Faith and Mission.* Downers Grove, Ill.: InterVarsity Press, 2001.

Okholm, Dennis L., and Timothy R. Phillips. *Four Views on Salvation in a Pluralistic World.* Grand Rapids, Mich.: Zondervan, 1996.

18

EASTERN THOUGHT
The Chimera of Pantheism

Ravi Zacharias

ONE DOES NOT GET FAR IN A CONVERSATION WITH A HINDU SAGE OR AN unsophisticated follower of Hinduism before one of them offers the familiar illustration of four blind people feeling an elephant in the dark and each one coming out with a different description of what it is he or she is feeling—a rope, a tree or some other object, depending on the tail or leg or whatever is being clasped. This story seems to be the best escape hatch to do away with any interpretive burden that keeps with the facts. Yet the obvious seems to escape the one giving the illustration: that smuggled into the analogy is the idea that it *is* an elephant that is under discussion and not any of those errant pronouncements made by the ones devoid of light and sight.

This illustration, however, is part and parcel of the enormous challenge of communicating across the huge divide of language, truth, logic and culture. I would like to focus on the last of these because much has been written about the other three. The biggest wall standing between the various ethnic groups and beliefs of our time is the catch-all term we call culture—especially if the reigning worldview behind the culture is Eastern pantheistic in its framework.

The famed theologian Paul Tillich once said, "Religion is the essence of culture and culture the dress of religion." At the core of every people-group is a belief of life's essence and meaning. These form the metaphysical givens in their worldview. The outworking of these beliefs is the attire of their culture.

Professor T. M. P. Mahadevan, who was professor of philosophy at Madras (now called Chennai) in the 1950s and also guest lectured at Cornell, Berkley and other such fine institutions, often described Indian philosophy as a "philosophy of values." His statement is echoed in one way or another, in the halls of Eastern learning. This is how he said it:

> Facts as such do not fascinate the Indian philosopher except as revealers of value. The discoveries of facts and the laws that govern them is the business of science and not of philosophy. Philosophical inquiry . . . must lead to the apprehension of value. Any metaphysical investigation which does not so lead is generally compared to such futile occupations as examining the teeth of a crow. Logic is a useful instrument of catharsis by means of which the philosopher rescues his intellect from obscure and conflicting conceptions, and from unreflective modes of thinking. It is of negative help insofar as it may clear away impossible ideas about the nature of reality, self-contradictory notions, and uncritical dogmas. It is the purified intellect that is said to become the instrument of intuition. . . . When logic degenerates into logic-chopping, reveling in a mere display of fine-spun theories, it is worse than useless to the philosopher, because it does not then aid in the process of discovering and realizing the supreme value. So it is that the Upanishads declare that wisdom is not obtained by intellectual acrobatics. A philosophy is to be judged by its fruits; and the final fruit of philosophy is the experience of value.[1]

One can see in this statement made over half a century ago, the long and ubiquitous shadow of the pantheistic worldview that stretched its reach through the second half of the twentieth century—transcendental meditation, the science of being and art of living, the New Age movement with its multiple offerings, Deepak Chopra's hybrid entity of science, philosophy and mysticism, and so on. This was the chimera waiting to be born that would give the religiously denuded West a semblance

---

[1]T. M. P. Mahadevan, "Social, Ethical and Spiritual Values in Indian Philosophy," in *The Indian Mind; Essentials of Indian Philosophy and Culture,* ed. Charles A. Moore (Honolulu: East-West Center Press, 1967), p. 152.

of religion with a sophistication of a supralogic. Today, any doctrine that smacks of biblical teaching is castigated as being divisive and a cultural imposition, while the fundamental beliefs that have spawned the nebulous world of value without doctrine are the grand elephant that the doctrinaire misconstrues as a rope or a tree trunk.

It does not take much to notice what this means in practical terms. Simply stated, one can make value statements with which someone of a different worldview agrees, but we had dare not go beyond the statement to the reason for its being true. That would be logic chopping and some kind of metaphysical voyeurism that is obscene to the one who intuitively deduces the value while denying the reason. In short, the foundations of argument have been replaced by the bullying force of culture, and the law of noncontradiction is used only when the opponent of the Christian faith wishes to demean the gospel in some way. Spirituality with an underpinning of pantheistic beliefs is portrayed as being serene, innocuous, all-embracing, mystical and wonderful. The Christian faith is portrayed as some kind of "been there, done that," hate-filled, judgmental, exclusionary and ideationally unfit dinosaur for our pluralistic times. The challenge has become immense and must be viewed with great caution and wisdom so that the bridge that has broken down may be reconstructed and crossed with effect and legitimacy.

The world is now being constructed on reclaimed land from the sea of faith in which we seek common values without finding common reasons from which those values stem. Yet the deeper one probes into the reasoning, the more one has to wonder whether this disjunction between values and reasons will sooner or later take away from us the water of life. "Stay with the platitudes," "Don't rock the boat," "Agree on the niceties." So what if it gradually erodes the source of life and truth? Many of us are familiar with the injunction "He is no fool who gives what he cannot keep to gain what he cannot lose." If that statement were to be repeated by a follower of Jesus Christ to a devout Hindu, the recipient would smile with utter glee and say, "That is exactly what I believe." Many such statements, even if lifted from Jesus' own words, evoke such a response. I even heard one man share his testimony at the Washington prayer breakfast that he was a Hindu Christian—whatever that meant.

Unfortunately, the terms do not come in a vacuum but are value-laden with two different worldviews in collision. It is imperative, therefore, that we try to understand what values permeate these cultures of the pantheistic worldview and seek some common ground from which to underscore what the truth is and why the truth matters. I take India as the microcosm of study because in many ways it has been the progenitor of such thinking and, in our time, even the beacon to guide the world of intuition into reclaiming religion from the sea of spirituality and constructing it on the sand of culture.

I must state from the outset that one can be gracious in disagreeing and that everyone has a right to his or her belief. What we must all remember, though, is that not everything a person believes is right—and one had better take his or her belief system to the scrutiny of truth.

A VAST HISTORY

Indian religious history evolves over several thousand years. This is in itself considered a badge of honor. One can go back well beyond two to three millennia B.C. into the development of the Vedas. As these were being formed one could detect the two strands that were clearly underpinning the thought: the doing and the being or the pragmatic and the meditative—the active and the contemplative. The Vedas are such a mix of sophistication and embarrassment that some scholars wondered how they ever came to be a corpus of such extremes. Some of the Vedic ideas incorporated even bizarre incantations and in turn invoked strong castigations from critics. Gautama Buddha, for example, denied the authority of the total Vedic teaching, and Mahatma Gandhi said he would like to remove some of its pages. The vast breadth from polytheism to henotheism to maybe even laying the groundwork for individual spirituality is the extent of its teaching. This paved the way for the Upanishads, where mystical experience and intuition overrode reason and even cast doubt upon the possibility of knowing ultimate truth.

After the Vedic period came the most formative stage of Indian culture. If every culture has a story, the Epic period of Hindu development became the stage. From about 500 B.C. to about A.D. 200 the Hindu epics of the Mahabharata and the Ramayana literally took center stage. Treatises on social philosophy and the laws and customs of life and culture were being imperceptibly etched into a people's consciousness. Whenever we read of the values of the four human ends intrinsic to reality, this is where they come from: wealth (artha), pleasure (kama), righteousness (dharma) and perfection or freedom (moksa).

This period also gave rise to various political treatises and ultimately the most beloved of all Hindu writings, the Bhagavad Gita. But interestingly enough, it was during this period that robust debate was stirred and significant movements emerged out of the bed of Hindu thought, yet into a world of different beliefs. Mahavira with his Jainism, Buddha with a different belief, and other systems sprang up. In the words of Radhakrishnan, "Doubt was no longer looked upon as dangerous." This springboard is what probably prompted Radhakrishnan's further statement that one could be a Christian, an atheist and a Buddhist but still be a Hindu.

But following this era there came an obvious thrust to find some systematization out of the disparate threads, and from this analysis there emerged six schools of thought.

> The Mimamsa school (ritualistic realism)
> The Vaisesika school (atomic pluralism)
> The Nyaya school (logical realism)
> The Vedanta school (idealistic, pantheistic monism)
> The Samkhya school (evolutional dualism)
> The Yoga school (dualistic meditative intuitionism)

In this vast spread of theory and practice lies the soul of Indian culture. One can see how difficult it is to make some cohesive sense of it.

FINDING SOMETHING SOLID TO BUILD ON

Junjiro Takakusu, in *The Essentials of Buddhist Thought,* first traces the development in Hinduism to show how Buddha departed from it. His delineation of the development is very succinctly put.

> In the Upanishads a pantheistic idea was already ripe and the universal principle was conceived also to be immanent in an individual. The Self (Atman) gradually became the individual principle. The Supreme God

which the Upanishadic philosophers objectively sought and found was now discovered subjectively in their own person. It was an Intellectual Reality, The Lord of Cognition, The Internal Guide, The Light of Mind, The True Light, The Highest Splendor. Where there is no sun, no moon, no star, no lamp, Atman alone shines in darkness, from whom all beings partake of the light. It was finally identified with the universal Self, which was also called Maha-purusa (Great Person) or Mahatman (Great Self). Finally, the mysticism of identity was realized: "Tat Tvam asi" (Thou art that), and "Aham Brahman asmi" (I am Brahman).[2]

Takakusu actually has a brilliant section that follows in showing how Buddha departed from these steps, one by one. It makes for a fascinating study. But any student of this philosophy and culture can see how the variegated strands of thought were interwoven till the colors and distinctives of each showed forth depending on the way one wanted to look at it. To shift the metaphor, this was truly thinking put into the blender so as to not lose anything, but the end result was a different product to what went in. Pantheism in Hindu thought is anything but monolithic. Just as the elephant lent itself to manifold descriptions, so does this world of belief. It is no wonder that one can walk only a few paces to engage another in a conversation and find it in a totally different description from the preceding one. The dress and the essence have intermixed till one does not know which is which.

When you add to the sheer weight of writings the massive size of this subcontinent in its socioeconomic struggle, you can see that systematization was merely a dream. It was this combination of complexities that gave rise to the three ways to attain the ultimate release: the way of knowledge, the way of works and the way of *bhakti* or devotion. It became a system where the religion could become all things to all people so that by all means it would save all. Bringing the exclusive claims of Jesus Christ into this mix was to put oil into water. No one wanted a rock in the shifting sands of epistemological chaos. Any mix retaining exclusivity was to ask for the impossible.

I would like to borrow, both from study and experience, what foun-

---

[2]Junjire Takakusu, "Buddhism as a Philosophy of Thusness," in *The Indian Mind*, p. 88.

dations of belief are disclosed when the weight of analysis is placed
upon it. Over the years I have learned more and more to appreciate the
culture in which I was cradled and the values that it imparted. I often
think back with nostalgia to the days of growing up, and yes, even the
late-night conversations we would have of a Hindu play or some event
that featured its thought. Now, through the lens of Jesus Christ, I have
learned to see how deep-seated all these things can be and that only the
power of the Holy Spirit can take truth and gently reveal the error of an
ingrained way of thinking. That gives the promise that we may see a few
glimmers of hope for effective communication.

An Ocean of Culture

Professor Charles Moore from the University of Hawaii, who passed
away in 1967, was instrumental in convening the East-West Philosophers
Conference, which since its inception in 1939 has met every ten years.
He went on to edit a very fine volume entitled *The Indian Mind,* which
gleaned from those gatherings that brought together some of the finest
scholars India had at that time. Professor Moore on one of those occasions presented an excellent paper, *The Comprehensive Indian Mind.* It
was obviously a very daring title with the very quick disclaimer that one
could offer such a description. But that aside, he captured several critical
aspects. I am indebted to his thought and added my own on the basis
of being cradled and raised in that thinking. These are not always studied deductions; rather for the vast majority they come down the distilling
mechanism of culture and get assimilated into the beliefs, hopes and ac-
ceptances of the way life is.

Here is that distillation.

The spiritual wellbeing as it is woven into life every day is a universal
and primary concern. From the early morning chants to the visits at the
temple, to the ash that lines the forehead, to the fears that dominate
before any new venture, it is all in the realm of spirit. The very greeting
in India with folded hands, to the sweets distributed on festive occasions: India's soul is wrapped up in the practice of spiritual beliefs. The
very name—Hindusthan—is the "land of the Hindus." From its Indus
Valley civilization to the present day teeming cities, life and spiritual sig-

nificance are attributed to everything, now encased in the multifaceted term called Hindu.

Karma, the moral law of cause and effect, is tacitly believed and assumed. Life carries its moral bills and they are paid in the cyclical pattern of rebirth till all dues are paid in full. The repercussions of fatalism and the indifference to the plight of others are inescapable but dismissed by philosophical platitudes that do not weigh out the consequences of such reasoning.

A prominent place is given to intuition. But this ought not to be overgeneralized. As a rule, such esteem is given to particular people whose influence or position has been recognized by some act or acts that seem to be in the realm of the extraordinary. This predisposition has made it the land of gurus and sages that manufactures a new one every so often. This alone sets India apart as the most religious nation on the face of the earth and may account for why there are 330 million gods in the Hindu pantheon and still counting. Intuition has bred both mystical reflection and bizarre discourses.

Religion is not a commitment to propositional truth or to the world as an object of reason. It is the response of the whole person to a way of life. In the words of Radhakrishnan, it is a nondiscursive, immediate cognition of the real (*aproksanubhuti lokkottarajnana*). This is not merely a glimpse into reality; it is a constant communion with it. That is why the sages and their sayings ought not to be cross-verified by any other empirical form of investigation. These noble experiences are within a world of different measuring sticks.

Moral purification is a necessary prerequisite to spiritual advancement.

There is a deep and passionate commitment to the ancient past, the immediate family and the pride of birth in the land of age-old teachings.

Life is a form of suffering. This is universal, and pain provides the context of our pursuit.

Yoga in one or many forms is considered essential to the pursuit of spiritual truth and the freedom of the spirit since it provides the mental concentration necessary for freedom from all distractions that rob us of spiritual purity.

A deep pride of the age of culture, and submission to the path itself rather than just the point of arrival, characterize the belief system.

A cultural commitment to the community, with a deep suspicion of any attempt to change its religious belief as an attack upon its cultural values, is common.

DISTORTIONS HINDERING THE HEARING OF THE GOSPEL

These ten underlying descriptions above well represent the basic ideas positively stated within the context of Indian thought. But I believe any scholar who leaves it at that has missed how one thinks within that culture in the reception of the gospel. Indeed, that is often the missing link in the evangelist who goes there and preaches the pure gospel or the scholar who responds with just this backdrop of understanding. There are also in the distilled mix beliefs that terribly distort the way one hears.

It is assumed that the Christian faith is something Western in its origin and that the West is bringing with it a cultural superiority that seeks to override the indigenous way of thinking. I well remember one of my Hindu friends remarking after my conversion to the Christian faith, "You have lost your originality." He made this comment, even though my commitment took place in India and on my own reflection of who Jesus was and is. To him, this was a defining statement as he thought that somehow something of my birthright was sold in the process. Hinduism is conveyed by birth. It is your lot in life assigned to you. The term used is *Dharti ka admi,* a "man of the soil." Notice the word in Hindi, *admi.* It means "man"—from the same root as Adam.

It took hours and hours of discussion to help my friend understand that the birthright sold was not of the one who came to know the Lord Jesus Christ but the first Adam who sold out to his own version of truth. Now in our setting we were selling our souls to a culture that is idealized even when it departed from God. The struggle is not East or West, north or south. The struggle is indeed internal—our way versus God's way. Hours and hours of talk lifted the veil a bit till he could see the difference. This is the element so often forgotten. Conveying the gospel in such settings demands protracted commitment of time and a willingness to even go round in circles till the Holy Spirit lifts the veil and the light shines in darkness. If one can show that it is not one culture against another but one will against God, the truth sinks in deeply.

The ingrained belief is that the colonial efforts of Western powers were motivated by and came accompanied by the missionary zeal to "convert the pagans." There seems an inability to separate the teachings of Jesus Christ from the sword of conquerors who came centuries ago. Mahatma Gandhi, Swami Vivekanada and India's most vitriolic critic of Christianity today, Arun Shourie, sound the same theme. Mr. Shourie, who is a member of India's parliament, spares no venom in his book *Harvesting Our Souls* to attack the proclaimer of the gospel as he heaps criticism upon criticism. As often happens in such efforts, his tendentious use of a counterapologetic would only convince the unstudied or the highly prejudiced. But without doubt he unblushingly attempts to take the gospel and its missionaries apart.

It is very important in understanding such presuppositions to patiently grant the mistakes and serious errors of those who did enter in with duplicitous motives or misguided zeal. But in granting such mistakes, the problem ought not to be further misrepresented in not seeing the difference between the Jesus of history and the politicized efforts of those who misused the gospel. But there is a very significant counterpoint not to be missed. I have often quoted to such a critic the statement that hangs emblazoned in Mahatma Gandhi's home in Ahmedabad. The statement is most fascinating and is that of Bertrand Russell. This is what he said: "It is doubtful that the method of Mahatma Gandhi would have succeeded except that he was appealing to the conscience of a Christianized people." This hangs on a banner in Gandhi's home. It is a stunning comment made by an atheist about a pantheist in his attempt to appeal to a theist. I remind the critic that the liberty he attained was because of the values appealed to, which could only have found legitimacy in a Christian theistic framework. There is a sobering silence when I make that comment.

With the increase in contact and travel, there is the belief that these factors make the gospel presentation easier. The fact is, they have actually made it harder. Those who come from these parts after getting closer to the culture that sent them the gospel begin to see the breakdown of life here. Just as they were unable to separate their religion from their culture, in the West they are unable to separate what the Christian faith is to what Western culture is. They think they are one and the same. Gandhi long before had said, "I like their Christ; I don't like their Christian." As disheartening as that is to hear, lands that have received the gospel accompanied by political exploitation have come to believe that religion was used for ulterior purposes.

All this being true, now that it is not so much the West on Eastern soil as it is the East on Western soil, the acquired wealth and prestige have served a different scenario. The Easterner has actually dug deeper into his or her own culture, for whatever motivation, in attempting to prove that the arrival here was purely for material motives and nothing more. This step deeper into cultural memory in a foreign setting is creating new tensions within their own families as the children of that transplantation become unsure of where they belong. In addition, the commercialized version of Christianity, the superficial presentation of simple truths in the popular media, appears to the listener from those parts as rather a simplistic look at a world of very complex issues.

These changes present many points of discussion in the presentation of the gospel to such a person. As such, it is imperative to point out, first of all, how the big picture of the culture of the West could only have been framed from a Christian worldview, giving possibilities of work and success. Yet second, the same freedoms also lend themselves to abuse, and the downward slide in Western culture is not a result of the Christian faith but the abuse of it. The small picture is the distortion of the big one and not the basis of it. In the words of Augustine, "One must never judge a belief by its abuse."

THE TENDER LIFE AND WORK OF THE SPIRIT

Last but not the least is that the life one lives out in his or her commitment to Jesus Christ is going to have greater apologetic value than the one who is mainly able to argue. To the younger generation the argument has more importance, which in turn helps them see why it is true. But to the older generation, the life becomes more important to help them see why it is what it claims to be. You see, deep within the heart of one raised in the context of Hindu thought is the recognition that the corruption that is endemic to the system and the stratification brought about by the caste system have left millions with nothing more than a hope and allegiance to a fragile strand of language and belief in life's suffering. But to change and to find answers does not seem to come from their religion itself. The gospel's power to offer forgiveness and individual hope that works for the betterment of the whole family is a precious truth we must not forget. Then we discover ways in personal contact to demonstrate that.

As can be deduced, one of the great struggles a person has when the gospel is received and understood is the next step of telling the family and not appearing a traitor to the culture. I have often drawn courage from the story of Naaman, the Syrian general who was healed of leprosy. You may recall after his healing he came to Elisha and asked him what he should do when his master takes him to the temple and leans on his arm during his worship. The Scriptures make a remarkable statement. Elisha says, "Go in peace" (2 Kings 5:19). There is no great pressure put on him in some how-to or some legislating command of doing it with immediacy and bravado. There is a keen understanding that God would go with the individual and guide that one to the how and when. Just as conversion is so tenderly handled by the Holy Spirit in our individual dispositions, so also the witness must be done in recognition of the individuality of the one to whom that message is then transmitted. This is especially true in upwards witness, that is, children to parents or in any age communication of the younger to the older. Culturally, this stands to reason.

We must ever remember the emotional cost of conversion within this cultural ethos. "I surrender to Jesus Christ" raises a plethora of questions for the individual—some great sage comes to their mind and they want to know if that person then is in an eternal condemnation for not having trusted Jesus Christ. "What about my father or my mother?" is the obvious question. Here too, a careful apologia is in order. I often remind them of how salvation is seen in the eyes of God. God is not calling us to be better people; rather he came to make us who were dead alive to him. Salvation is always seen in a sequence: redemption, righteousness and worship. It is never altered. Once they grasp this, they see the world of difference between that and a culture that makes worship the means of salvation. A careful reminder to them that God is the ultimate judge and will do what is right sets their heart at peace.

I recall on one occasion a young Pakistani student at an English university who stayed back after a meeting to share the deep distress in his heart. He had made a commitment to Jesus Christ but felt terribly guilty because his entire education was paid for by his father and this commitment was seen as a thoroughgoing betrayal of the family's heritage. To make matters worse, the father suddenly passed away, and the son was wondering whether this was some kind of judgment meted out to him. He actually suggested that he take his degree and go to his father's grave and bury it there in some reverential expression. The emotional weight of conversion is great. A tender and caring heart must come alongside, listen and through a grounding in the Word bring sustenance to the soul. Many churches are just not equipped to handle this kind of need and many a new convert is lost in the absence of discipleship.

We must never lose sight of the fact that after all the philosophizing has been done there is nothing different in principle to the description the apostle Paul gives of all of humanity in Romans 1:21-23: "For although they knew God, they neither glorified him as God nor gave thanks to him, but their thinking became futile and their foolish hearts were darkened. Although they claimed to be wise, they became fools and exchanged the glory of the immortal God for images made to look like mortal man and birds and animals and reptiles." When one reads this, is it any different to Professor Takakusu's description of how the Vedic concepts led to the Upanishadic spiral into individual self-deification?

The final point I make is to realize why pantheism does seem so attractive. One must remember how even C. S. Lewis battled this possibility as the only other alternative. The attraction is manifold. It lends itself more pliable to any scientific theorizing, and many of these cultures have that bent. It also gives one a moral reasoning without the need to invoke God. But in the final analysis, it is existentially impoverished when one needs to talk about the deepest struggles of the soul. Hindu scholars even admit this creation of a path to satisfy the inescapable existential hunger. Professor P. T. Raju of the University of Rajasthan, in an essay entitled "Metaphysical Theories in Indian Philosophy," puts it this way:

> But neither the way of knowledge nor the way of action satisfies man's need for love, confidence, and faith. Man is not only an intellectual and active being but also an emotional creature. If he is to treat the Supreme Being as the source of his intellect and as the goal of his action, he is to treat it as the object of his love also. Thus, another way was made open to man, the way of love or devotion. Ramanuja says that *dharma* (right action) leads to *jnana* (right knowledge), and knowledge leads to *bhakti* (love, devotion).[3]

It is not at all surprising that the Hare Krishna movement gained such currency during the heyday of cultural shift to the East. All the talk about meditation did not give the soul its relational hungers. Krishna consciousness stepped into that vacuum and offered a devotional and relational substitute, ratcheting up pantheism a notch to a contradiction of "ism."

It is here that a very keen understanding is needed. You see, Krishna is the avatar that, at best, brings God to man. But a huge chasm still remains. How does one bring man to God? For this there is only one way—the way of the cross. A profound and studied presentation of the cross, and what it means, is still the most distinctive aspect of the Christian faith. Even Gandhi said it was the most enigmatic thing to him and was unparalleled. For the Christian, the cross of Jesus Christ is the message "to the Jew first and also to the Greek"—to the moralist and the pantheist, to the religious and the irreligious. The cross of our Lord is the message we have.

In summary, one discovers that while the dress differs in religious culture, the heart remains the same everywhere. The foundational sands rescued are just that: fragile, weak and unable to hold the edifice of truth. They only manage to keep a temple erected to humankind. That is why we see the depravity and the horrors with which our world lives,

---

[3]P. T. Raju, "Metaphysical Theories in Indian Philosophy," in *The Indian Mind,* p. 194.

for there is no culture that can steal from the sea of faith with impunity, while neglecting the ocean of truth. What is brought to land really is a hybrid monster that ultimately devours the one who brought it forth. The words of Pascal come to mind: "What a chimera, then, is man! What a novelty, what a monster, what a chaos, what a subject of contradiction, what a prodigy! A judge of all things, feeble worm of the earth, depositary of the truth, cloaca of uncertainty and error, the glory and the shame of the universe."[4]

Only in Jesus Christ can that glory be rescued and the shame be dealt with. The problem is not pantheism. The problem is the human will's tendency to play God. That is not the distinctive of any culture. We are all *Dharti ke admi,* the Adam of the soil. For that ailment only Jesus Christ, the second Adam who as God became man, can lift us to terrain greater than that of our own making.

The hymn writer put it well:

We've a story to tell to the nations
That shall turn their hearts to the right,
A story of truth and mercy,
A story of peace and light.[5]

A LIFE WELL LIVED

As I close, I wish to pay tribute to Norman Geisler for the share he has had in my life. He was my professor and, in my estimation, is one of the finest apologists ever. He brings that depth because his philosophical prowess never overrode his deep commitment to the Scriptures. His strength lay in his theology that withstood the tests of philosophy. His blend between both historic and systematic theology and profound philosophical inquiry made him the defender of the faith that he is. Every generation needs a voice like his. One that never forgets the past but speaks to the present in preparation for the future. May God give us more and bless Norman Geisler and his family. It is my privilege to have this small share and pay this brief tribute.

---

[4]Pascal *Pensées* 12.434.
[5]"We've a Story to Tell to the Nations," words and music by Henry E. Nichol (London: 1896).

FOR FURTHER READING

Amano, Yutaka J., and Norman L. Geisler. *The Infiltration of the New Age.* Wheaton, Ill.: Tyndale House, 1989.

Beckwith, Francis J., and Stephen Parrish. *See the Gods Fall: Four Rivals to Christianity.* Joplin, Mo.: College Press, 1997. Chapter 6.

Clark, David K., and Norman L. Geisler. *Apologetics in the New Age: A Christian Critique of Pantheism.* Grand Rapids, Mich.: Baker, 1990.

Zacharias, Ravi K. *Jesus Among Other Gods: The Absolute Claims of the Christian Message.* Nashville: Word, 2000.

———. *The Lotus and the Cross: Jesus Talks with Buddha.* Sisters, Ore.: Multnomah, 2001.

19

MORMONISM

Carl Mosser and Paul Owen

PERHAPS MORE THAN ANY OTHER NEW RELIGIOUS MOVEMENT, MORMONISM presents a challenge to the health and growth of authentic Christianity.[1] It is also the most insistent of these groups in its claim to be Christian. As evidence for their claim Mormons cite the official name of their church: the Church of Jesus Christ of Latter-day Saints. They point out that the subtitle to the Book of Mormon is "Another Testament of Jesus Christ" and that according to its title page, it was compiled for "the convincing of Jew and Gentile that Jesus is the Christ." Latter-day Saints (LDS) affirm the divinity of Christ, his earthly ministry and resurrection from the dead. They believe he is the savior of the world and seek to follow him. This devotion to Christ, they insist, is more than sufficient for Mormonism to be considered an authentic Christian faith.

Latter-day Saints regularly tell potential converts that many Christian churches have part of the truth, maybe a lot of it. But only Mormonism, the restoration of earliest Christianity, has the "fullness of the gospel." LDS leaders encourage Christians to "bring all the good that you have and let us see if we can add to it." This gives the impression that Mormonism is basically Christian, differentiated from other forms of Christianity primarily by additions and modifications. For example, regular

---

[1]Recent decades have witnessed a renaissance of Christian philosophy and apologetics. Among conservative evangelicals no one has been more influential than Norman L. Geisler in fostering this renaissance or more deliberate in encouraging young scholars to enter these fields. We dedicate this essay to him in grateful recognition.

Christians accept the Bible as revealed Scripture. Mormons believe this but also accept the Book of Mormon, Doctrine and Covenants, and Pearl of Great Price. Christians believe the Father, Son and Spirit are one God united in their very being. Mormons believe their unity is not one of being but of purpose, power and will. Christians baptize; Mormons baptize and undergo proxy baptisms for the dead. Traditional Christians believe in marriage "until death do us part" and stress strong family values. Mormons believe in marriages both for time and eternity; the family unit can continue forever.

These examples illustrate Mormonism's heavy indebtedness to Christianity in terms of its doctrinal skeleton and categories. Both communities can talk about doctrines of Scripture, doctrines of baptism, doctrines of the Godhead, and so on. They further illustrate that Christian categories undergo mutation and transformation under the influence of modern revelation in LDS theological discourse.[2] This leads to some significant challenges for Christian mission.

CHALLENGES TO EFFECTIVE APOLOGETICS

Two challenges stem directly from the fact that in LDS teachings we encounter beliefs that are structurally similar to biblical beliefs, yet at the same time substantively different. Often Christians only mention differences and neglect the similarities. The result is caricatured descriptions of LDS doctrine. When Latter-day Saints come across these caricatures, they assume that Christians are intentionally distorting LDS theology. At that point one loses all credibility. The first challenge for apologists, pastors, missionaries and lay evangelists is to distinguish between Christian teaching and LDS teaching on the various loci of theology without exaggerating the disparities.

Second, the structural and categorical similarities lead many Christians to engage Mormons on doctrinal issues in the same way that they engage fellow Christians on in-house disputes over issues like Arminianism versus Calvinism, women in ministry or speaking in tongues. Mormon-

---

[2]For a helpful overview and comparison, see Stephen E. Robinson, "LDS Doctrine Compared with Other Christian Doctrines," in *Encyclopedia of Mormonism*, ed. Daniel H. Ludlow, 5 vols. (New York: Macmillan, 1992), 1:399-402.

ism is thus effectively treated as if it were a heresy internal to the Christian community. This makes it appear as if disagreements are about secondary issues within broader areas of agreement. Consequently it is very difficult for Latter-day Saints and others to see Mormonism as anything other than an idiosyncratic form of Christianity whose particular interpretations of Christian doctrines happen to be objectionable to some other Christians. The challenge here is to distinguish between Christian and LDS teachings in a way that adequately depicts the theological gulf that separates Mormonism from Christianity. This requires that we focus not only on doctrinal issues but also on deeper worldview issues.

This immediately leads to the challenges of the Mormon worldview and worldview disparity. As with any religion, Mormonism provides its adherents with answers to ultimate questions about God, the world, humanity and the human condition. Those answers have been developed and systematized enough to portray a basic vision of reality. We can therefore speak of a Mormon worldview. However, because of a tendency to eschew systematic theology and philosophical reflection, the Mormon worldview is not always well-developed. At many points it is internally inconsistent and it lacks the kind of precision that Christians are accustomed to. Moreover, the Mormon worldview seems to imply many things that most Latter-day Saints have never considered and do not believe. For these reasons studying the Mormon worldview is a challenging task.[3]

Not engaging in systematic reflection of their faith is an important cause of LDS worldview disparity. A second comes from the fact that many Latter-day Saints are converts from nominal Christian backgrounds who have not been fully indoctrinated into Mormonism. Another is the influence that can be exerted upon a Mormon's thinking by Christian writers popular in LDS circles like C. S. Lewis. Thus it should come as no surprise that many Latter-day Saints assume things

---

[3]Few works on Mormonism attempt to describe Mormonism's fundamental worldview commitments, and fewer offer any significant critique. Several essays from a Christian perspective that do both can be found in Francis J. Beckwith, Carl Mosser and Paul Owen, eds., *The New Mormon Challenge: Responding to the Latest Defenses of a Fast-Growing Movement* (Grand Rapids, Mich.: Zondervan, 2002). The main LDS literature focused on worldview issues is referenced on p. 416 n. 58; p. 417 n. 59; p. 456 n. 12.

about God, humanity and the world that are actually at odds with Mormonism's basic worldview commitments. Often these personal assumptions are genuinely similar to Christian teachings. One must be keen to discern the degree to which individual Latter-day Saints understand and accept the Mormon worldview and its implications and the degree to which they share Christian assumptions.

The final challenge to be mentioned here is the challenge of Mormon apologetics. In recent years Mormon scholars with advanced degrees in relevant disciplines have produced a body of sophisticated apologetic literature defending Mormonism. Mormonism's fundamental truth claim is that Christianity went apostate in the first century or shortly thereafter and was restored to the earth through the prophet Joseph Smith in 1830. Because of the nature of this claim, arguments in favor of Mormonism often include direct challenges to the truth claims of orthodox Christianity. During encounters with Mormons it is increasingly the Christian who is put on the defensive. One must therefore be prepared to defend such things as early Jewish and Christian monotheism, the development of Christian theology, the doctrine of creation and the doctrine of the Trinity.

The Christian who wishes to engage Latter-day Saints apologetically should have a solid grasp of the Mormon worldview. It is only by contrasting the Mormon and Christian worldviews that one is able to effectively depict the gulf that separates Mormonism from Christianity. One should also be prepared to expose the Mormon worldview's inconsistencies, radical implications and shortcomings. Doing this is sometimes much more effective than the typical strategy of attempting to debunk Joseph Smith and the Book of Mormon. At the same time, one must be prepared to engage in doctrinal discussions with Mormons who have not internalized much of the Mormon worldview or whose beliefs have been influenced in an orthodox Christian direction. In these cases one can frequently employ areas of genuine agreement as building blocks for fruitful theological discussions. One must also be prepared to defend Christian doctrines against LDS criticism.

WORLDVIEWS AND AUTHENTIC CHRISTIAN CONFESSION

Given Latter-day Saints' devotion to Christ, one might be tempted to think that this is sufficient to qualify Mormonism as Christian or that differences between the Christian and Mormon worldviews are about matters inconsequential to genuine reception of the gospel and salvation. However, according to the New Testament, confronting erroneous teachings about God, humanity and the world is not peripheral to the proclamation of the gospel. For example, in Romans 1:16-32 the apostle Paul contrasts the message of the gospel which brings salvation (Rom 1:16-17) with the plight of a fallen humanity that stands under divine wrath (Rom 1:18-32). In the verses that follow Paul emphasizes that the specific reason for divine wrath is humanity's distorted view of God (Rom 1:19-21, 28), the created world (Rom 1:23, 25) and humanity itself (Rom 1:22, 32). But the message of the gospel breaks into the structures of this world and overcomes the idolatry of humankind's "depraved mind" (Rom 1:28). Thus a central component of the proclamation of the Christian gospel is precisely the calling of human beings to abandon idolatrous beliefs and practices and to view reality through the lens of divine revelation rather than the distorted perceptions of the fallen world around us. It follows from this that messages which reflect these distorted perceptions cannot be meaningfully described as Christian.

In the second century the early church father Irenaeus described the summary of Christian truth that had been delivered to his generation by the disciples of the apostles. Termed the rule (*regula*) of faith or truth, it serves two important functions. First, the rule is an encapsulation of the fundamental Christian vision about God, the world, humanity and salvation as it was understood by the immediate heirs of the apostles. As do the later ecumenical creeds, it serves to demarcate authentic Christianity from various religious movements whose teachings contain Christian elements but are nonetheless profoundly incompatible with the apostolic faith. Today this fundamental vision is held in common by all confessionally orthodox Catholics, Protestants and Eastern Orthodox. Second, the rule lays out the basic theological parameters within which a proper Christian interpretation of Scripture occurs. Interpretations that violate these parameters have no claim to the title *Christian* because they deny the realities that lie behind the Scriptures themselves.

In introducing the rule, Irenaeus reminds his reader that Christians are people who have been baptized in the name of the Father, Son and Holy Spirit as a seal of eternal life and rebirth unto God. This new life is theirs by virtue of the fact that Jesus was incarnate as "a man among men," died and was raised from the dead.[4] But affirming Jesus as Savior and being baptized do not guarantee one's faith is Christian. One must also believe rightly about the nature and identity of the persons into whose shared name the Christian has been baptized. Otherwise "falseness enters the soul" and it "becomes broken and spoilt, not being whole." This is analogous to the way in which immorality ruins godliness. According to Irenaeus, it is useless for one to give verbal affirmation to true doctrines while living a life of immorality. It is likewise of little use if one lives morally without truth in the soul.[5] Heresy and immorality separate one from God. So how one lives and what one believes are both important to one's eternal well-being. This same point is implied by the apostle Paul's exhortation for Timothy to watch his life and teaching closely (1 Tim 4:16).

Irenaeus reports that according to the rule of truth there are three main articles necessary for authentic Christian faith. The first, which informs the other two, is "God, the Father, uncreated, uncontainable, invisible, one God, the Creator of all." The keystone to an authentic Christian worldview is the insistence that "the origin of all is God, for He Himself was not made by anyone, but everything was made by Him." Thus there is one "uncreated, invisible, Creator of all, above whom there is no other God, and after whom there is no other God."[6] God is unique in his being and the only being properly termed "God."[7] The other two articles focus on the persons and redemptive work of the Word of God and the Holy Spirit. The trinitarian structure of the rule is not accidental. From the moment one is initiated into the Christian community through

---

[4]Demonstration of the Apostolic Preaching [*Demonstratio*], 3, 6. The translation is from St. Irenaeus of Lyons, *On the Apostolic Preaching,* trans. John Behr (Crestwood, N.Y.: St Vladimir's Seminary Press, 1997). All other patristic quotations are taken from the translations in the Ante-Nicene Fathers or the Nicene and Post-Nicene Fathers series.

[5]Irenaeus *Demonstratio* preface 2.

[6]Irenaeus *Demonstratio* 4, 5.

[7]Irenaeus *Against Heresies [Adversus Haereses],* 3.6.3; 3.19.2; 4.1.2.

baptism in the triune name one must think of God in trinitarian terms. The Trinity is not an add-on to the Christian doctrine of God but its very heart. Irenaeus may not express himself with the later Nicene terminology, but, as Iain MacKenzie rightly observes, "there is little, if anything, in the Nicene formulae which is not present in embryonic or directional form in the works of Irenaeus."[8] (Below we will argue that the same can be said of the New Testament.)

The earliest Christians recognized that God and humans are fundamentally different kinds of beings. Unlike the Word of God who became a man, human beings are not uncreated and did not always coexist with God.[9] God is a creator; humans are created beings. God contains and transcends all reality; humans are contained and limited by the world around them. Humans are contingent creatures whose very existence depends upon the creative will of the uncreated God.[10] While God created humanity without sin with the possibility of immortality, the human race disobeyed his commandment. In doing so they rebelled against God's lordship and became sinners subject to corruption and death.[11] The human condition is characterized by humanity's rebellion against God, by sin and its fatal effects. It is this which Christ came to overcome in order to reconcile God and humanity.

Devotion to Christ is obviously necessary for a religious movement to be considered Christian. But is it in itself sufficient? The New Testament and early Christian writers recognized that it is not—one's understanding of Jesus must be informed by a biblical understanding of reality. They also recognized that unbiblical worldviews can undermine one's understanding of Jesus in ways that inhibit true knowledge of God, thereby imperiling salvation. Erroneous worldviews are expressions of the idolatry that the gospel calls upon everyone to abandon. Groups like the Gnostics were refused the label *Christian* not just because they had a deficient Christology or erred on this or that secondary theological point,

---

[8]Iain M. MacKenzie, *Irenaeus's Demonstration of the Apostolic Preaching: A Theological Commentary and Translation* (Aldershot, England/Burlington, Vt.: Ashgate, 2002), p. 29.
[9]Irenaeus *Adversus Haereses* 2.25.3.
[10]Irenaeus *Adversus Haereses* 4.11.2.
[11]Irenaeus *Demonstratio* 15-16.

but because they promoted worldviews fundamentally at odds with Scripture, the apostolic witness and sound reason.

THE MORMON WORLDVIEW

In continuity with earliest Christianity, the tradition of Christian orthodoxy has always insisted that devotion to Christ is not sufficient in itself to qualify a religious movement as authentically Christian. This devotion must occur within the broader biblical vision of reality. At the absolute center of this worldview is the truth that there is one true and living God who is unique in his being and Creator of all things. God did not come into existence but has always existed as God. He created the world *ex nihilo* (out of nothing) and sustains its continued existence. There are no beings, metaphysical principles or laws of nature whose existence is independent of God's being or creative will. As the origin of its existence, God transcends the space-time cosmos. He alone is ultimate reality and is subjected to nothing beyond himself. As the unique, eternal, transcendent Supreme Being, God knows all things and rules over all things as Lord and King. In contrast, humans are contingent beings who have been created by God. Though created good, the human race is in a state of rebellion against its Creator and is sinful and corrupt. The good news of the gospel is that because of the incarnation, death and resurrection of Jesus, human beings can be forgiven of their sins, reconciled to God and regenerated to share in the life and love of the Father, Son and Holy Spirit.

Traditional Mormonism presents a very different worldview. In the Doctrine and Covenants (D&C) we are informed that Jesus existed "in the beginning" with the Father (D&C 93:21). But the passage goes on to say that "man was also in the beginning with God" (D&C 93:29; cf. 93:23). This means that humans are uncreated and eternal in their most basic part (in LDS literature this is often referred to as an intelligence). We are also informed that "Intelligence, or the light of truth, was not created or made, neither indeed can be." Furthermore, the basic building blocks of the universe have always existed: "the elements are eternal" (D&C 93:33). In another text we read that "there is no such thing as immaterial matter," that is, immaterial substance. Furthermore, "all spirit is matter, but it is more fine or pure, and can only be discerned by purer eyes. We cannot see it, but when our bodies are purified we shall see that it is all matter" (D&C 131:7-8). It follows that even God is a material being.

Elsewhere Mormonism's founding prophet taught similar things. God did not create the world *ex nihilo;* rather, "God had materials to organize the world out of chaos—chaotic matter, which is element, and in which dwells all the glory. Element had an existence from the time he had."[12] Both the matter and the principles that govern it are eternal and cannot be destroyed. The "elements are eternal . . . any principle which is not eternal is of the devil. . . . The first step in [the] salvation of man is the laws of eternal and self-existent principles."[13] "The pure principles of element are principles which can never be destroyed; they may be organized and re-organized, but not destroyed. They had no beginning, and can have no end."[14] He affirmed that "the spirits of men are eternal."[15] In his most famous sermon Joseph Smith stated it this way: "We say that God himself is a self-existent being. Who told you so? It is correct enough; but how did it get into your heads? Who told you that man did not exist in like manner on the same principles? Man does exist upon the same principles. . . . The mind or intelligence which man possesses is co-equal [i.e., co-eternal] with God himself."[16]

Thus, according to the Mormon worldview, God did not create the matter of which the cosmos is composed or the various eternal laws that govern it at the most fundamental level. Neither did he create human beings in their most basic constitution. All of these things, like God, are part of ultimate reality, self-existent and eternal. God is powerless to bring any of them to an end or change their fundamental natures because they exist independent of his creative power. They also limit his power. As Sterling McMurrin explains, "For Mormonism the universe is a 'pluriverse' of both personal and impersonal elements, and these all

---

[12]Joseph Smith, *Teachings of the Prophet Joseph Smith,* comp. Joseph Fielding Smith (Salt Lake City: Deseret Book, 1976), p. 351. Hereafter abbreviated *TPJS.*

[13]*TPJS,* p. 181.

[14]*TPJS,* p. 351-52.

[15]*TPJS,* p. 208.

[16]*TPJS,* pp. 352, 353.

have ultimate reality and they genuinely condition one another."[17] While God is very powerful, the fact that there are things which he did not create entails that "omnipotence" in the Mormon worldview "means God has all the power it is possible to have in a universe—actually a pluriverse—of these givens."[18] Just how much these givens limit God's power is debated, but it is clear that Mormonism's metaphysical pluralism implies a version of finite theism.

God the Father is understood to have a glorified body of flesh and bones. LDS scholar Kent P. Jackson observes that it is significant to LDS theology that God specifically has a body of flesh and bones, not just a material body. This "suggests something of the relationship between deity and humans."[19] In LDS theology God is literally an exalted man—of the same species as all men. Joseph Smith taught this when he declared, "God himself was once as we are now, and is an exalted man, and sits enthroned in yonder heavens! That is the great secret."[20] Thus Jackson agrees that "the doctrine of God and the doctrine of humanity are virtually the same in Mormon theology."[21] God and human beings are very different from one another, to be sure, "but the difference is not a difference in the kind of beings they are but a difference in their respective locations in a universal process that perfects intelligent life."[22]

Humans are naturally like God in being self-existent entities who have always existed (even if we can't remember anything before this life). They also share God's nature because they were begotten by him in a pre-mortal state to be his "spirit children." (It is unclear how begetting self-existent beings works.) In a doctrinal exposition by the LDS First Presidency, we are told that "the Church of Jesus Christ of Latter-day

---

[17]Sterling M. McMurrin, *The Philosophical Foundations of Mormon Theology* (Salt Lake City: University of Utah Press, 1959), p. 24.

[18]John Cobb and Truman G. Madsen, "Theodicy," in *Encyclopedia of Mormonism,* ed. Daniel H. Ludlow, 5 vols. (New York: Macmillan, 1992), 4:1473.

[19]Kent P. Jackson, "Are Mormons Christians? Presbyterians, Mormons, and the Question of Religious Definitions," *Nova Religio* 4, no. 1 (2000), p. 57.

[20]*TPJS,* p. 345.

[21]Jackson, "Are Mormons Christians?" p. 58 (favorably quoting "Relations with the Church of Jesus Christ of Latter-day Saints and Its People: Position Paper" [Salt Lake City: The Presbytery of Utah, Presbyterian Church (U.S.A.), 1995], p. 12).

[22]Jackson, "Are Mormons Chritians?" p. 58.

Saints, basing its belief on divine revelation, ancient and modern, pro-
claims man to be the direct and lineal offspring of Deity. . . . All men
and women are in the similitude of the universal Father and Mother, and
are literally the sons and daughters of Deity. . . . Man, as a spirit, was
begotten and born of heavenly parents."[23] Having been begotten by
God, the potential for godhood is inherent in every person on earth.
Thus, "man is the child of God, formed in the divine image and endowed with divine attributes, and even as the infant son of an earthly
father and mother is capable in due time of becoming a man, so the un-
developed offspring of celestial parentage is capable, by experience
through ages and aeons, of evolving into a God."[24]

In the traditional LDS worldview the fundamental problem for human
beings is not sin but the fact that they exist in an unexalted state. That
is, humans are divine beings in embryonic form who have not yet fulfilled their potential. Their innate desire is to become adult sons and
daughters of God, but first they must grow, learn and mature. We are
like acorns yearning to become oaks. Only by achieving exaltation can
our chief problem be overcome. Those who are exalted receive a "fulness of joy" and experience an "eternal increase" in the same manner as
God the Father. This is understood to include the opportunity for exalted
humans to continue in family units and, like God the Father, have the
ability to procreate spirit children after the resurrection (cf. D&C
132:63).[25]

God and human beings share the same divine nature. The chief difference between us is that God has actualized far more of his divine potential than we have. In our current state we are but gods in embryo. On
the more traditional reading of Mormon theology, God has not always
existed as God. Rather, at one time he was like we are now. By obeying
the laws of eternal progression he was exalted to the status of a God by
the God above him. Human beings can become gods by following the

---

[23]Joseph F. Smith, John R. Winder and Anthon H. Lund, "The Origin of Man," in *Encyclopedia of
    Mormonism,* ed. Daniel H. Ludlow, 5 vols. (New York: Macmillan, 1992), 4:1669, 1667, 1668.
[24]Ibid., 4:1669.
[25]See further the following entries in the *Encyclopedia of Mormonism:* "Degrees of Glory;"
    "Eternal Lives, Eternal Increase;" "Exaltation;" "Eternal Progression;" "Godhood."

same path of obedience that our God and all the Gods followed to become what they are.[26] An increasing number of Latter-day Saints are uncomfortable with the idea that there are Gods above God the Father. Some are convinced that the idea is incompatible with their scriptures. Joseph Smith's statements that teach this were made at the end of his life, and he did not have opportunity to explain further what he meant. For this reason, and because they are not part of the LDS standard works, some Mormons feel free to dismiss these statements and view God as the Supreme Being not just for our world but for the entire cosmos. Nonetheless, they still see God as a progressive material being within a cosmos whose fundamental elements and principles he did not create.

Paul K. Moser and David Yandell observe that naturalism takes various forms but the core ontological belief is that "every real entity either consists of or is somehow ontologically grounded in the objects countenanced by the hypothetically completed empirical sciences (that is, in the objects of a natural ontology)."[27] Defined in this way Mormonism is clearly a form of metaphysical naturalism. It is unusual in affirming the existence of deities and angels, but within Mormonism these beings are understood naturalistically. They are entirely material, finite beings who exist as part of the cosmos and are subject to the fundamental eternal laws that govern it. Latter-day Saints have themselves described their beliefs as naturalistic. For example, philosopher David L. Paulsen says that as "a corollary to its materialistic (or physicalistic) metaphysic, Mormon theism has a strong naturalistic bent" and refers simply to "Mormon naturalism."[28] Scientist David Bailey speaks of the LDS "notion of a finite, naturalistic, material God" and of LDS theology's "rich tradition of naturalism."[29]

Despite its idiosyncrasies, Mormonism shares many of the problems

---

[26]Cf. *TPJS*, pp. 345-47, 370, 373.

[27]Paul K. Moser and David Yandell, "Farewell to Philosophical Naturalism," in *Naturalism: A Critical Analysis,* ed. William Lane Craig and J. P. Moreland (London: Routledge, 2000), p. 4.

[28]David L. Paulsen, "Comparative Coherency of Mormon (Finitistic) and Classical Theism" (Ph.D. diss., University of Michigan, 1975), p. 73.

[29]David Bailey, "Scientific Foundations of Mormon Theology," in *The Search for Harmony: Essays on Science and Mormonism,* ed. Craig J. Oberg and Gene A. Sessions (Salt Lake City: Signature Books, 1993), pp. 8, 14.

that afflict all forms of naturalism. When subjected to critical scrutiny it has been shown that the Mormon worldview has great difficulty grounding the existence of objective moral values.[30] It cannot adequately account for the philosophical and scientific evidence that confirms the Christian doctrine of creation *ex nihilo.*[31] It does not explain why God exists, why anything else exists, why anything continues to exist or why the universe is orderly and governed by law.[32] Its odd physicalist understanding of human persons cannot account for the unity of persons, genuine mental events and other things that we know about ourselves through introspection.[33] One could also argue that the metaphysical commitments of the Mormon worldview are incompatible with scientific realism, cast doubt on the reliability of our cognitive faculties and may even preclude the very possibility of truth and knowledge. In more specifically theological areas, the Mormon worldview exacerbates the problem of evil by undermining our warrant for believing that God can eventually overcome evil. Indeed, evil seems to be one of the eternal elements of the Mormon cosmos. Trust in God is also made tenuous because the Mormon God is neither the source of moral values nor is he good necessarily. The Mormon God could go wrong and fall from his position as God, a point Joseph Smith acknowledged.[34]

By now it should be very clear that Mormonism represent a worldview far removed from that of the earliest Christians and the orthodox

---

[30]Francis J. Beckwith, "Moral Law, the Mormon Universe and the Nature of the Right We Ought to Choose," in *The New Mormon Challenge: Responding to the Latest Defenses of a Fast-Growing Movement,* ed. Francis J. Beckwith, Carl Mosser and Paul Owen (Grand Rapids, Mich.: Zondervan, 2002), pp. 219-41.

[31]Paul Copan and William Lane Craig, "Craftsman or Creator? An Examination of the Mormon Doctrine of Creation and a Defense of Creatio ex nihilo," in *The New Mormon Challenge: Responding to the Latest Defenses of a Fast-Growing Movement,* ed. Francis J. Beckwith, Carl Mosser and Paul Owen (Grand Rapids, Mich.: Zondervan, 2002), pp. 127-52.

[32]Stephen E. Parrish, "A Tale of Two Theisms: The Philosophical Usefulness of the Classical Christian and Mormon Concepts of God," in *The New Mormon Challenge: Responding to the Latest Defenses of a Fast-Growing Movement,* ed. Francis J. Beckwith, Carl Mosser and Paul Owen (Grand Rapids, Mich.: Zondervan, 2002), pp. 204-11.

[33]J. P. Moreland, "The Absurdities of Mormon Materialism: A Reply to the Neglected Orson Pratt," in *The New Mormon Challenge: Responding to the Latest Defenses of a Fast-Growing Movement,* ed. Francis J. Beckwith, Carl Mosser and Paul Owen (Grand Rapids, Mich.: Zondervan, 2002), pp. 243-66.

[34]See Van Hale, "The Doctrinal Impact of the King Follett Discourse," *BYU Studies* 18, no. 2 (1978), p. 218. Cf. Alma 42:13, 22, 25.

tradition. We cannot accept its claim to restore earliest Christianity. To be sure, at the doctrinal level Mormonism has a structure similar to Christianity's, and its devotion to Jesus is sincere. Both, however, are nested in a worldview that undermines true knowledge of God and salvation. Like those of the Gnostics, many Mormon teachings are antithetical to a Christian vision of reality. Mormonism rejects both the main doctrinal affirmations of what Lewis termed "mere Christianity" and the fundamental vision of reality that informs them. The "restored gospel" of Mormonism must be clearly distinguished from the biblical gospel. For these reasons Mormonism cannot be meaningfully or properly classified as a Christian faith.[35]

THE DOCTRINAL CHALLENGE: THE TRINITY

It was noted above that increasingly one comes across Latter-day Saints who are uncomfortable with the idea that there is an infinite chain of Gods above God the Father. Many of these are Mormons whose assumed worldviews are not consistent with Mormonism's basic worldview commitments. Others are uncomfortable because they have studied their scriptures and have concluded that this idea is incompatible with them. While one can find many Mormons who hold to the traditional views, one must also be prepared to address the objections of those who wish to see the Father, Son and Spirit as in some sense the only God or Godhead that there is. In both cases one will likely have to defend Nicene trinitarianism and its insistence that the persons of the Trinity are *homoousios* (one and the same Being). Mormons of both stripes assert that this is an unbiblical notion that was imported into Christianity from pagan Greek philosophy. Yet the doctrine of the Trinity, as maintained in historic orthodoxy, is fundamental to the Christian understanding of the identity of God and hence to the framework which supports the Christian vision of reality. In what follows we will illustrate how one can defend this important doctrine and show how it strikes at the heart of the theological gap that presently sep-

---

[35]In books on the world's religions, discussion on Mormonism naturally occurs in the section on Christianity, not in the section on Judaism, Islam or another of the world's religions. This is appropriate given the kinds of broad phenomenological definitions these works employ, but it is theologically irrelevant.

arates all varieties of Mormonism from Christianity.

To begin with, it must be acknowledged that both Christians and Latter-day Saints affirm a Godhead consisting of three persons—Father, Son and Holy Spirit. (Many Mormons affirm this but limit God's rule to this system of worlds rather than the whole of reality.) Each person in the Godhead is distinguishable from the other persons, and yet the three persons considered together are viewed as one God. In engaging the LDS on this matter, it will not prove fruitful to simply argue the point that the Bible teaches that the Father, Son and Holy Spirit are one God. The LDS already agree with this claim in a sense.[36] What must be argued is that the three persons of the Trinity are *only* one God; in other words that they are one God *only,* and not in any sense *also* three Gods.

In the Mormon view, from one standpoint the persons of the Godhead are one God, yet from another standpoint they are three Gods.[37] Christians see it as a contradiction to say that the Father, Son and Holy Spirit are at the same time one God and yet three Gods. The LDS generally do not understand the oneness of the Godhead ontologically but rather functionally and experientially.[38] Stephen Robinson captures the

---

[36]See Craig L. Blomberg and Stephen E. Robinson, *How Wide the Divide? A Mormon and an Evangelical in Conversation* (Downers Grove, Ill.: InterVarsity Press, 1997), pp. 128-29.

[37]Even Blake Ostler, whose views on the Godhead are perhaps closer to orthodox Christianity than any other contemporary Mormon thinker, can write: "We may say that God the Son and God the Father are both properly considered as Gods. When asserted in this sense, the Son and the Father, though separate, belong to the same class or kind of being" (*Exploring Mormon Thought: The Attributes of God* [Salt Lake City: Greg Kofford Books, 2001], p. 6, emphasis in the original). In Ostler's version of social trinitarianism, none of the divine persons possesses the properties of God in a unique and absolute sense, since the Godhead is not ontologically one substance. In fact, each person in the Godhead depends upon the other persons for their experience of possessing the properties of God (i.e., each person possesses the divine properties contingently upon the others). The properties that distinctively belong to God arise from the unity of the persons of the Godhead; they are not rooted in one divine Being or substance. See Blake Ostler, "Re-visioning the Mormon Concept of Deity," *Element: An E-Journal of Mormon Philosophy and Theology* 1, no. 1 (2000), pp. 3, 7. On the varieties of thought within social trinitarianism, including a critique of all of them, see Brian Leftow, "Anti Social Trinitarianism," in *The Trinity: An Interdisciplinary Symposium on the Trinity,* ed. Stephen T. Davis, Daniel Kendall and Gerald O'Collins (Oxford: Oxford University Press, 1999), pp. 203-49. For a defense of continuing to employ substance metaphysics in formulating the doctrine of the Trinity, see William P. Alston, "Substance and the Trinity," in *The Trinity,* pp. 179-201.

[38]B. H. Roberts did speak of God as ontologically one in the sense of one "governing force" or "Spirit" whose influence "permeates the universe" (*The Mormon Doctrine of Deity* [Bountiful, Utah: Horizon, 1903], pp. 137, 168). Elsewhere he describes the persons of the Trinity as incarnations of "the one God-Nature" (*The Truth, the Way, the Life* [Provo, Utah: BYU Studies,

essence of the theological chasm that separates Mormonism from Christianity when he writes that "we believe that the oneness of these three is not an ontological oneness of being (this is a creedal rather than a biblical affirmation), but a oneness of mind, purpose, power and intent. . . . What is not said in the Bible, but is said at Nicaea and is rejected by Mormons, is that these three persons are ontologically one *being*."[39]

Robinson has a point, in the sense that orthodox Christians do not simply read the Bible through the lens of their own insight or purported modern revelations; rather, we read the sacred text collectively in sympathy with the ecumenical voice of Christians through the centuries who have reflected on the same biblical materials.[40] What must be argued in interacting with the LDS is not simply that the three persons of the Godhead are in some way one (a point to which they consent), but that they are one in precisely the sense which is set forth in the Nicene Creed.[41] This shifts the grounds from arguing with Mormons about the outward structure of our respective beliefs, which is actually quite similar, to the

---

1994], pp. 166-68). Although Roberts views all personal Intelligences as incarnations of the "God-Nature" (p. 171), his language bears superficial similarities with orthodox distinctions between the one *substantia* (substance) and the three *personae* (persons) of the Trinity; however, in Roberts's model, the persons emanate from the divine nature, so that "God" is the collective unity of all divine Intelligences. This is why the persons of the Godhead are separable substances in Roberts's understanding, which is influenced by Orson Pratt (cf. *Mormon Doctrine of Deity*, pp. 162-63; and Pratt, "Absurdities of Immaterialism," in *Orson Pratt's Works*, vol. 2, *Important Works in Mormon History* [Orem, Utah: Grandin Book Company, 1990], p. 30). Orthodox trinitarianism does not view the persons of the Trinity as emanations from an ontologically prior divine nature (cf. Athanasius, *Statement of Faith [Expositio Fidei]* 1; *Defense of the Nicene Definition [De Decretis]* 3.11).

[39]Blomberg and Robinson, *How Wide the Divide?* p. 129, emphasis in the original.

[40]Further on this point see Thomas C. Oden, *The Rebirth of Orthodoxy* (New York: HarperCollins, 2003); D. H. Williams, *Retrieving the Tradition and Renewing Evangelicalism: A Primer for Suspicious Protestants* (Grand Rapids, Mich.: Eerdmans, 1999); and Christopher R. Seitz, ed., *Nicene Christianity: The Future for a New Ecumenism* (Grand Rapids, Mich.: Baker, 2001).

[41]For a model of how to go about demonstrating this, see the brilliant study of David S. Yeago, "The New Testament and the Nicene Dogma: A Contribution to the Recovery of Theological Exegesis," in *The Theological Interpretation of Scripture*, ed. Stephen E. Fowl (Cambridge, Mass./Oxford: Blackwell, 1997), pp. 87-100. See also Colin Gunton, "And in One Lord, Jesus Christ . . . Begotten, Not Made," in *Nicene Christianity: The Future for a New Ecumenism*, ed. Christopher R. Seitz (Grand Rapids, Mich.: Baker, 2001), pp. 35-48. The most thorough and articulate modern discussion of the doctrine of the Trinity, blending together biblical analysis with discussion of Patristic doctrine, with which we are familiar is Thomas F. Torrance, *The Christian Doctrine of God, One Being Three Persons* (Edinburgh: T&T Clark, 1996).

inward substance of orthodox Christian faith.

It is important to recognize that the Nicene doctrine, which maintains that the Lord Jesus Christ is *homoousion tō patri* ("of one substance with the Father"), is no mere triviality but strikes at the very heart of the Christian faith. This is true for several reasons. First of all, it maintains biblical monotheism without sacrificing the divine identity of Jesus. It is clear that the New Testament ascribes to Jesus a status and role in religious devotion which is reserved for God alone (Phil 2:9-11; Rev 5:13; cf. Rev 22:9).[42] If Jesus is to be understood as a second and subordinate god, then the worship of the early church must be understood as abandoning the most fundamental principle of Old Testament religion (Deut 6:4; Is 43:10)—the incomparability of God. Israel's prophets understood that no created thing was comparable to God (Is 46:5) or worthy of worship (Is 42:8). Yet the Christian church worshiped Jesus. By Old Testament and Jewish standards, the religion of the apostolic church would have to be rejected as idolatrous (Ex 20:3-6). If the Nicene doctrine were not true, then Christianity would forever be separated from its Judaic roots, only to join the plethora of heathen religions, which distribute their religious devotion among a plurality of deities.

Second, the Nicene doctrine preserves the true knowledge of God in religion as opposed to secondary knowledge. The whole point of the incarnation was paradoxically to make the unknowable God the direct object of religious knowledge (Jn 1:18; 2 Cor 4:6). A common belief of pagan philosophy was that there was one supreme God, beyond knowledge, from whom gods and men derived their being. But such a philosophical abstraction could not be worshiped. This gap was filled by the pantheon, which provided practical objects of religious devotion. The question that framed the Nicene debate was precisely which side of this divide would the church fall upon. Would the Christians agree with the pagans that the one supreme God remained beyond contact with our

---

[42]On the compatibility of monotheism with the acknowledgment of Jesus' divine status, see further Paul Owen, "Monotheism, Mormonism and the New Testament Witness," in *The New Mormon Challenge: Responding to the Latest Defenses of a Fast-Growing Movement,* ed. Francis J. Beckwith, Carl Mosser and Paul Owen (Grand Rapids, Mich.: Zondervan, 2002), pp. 271-314; and in much more detail, Larry W. Hurtado, *Lord Jesus Christ: Devotion to Jesus in Earliest Christianity* (Grand Rapids, Mich.: Eerdmans, 2003).

world and beyond the bounds of religious knowledge? Or would they maintain that God himself, and not merely a quasi divine intermediary, had actually revealed himself and become the object of religious knowledge in the person of Christ (Mt 11:27; Jn 14:6-11)? For Arius, God still remained beyond the reach of human knowledge and could have no direct contact with the created world. In the Son we get only an indirect reflection of what God is like through an appointed intermediary. For Athanasius, God actually entered into our world and was made available to be directly known and experienced in the person of the Lord Jesus Christ, who is none other than God himself, truly revealing himself through himself.

Third, the Nicene doctrine maintains the *eschatological vision* of the Old Testament. It was a fundamental vision of Hebrew eschatology that one day God himself would enter our world and bring salvation to his wayward people (Zech 14:1-5; Is 40:3, 9-11; 59:16-20). The New Testament clearly understands Jesus to be the fulfillment of that prophetic vision (Mt 1:21-23; Lk 3:4-6, 16-17). If the opponents of the Nicene doctrine are correct, then Jesus did not truly fulfill the eschatological hopes of the Hebrew Bible. God himself did not come into our world to bring salvation; instead he sent a lesser deity to represent him. In a way, Mormonism also maintains this prophetic vision of God coming into our world—but at a very high cost. Because of their denial that the Father and the Son are *homoousios,* Mormons are often forced into the quasi-Gnostic heresy of separating the God of the Old Testament *(Yahweh)* and the Most High God *(El).* For the Mormons, while the God of the Hebrew prophets did become incarnate in the historical life of Jesus Christ, there was yet another God, higher on the scale of being, who remained outside our world.

Particular texts in the New Testament are especially relevant to establishing the biblical basis of Nicene trinitarianism, and in particular the doctrine that the persons of the Trinity are *homoousios* (one and the same Being or substance).[43] We will briefly examine five such texts below.[44]

---

[43]For the text and discussion of the Nicene Creed, see Philip Schaff, *The Creeds of Christendom,* 3 vols. (Grand Rapids, Mich.: Baker, 1993), 1:24-29.
[44]Scripture quotations are taken from the New American Standard Bible (NASB).

Matthew 28:19. This text is theologically crucial, not simply because it points to a Godhead that includes three persons (which the Mormons also believe), but because it identifies the singular "name" of God as Father, Son and Holy Spirit. The singular name *Yahweh* known from the Old Testament (cf. Ex 3:15; 6:3), has been reshaped into a name that includes more than one divine person, hence showing that in the development of biblical revelation, the divine identity of the one God is seen to include three persons.[45] A "name" specifies the identity of someone, so to say that the Father, Son and Holy Spirit share God's name is to say that they share a common divine identity—which is ultimately what it means for the three persons to be *homoousios*.[46]

John 1:1. This verse is an explicit endorsement of what would become Nicene orthodoxy. It identifies the preexistent Word as both being God and yet as standing in intimate relationship with God. In the terms of the Nicene Creed, the Word is "very God of very God." To say that the Word is at one and the same time God and yet distinguishable from God the Father is to state the content of Nicene dogma. Had John intended to say that the Son was a second and subordinate God alongside the Father (albeit united in mind, will and purpose), he could have used the Greek term *theios* in John 1:1 ("and the Word was divine/was a god") rather than *theos*.[47] Alternatively, we might have expected John to plainly state that the Word was a "second God" *(deuteros theos)* had that been his intent. (This would have been much more transparent than a Greek construction that merely lacks the definite article.) As the text stands, it expresses precisely what the Nicene fathers intended to articulate—that although the Father and the Son are distinguishable persons, they are one Being.[48] The Father and the Son are *homoousios*—each per-

---

[45]See Richard Bauckham, *God Crucified: Monotheism and Christology in the New Testament* (Carlisle: Paternoster, 1998), p. 76; cf. Hurtado, *Lord Jesus Christ,* pp. 381-89.

[46]See Bauckham, *God Crucified,* pp. 78-79.

[47]See Murray J. Harris, *Jesus as God* (Grand Rapids, Mich.: Baker, 1992), p. 66. On the grammatical unlikelihood of translating John 1:1c "and the word was a god," see Daniel B. Wallace, *Greek Grammar Beyond the Basics* (Grand Rapids, Mich.: Zondervan, 1996), pp. 266-67.

[48]It is important to distinguish between the terms *being* and *person* in theological discourse. A particular being is who one is by virtue of one's nature or essence. A particular person is who one is by virtue of one's relation to others. In other words, a person is a being-in-relation to others. Each human being stands in one distinctive set of relations in the world that cannot

son is God (not *a* God), yet they are distinguishable persons.[49]

It is important to note that John 1:1 does not say that together the Father and the Son are God in the sense of one united Godhead. John 1:1b identifies God specifically as the Father ("and the Word was with God"); the third clause then goes on to state that what the Father was (i.e., God), so was the Son (i.e., God). When Mormons speak of the persons as "one God" they are referring to the unified mind, will and action of the persons; when orthodox Christians speak of the persons as "one God" they are referring to the identity of divine Being shared by the Son and the Father. So one must either accept the Nicene understanding of this verse or else argue for an alternative translation of the clause.[50] John 1:1c cannot at the same time be translated "and the Word was God" and be understood in the Mormon sense of a unified Godhead, since the Word is not God in that sense—only the three persons together are God in the sense of one Godhead.

John 8:58. It is commonly agreed that when Jesus states "before Abraham was born, I am," he is alluding to the language of Exodus 3:14. Within the structure of John's Gospel, Jesus' discourses about God are normally understood to refer to God the Father, and this is certainly the case with the context of John 8:58 (cf. Jn 8:39-42, 54).[51] So when Jesus takes the name "I am" and applies it to himself, he is understood to be making a claim that would only be appropriate for God the Father. This

---

be duplicated by another person. The mystery of the Trinity lies in the fact that the one Being of God experiences three modes of being-in-relation to others. Finite beings each experience only one mode of being-in-relation to others. It is here that human experience and divine experience break down. See *modus subsistendi, relatio personalis* and *Trinitas* in Richard A. Muller, *Dictionary of Latin and Greek Theological Terms* (Grand Rapids, Mich.: Baker, 1985), pp. 195, 261, 306-10.

[49]"Having distinguished the Logos from the Father [*ton theon,* 1:1b], John wished to point to their commonality, not merely in purpose but in being [*theos*]. Like the Father, and equally with him, the Logos may be included within the category of Deity as a partaker in the divine essence" (Harris, *Jesus as God,* p. 67).

[50]Mormons might opt for the translation "and the Word was divine" and argue that it simply means that the Father and the Son share a common divine nature in the generic sense of having the properties of God. However, John did not use the term *theios,* which could have denoted this notion, and it is highly unlikely that John would switch mid-verse from a substantival use of *theos* in Jn 1:1b to an adjectival use in Jn 1:1c. See Harris, *Jesus as God,* pp. 63-64.

[51]This point needs to be made to cut off the possible LDS claim that Ex 3:14 has in view only Jehovah/God the Son and not God the Father.

is why the Jews attempt to stone him (Jn 8:59).

It is significant that Jesus uses a verb of "being" to describe his identity with the Father as the God of the Exodus story. Who is the "I AM" of Exodus 3:14? The "I AM" is both the Father and the Son. Long ago, the church father Athanasius made the link between the term *ousia* ("being") and the divine "I AM" of Exodus 3:14.[52] Athanasius observed the usage of this same divine name in Jesus' "I am" sayings (e.g., Jn 14:6) and pointed out that this indicates an identity of *ousia* between the Father and the Son.[53] Jesus' claim in John 8:58 amounts to a claim to be of one and the same *ousia* as God the Father—the God who IS, is both the Father and the Son. In biblical idiom, Jesus and the Father share the divine name "I AM"; in Nicene language the Father and the Son are "one and the same Being" *(homoousios).*[54]

John 10:30. In this verse, Jesus explicitly claims to be "one" with the Father. Is this claim to be understood ontologically or only functionally? Clearly, Jesus is not only claiming here to be one in "mind, purpose, power and intent," because the audience understood his words in terms of a claim of identity: "You, being a man, make Yourself out to be God" (Jn 10:33). Jesus was not making an assertion about his thoughts, goals, abilities or intentions—rather, he was making a claim about who he was, his identity.[55]

How is it that the word *one* would signal to his Jewish audience that he was making a unique claim of identity, that he was in fact claiming to be God? Because they heard in Jesus' words an echo of Deuteronomy

---

[52]Councils of Ariminum and Seleucia *[De Synodis],* 35. The Greek noun *ousia* is derived from the feminine participle *(ousa)* of the verb *eimi* ("I am").

[53]*De Synodis,* 41. cf. *Against the Arians [Orationes contra Arianos 4],* discourse 1.12.

[54]See Torrance, *Christian Doctrine of God,* pp. 118-19.

[55]Robinson suggests that the oneness of the Father and the Son should be interpreted in light of the oneness believers enjoy in John 17:21-22 (Blomberg and Robinson, *How Wide the Divide?* p. 130). But this ignores clear distinctions John's Gospel makes between our oneness with God and the oneness of God. First of all, Jesus' words are already defined contextually in Jn 10:30 as making a claim of divine identity (cf. Jn 10:33). Yet there is no hint that Jesus is telling believers that they can be God in Jn 17:21-22. Second, Jn 17:21-22 makes it clear that the oneness we enjoy is an experience to be entered into. By way of contrast, John's Gospel gives no hint of a time when Jesus became one with the Father (cf. Jn 1:1-2; 8:58; 17:5, 24). This indicates that the ontological relationship that the Father and the Son enjoy provides a pattern which believers can then enter into by analogy—but this is not to equate the oneness of believers and the oneness of the Trinity.

6:4: "Yahweh is one." That there is only one God was a fundamental belief of Judaism, yet Jesus was somehow claiming that the "one God" of the Shema (Deut 6:4) must be understood in such a way as to include himself within that unique divine identity. In light of the reaction of the audience and the allusion to Deuteronomy 6:4, it becomes necessary to understand the oneness between Jesus and the Father ontologically. The Father and the Son share more than a common purpose and will; they share a common divine identity. In short, they are *homoousios* (one and the same Being).

Hebrews 1:3. The first two clauses of this verse support what the Nicene fathers claimed to be true—that the Father and the Son share the same divine essence and are the same substance. First of all, how can the Son be "the radiance of [the] glory" of God unless his identity is intrinsic to God's own Being? Can you separate a source of light from the radiance that it sends forth from itself? Are not the sun and its shine one light? As Athanasius pointed out long ago:

> Or let a man venture to make the distinction, that the sun and the radiance are two lights, or different essences; or to say that the radiance accrued to it over and above, and is not a simple and pure offspring from the sun; such, that sun and radiance are two, but the light one, because the radiance is an offspring from the sun. But, whereas not more divisible, nay less divisible is the nature of the Son towards the Father, and the godhead not accruing to the Son, but the Father's godhead being in the Son, so that he that hath seen the Son hath seen the Father in Him; wherefore should not such a one be called Coessential [i.e., *homoousios*]?[56]

But did the writer of Hebrews intend to make concrete ontological claims about the relationship between God the Father and the Son in this passage? Is he not merely saying that we see a reflection of God in the person of Jesus? We can be sure that the writer intended his words to be understood as making ontological claims, for he goes on to say that the Son is "the exact representation of His nature." The Greek term that is translated "nature" here *(hypostasis)* in first-century usage meant "sub-

---

[56] *De Synodis*, 52.

stantial nature, essence, actual being, reality."[57] In other words, what God is in his "substantial nature" or "being," so is the Son. If the Father and the Son were not identical in essence *(homoousios)*, then the writer of Hebrews could not have claimed that Jesus was the "exact representation of [God's] nature."[58] In combination with each other, the twin assertions of the first two clauses of Hebrews 1:3 provide solid support for the Nicene doctrine of the Trinity.[59]

Some Apologetic Principles

The doctrine of the Trinity represents only one of the theological challenges that Mormonism poses to Christianity. Similar examples could be multiplied in the areas of monotheism, creation, christology and soteriology. A number of principles can be drawn from the preceding study that apply across the spectrum of theological loci. They can also be applied in apologetics to any heterodox religious movement that claims to be Christian.

First, apologetics aimed at non-orthodox groups should be unashamedly confessional. We should be up front in our apologetics with nonorthodox groups and let it be known that what is required of them is not simply giving assent to the teaching of particular Bible passages (which they believe they already do). What we are actually asking them to affirm is what Christians through the centuries have understood and defined as biblical teaching as outlined in the church's definitional creedal statements. The Bible *by itself* is not the sole object of theological reflection, but rather the Bible as interpreted within the framework of ecu-

---

[57]Walter Bauer, W. F. Arndt and F. W. Gingrich, *A Greek-English Lexicon of the New Testament and Other Early Christian Literature* (Chicago: University of Chicago Press, 1979), p. 847.

[58]The writer chooses his words carefully. The word translated "exact representation" is the word *charactēr*, which means something like "exact likeness, full expression." He does not say that the Son is "the copy of His nature." Had he intended this, he would have chosen the Greek word *hypodeigma* or *antitypos* (cf. Heb 9:23-24).

[59]The words of the first clause ("He is the radiance of His glory") further guard the reader from misunderstanding the Son's representation of God's nature in terms of a second Being who replicates the first Being. The writer does not speak of two glories or sources of light (the one a copy of the other) but rather of God's glory shining in the person of the Son (cf. 2 Cor 4:6). The only way God the Father's glory can shine in the person of the Son is if they are *homoousios* (identical in essence). If the persons of the Godhead were ontologically separate, the writer would have to say that the Son is "a copy of the radiance of His glory."

menical Christian orthodoxy. Recognizing this will avoid frustrating encounters with groups like the Mormons, who see us as disingenuous when we ask them to simply affirm biblical statements.

Many Protestants, operating with a distorted and exaggerated understanding of the principle of *sola Scriptura,* have wrongly operated on the assumption that only the Bible itself, and not ecumenical summaries of its teaching, can be set forth as binding and obligatory for authentic Christian faith. Yet the Reformed and Lutheran churches, unlike the Catholic and Eastern Orthodox churches, have never maintained that the Bible functions as a theological norm outside of and separated from the rule of faith and ecumenical creeds. These do not function as inspired sources of authority alongside Scripture but as the hermeneutical norm that guides the church in its reading of Scripture.[60] They enable us to read Scripture in communion with the saints of all ages and to benefit from the insight the Spirit gave to previous generations of Christians. Just as Protestants affirm that justification is by faith alone, but not by a faith that is alone, so we must maintain that authentic Christian doctrine is established by Scripture alone, but not by a Scripture that is alone.

Second, our apologetics should be exegetically sophisticated. It is necessary to do more than quote verses as proof of our position. We must demonstrate in detail how our theological stance is supported by the wording and subtleties of key texts that bear upon the particular issue being discussed.

Third, our apologetics must avoid exaggerating differences between our own theological views and those of other groups. This will both enable us to build upon our points of skeletal agreement in our doctrinal stances as well as move beyond those general agreements to analyze the substantial differences that separate our religions.[61]

---

[60]See further the excellent study of Keith A. Mathison, *The Shape of Sola Scriptura* (Moscow, Id.: Canon Press, 2001).

[61]Contrary to much ill-informed criticism, it is to the credit of *How Wide the Divide?* that Blomberg and Robinson attempted to acknowledge genuine areas of skeletal agreement in key doctrines, without glossing over important differences where they existed under the surface. For another model of principled and respectful dialogue that explores differences of opinion with another viewpoint without engaging in caricature, see Norman L. Geisler and Ralph E. MacKenzie, *Roman Catholics and Evangelicals: Agreements and Differences* (Grand Rapids, Mich.: Baker, 1995).

Fourth, our apologetics must be confident in the biblical basis of Christian orthodoxy. We must avoid the temptation to view later orthodox positions as anachronistic additions to the content of New Testament teaching. We should analyze key doctrinal texts with the full confidence that orthodox distinctives arise naturally from the soil of the Bible. The secular bias against systematization and the chronological priority of orthodoxy is a subtle influence which permeates the academic community; its influence must be resisted by Christian apologists, without sacrificing intellectual and scholarly integrity in our appropriation of biblical texts.

Fifth, we should utilize the richness of the Christian tradition. Theological insights and arguments are not like computers or cars. They do not get outdated. They may fall out of fashion, but that does not affect their validity, soundness or truth. We are wise to drink deeply from the wells dug by our forbearers in the faith. Church fathers like Irenaeus and Athanasius still have much to offer in contemporary discussions. The same can be said of many others in the Christian tradition (e.g., Augustine, Anslem, Aquinas, Calvin).

CONCLUSION

One can readily cite many noble features of the Mormon religion. There are genuine areas of agreement between Latter-day Saints and orthodox Christians, especially with respect to moral and social concerns. These should be openly acknowledged, and Christians should feel free to work with Latter-day Saints on issues of common concern within society. However, Mormonism denies the distinctively trinitarian worldview of early Christianity and the orthodox tradition. Mormonism's founder Joseph Smith correctly perceived that "the creeds set up stakes, and say, 'Hitherto shalt thou come, and no further.'"[62] Smith would not subscribe to these boundaries and thereby erred in his interpretation of the Bible and departed from the boundaries of Christian faith. Christians have a duty to share the gospel with their LDS friends, to call upon Mormonism to reconsider its teachings in light of Scripture, and to do so in such a

---

[62]*TPJS*, p. 327.

way that Latter-day Saints are attracted to the truth of our apostolic message.

FOR FURTHER READING

Beckwith, Francis J., Carl Mosser, and Paul Owen, eds. *The New Mormon Challenge: Responding to the Latest Defenses of a Fast-Growing Movement*. Grand Rapids, Mich.: Zondervan, 2002.

Beckwith, Francis J., and Stephen Parrish. *The Mormon Concept of God: A Philosophical Analysis*. Studies in American Religion. Vol. 55. Lewiston, N.Y.: Edwin Mellen, 1991.

Blomberg, Craig, and Stephen Robinson. *How Wide the Divide?: An Evangelical and a Mormon in Conversation*. Downers Grove, Ill.: InterVarsity Press, 1997.

Ludlow, David H., ed. *Encyclopedia of Mormonism*. 5 vol. New York: Macmillan, 1992.

Millet, Robert. *The Mormon Faith: A New Look at Christianity*. Salt Lake City: Shadow Publishing, 1998.

Ostling, Richard N., and Joan K. Ostling. *Mormon America: The Power and the Promise*. San Francisco: HarperCollins, 1999.

20

ISLAM

Abdul Saleeb

LIVING IN THE REALITIES OF THE POST-SEPTEMBER 11 WORLD, WE HAVE BECOME all too familiar with the challenge of Islam, especially in regard to the sociopolitical threats that we face from radical Muslim factions around the globe on a regular basis. Books on Islam, especially in evangelical circles, have been flooding the market in the last two years. Many of these books seem to have been written with a one-sided emphasis on the negative aspects of Islam and in particular with a focus on the themes of violence in Islamic scripture and history.

Although the multifaceted political, social, economic and even military threats of Islam are very real and present dangers (a fact often ignored in books written by Muslim or nonevangelical authors), the most significant challenge of Islam to the Christian faith has to do more with Islamic theology than any other area in the world of Islam. It is in Islamic theology that we find the source of Islam's fundamental opposition to Christianity. Unless we grasp what it is that Muslims believe, how that belief confronts the truth claims of the Christian faith and how to respond to the Islamic charges against Christianity, we have not succeeded in understanding Islam or providing Muslims with an adequate Christian response.

Our purpose in this chapter is to focus on the most significant doctrinal differences between Islam and Christianity. After a brief survey of Islamic theology, we will demonstrate how Islam challenges every single foundational doctrine in the Christian faith and how as Christians we can respond to the Islamic charges.

THE BASICS OF ISLAMIC THEOLOGY

Islamic theology is based on five articles of faith.[1] The significance of these articles of faith is reflected in Qur'anic passages such as sura 2:177: "It is righteousness to believe in God and the Last Day, and the Angels, and the Book and the Messengers," or sura 4:136: "Any who denieth God, His angels, His Books, His Apostles, and the Day of Judgment, hath gone far, far astray."

The oneness of God. The first and by far the most important belief is in the absolute oneness of God. "There can be no doubt," wrote Isma'il al-Faruqi (1921-1986), one of the most prominent Muslim thinkers in the West, "that the essence of Islam is *al tawhid,* the act of affirming Allah to be the One, the Absolute, transcendent Creator, the Lord and Master of all that is."[2] Another well-known Muslim intellectual in the United States, Seyyed Hossein Nasr, also writes, "At the heart of Islam stands the reality of God, the One, the Absolute and the Infinite, the Infinitely Good and All Merciful."[3] The absolute oneness and sovereignty of Allah is the unifying theme of Islam. In fact throughout their history, Muslims have viewed their confession of faith that "there is no god but Allah, and Muhammad is Allah's messenger" as an adequate summary of Islam and what it stands for. The Qur'an is filled with passages that urge the readers to abandon pagan and polytheistic beliefs and turn with faith and submission to the sovereignty of the one true God.

Messengers of God. Although human beings are not fallen or sinful by nature according to Islam, they are very prone to be led astray from the straight path of true worship. Thus God has sent prophets and messengers throughout history to all people groups to teach and guide humanity to the straight path. The Qur'an mentions approximately twenty-five prophetic names, but according to Islamic tradition, God has sent 124,000 messengers to all human cultures and languages. All prophets

---

[1]For a more extensive treatment of Islamic theology and its historical beginnings, see Norman Geisler and Abdul Saleeb, *Answering Islam: The Crescent in the Light of the Cross,* rev. ed. (Grand Rapids, Mich.: Baker, 2002) chaps. 1-6.

[2]Isma'il Raji al-Faruqi, *Al Tawhid: Its Implications for Thought and Life* (Verndon: International Institute of Islamic Thought, 1995), p. 17.

[3]Seyyed Hossein Nasr, *The Heart of Islam: Enduring Values for Humanity* (San Francisco: HarperSanFrancisco, 2002), p. 3.

have brought the same essential message of Islam or submission to God and thus are worthy of respect. As the Qur'an puts it in sura 2:136, Muslims must acknowledge that "we believe in God and the revelation given to us and to Abraham, Isma'il, Isaac, Jacob, and the Tribes, and that given to Moses and Jesus, and that given to (all) prophets from their Lord. We make no difference between one and another of them and we bow to God [in Islam]" (cf. sura 3:84; 4:163-65; 6:84-87). Of course, despite the claimed equality, most Muslims believe that Muhammad was the final and the greatest prophet of God and his message of Islam is the only uncorrupted, complete and thus the only universally valid message for all humanity.

The books of God. Not only has God sent messengers for the purpose of guidance, but he has also given scriptures to some of those messengers in order to convey the will of God to the people of their time. Not all the messengers brought forth a divine book, but some of the ones that are mentioned in the Qur'an to have been given books are Abraham, Moses, David and Jesus. But as Hammadah Abdalati puts it, "Long before the revelation of the Qur'an to Muhammad, some of those books and revelations had been lost or corrupted, others forgotten, neglected or concealed. The only authentic and complete book of God in existence today is the Qur'an."[4] Muslims believe that the Qur'an, revealed on various occasions during a period of about twenty-three years to prophet Muhammad (A.D. 610-632) and collected and edited some years after his death, is the literal words of God, dictated to Muhammad through the angel Gabriel.

The angels of God. Belief in angels, as invisible agents of God, plays an important part in Islamic faith and practices of Muslims. Angels continually serve and worship God and are often believed to be involved in interacting with human beings such as providing protection from evil, recording their deeds and receiving their souls at the moment of death. Gabriel, in particular, has a high honor since he is the agent of revelation. It is he who brings down the word of God to the prophets.

The judgment of God. Along with the insistent belief in the oneness

---

[4]Hammadah Abdalati, *Islam in Focus* (Indianapolis: American Trust Publications, 1975), p. 12.

of God, the Qur'an is also continually warning its readers that there is a day of judgment in which people have to give an account for their life. Life has a moral purpose and those who fulfill their purpose with true worship and righteous deeds earn eternal paradise. Those who reject God's message of guidance and whose bad deeds outweigh their good deeds will suffer eternally in hell.

It is in this context that we have to understand the practices and rituals of Islam. Along with the articles of faith, there are also the so-called five pillars of Islam. These are the deeds (along with many other meritorious acts) that Muslims are commanded to do in order to progress in the path of righteousness. These pillars include the Islamic confession of faith by which a person becomes a Muslim, the observance of daily prayers five times a day, the payment of religious tax or alms to the poor, fasting during the month of Ramadan from dawn to sunset, and going on a pilgrimage to the city of Mecca at least once in a lifetime if one is physically and financially able. Thus earning one's salvation by accumulating merits and good works is an essential aspect of the Muslim life.

THE BASICS OF ISLAM'S THEOLOGICAL CHALLENGE

For many people today, especially at first glance, there seems to be many similarities between Islam and Christianity. Diana Eck's comment reflects the attitude of many in our society when she writes, "Islam, like Judaism and Christianity, traces its heritage to the prophet Abraham. . . . It is strongly monotheistic, looks to Moses and Jesus as communicators of God's message to humankind, and has an ethic of equality and justice for all."[5]

It is true that Islam seems to share many similar doctrines with Christianity, such as belief in God, creation, prophets (most of the prophets mentioned in the Qur'an are biblical characters), revelation, the Old and New Testament as divine Scriptures, angels, the day of judgment, heaven and hell, and so on. Compared with many other religions and worldviews, Islam and Christianity appear to be truly much closer to each other than many might at first have imagined. The Qur'an itself seems to support

---

[5]Diana Eck, *A New Religious America* (San Francisco: HarperSanFrancisco, 2001), p. 232.

such a position when it addresses Jews and Christians in sura 3:64,

> Say: "O People of the Book! Come to common terms as between us and
> you. That we worship none but God; that we associate no partners with
> Him; that we erect not from among ourselves Lords and patrons other
> than God."

And in sura 29:46 Muslims are told not to dispute with people of the
book but to say, "We believe in the Revelation which has come down to
us and in that which has come down to you; Our God and your God is
One; and it is to Him we bow [in Islam]."

However, if we take some time to look deeper under the surface, we
realize that despite many superficial similarities, a vast gulf separates Islamic teachings from the Christian faith. Despite all the lip service that
many Muslims and others pay to the closeness between Islam and Christianity, orthodox Islam challenges and refutes every major foundational
doctrine of the Christian faith.

Islam denies the Christian doctrine of God, especially the biblical
view of the fatherhood of God and the doctrine of the Trinity. Islam denies the Christian view of human beings, in particular the doctrines of
sin and salvation. Islam unequivocally disputes the biblical view of
Christ in regard to his death and deity. And finally Islam rejects the authenticity and authority of the Christian Scriptures.

What is important to realize is that Muslims, especially in our day, feel
a great sense of intellectual justification for their rejection of orthodox
Christianity. They can point to the fact that the theological challenges
that they have brought against Christianity for most of their history have
been echoed by Western liberal tradition in biblical studies for at least
the past two hundred years. In addition to Islam, and especially since
the Enlightenment, there has been a host of other intellectual movements from inside and outside the church that have rejected the doctrines of historic Christianity.[6]

One typical example is Misha'al ibn Abdullah's book *What Did Jesus*

---

[6]For specific examples of the convergence between Islam and the Western liberal tradition
against orthodox Christianity, see the introduction to R. C. Sproul and Abdul Saleeb, *The Dark
Side of Islam* (Wheaton, Ill.: Crossway, 2003).

Really Say? After quoting from a British article in which it is claimed that "more than half of England's Anglican bishops say that Christians are not obliged to believe that Jesus Christ was God" and that many of the bishops "think that Christ's miracles, the virgin birth and the resurrection might not have happened exactly as described in the Bible," Abdullah confidently concludes,

> With every passing day, the most learned among the Christian community are slowly recognizing the truth and drawing closer to Islam. These are not Muslims who issued this statement. These are not "liberal" Christians. These are the most learned and most highly esteemed men of the Anglican Church. These men have dedicated their whole lives to the study of the religion of Jesus, and their study has driven them to the truth which God had already revealed to them in the Qur'an 1400 years ago: That Jesus was not God. That God is not a Trinity. And that the stories of the ministry of Jesus in the Bible have been extensively tampered with by the hands of mankind.[7]

Let us now turn our attention to the four specific theological challenges of Islam against the Christian faith and explore ways that we can "give the reason for the hope" that is within us (1 Pet 3:15).[8]

THE DOCTRINE OF GOD

The heart of all theistic faiths is the question of God. The reality and the nature of God are of fundamental importance in the structure of any religious system. Each theistic religion finds its most basic identity in its particular view of God and God's relationship to humanity. As A. Montes correctly points out, "The historical controversy between the two religions [Islam and Christianity] is centered theologically on the concept of God."[9]

---

[7]Misha'al ibn Abdullah, *What Did Jesus Really Say?* (Ann Arbor, Mich.: Islamic Assembly of North America, 1996), pp. 66-67.

[8]Because of the space limitations of this chapter, we can do no more than suggest a broad outline of possible Christian responses. Also, our concern here is not only theological and apologetic but also practical and evangelistic.

[9]A. Gonzales Montes, "The Challenge of Islamic Monotheism: A Christian View," in *Islam: A Challenge for Christianity* (London: SCM Press, 1994), p. 68.

Islam sees itself as God's final religion to humanity with the basic message that there is no god but the One true God (Allah). As one Muslim author puts it, "The Unity of Allah is the distinguishing characteristic of Islam. This is the purest form of monotheism, i.e., the worship of Allah who has neither begotten or beget nor had any associates with Him in His Godhead. Islam teaches this in the most unequivocal terms."[10]

Because of this emphasis on the absolute oneness, transcendence and sovereignty of God, it is quite understandable why Islam rejects such Christian notions such as the fatherhood of God or the Christian understanding of the triunity of God. For a Muslim, such doctrines bring dishonor to the glory and majesty of God by bringing God to a human level and introducing logical contradiction to pure monotheism. The Qur'an in fact is filled with warnings against Christians and others who adhere to these doctrines.[11]

Before providing certain lines of Christian response, it is important to point out that although many of the Islamic objections stem from genuine disagreements between Islam and Christianity, some of the "objections are based on a fundamental misunderstanding of what the Christian doctrine actually teaches. In other words, the Muslim is not rejecting the doctrine itself but a caricature of the doctrine."[12]

Therefore, in our witness to Muslims, our first job is to clarify some of the misunderstandings that create obstacles in communicating the gospel. For example, we must be emphatic that our understanding of God's fatherhood is not about a physical relationship but a spiritual relationship. There is no hint or suggestion in the Christian faith that God had any sexual relationship with Mary which resulted in the conception of Jesus.[13]

---

[10]Alhaj Ajijola, *The Essence of Faith in Islam* (Lahore: Islamic Publications, 1978), p. 55.

[11]For Qur'anic warnings against the Trinity, see sura 4:171; 5:76. The Qur'anic rejection of God's fatherhood can be seen in many passages, including sura 112; 19:35; 6:101.

[12]Timothy Tennent, *Christianity at the Religious Roundtable* (Grand Rapids, Mich.: Baker, 2002), pp. 153-54. Tennent provides us with an excellent model of evangelical-Muslim dialogue.

[13]In a commentary footnote on sura 2:116, Yusuf Ali, the most famous translator of the Qur'an into English language, writes, "It is a derogation from the glory of God—in fact it is a blasphemy—to say that God begets sons, like a man or an animal. The Christian doctrine is here emphatically repudiated. If words have any meaning, it would mean an attribution to God of a material nature and of the lower animal function of sex." Our misunderstanding of each other is often much deeper than we realize!

In the same way, it is of vital importance to demonstrate to a Muslim that there is no contradiction in the orthodox formulation of the doctrine of the Trinity. In a Qur'anic commentary written by two Indian Muslim scholars, we read, "So how can God be one and three at the same time? It is absurd, rationally impossible, mathematically wrong. Unity and Diversity cannot gather together."[14] What needs to be pointed out here is that in the doctrine of the Trinity, Christians do not affirm God to be one and three at the same time and in the same sense (that would be a contradiction). What Christians claims is that in one sense God is one (he is one in essence or being) and in a very different sense there is a divine plurality (three eternal "persons" or distinctions or relationships or dimensions).[15] Thus there can be no charge of logical contradiction against this doctrine.

At this point, many Muslims might complain about the incomprehensible mysteries of Christianity. Whereas Islam seems so rational and simple to understand and explain, Christianity is filled with such complex and confusing doctrines that even most Christians have trouble understanding.[16] We need to remind Muslims that it is not the case that everything about God is completely clear and understandable. If Muslims reflect more deeply on their own affirmation of *Allahu Akbar* (God is greater) and study the heated theological debates in the history of Islam concerning Qur'anic passages that speak of God's hands and eyes and throne, they will probably agree with Christians that God as God (Trinity or not) is a mystery and beyond being exhaustively cap-

---

[14]Shabir Ahmad Usmani, *The Noble Qur'an: Tafseer-e-Usmani* (New Delhi: Idara Isha'at-e-diniyat, 1990), 1:ii. Another fairly typical misstatement of the Trinity by a Muslim is the comment of Misha'al ibn Abdullah. In summarizing the Christian understanding of the Trinity he writes, "God is three gods merged into one God. This one God is called a Trinity. However, to say that God is three is blasphemy of the highest order. All three parts of the Trinity are 'coequal,' co-eternal' and 'the same substance.' For this reason, this doctrine is described as a 'mystery'" (*What Did Jesus Really Say?* p. xiii).

[15]The literature in this field is enormous and growing every year. For a recent book on the Trinity with an impressive bibliography, see Roger Olson and Christopher Hall, *The Trinity* (Grand Rapids, Mich.: Eerdmans, 2002). Two recent scholarly evangelical books on the doctrine of God are also very helpful. See John Frame, *The Doctrine of God* (Phillipsburg, N.J.: P&R, 2002); John Feinberg, *No One Like Him* (Wheaton, Ill.: Crossway, 2001).

[16]This point is eloquently made by the Muslim writer Shabbir Akhtar, *A Faith for All Seasons* (Chicago: Ivan R. Dee Publisher, 1990), p. 179.

tured by our human understanding.

After clearing the ground of these charges, we now come to the heart of the issue. Ultimately, this peculiar Christian doctrine is not about logic or arithmetic. The doctrine of the Trinity is a summary of the encounter of Christians with the one living God.[17] This doctrine is the feeble attempt of Christians to explain how from the very beginning as monotheistic Jews to this day, they have encountered the one true God as their loving Creator and Father, as their Redeemer in Jesus Christ and as their Sanctifier in the presence of the Holy Spirit. As C. S. Lewis put it in very simple language:

> And that is how theology started. People already knew about God in a vague way. Then came a man who claimed to be God; and yet He was not the sort of man you could dismiss as a lunatic. He made them believe Him. They met Him again after they had seen Him killed. And then, after they had been formed into a little society or community, they found God somehow inside them as well: directing them, making them able to do things they could not do before. And when they worked it all out they found they had arrived at the Christian definition of the three-personal God.[18]

In a similar vein, Alister McGrath explains:

> A helpful way of looking at this [the doctrine of the Trinity] is to say that *three essential models* must be used if the full depth of the Christian experience and understanding of God is to be expressed adequately. No one picture, image or model of God is good enough—and that these models are essential if the basic outline of the Christian understanding of God is to be preserved. The first model is that of the transcendent God who lies beyond the world as its source and creator; the second is the human face of God, revealed in the person of Jesus Christ; the third is that of the immanent God who is present and active throughout his creation. The doctrine of the Trinity affirms that these three models combine to define the

---

[17]Because of the often-repeated charge that the doctrine of the Trinity is the result of pagan influence that imposed itself on Christianity through the actions of church councils in the fourth century, it is important in our witness to Muslims to emphasize the experiential and biblical root of this doctrine.

[18]C. S. Lewis, *Mere Christianity* (1952; San Francisco: HarperSanFrancisco, 2001), p. 163.

essential Christian insights into the God who raised Jesus Christ from the dead. None of them, taken on its own, is adequate to capture the richness of the Christian experience of God.[19]

The above discussion sheds light on a crucial but often neglected issue between Islam and Christian faith. Our disagreement about the Trinity is rooted in our disagreement about the very character of God. For example, many people might have the impression that since, classically, both Islam and Christianity have defined God as the omnipotent, omniscient and omnipresent Creator of the world, that Muslims and Christians agree on almost everything about God except the contentious and mysterious doctrine of the Trinity. But on closer inspection we realize that Islam and Christianity disagree fundamentally on who God is, what he has done and his purposes in history.

The building blocks of such peculiar Christian doctrines as the Trinity, incarnation and atonement are all founded on who God is. The God who encounters us in the pages of the biblical narratives is a God who has revealed himself, and thus his acts in history tell us true things about who he is in himself (unlike the Islamic emphasis on God only revealing his will). The God of the Bible wants to be known in a personal and intimate relationship with his people (unlike the Islamic emphasis on the utter transcendence of God). He is a God who is engaged with the suffering of human beings due to the sinfulness of humanity (as opposed to the Islamic portrayal of God simply as a Judge), a God who loves unconditionally (not just loving God-fearing people as stated in the Qur'an) and a God who is perfect in holiness (and thus cannot simply disregard the sinfulness of human beings). These are the biblical convictions that mature into the theological formulations of the Trinity, incarnation and

---

[19]Alister McGrath, *Understanding the Trinity* (Grand Rapids, Mich.: Zondervan, 1988), pp. 136-37. This is an excellent popular treatment of the Trinity. Elsewhere McGrath writes, "The doctrine of the Trinity can be regarded as the outcome of a process of sustained and critical reflection on the pattern of divine activity revealed in Scripture, and continued in Christian experience. . . . Scripture bears witness to a God who demands to be understood in a Trinitarian manner." Furthermore, "Far from being a rather pointless piece of theological speculation, the doctrine of the Trinity is grounded directly in the complex human experience of redemption in Christ, and is concerned with the explanation of this experience" (Alister McGrath, *Christian Theology: An Introduction* [Oxford: Blackwell, 1994], pp. 294, 296-97).

atonement.[20]

This approach helps us to discern that before getting into any discussion about the philosophical or logical ramifications of the Trinity, we must start and center our discussion on who God is and what he has done for us in history and especially through Jesus Christ. Unless there is a "plausibility structure" rooted in the very character of God that opens the space for a trinitarian understanding of God, Christians will continue to fail in communicating to Muslims the meaning and significance of this crucial doctrine.

HUMAN BEINGS

The Qur'an views human beings as the special creations of God who were created to serve and worship God alone. But since human beings are easily and constantly led astray by Satan and their own carnal desires, God has continually sent his prophets and messengers to guide people to the straight path of submission and surrender. However, despite the fact that there are a number of Qur'anic passages that resemble the Genesis account of the creation and the fall of human beings (sura 2:30-39; 7:19-25), Islamic theology strongly disagrees with the Christian understanding of sin, especially original sin, and thus the Christian remedy of salvation. As Isma'il al-Farqui explains, "In the Islamic view, human beings are no more 'fallen' than they are 'saved.' Because they are not 'fallen,' they have no need of a savior. But because they are not 'saved' either, they need to do good works—and do them ethically—which alone will earn them the desired 'salvation.'" He further notes, "Islam teaches that people are born innocent and remain so until each makes him or herself guilty by a guilty deed."[21]

In spite of the fact that there is no assurance of salvation in Islam, many Muslims hope that by doing plenty of good works and trusting in God's compassion and mercy they can attain salvation in the hereafter.

---

[20]See, for example, "The Character of God in the Bible and the Qur'an," <http://answering-islam.org/God/character.html> (July 27, 2003). Also see Timothy George, *Is the Father of Jesus the God of Muhammad?* (Grand Rapids, Mich.: Zondervan, 2002), and Geisler and Saleeb, *Answering Islam,* chap. 7.

[21]Isma'il al-Faruqi, *Islam* (Nils: Argus Communications, 1984), p. 9.

One popular imagery of the Qur'an in regard to God's basis of judgment is found in sura 23:102-3. On the day of God's judgment, "those whose balance [of good deeds] is heavy, they will attain salvation, but those whose balance is light, will be those who have lost their souls; in Hell will they abide." In such a theological system, it is clear that there is no room for any biblical concept of atonement or a salvation based solely on God's grace through faith.

Although it should be obvious that we cannot prove the particular Christian understanding of human sinfulness and God's gracious salvation in Christ, there are certain important truths that we need to highlight in our discussion with Muslims.

Someone has wisely commented that the doctrine of original sin is the one Christian doctrine with the most empirical verification in its favor. It is beyond doubt and a matter of simple observation that human beings and the social environments that they create have been and continue to be deeply flawed and broken. If people are born in a total state of innocence as Muslims claim, then why is there an almost universal recognition that nobody is perfect and everybody sins? Or why isn't there at least a significant percentage of the world population that would stay sinless as they grow, since 100 percent were born sinless to begin with? Due to the force of these observations, Abdolkarim Soroush, the most prominent Iranian Muslim intellectual today, suggests that "our definitions of humanity need to be soberly and somberly examined in view of the amount of greed, cruelty, wickedness, and ingratitude that humans have caused—all of which they have done willingly and in accordance to their nature, not because they have been coerced or perverted."[22] He goes on to say, "It is true that we do not relish seeing humans as tyrannical, unappreciative, unjust, and foolish and that we hope they will not be so. Yet we must recognize these defects as part of human nature. Iniquity must be recognized as a natural and permanent part of human nature and not as an erasable or incidental facet of it."[23]

Furthermore, it should also be pointed out that the Qur'an itself is not

---

[22]Mahmoud Sadri and Ahmad Sadri, eds., *Reason, Freedom, and Democracy in Islam: Essential Writings of Abdolkarim Soroush* (Oxford: Oxford University Press, 2000), p. 191.
[23]Ibid., pp. 191-92.

nearly as optimistic about human nature as some Muslim theologians would like us to think. The Qur'an is filled with passages that describe human beings as unjust, foolish, ungrateful, wicked, boastful and rebellious.[24]

We should also mention that in regard to the doctrine of atonement, it is not Christianity that has deviated from the path of God's previous prophets, but Islam. By denying the necessity of atonement and insisting that good works is all that is needed to obtain salvation, Islam has completely disregarded the entire witness of the Old Testament Scriptures and the consistent teaching throughout the Torah (found especially in the sacrificial system of Leviticus) that the sinful human being cannot approach a holy God without the provision of a sacrificial atonement. It is the Christian view of the cross that is the reasonable and climactic conclusion of God's revelation in the Old Testament, not the Islamic denial of it.

As we mentioned earlier, our fundamental disagreement is rooted in the character of God. If God is too holy to let us minimize the depth of our sinfulness and too loving to let us perish on our own, then there is very little difficulty in understanding the Christian doctrines of sin and salvation. By denying the extent of God's holiness and depth of his love, it becomes impossible for Islam to appreciate or understand these foundational doctrines of the Christian faith.[25]

JESUS CHRIST

Nowhere does the opposition between Islam and Christianity come into sharper focus than when we reach the person of Jesus Christ. Although the Qur'an acknowledges many truths about Christ, such as his virgin birth and his ability to do miracles, and honors him with many titles such as the "Messiah," "a word from God," "the Spirit of God" and "sign unto

---

[24]For an excellent discussion of this point, see J. Dudley Woodberry, "Different Diagnosis of the Human Condition," in *Muslims and Christians on the Emmaus Road,* ed. J. Dudley Woodberry (Monrovia, Calif.: MARC, 1989), pp. 149-60.

[25]This can explain why for many Muslims who come to Christ, two of the most attractive features of the New Testament are the Sermon on the Mount, which throws fresh light on the sinfulness of the human heart, and the New Testament emphasis on the unconditional love of God, which is radically opposed to the Qur'anic portrayal of God.

men and a mercy from God," the Qur'an is adamant in its denial of Jesus' deity and death.[26] The Qur'an states:

> They do blaspheme who say: "God is Christ the son of Mary." But said Christ: "O Children of Israel, worship God, my Lord and your Lord." Whoever joins other gods with God, God will forbid him the Garden, and the Fire will be his abode. (sura 5:75)
>
> Christ the son of Mary was no more than an Apostle; many were the apostles that passed away before him. His mother was a woman of truth. They had both to eat their (daily) food. See how God doth make His signs clear to them; yet see in what ways they are deluded away from the Truth. (sura 5:78)
>
> And the Christians call Christ the Son of God. That is a saying from their mouth; (in this) they but imitate what the Unbelievers of old used to say. God's curse be on them; how they are deluded away from the Truth. (sura 9:30)
>
> That they said (in boast), "We killed Christ Jesus the son of Mary, the apostle of God," but they killed him not, nor crucified him, but so it was made to appear to them, and those who differ therein are full of doubts, with no (certain) knowledge, but only conjecture to follow, for of a surety they killed him not. (sura 4:157)

Once again, before making our response, we need to make sure that we have clarified any of the misunderstandings that might be in the mind of a Muslim. So, for example, we must emphasize that Christian theology has not elevated a human being to the status of God or God's partner, and that Jesus is not the Son of God in any physical or biological sense. Shabir Akhtar rebukes his fellow Muslims when he writes,

> Most Muslims, including educated ones, know next to nothing about Christology. Few Muslims can distinguish clearly between the view that a

---

[26]Many Muslims are genuinely baffled with the lack of Christians' enthusiasm about the great place that the Qur'an and Islamic tradition give to the prophet Jesus. In order to help Muslims understand the Christian position, it would be helpful to ask a Muslim how he or she feels if we say that Muhammad was a great political and military leader; he was an inspiring and courageous character, but he was not a prophet of God. In the same way, Christians do not believe that by denying the two most important aspects of Christ's person and work (i.e., his deity and death), Muslims in fact are honoring Christ as he truly is.

man claims to be divine—a blasphemy—and the entirely different view according to which God volunteers to become human—the orthodox Christian conviction. And both of these views are routinely confused with the heretical doctrine that God "adopted" a son.[27]

As this Muslim author correctly points out, the orthodox Christian conviction is that God, in Jesus Christ, took on human nature. Why did Christians, all of whom were originally devout monotheistic Jews, come to hold and die for such a peculiar conviction? The short answer is that Jesus' closest disciples came to this conclusion because Jesus himself, by his claims and his deeds, claimed to be God incarnate. One cannot read the New Testament without prejudice and not see the amazing divine claims that Jesus, and later his followers, are making on his behalf.[28]

In numerous ways Jesus puts himself in the place of God (truly a blasphemy if he was merely a human being or even a great prophet). Jesus claims that he and the Father are one (Jn 10:30), that he who has seen him has seen the Father (Jn 14:9). He is the only one who truly knows the Father, and it is only him who can reveal the Father (Mt 11:27). He claims to be the judge on the day of resurrection (Jn 5:22); he forgives sins (Mk 2:10) and teaches with the authority of God himself (Mk 13:31). He receives worship (Mt 28:17) and describes himself with a host of titles and imageries used only for God in the Old Testament.[29]

Therefore, quite naturally, his disciples also reflect Jesus' own understanding of himself throughout the whole New Testament. They come to believe in and worship him as nothing less that Yahweh (personal name of God) in person. As William Lane Craig points out, based on all the available historical evidence that we have, "within twenty years of the crucifixion a full-blown Christology proclaiming Jesus as God incar-

---

[27]Akhtar, *Faith*, p. 182.

[28]Since the Qur'an acknowledges the legitimacy of Jesus' disciples and in fact puts God's blessing on them and their message (see sura 61:14), their testimony to the identity of Jesus becomes also very significant.

[29]An excellent, though quite technical, treatment of the New Testament evidence for the deity of Christ is Murray Harris, *Jesus as God: The New Testament Use of Theos in Reference to Jesus* (Grand Rapids, Mich.: Baker, 1992). See especially the helpful appendix, "An Outline of the New Testament Testimony to the Deity of Christ," pp. 315-17. On a popular level, another helpful book is Josh McDowell and Bart Larson, *Jesus: A Biblical Defense of His Deity* (San Bernardino, Calif.: Here's Life Publishers, 1983).

nated existed." He goes on to say,

> The great church historian Jaroslav Pelikan points out that all the early Christians shared the conviction that salvation was the work of a being no less than Lord of heaven and earth and that the redeemer was God himself. He observed that the oldest Christian sermon, the oldest account of a Christian martyr, the oldest pagan report of the Church and the oldest liturgical prayer (I Cor. 16:22) all refer to Christ as Lord and God. He concludes, "Clearly it was the message of what the church believed and taught that 'God' was an appropriate name for Jesus Christ."[30]

Many Muslims, like the well-known apologist Jamal Badawi, bend over backwards to explain away all the New Testament evidence for the deity of Christ and then ask why Jesus never clearly claimed to be God and asked for worship.[31] The fact of the matter is that Jesus was more than clear about his divine status throughout his ministry and was as clear as it was possible to be in a first-century Jewish monotheistic context and in accordance with his mission of humble self-sacrifice (see Phil 2:6-11).[32] He was even clearly understood by his enemies (Jn 5:18; 10:33)! (See chapter nine of this book by Ben Witherington III.)

We conclude our brief discussion on this point with one important clarification. When Christians claim "Jesus is God," they need to be aware that they are using a theological shorthand. Christians do not claim that Jesus and God are numerically identical and thus everywhere we see the word *Jesus* in the New Testament, we can replace that with the word *God*. Jesus is not numerically one with God (therefore, he can genuinely pray to the Father and claim to have come from the Father), but he is essentially one with God. Jesus is God in essence.

---

[30]William Lane Craig, *A Reasonable Faith*, rev. ed. (Wheaton, Ill.: Crossway, 1994), p. 243.

[31]For one example, see <www.geocities.com/Athens/Acropolis/6808/Jesus.html> (July 27, 2003).

[32]Some years ago, in a speech at Emory University in Atlanta, Dr. Seyyed Hossein Nasr commented how Jesus claimed to be the truth, whereas Muhammad could only claim to be truthful, since according to Islam only God can say he is the truth! The Gospels are filled with these kind of references to Jesus' self-designation. When Jesus says he is the Lord of the sabbath or the true temple, he is making nothing short of a radical claim to divinity. What would happen to a Muslim religious leader if he claimed to be the Lord of the Ka'ba (the "house of God" in Mecca, Saudi Arabia), or the master of the day of judgment?

Let us use a helpful analogy, acknowledging that no human analogy can perfectly convey spiritual truths. Let us suppose God to be like an ocean. No one can experience the ocean, since it is far beyond our limited human horizon. Now imagine that a glass of water coming from the ocean is offered to us. The water in the glass has all the characteristics of the ocean. There is nothing in the chemical makeup of the ocean that is not represented in that glass of water. He who tastes the water in the glass can truly say he has tasted the ocean. The water in the glass is one in its essence with the ocean, although it is also distinct from it since it is in a glass. But the ocean is still there and has not disappeared. This analogy helps us better understand the New Testament proclamation, "For in Christ all the fullness of the Deity lives in bodily form" (Col. 2:9 NIV).[33]

When we come to the topic of Jesus' crucifixion, we can be confident that we are standing on the firmest historical grounds of our faith, whereas, exactly at this point, the Qur'an faces its weakest historical claim.[34] If there is one thing that all biblical scholars across the whole theological spectrum agree about the historical Jesus, even all the liberal scholars whom Muslims love to quote, is the fact that Jesus of Nazareth died on the cross. The significance and the aftermath of the cross are hotly debated issues, but the fact of his death by crucifixion is beyond historical doubt.

In order to shed more light on the whole context of the Islamic rejection of the cross, we can refer to Kenneth Cragg's analysis that for Muslims, "there is the historical denial of its [the crucifixion] actuality, the

---

[33]It is beyond the limits of this chapter to deal with the issues of philosophical coherence of the incarnation. For a helpful discussion see Paul Copan, *That's Just Your Interpretation* (Grand Rapids, Mich.: Baker, 2001), pp. 127-37, and its related bibliography. See also Thomas V. Morris, *The Logic of God Incarnate* (Ithaca, N.Y.: Cornell University Press, 1986). We should also heed the insightful reminder of N. T. Wright, "When people ask the question, 'Is Jesus God?', they tend to assume that we know who *God* is; the question means, Can you fit Jesus into your God-picture? Well, the best Christian answer has always been: we *don't know,* off the top our heads, exactly who God is; but we can discover him by looking at Jesus. You could say that at the heart of Christian faith is the view, not that Jesus is more or less like God, or part of God, but that the being we refer to as 'God' was, and is, fully present, and fully discoverable, in and as Jesus of Nazareth" (*The Original Jesus* [Oxford: Lion Publishing, 1996], pp. 78-79).

[34]The attempt of some Christians who try to reinterpret the Qur'anic denial of the crucifixion in order to find Qur'anic support for the cross is not in the least convincing.

moral refusal of its possibility and the doctrinal rejection of its necessity."[35] It seems that the Qur'anic denial of the historicity of the cross is mainly because of the belief that God would always protect his honored prophets and would ultimately rescue them from their enemies and also the conviction that human beings only need guidance and obedience in order to earn salvation. But Muslims cannot dismiss historical facts based on dubious theological assumptions, assumptions that are completely opposed to the biblical understanding of prophethood and means of salvation.

The Islamic denial of the cross confronts three major problems, for which Muslims have failed to provide any satisfactory answers. First, if Jesus was not crucified, how can we account for the conviction of every disciple and writer of the New Testament that the crucifixion is the cornerstone of the Christian faith? The cross is not just one detail in the distinguished career of a great teacher and prophet. For the writers of the New Testament, the cross is the absolute foundation for understanding who Jesus is and what he has done for humanity.

Second, without the cross, there is obviously no resurrection. If someone else died on the cross instead of Jesus (the popular Islamic suggestion based on sura 4:157), then how do Muslims account for all the resurrection appearances in the Gospels and the foundational belief in the resurrection by all early Christian communities? Without the resurrection, there would have been no Christian faith to start with (1 Cor 15:12-19). Muslims need to understand that Christianity as a historical movement did not start with preaching about Jesus inviting people to a "straight path" but with the message that "God has raised this Jesus to life, and we are all witnesses of the fact" (Acts 2:32).[36]

Finally, Muslims need to reflect on the implication of their rejection of the cross for the character of God. If God really rescued Jesus from suffering on the cross and instead made it only appear like that to the people (as Muslims believe), wouldn't this act involve God in the great-

---

[35]Kenneth Cragg, "Islamic Theology: Limits and Bridges," in *The Gospel and Islam,* ed. Don Mc-Curry (Monrovia, Calif.: MARC, 1979), p. 202.

[36]For the latest treatment of this topic, see N. T. Wright, *The Resurrection of the Son of God* (London: SPCK, 2003).

est act of deception in human history? Muslims must thus conclude that God not only deceived the disciples of Jesus and all the subsequent generations of Christians from the very beginning, but also that he allowed this deception to continue unchallenged for six hundred years till the advent of the Qur'an. These are very serious questions that most Muslims would rather ignore than face with honesty and historical scholarship.

THE BIBLE

The underlying conviction behind all the Muslim charges against Christian theology is the Islamic rejection of the Christian Scriptures. Misha'al ibn Abdullah accurately summarizes the mainstream Muslim attitude toward the Bible when he writes,

> Muslims believe in the books of the previous prophets including the "Torah" which was sent to Moses, the "Zaboor" (Psalms) which were given to David, the "Injeel" (Gospel) which was given to Jesus, and the Qur'an which was given to Muhammad. However, Muslims are told that the previous scriptures were tampered with by mankind and the Bible should only be accepted in as far as it is confirmed by the Qur'an. It is to be treated with respect, however any statements which clearly oppose those of the Qur'an are to be rejected as the work of mankind.[37]

In other words, because the Bible has been corrupted and is no longer in its pure and original form that was revealed by God to the prophets, the Bible is no longer authoritative for today. The only authentic, final and authoritative revelation of God for humanity today is the Qur'an. As I mentioned earlier, Muslims feel intellectually vindicated because they can find a great deal of support in critical and liberal Christian scholarship for their rejection of the authenticity and authority of the Scriptures.

Since defending the integrity of the biblical revelation and responding to the challenges against the Bible by critical scholarship are beyond the scope of this chapter, we will limit ourselves to two main lines of response in dealing with the Islamic charge of the corruption of our Scriptures.

---

[37]Abdullah, *What Did Jesus Really Say?* pp. xiv-xv.

First, the dilemma of the Muslim position becomes obvious when we look at the Qur'an itself and realize how positively the Qur'an speaks of the Jewish and Christian Scriptures. The Qur'an refers to the Bible as "the Book of God," "the Word of God," "a light and guidance to man," "a guidance and mercy" and other descriptions confirming its divine origin and continuing authority. The Qur'an repeatedly tells its readers that it has come in confirmation of the previous scriptures (sura 2:41, 89, 101). Muslims are commanded to believe in the previous Scriptures (sura 2:136). Muhammad is even encouraged by God to test the genuineness of his own message with the contents of the Jewish and Christian Scriptures (sura 10:94)! Christians and Jews are also commanded, "you have no ground to stand upon unless you stand fast by the Law, the Gospel and all the revelation that has come to you from your Lord" (sura 5:71, also 5:50).[38]

How is it possible for Jews and Christians to have such totally corrupt Bibles and yet receive such glowing recommendation and confirmation by the Qur'an? If the Bible had been corrupted before the advent of the Qur'an, then the Qur'an is not only completely silent about it, but it is actually giving legitimacy to a corrupt Scripture. However, if Muslims claim that the Bible was corrupted afterwards, then obviously we can point to the many manuscripts of the Old and New Testaments that predate the Qur'an by several centuries and form the basis of all modern translations today.[39]

Finally, we must briefly address a popular strategy in attacking the Bible by Muslim apologists. Often times, Muslim writers select a handful of quotes from liberal Western scholars that raise doubts about the historicity of the Bible. Almost always, what are missing from the quotations of these scholars are the philosophical presuppositions and highly critical methodologies employed to reach those conclusions.

What needs to be pointed out is that the same philosophical and

---

[38]We can tell our Muslim friends that the Qur'an itself tells us to go back to the gospel and stand firm on it. When we go to the gospel, we then see that the gospel leaves no room for the coming of another revelation after Christ (Heb 1:1-3).

[39]Historically, Muslims came to their belief in the corruption of previous Scriptures some centuries after Muhammad, when they realized that contrary to the assertions of the Qur'an, the message of the previous prophets found in the Bible was not at all the same as the message of the Qur'an.

methodological biases lead to conclusions that also contradict the
Qur'an. For example, if genuine miracles do not happen as a matter of
principle, a belief held by most critical scholars, then it is a forgone conclusion that the accounts of Jesus' virgin birth, his miraculous ministry
and his resurrection, along with any biblical prophecies are later legendary creations. But these conclusions also contradict what the Qur'an affirms about Jesus and thus can be used as much against the Qur'an as
they are used against the Bible.[40]

CONCLUSION

Although this chapter has been mostly a summary survey of major Islamic
doctrines and the main points of difference between Islam and Christianity, our hope is that it can be used as a good beginning in learning to
defend the faith against the theological challenges of Islam. In light of today's realities of war and terrorism, we must not forget that our primary
battle is the battle over minds and ideas. We should once again be re-
minded of the apostle Paul's exhortation, "For though we live in the
world, we do not wage war as the world does. The weapons we fight
with are not the weapons of the world. . . . We demolish arguments and
every pretension that sets itself up against the knowledge of God, and we
take captive every thought to make it obedient to Christ" (2 Cor 10:3-5).

FOR FURTHER READING

Deedat, Ahmad, and Josh McDowell, with John Gilchrist. *The Islam Debate.* San
     Bernadino, Calif.: Here's Life Publishing, 1983.
Geisler, Norman L., and Abdul Saleeb. *Answering Islam: The Crescent in the
     Light of the Cross.* Rev. ed. Grand Rapids, Mich.: Baker, 2002.
Gilchrist, John. *The Textual History of the Qur'an and the Bible.* Villach, Austria:
     Light of Life, 1988.
Cragg, Kenneth. *Jesus and the Muslim: An Exploration.* London: George Allen &
     Unwin, 1985.
Montgomery, John Warwick. "How Muslims Do Apologetics: The Apologetic

---

[40]In fact, in certain Western academic circles, especially in the writings of John Wansbrough,
Patricia Crone and Michael Cook, the same critical methodologies are being used on the
Qur'an and early Islamic history. The results have been devastating to the traditional Islamic
beliefs about the authorship and compilation of the Qur'an.

Approach of Muhammad Ali and Its Implications for Christian Apologetics."
In *Faith Founded On Fact*. Nashville: Thomas Nelson, 1978.

Sproul, R. C., and Abdul Saleeb. *The Dark Side of Islam*. Wheaton, Ill.: Crossway, 2003.

CONCLUSION

J. P. Moreland

IT IS TIME TO WRAP UP OUR CASE AND PONDER SOME FINAL THOUGHTS. IN THE preceding pages we have taken you on quite a journey. In part 1 we provided insights about faith, reason and the importance of apologetics for the vibrancy of the church. Part 2 laid out a well-reasoned examination of the considerable evidence for monotheism. Part 3 zeroed in on the exciting evidence for why Christianity is the most reasonable form of monotheism. Christianity is supported by solid historical evidence for the reliability of the New Testament and the miracles it records. Parts 4 and 5 responded to philosophical, cultural and religious challenges that are often raised against Christianity.

We have argued that there is more than adequate evidence to persuade an open-minded unbeliever to become a disciple of Jesus Christ and to encourage a believer to dedicate more of his or her life to living as one of Jesus' bondslaves. It is important that you not read this book merely as an intellectual exercise. The evidence we have presented calls for action on your part. Your decision about what to do with Jesus Christ must be approached in light of four questions that every human being must answer:

1. What is real?
2. Who is well-off? What is the good life?
3. Who is a really good person?
4. How does one become a really good person?

We are all somewhere between birth and death and have a life we must live. It is a simple fact that life cannot be lived without some orientation. To be disoriented can bring great harm to a person, even premature death. One's answers to these four questions provide the fundamental orientation of one's whole life.

Currently, a three-way worldview struggle rages in our culture among Christianity, scientific naturalism and postmodernism. Since we have described and argued against scientific naturalism and postmodernism in previous chapters, we will not do so here. Instead, we shall briefly characterize each and their answers to the four questions above.

First, scientific naturalism takes the view that the physical cosmos science studies is all that exists. Scientific naturalism has two central components, one metaphysical and one epistemological. Metaphysically, scientific naturalism implies that everything that exists is composed of matter or emerges out of matter when it achieves a suitable complexity. Among other things, this amounts to a denial of the soul and the possibility of disembodied existence after death. Epistemologically, it implies that physical science is the only, or at least a vastly superior, way of gaining knowledge. In regard to the four questions, the naturalist says that the physical world is all there is; that the good life is a life of social recognition and success, most likely, financial, academic or artistic success; that a really good person is one who is true to one's own ideals (whatever they are) and is tolerant of others; and there is virtually no advice given for how to become a good person.

The second worldview is postmodernism. This contains a very complicated set of ideas, and no short characterization of it would be entirely adequate. Still, we may safely say that postmodernism is a form of cultural relativism. According to postmodernism, truth/falsehood, real/unreal, right/wrong, rational/irrational, good/bad are dichotomies relative to different linguistic communities. What is true, real and so forth, for one community may not be so for another. In regard to the four questions, reality, the good life and the nature of a good person are whatever your community arbitrarily takes them to be. Moreover, there is no clear advice given as to how to become a good person.

Not only are naturalism and postmodernism false, but seen in light of these four questions, they are exposed as the shallow, destructive frauds that they really are. By contrast, the worldview of Jesus provides deep, satisfying, true answers to these questions. For Jesus, the basic reality is the triune God and his wonderful kingdom. The well-off person is any-one who is alive in the kingdom of God, irrespective of his or her life's circumstances. The good person is the one who is pervaded with agape love and who manifests the fruit of the Holy Spirit (love, joy, peace, pa-tience, kindness, goodness, faithfulness, gentleness and self-control). The way to become a good person is to enlist as an apprentice of Jesus in kingdom living. By comparison with the other worldviews, it becomes obvious that the way of Jesus is the only game in town! Today, Jesus stands at the center of the world and its history, just as he predicted he would. Jesus simply towers over any other figure in world history. In the last fifty years, his church has experienced its greatest expansion in two thousand years, and there are no signs that this harvest is going to slow down.

Still, many in Western culture have a suspicion that Christianity has been weighed in the intellectual balance and found wanting. As Dallas Willard notes,

> the crushing weight of the secular outlook . . . permeates or pressures ev-ery thought we have today. Sometimes it even forces those who self-iden-tify as Christian teachers to set aside Jesus' plain statements about the reality and total relevance of the kingdom of God and replace them with philosophical speculations whose only recommendation is their consis-tency with a "modern" [i.e., contemporary] mindset. The powerful though vague and unsubstantiated presumption is that *something has been found out* that renders a spiritual understanding of reality in the manner of Jesus simply foolish to those who are "in the know."[1]

In fact, nothing could be further from the truth. Christianity has not been weighed and found wanting. It has been inadequately defended and proclaimed and, thus, too frequently ignored. But that is changing, and this book is an attempt to set the record straight. For several decades Norman Geisler has tirelessly been a voice of reason in a religiously il-

---

[1]Dallas Willard, *The Divine Conspiracy* (San Francisco: HarperCollins, 1998), p. 92; cf. pp. 75, 79, 134, 184-85.

literate culture and a church that too often had no acquaintance with apologetics. The contributors of this volume owe him a great debt. And we, along with Geisler, have made our decision about Jesus of Nazareth. What about you? What have you decided regarding Jesus? Our prayer is that you will decide to abandon everything and follow him. If you do, you will find that he is, indeed, "the way, the truth and the life" (Jn 14:6).

About Norman L. Geisler

Educational Background

William Tyndale College, 1950-1955

University of Detroit, 1956-1957

Wheaton College, 1958 (B.A. in philosophy)

Wheaton Graduate School, 1960 (M.A. in theology)

William Tyndale College, 1964 (Th.B.)

Wayne State University Graduate School, 1964 (work in philosophy)

University of Detroit Graduate School, 1965-1966 (work on M.A. in philosophy)

Northwestern University, Evanston, 1968 (work in philosophy)

Loyola University, Chicago, 1967-1970 (Ph.D. in philosophy)

Academic Appointments

Graduate Assistant in Bible-Philosophy Department, Wheaton College, 1959

Part-time Instructor in Bible at Detroit Bible College, 1959-1962

Full-time Assistant Professor of Bible and Apologetics at Detroit Bible College, 1963-1966

Full-time Associate Professor of Philosophy at Trinity College, 1966-1971

Visiting Professor of Philosophy of Religion, Trinity Evangelical Divinity School, 1969-1970

Chairman of Philosophy of Religion, Trinity Evangelical Divinity School, 1970-1979

Professor of Systematic Theology, Dallas Theological Seminary, 1979-1988

Dean of Liberty Center for Research and Scholarship, Lynchburg, Virginia, 1989-1991

President of Southern Evangelical Seminary, Charlotte, North Carolina (which he cofounded in 1992), 1992-present

Pulpit Ministry

Director of Northeast Suburban Youth for Christ, near Detroit, 1952-1954

Pastor of Dayton Center Church, Silverwood, Michigan, 1954-1957 (ordained there 1956)

Assistant Pastor of River Grove Bible Church, River Grove, Illinois, 1958-1959

Pastor of Memorial Baptist Church, Warren, Michigan, 1960-1963

President of Alumni of Detroit Bible College, 1961-1962

Several interim pastorates in Michigan, Illinois, Texas and North Carolina, 1965-present

"Quest for Truth," radio ministry, 1981-1991

Speaker at churches, retreats, pastors' conferences, universities, on radio and television, 1960-present

Memberships

Evangelical Theological Society, 1964-2003

American Philosophical Society, 1968-present

Evangelical Philosophical Society, 1976-present

American Scientific Association, 1980-present

American Theological Society, 1980-present

American Academy of Religion, 1982-present

Honors and Recognitions

Graduated with honor from Wheaton College (1958)

Chosen as an "Outstanding Educator of America" (1975)

Philosophy of Religion text chosen as a "Choice Evangelical Book of the Year" by *Christianity Today* (1975)

First president of Evangelical Philosophical Society (1976)

Elected to the Wheaton Scholastic Honor Society (1977)

Listed in *Who's Who in Religion, Writers Who's Who* and *Men of Achievement*

Honored as Alumnus of the Year (1982), William Tyndale College (June 14, 1981)

General Introduction to the Bible won the Cornerstone Magazine book of the year award in its category (1986)

When Skeptics Ask was nominated for the ECPA Gold Medallion Award in the category of Missions/Evangelism (1991)

President of Evangelical Theological Society (1998)

Won ECPA Gold Medallion Award for *Legislating Morality* (1999)

Won ECPA Silver Medallion Award for *Baker Encyclopedia of Christian Apologetics* (2000)

Travel Experience

Dr. Geisler has lectured and traveled in fifty states and twenty-five countries on six continents.

Family

Wife, Barbara Jean, is a graduate of Fort Wayne Bible College (B.S.M.). They have six children and eleven grandchildren.

Published Books

An "*" represents a revision or reprinting. A "+" represents a coauthored or edited work. An "ˣ" represents a booklet.

+*General Introduction to the Bible* (Moody Press, 1968)

Christ: The Theme of the Bible (Moody Press, 1968)

Ethics: Alternatives and Issues (Zondervan, 1971)

The Christian Ethic of Love (Zondervan, 1973)

Philosophy of Religion (Zondervan, 1974)

+*From God to Us* (Moody Press, 1974)

Christian Apologetics (Baker, 1976)

A Popular Survey of the Old Testament (Baker, 1979)

The Roots of Evil (Zondervan, 1978)

*To Understand the Bible, Look for Jesus (Baker, 1979)

+*Inerrancy* (Zondervan, 1979)

+*Introduction to Philosophy* (Baker, 1980)

Options in Contemporary Christian Ethics (Baker, 1981)

+*Biblical Errancy* (Zondervan, 1981)

Decide for Yourself (Zondervan, 1982)

+*The Creator in the Courtroom—Scopes II* (Baker, 1982)

What Augustine Says (Baker, 1982)

Miracles and Modern Thought (Zondervan, 1982)

Is Man the Measure? (Baker, 1983)

Cosmos: Carl Sagan's Religion (Quest Publications, 1983)

ˣExplaining Hermeneutics (ICBI, 1983)

Religion of the Force (Quest, 1983)

To Drink or Not to Drink (Quest, 1984)

+*Perspectives* (Here's Life Publications, 1984)

+*Christianity Under Attack* (Quest, 1985)

False Gods of Our Time (Harvest House, 1985)

*+*General Introduction to the Bible* (revised, Moody, 1986)

+*Reincarnation Sensation* (Tyndale, 1986)

+*Origin Science* (Baker, 1987)

*+*The Bible: From God to Us* (ICBI, 1987)

*+*Philosophy of Religion* (revised, Baker, 1988)

Signs and Wonders (Tyndale, 1988)

Christian Ethics (Baker, 1989)

*+*Worlds Apart* (Baker, 1989)

Knowing the Truth About Creation (Servant, 1989)

+*The Infiltration of the New Age* (Tyndale, 1989)

The Battle for the Resurrection (Thomas Nelson, 1989)

+*Apologetics in the New Age* (Baker, 1990)

+*Come Let Us Reason* (Baker, 1990)

+*Gambling: A Bad Bet* (Fleming H. Revell, 1990)

+*When Skeptics Ask* (Victor, 1990)

+*The Life and Death Debate* (Greenwood, 1990)

ˣ*Civil Disobedience* (Quest, 1990)

In Defense of the Resurrection (Quest, 1991)

Thomas Aquinas: An Evangelical Appraisal (Baker, 1991)

+*Matters of Life and Death* (Baker, 1991)

**Miracles and the Modern Mind* (Baker, 1992)

+*When Critics Ask* (Victor, 1992)

+*Answering Islam* (Baker, 1993)

**In Defense of the Resurrection* (rev. by Witness, Inc., 1993)

+*Roman Catholics and Evangelicals* (Baker, 1995)

+*Love Is Always Right* (Word, 1996)

Creating God in the Image of Man? (Bethany House, 1997)

+*When Cultists Ask* (Baker, 1997)

+*The Counterfeit Gospel of Mormonism* (Harvest House, 1998)

+*Legislating Morality* (Bethany House, 1998)

Baker Encyclopedia of Christian Apologetics (Baker, 1999)

Chosen but Free (Bethany, 1999)

+*Unshakeable Foundations* (Bethany, 2001)

+*Why I Am a Christian* (Baker, 2001)

+*Battle for God* (Kregel, 2001)

+*Living Loud: Defending Your Faith* (Broadman & Holman, 2002)

Systematic Theology, vol. 1 (Bethany, 2002)

*+*Answering Islam* (revised, Baker, 2002)

+*Who Made God?* (Zondervan, 2003)

+*Is Your Church Ready?* (Zondervan, 2003)

Systematic Theology, vol. 2 (Bethany, 2003)

+*I Don't Have Enough Faith to Be an Atheist* (Crossway, 2004)

Systematic Theology, vol. 3 (Bethany, 2004)

About the Contributors

Michael Bauman is Professor of Theology and Culture and Director of the Christian Studies Program, Hillsdale College. He earned a Ph.D. in theology and literature from Fordham University and an M.A. in Old Testament from McCormick Theological Seminary.

W. David Beck is Professor of Philosophy and Associate Vice President for Academic Affairs, Liberty University. He is a graduate of Boston University (Ph.D., philosophy) and Trinity Evangelical Divinity School (M.A., philosophy of religion).

Francis J. Beckwith is Associate Professor of Church-State Studies and Associate Director of the J. M. Dawson Institute of Church-State Studies, Baylor University, where he is also the associate editor of the *Journal of Church and State*. He is a graduate of Fordham University (Ph.D., philosophy) and the Washington University School of Law, St. Louis (M.J.S.).

David K. Clark is Professor of Philosophy and Theology and Dean of the Center for Biblical and Theological Foundations, Bethel Theological Seminary (St. Paul). He holds a Ph.D. in philosophy from Northwestern University as well as an M.A. in philosophy of religion from Trinity Evangelical Divinity School.

Paul Copan is the Pledger Family Professor of Philosophy and Ethics, Palm Beach Atlantic University. He earned a Ph.D. in philosophy from Marquette University, as well as an M.Div. from Trinity Evangelical Divinity School.

Winfried Corduan is Professor of Philosophy and Religion, Taylor University. His Ph.D. (philosophy) is from Rice University, and his M.A. (philosophy of religion) was earned at Trinity Evangelical Divinity School.

William Lane Craig is Research Professor of Philosophy, Talbot School of Theology, Biola University. President of the Evangelical Philosophical Society, he holds a Ph.D. in philosophy from the University of Birmingham (U.K.) and a D.Theol. from the University of Munich.

William A. Dembski is Associate Research Professor in the Conceptual Foundations of Science, Baylor University. Among his degrees are a Ph.D. in philosophy (University of Illinois, Chicago), a Ph.D. in mathematics (University of Chicago) and an M.Div. (Princeton Theological Seminary).

R. Douglas Geivett is Professor of Philosophy, Talbot School of Theology, Biola University. He is a graduate of the University of Southern California (Ph.D., philosophy) and Dallas Theological Seminary (M.A.B.S.).

Douglas Groothuis is Professor of Philosophy of Religion and Ethics, Denver Theological Seminary. He holds a Ph.D. in philosophy from the University of Oregon and an M.A. in philosophy from the University of Wisconsin, Madison.

Gary R. Habermas is Distinguished Professor of Philosophy and Theology, Liberty University. He holds a Ph.D. in interdisciplinary studies (religion, history and philosophy) from Michigan State University and a D.D. from Emmanuel College, Oxford.

Craig J. Hazen is Associate Professor of Comparative Religion and Apologetics, Biola University, where he is the founding and current director of the M.A. program in Christian Apologetics. Editor of *Philosophia Christi* (journal of the Evangelical Philosophical Society), he earned a Ph.D. in religious studies from the University of California, Santa Barbara.

Richard G. Howe is a Ph.D. candidate (in philosophy) at the University of Arkansas and has an M.A. in philosophy from the University of Mississippi.

Thomas A. Howe is Professor of Bible and Biblical Languages, Director of the Apologetics Program and Director of the External Studies Program, Southern Evangelical Seminary. He is a graduate of Southeastern Baptist Theological Seminary (Ph.D., philosophy), Liberty University (M.A) and Luther Rice Bible College (B.D.).

Gregory P. Koukl is President and CEO, Stand to Reason Ministries. He holds an M.A. in Christian Apologetics from Simon Greenleaf University (which has since merged with Trinity International University).

Josh McDowell is President of Josh McDowell Ministries (Richardson, Texas). He is a graduate of Wheaton College as well as the Talbot School of Theology at Biola University (M.Div.).

J. P. Moreland is Distinguished Professor of Philosophy, Talbot School of Theology, Biola University. He also serves as director of Eidos Christian Center. He holds a Ph.D. in philosophy from the University of Southern California, as well as a Th.M. from Dallas Theological Seminary.

Carl Mosser is a Ph.D. candidate in New Testament at the University of St. Andrews (Scotland). He is a graduate of Fuller Theological Seminary (Th.M., philosophy) and Talbot School of Theology (M.A., theology; M.A., philosophy of religion and ethics; M.A., New Testament).

Ronald H. Nash is Professor of Christian Philosophy, Southern Baptist Theological Seminary (Louisville). He is a graduate of Syracuse University (Ph.D., philosophy) and Brown University (M.A., philosophy).

Paul Owen is Assistant Professor of Biblical Studies, Montreat College. He holds a Ph.D. in New Testament from University of Edinburgh (Scotland) and an M.A. in New Testament from Talbot School of Theology.

Abdul Saleeb is a pseudonym for a former Muslim who converted to Christianity.

Ben Witherington III is Professor of New Testament, Asbury Theological Seminary. He is a graduate of the University of Durham (U.K.), where he earned a Ph.D. in New Testament, as well as Gordon-Conwell Theological Seminary (M.Div.).

Ravi Zacharias is President of Ravi Zacharias Ministries and Distinguished Visiting Professor of Religion and Culture, Southern Evangelical Seminary. He is a graduate of Trinity Evangelical Divinity School (M.Div.) and Ontario Bible College (B.Th.) and has been awarded honorary doctoral degrees from Asbury College and Houghton College. He is a convert to Christianity from Hinduism.

Index of Names

Index of Subjects